COLOSSUS

COLOSSUS
Bletchley Park's Greatest Secret

Paul Gannon

Atlantic Books
LONDON

First published in Great Britain in 2006 by Atlantic Books,
an imprint of Grove Atlantic Ltd.

9 8 7 6 5 4 3 2 1

A CIP catalogue record for this book is available from the British Library.

1 84354 330 3

Printed in Great Britain by MPG Books Ltd, Bodmin, Cornwall

Typeset and Design by AvonDataSet Ltd, Bidford on Avon, Warwickshire

Atlantic Books
An imprint of Grove Atlantic Ltd
Ormond House
26-27 Boswell Street
London WC1N 3JZ

For Frances and Mackie

Contents

Contents

PART THREE – APPENDICES

List of Illustrations

List of Illustrations

A Word about Words

Any account of the birth of Colossus and the computer age must involve three particularly jargon-ridden subjects – information and communications technology, codebreaking, and military history. I have tried not to be too pedantic in the use of jargon, preferring to use everyday words wherever possible, which has meant simplifying some technical terms. I have also tried to use contemporary rather than modern terminology. Occasional notes in the text will point to variations and possible confusions.

One particularly hard decision was what to call the 'units' of the Baudot code (see Chapter two). Telecommunications engineers called them units, but during the Second World War the British codebreakers used the term 'impulses'. After the war, the term 'bit' (from BInary digiT) came into universal use. In many ways, it would have been easiest to use the now familiar 'bit', but it creates a false historical impression (in its use before its time). As 'impulse' is potentially confusing, I have used 'unit' throughout.

Codebreaking, in particular, suffers from problems of terminology. 'Codebreaking' is itself a good example. It clearly means breaking a code, but it is also widely used to mean 'cipher breaking' (which can also be called 'cryptanalysis'). Codes and ciphers are generally different things (see Chapter two), but 'codebreaker' has come to mean people who crack ciphers as well as codes. By extension, what should properly be called a 'decrypt' (i.e. an enciphered message for which the key has been worked out and used to decipher the message to reveal its plain-language content) was usually known at Bletchley Park as a 'decode', a term which I have thus adopted. I have also sometimes used the term 'intercept' to mean the same as a decode and decrypt. One particularly misleading term is 'plain language' ('plain', 'in plain', etc. and also as 'clear language', 'clear', 'in clear', etc.). The plain-language version of intercepted messages was usually far from plain, consisting of German military terms and abbreviations and often highly formatted reports consisting of figures and punctuation, as a glance at Appendix C – Whiting decode, 5 February 1945 will show. To make matters more difficult, the interaction between the transmission code and the cipher, both of which lay at the centre of the Colossus story, made the plain language even less plain by inserting machine commands (see Chapter two).

Introduction

Towards the end of the Second World War, civilian and military staff who had been employed at Britain's highly successful codebreaking organization the Government Code and Cipher School (GC&CS), based at Bletchley Park, were all advised that, even after the end of hostilities, they were bound to secrecy about their wartime work. Bletchley Park had been the centre of a massive interception and codebreaking operation that had helped the Allies win the war. Decrypts of German enciphered military messages, revealing strategy and tactics, had been passed to Allied operational commands from as early as 1939 under the name of Ultra. By and large, there were no serious security breaches during the war and, despite the occasional scare, the German armed forces remained wholly unaware of the extent of Allied codebreaking. Now it was essential that tight security be maintained.

The staff were told, 'The end of the German war is now in clear view. The several strands of keenness, discipline, personal behaviour and security have been admirable and have combined to produce a direct and substantial combination in winning the war.' However, there were still things to do: the war against Japan had to be won; there was the need to ease the transition from war to peace for everyone; and, most important of all, it was essential 'to ensure that nothing we do now shall hinder the efforts of our successors… I cannot stress too strongly the necessity for the maintenance of security... At some future time we may be called upon to use the same methods. It is therefore as vital as ever not to relax from the high standard of security that we have hitherto maintained. The temptation to "own up" to our friends and families as to what our work has been is a very real and natural one. It must be resisted absolutely.'[1] Another document was more forceful: 'All persons concerned must remember that they are bound by honour as well as law to maintain secrecy of Ultra in Peace as well as in time of War.' Not even their husbands (the majority of GC&CS staff were women) or, for that matter, their wives could be told. The most severe penalties would follow if anyone so much as dared to publicize what they had done or seen. A trial, with a complete ban on any reporting of it, would end with a very long prison sentence and a sorry future.

Naturally, the wartime secrecy was essential – any hint that Britain and the United States were successfully decoding German signals would have led to a tightening of German wireless security and the loss of the intelligence the Allies gleaned from the intercepted messages. Yet the blanket ban was to be held in place for nearly three decades and, during that entire period, histories of the Second World War were written without any awareness of how the Allies managed to achieve some of their most significant victories. The comprehensive history of codes, ciphers and decryption remains *Codebreakers*, a massive tome written by the American historian David Kahn. Kahn records in conscientious detail the activities of codebreakers through the ages, culminating with the world wars of the twentieth century, and in the first edition of the book, published in 1967, he reported on how, in the Second World War, 'Some of the most important British communications intelligence resulted, however, not from the scribblings and quiet cogitations of reticent cryptanalysts, but from the explosive sexual charms of a British secret agent in America.'[2] The reality was otherwise: since the beginning of the twentieth century, spies, regardless of their sexual charisma, have been far less productive than backroom codebreakers in providing intelligence to both the military and governments – a notable exception, perhaps, being the success enjoyed by the Soviet Union in recruiting agents in both Britain and America. Yet such tales of voluptuous agents made more attractive reading and, more importantly, they led the trail away from codebreaking. For interception and decryption operations were undergoing a massive and continuous growth as the Cold War intensified, with nuclear weapons presenting a threat to humanity many times greater than any posed by even Hitler at his most rampant, and those running these operations were determined that the whole subject must remain wholly secret – or see its usefulness destroyed.

But hints that the German Enigma cipher machine had been broken eventually started to come out abroad, beyond the jurisdiction of Britain's Official Secrets Act. In Poland and France, the few individuals aware of the essential contributions made by Poles and the French to cracking the Enigma machine were no longer willing to remain silent. And a sort of reverse pride was at work in Italy, where, unlike in Britain, you can be prosecuted for libelling the dead. The Italian navy had long simmered with anger at accusations by the Germans that it had allowed a spy to acquire the information that led, in 1942, to a successful attack on Italian naval ships that had been intended to supply German troops in North Africa. The Germans blamed the incident on a spy who used sex to gain information from a fallible Italian admiral, who in due course died. In the early 1970s, when the admiral's surviving relatives threatened to sue for libel the author of a book that repeated these charges, it seemed likely that the whole codebreaking story would start to emerge. And, indeed, once speculation about whether the Allies had broken Axis codes began to surface in books published in Germany, as well as in France, Poland and Italy, the wall of secrecy built up around the whole affair began to crumble.

The British authorities reluctantly decided that they had no choice but to allow censored versions of the story of wartime codebreaking activities to be published and, in 1974, the total ban on any mention of these activities was relaxed. After all, it had been an astounding success for the British, and an unregulated flood of rumours might not only tarnish that success but also threaten to provide details of areas about which it was essential to remain silent. It was therefore essential to monitor carefully the release of information. So a spate of personal reminiscences, first among them Fred Winterbotham's pioneering account, *The Ultra Secret*, published in 1974, alerted the wider world to the existence of Bletchley Park and its cast of eccentric characters and to the breaking of the Enigma cipher machine. Another popular book, Anthony Cave Brown's *Bodyguard of Lies*, helped to disseminate the story. (Both these books were marred by numerous errors and are now considered very unreliable.) A rash of other books followed, of varying quality and openness, and the authorities made every effort to ensure they were published under strict guidelines: what could and could not be said was carefully controlled. Those who overstepped the boundary were punished, even if they had moved beyond the jurisdiction of the Official Secrets Act. In the early 1980s, Gordon Welchman, who along with Alan Turing had played a key role in the Enigma story, had to publish his account in the USA to avoid British censorship laws. Nonetheless, Welchman's security clearance was removed and he was unable to continue working as a cryptographic consultant to companies that had contracts with the US Department of Defense.

What could, however, be allowed to circulate without compunction was the story of Alan Turing and his repressed homosexuality (repressed by the authorities, that is, not by himself). This story, with its tragic end, displaced the tales of the more orthodox sex offered by those lascivious female spies who had been the staple of the yarns the spymasters had previously spun out. Turing's well-rehearsed eccentricities – cycling in a gas mask to mitigate the effects of hay fever and so on – strengthened his appeal as the harmless crackpot-cum-genius who had saved Britain in the secret war. The other codebreakers, and the thousands of machine operators and wireless intercept operators, appeared only as a backdrop to the flawed star. Indeed, the story of the cracking of the Enigma codes eventually gained wide currency, even leading to a blockbuster novel, a play and a big-screen spin-off. Oh, and a thing called Colossus was also mentioned.

The release of information remained partial, however, and it was designed to confuse and to conflate – in effect, to subsume the Colossus story into that of Enigma. Photographs of the machine were released, along with some captions outlining its basic functions. An extremely detailed description was offered of Colossus's 'Bedstead' paper tape-reading mechanism – as if this feature represented the greatest breakthrough in information technology since the cuneiform mud tablet. But nothing was said about what Colossus actually *did*. It was apparently designed 'to help solve a specific cryptanalytic operation', and that was more or less that. No hint was given of the real importance of the machine.

However, if the details of what it did were kept secret, the claims made for Colossus were not modest and they were bound to attract attention: it was lauded as the world's first electronic computer and the forerunner of all the machines that the electronics revolution has spawned in the years since the end of the most lethal war in history. Even the closest observers remained confused, however, wondering what exactly was the relationship between Colossus and Enigma, and they duly offered many misleading interpretations that have been widely repeated. It was assumed, for instance, that Colossus had been involved in decoding Enigma messages. According to one recent book, 'Turing's decoding machine was known as Colossus' and it 'cracked German Enigma codes'.[3] As it was, Turing did indeed design a decryption machine used on Enigma messages, but it was called the Bombe and it was electro-mechanical. Furthermore, Turing was only one of the people who worked on the cipher problem for which Colossus was built and his role was tangential at best (indeed, Turing developed a hand or manual method of breaking the relevant cipher, not the machine method for which Colossus was invented).

In fact, Colossus was used to crack a quite different cipher machine, known as the Geheimschreiber or secret writer, not Enigma's Morse messages. This confusion is understandable – it was precisely the intention of Britain's modern eavesdroppers that their predecessors' secret techniques and the real story of Colossus should be confused with that of Enigma. In reality, Enigma was only half the story. The Geheimschreiber was used to link Hitler's high command with his army commanders in the field and it gave the Allies intelligence of vital strategic importance during the war. But the story of Colossus is not just the other half of the Enigma story; it actually forms the major part of Bletchley Park's Ultra output in terms of intelligence value.

However, the decades of post-war secrecy meant that it was not just the role of Colossus in the Second World War that was hidden away from view. For the history of the computer is also the history of a secret: the true history of the birth of the computer age was also concealed and then deliberately distorted by confusing it with Enigma. This book is an attempt to reconstruct the history of why and how Colossus was born, and to provide an account of its role during the Second World War, using documents that have been declassified since the late 1990s. Until now, there has been a sizeable gap in our knowledge of the birth of the computer age. These documents allow us not only to fill in much of that gap, but also to review our understanding of the historical context in which the computer was born. We can look back further and view the pre-war years from a somewhat different perspective, identifying the roots of the invention of the machine that in effect changed the world. In fact, this book searches for those roots in the meshing of cryptography, telecommunications and the military, a vital aspect of the industrialization of war, especially in the great Wireless Wars of 1914–18 and 1939–45. This retrospective view also offers the opportunity to follow the set of technical threads that intertwine to make the history of Colossus not only an issue pregnant with implications for the post-war world but also a thoroughly engrossing story in its own right.

I first heard of Colossus in the late 1970s while working for British Telecom, then still part of the Post Office and a government department. It was a time of dramatic change in the industry. Electro-mechanical technology was progressively being displaced by computerized switching and transmission systems; there was increasingly widespread deployment of computers in running the network and the organization; and in addition there were big changes in the structure of the industry as it prepared to cease being a government monopoly and become a private company in a competitive market. I worked with various generations of computers at British Telecom, and I was both surprised and fascinated when I learned that a Post Office engineer had invented the computer. Some years later, when I started writing about information and communications technology for a living, I developed an interest in computer history. However, it seemed there was one area of the history of the computer that would forever remain a mystery – Colossus. Although more information was made available about Colossus in the 1990s, the real details of the story and its relation to Enigma remained opaque, hidden behind half-truths. Here, it seemed, was one area of the history of the computer that would forever remain a mystery.

Whenever possible, I attended the always interesting meetings on the history of the computer organized by a specialist sub-group of the British Computer Society, the Computer Conservation Society. Indeed, I made sure that I could attend a meeting in May 2002 entitled 'Beyond Colossus: More Wartime Coding Machines' at the Science Museum in London. The two speakers, Brian Oakley and Tony Sale, gave an inspiring talk, shedding new light on the story and referring to a large number of newly released documents at the National Archives (formerly the Public Record Office) at Kew, West London. Brian Oakley, who had been head of the Alvey information technology research and development programme and then head of the software company Logica, said that there was a wealth of material in these archives and that it cried out for someone to examine them and write a book. It was a pleasant day and I had cycled to the museum from my home in North London. I recalled nothing of the ride home, via Hyde Park, Regent's Park and Regent's Canal, thinking instead of Colossus and, by the time I arrived home, I had already resolved to take up the challenge, or at least to initiate some investigations.

I started research at the National Archives with modest expectations; I thought I might perhaps be able to provide something for a specialist audience. But I was immediately hooked, and the deeper I delved, the more the story started to come together, often in surprisingly fascinating detail (even if significant gaps do remain). Many more important documents were released as I continued my research and wrote the early drafts of this book, and indeed I learned of several more made public only a few days before my manuscript was due to be submitted to my publisher. No doubt, further documents will follow.

One or two specialist codebreaking publications about the Vernam cipher, which Colossus was designed to break, have been published, but no one has so far attempted to place the Colossus story in a wider context. This book is my attempt to do that. Special thanks, therefore, go to Brian Oakley for first suggesting this book and for reading the whole of a draft version, commenting in detail on it and suggesting significant improvements as well as saving me from some silly errors. Tony Sale's reconstruction of Colossus, now housed at the Bletchley Park Museum, provided further inspiration. (Information received at the time of writing indicates that the Colossus reconstruction is no longer open to the public and its future at Bletchley Park Museum is in doubt.) Jean Dollimore,

George Colouris, William Newman, Andrew Emmerson, Richard Handford, Reginald Atherton and Debbie Neal also read large parts of the draft and their comments have been of immense value. John Chamberlain kindly gave me a copy of his father Arthur Chamberlain's reminiscences of Bletchley Park and the Newmanry. Andrew Hodges and Kenneth Macksey commented on particular issues. Andrew Emmerson also provided numerous important references and information on telecomms history. Several people have discussed the contents and given support and encouragement, including Tim Matschak, Clair Drew, Peter Wills, Peter Norman, Peter Landin, Tony Ward and others. Robert Dudley agreed to act as my agent when the book was at an early insubstantial stage and followed it through with dedication. Angus MacKinnon, Bonnie Chiang, Clara Farmer, Sarah Norman and Toby Mundy at Atlantic Books have given enthusiastic attention to the book from the outset. My thanks also go to the helpful and friendly staff of the National Archives, the Science Museum Library, Imperial College and the Imperial War Museum; also to Jonathan Harrison of the Library at St John's College, Cambridge, where the Max Newman Papers are held. William Newman and Helge Fykse have contributed photographs, as have British Telecom Archives, Siemens and Marconi Corporation. Frank Dobson, MP, supported my unsuccessful application that retained documents be opened to public view. Peter Freeman of GCHQ spent much time checking those retained documents for me and provided copies of certain non-sensitive pages. Finally, I must thank Daniel R Headrick, an author I have never met, for providing me with the historical framework which I have borrowed (and no doubt badly battered) and within which I have set the Colossus story. Headrick's pioneering work on the international politics of telecommunications, *The Invisible Weapon*, deserves a wider readership.

I have found the process of uncovering the Colossus story and setting it in its historical context fascinating, and I hope the reader will come to share some of that fascination with the story of how and why the most important machine of the modern age was born as a weapon of war. The Second World War, despite the immense destruction it wrought, created much of the modern world. Furthermore, the lessons of the Colossus story – the role of intelligence in war the ubiquity of eavesdropping and hacking in our digital networks, and the role of the computerized machine in society – are just as relevant to the world since the collapse of the bipolar world order as to the years of the Cold War itself. In this sense, and in many others, Colossus is a story whose telling is all too timely.

part one – interception

chapter one

Wireless War One

In August 1914, a few days after the start of the First World War, the assistant district commissioner of Fanning Island, one of the most remote outposts of the British Empire, donned his symbol of authority – a pith helmet – and walked down to the beach to welcome a French warship.[1] The island had no harbour, not even a jetty, so the warship lowered a small boat, and a landing party rowed towards and then past the coral reef that constrained the approach of larger vessels. Some of the workers who collected copra on the island dashed out into the surf to meet the party: it was the practice for visitors to be carried ashore so that they need not wet their feet. But, as the workers waded out to the boat, a uniformed officer jumped from it, ran past the porters up to the beach and the waiting assistant district commissioner. He then pulled out a pistol, waved it around for all to see and, pointing it at the commissioner's stomach, announced, 'You are my prisoner.' Out beyond the coral reef, the French flag was lowered and a German one raised in its place: the warship was, in fact, the light cruiser *Nuernberg*.

Fanning Island, located at latitude 3 degrees, 51 minutes North, longitude 159 degrees, 21 minutes West, is sixty-five kilometres (forty miles) south of the Equator and 1,900 kilometres (1,200 miles) from Hawaii. It is a typically tiny spot on the map of the

3

Pacific at fifteen kilometres long by six kilometres wide, and very low – largely just about a metre above sea level, rising to a maximum of just over three metres. A few dozen natives of other Pacific islands were employed there by a British company to collect copra, the dried kernel of the coconut from which coconut oil is extracted, and until the beginning of the twentieth century the island had been otherwise unoccupied. However, the purpose of the German ship's visit was not to seize a source of copra. Rather, it was to destroy a telegraph-cable relay station. For the island was the first landing stage of the British transpacific telegraph cable, laid in 1902, as it headed away from Canada towards Australia and New Zealand. A staff of ten to twelve people kept the cable open to telegraph traffic day and night, all year round.[2] The remote island was a tough posting for telegraph staff where, at least until the arrival of the German ship, little tended to distinguish one day from another.

The Pacific cable was the latest link in the network of All-Red Routes, owned and operated by British companies, which encircled the globe and provided the communications that both bound together the British Empire and supported every other developed country's international trade and commerce. The 'All-Red' label derived from the colour used on British maps to show the territories of the Empire, a practice that would endure until the 1960s. The main cable routes in the network touched land only on the territories of the Empire. Where there was no British territory, land was annexed – as had happened with the remote Fanning Island, no nation having previously seen the copra as being worth the effort of claiming the island, or discerning any strategic or tactical value in its possession. But the coming of the cable made it a significant location, there being no other suitable British possession in the mid-Pacific. The distance from Fanning Island to the western coast of Canada still required a single cable span of 5,600 kilometres (3,500 miles), then 'very much longer than any in existence'.[3] The next link, between Fanning Island and Fuji, was another 3,200 kilometres (2,000 miles), while the entire cable length was 11,900 kilometres (7,400 miles). Indeed, it was with the completion of the Pacific cable that the Imperial Defence Committee was able to report to the British government, 'The dependence of the United Kingdom on cable stations situated upon foreign territory has been generally eliminated.'[4]

At the end of the nineteenth century, Britain dominated the international cable networks. No other country possessed such an extensive network. One company, the Eastern Telegraph Company, controlled almost 50 per cent of the world's submarine cables, while other British companies owned another 30 per cent of the cable routes.[5] These figures underestimate the extent of British domination of worldwide telegraph traffic, because, apart from a number of transatlantic cables, most of the submarine cables owned by non-British companies were local links, connecting to British long-distance routes. For a while, writes Daniel Headrick, historian of the politics of telecommunications, this British domination of cable networks 'aroused the admiration and envy of foreigners, but little hostility. In an age of free trade, nations tolerated each other's comparative advantages. As long as the European powers were preoccupied with Continental problems and the United States with its own westward expansion, the seas were Britain's special sphere... The benefit of the telegraph for colonial administration, news and world trade were so evident that the ownership of the cables was seen as a minor issue.'[6] In this spirit, in 1885, the Committee for Colonial Defence (later renamed the Imperial Defence Committee) had declared that submarine cables should be treated as neutral assets that would not be interfered with during a conflict.[7]

These laissez-faire attitudes were to disappear as the nineteenth century drew to an end. Conflict between European nations, for example, in the rush to acquire colonies made foreign governments and their traders more resentful of British control. Several incidents – such as that at Fashoda in 1898 when British and French colonial forces came close to clashing in the Sudan – demonstrated that the

British were quite happy to make use of their dominance to read the telegrams of other countries and to use the information thus gleaned for political, military or commercial advantage. (Non-British telegrams were given lower priority than British ones and could be delayed as well as read.) This growing resentment of British control clearly signalled that the cable network would be at risk in the event of war, and so the Imperial Defence Committee turned its attention to how the cables could be protected. Its policy of treating cables as neutral assets shifted towards one of attacking other countries' cables, regardless of whether they were owned by enemies or neutrals.

> According to practice, which, in the absence of any provision dealing specifically with cable-cutting, must be regarded as the international law on the subject, it is open to a belligerent to cut cables connecting a point on the territory of the belligerent and a point on the territory of a neutral, as well as those connecting points on belligerent territory... It may be expected that an enemy such as Germany will cut as many as possible of the cables serving British interests, whether they connect points on neutral territory or not... In these circumstances, and seeing that there are places which it would be desirable for naval and military reasons to cut off from telegraphic communication in the war with Germany, or with Germany and her allies, the [Committee] are of opinion that the right to cut cables, whether neutral connecting points or not, should be exercised whenever the exigencies of war demand it... Generally speaking, if France and Russia were in alliance with this country, it would be possible to isolate Germany from practically the whole world, outside Europe, by cutting the cables to the Azores, Tenerife, and Vigo and the three cables on Yap Island.[8]

The policy of communications neutrality had in effect been replaced by the use of cables and communications as a weapon of war. Other states, including Germany and the United States, were to take the same view.[9] And it was for this reason that, in August 1914, out in the mid-Pacific, two German ships, the *Nuernburg* and the *Titania*, headed for Fanning Island, planning to use deception and the French flag to gain a bloodless landing on the island. The German officer explained that his orders were to destroy the cable station and that, if no one got in his way, no one would be hurt. The German seamen used hand grenades to blow up the powerhouse and then they smashed equipment in the operating room, spilling battery acid all over the floor. But the acid prevented them from continuing their destructive spree in an adjoining room that held sensitive equipment allowing the cable to work in both directions simultaneously. It would have taken some months to get this equipment set up again if it had been damaged, but, ironically, the careless spilling of the acid saved it.

Meanwhile, out at sea the cable itself was under attack. The *Titania*, which carried cable-cutting gear, had already hacked through the windward cable in several places and dragged the end out to deep water. The *Nuernburg* started fishing up the other cable link. But this operation was also botched. The light cruiser lacked specialist grappling equipment and so the cable had to be raised in shallow water: although it was cut, its severed ends could nonetheless be recovered fairly easily. Had the long cable end been dragged out over the edge of the reef, it could only have been lifted by a cable-repair ship. As it was, no sooner had the Germans left than the cable was recovered by staff from the plantation using a rowing boat and a grappling hook fashioned out of a pickaxe.[10] Engineers patched up a temporary connection and informed the next relay station at Suva, Fiji, of what had happened. Suva passed the message on, just in time, for it was the next port of call for the *Titania* and the *Nuernburg* and suffered similar damage. However, a cable-repair ship was dispatched from Auckland with the equipment needed to get both relay stations back into operation. It took several weeks to repair the damage, but neither relay station was attacked again and both provided normal service for the duration of the war.

The only other attempt to disrupt British strategic communications was an attack on another relay station in South West Africa where the staff were held as prisoners for a year. But the loss of the relay station did not matter. Britain had long before laid down second 'parallel' routes in its All-Red network, precisely to guarantee that communications would not be disrupted by the loss of a link or two. British maritime supremacy over the German surface fleet secured Britain's network and chased the raiders from the seas. (The *Nuernberg* herself was sunk near the Falklands Islands a few months later, along with all but one of German Admiral Graf von Spee's squadron.) Britain's cable network could now become a fully fledged weapon of war.

Even before the two German ships had approached Fanning Island, Germany itself had already been effectively isolated. Its cables were cut not haphazardly, or just at one or two remote points, but systematically and permanently. Britain, with its open economy, needed its global network to harness the resources of its Empire for the war. Constraining Germany's cable communications would undermine German efforts to win support in the USA and Latin America, as well as the Middle East and Asia, by closing down and controlling the channels that allowed Germany to gather intelligence and disseminate propaganda. The British cable ship *Telconia* executed one of Britain's first military actions of the war when it cut the five cables that linked Germany to the Americas and elsewhere. Shortly afterwards, Russia severed land cables that enabled Austria and Germany to communicate with the Middle East. Then Britain turned on Germany's overseas wireless stations, destroying those at Dar-es-Salaam and Yap in the Caroline Islands; others were destroyed in the Pacific or taken over by the Japanese, then Britain's allies. It took time to close the last loopholes, but eventually Germany was cut off from cable communication with the outside world for the remainder of the war. And the only links that remained open – courtesy of neutral governments which allowed German coded messages to be bundled in with their own diplomatic traffic – were closely monitored by the British as, at some point in their journey, they went over a British cable. This stranglehold on German international communications eventually had a decisive effect on the outcome of the war.

At the end of July 1914, a group of wireless engineers from the British Marconi Company visited their counterparts and competitors at the Telefunken Company, and were shown around its factories and research laboratory near Berlin. The most impressive demonstration was saved for the last day when the British engineers were taken to the new high-power wireless station at Nauen some fifteen kilometres from the German capital. Nauen was the most powerful wireless station in the world and an equally powerful statement of Germany's ambitions to neutralize the stranglehold exercised by Britain on cable communications. The British team saw the massive new antennas and the 200 kW high-frequency alternators that powered the transmitter. The trip had been the initiative of Telefunken and the German government, for such wireless technology promised to break the British cable monopoly and Germany wanted Britain to know it. According to the Marconi Company's official history, 'Immediately [the British] left the station, Nauen closed down its normal commercial operations and the military, who had been awaiting the visitors' departure, took over control.'[11] Later, on 31 August 1914, Nauen sent out a message, on behalf of the Imperial Admiralty, for re-transmission by the chain of German wireless stations to 'all ships and wireless stations'. Germany, it said, was 'threatened with danger of war. Enter no English, French or Russian harbours'.[12]

Germany, realizing that it lagged behind Britain in the control of cable communications, had eagerly embraced the idea of wireless. The new technology promised that Germany no longer had to endure the British intercepting, delaying and, worst of all, reading its messages. Unlike cables, which run from point to point, wireless can communicate with any number of points within its transmission range. It is quicker and easier to set up, and soon it was able to cover great distances. Wireless, an electrical technology, was an area in which German companies were expected to excel. In the latter half of the nineteenth century, the rapid advance of the German telephone and electrical industry, a key sector in the second industrial revolution, challenged British supremacy in telecommunications. The new wave of industrial and technological innovations demanded a much closer link between science and technology than in the industries that Britain had pioneered, and it was in Germany that the first industrial research laboratories appeared, marking an important stage in the development of industrial production. As a relative newcomer to industrialization, Germany found it easier to adopt the more coherent approach now needed, while British companies were slower to change and adapt.[13] 'Beyond question, the creation of this [electrical] industry was the greatest single achievement of modern Germany,' wrote the economic historian J H Clapham.[14] (In 1895, Germany employed 26,000 in its electrical industry; by 1906, the figure was 107,000. In 1913, Britain's electrical industry was about half the size of that of Germany.) The leading German electrical companies Siemens & Halske and AEG were encouraged to merge their wireless operations in the national interest, thereby creating Telefunken. By 1906, transatlantic wireless telegraphy was possible and Germany rapidly created a chain of international long-distance wireless stations, with Nauen at the centre of the web linking German possessions in Africa and the Pacific, along with one station in the United States. At a stroke, Germany was free of Britain's hard-won dominance of global communications.

But it was an illusion. The message cited above warning German naval and commercial ships of the approach of war, along with the messages below and many more transmitted later on, were inter-cepted by British wireless operators and decoded by British navy cryptanalysts. They provide a window on how Germany exper-ienced the start of the communications war. On 1 August 1914, the message was sent out: 'Mobilization of the Army and Navy is ordered. The first day of mobilization being August 2. Outbreak of war is imminent. Our opponent in the first instance is Russia. France and Great Britain not yet decided.' The next day, messages reminded cable and wireless stations that all communications needed to be protected from casual interception: all 'cable tele-grams to be ciphered, also wireless telegrams in case political situation becomes more acute. Put catchword Delta before the greeting'. But, within a month or so, the tone of the messages changed. 'All lines of communication compromised except perhaps No 163,' reads a wireless transmission of 20 September recording Britain's success in cutting German cables. Then, on 14 November, an even more serious development is recorded: 'Line Trinidad… compromised. HVB and key fallen into the hands of the enemy.' HVB was one of the main codes used by the German imperial and merchant fleets. This warning was followed by a flurry of messages instructing wireless operators to use a different code and key. The British attack on German communications was still wreaking havoc at the end of the year as German wireless operators tried to get new codes distributed and organized for use. On 24 December, a message from the German consulate in San Francisco to Bangkok was intercepted: 'With the German cipher here No 5950 I cannot decipher your communication. Please repeat or perhaps use the Marine Code.' And on 15 January 1915, German communications were again constrained by attacks on German wireless and cable stations in Africa, as this message from Nauen to the sole remaining German wireless station, in Windhoek, South West Africa, illustrates: 'Number your telegrams. Cipher telegrams referring to the occupa-tion of Luederitz Bay and Walfisch Bay received and understood.

Use Marine Code (VB). The HVB is compromised. Please report telegrams for several days.'[15]

Germany enjoyed no more success with its strategic wireless communications than it did with cable warfare. Japan took control of the German wireless stations in China and at Yap, Truk and elsewhere in the Pacific. The Germans blew up their own important relay station at Kamina, Togoland, to avoid it falling into British hands. Britain and Australia attacked a number of other stations in Africa and in the Pacific, among them those on Samoa, New Pommern and at Nauru in the Marshall Islands. In September 1914, it was the turn of the station at Duala, Cameroon, to be taken off the air. And in May 1915, South African forces closed down the station at Windhoek, South West Africa. So Germany was left with its own station at Nauen and a single station on neutral territory that was safe from a British attack – Sayville, in the USA. Even here there were limits. The US government insisted that all messages had to be 'in clear' – codes and ciphers were forbidden. Britain's stranglehold was thus almost as tight in the ether as it was around the cable networks. The British could read cables and intercept wireless messages, and they had also developed the capability to break codes if messages were not in plain language. All this was to give the British a clear military advantage as well as considerable bene-fits in diplomacy and the propaganda war, especially in the USA.

Wireless technology was over a decade old by the outbreak of the First World War, but wireless sets still tended to be large and un-wieldy, suitable only for use on ships and at land-based head-quarters. In the west, the German offensive through Belgium was eventually stopped at the first battle of the Marne, during which the British army intercepted and made good use of plain-language German wireless communications. The successful halting of the German advance was followed by a series of attempts by the two sides to outflank each other to the north-west, a process only interrupted by the Channel coast. Then trench lines were prepared and the ensuing, largely static war meant that wireless use declined. Much effort, however, was put into tapping phone and telegraph cables at the front, and army commands came to appreciate that signals intelligence operations needed to be carried out systematically. On the eastern and southern fronts, where Germany and the declining Austro-Hungarian Empire were pitched against the Russian Empire and Italy, the war was more mobile. In the autumn of 1914, the German army achieved a devastating encirclement of the Russian forces at Tannenberg. This time, it was the German army that made successful use of Russian plain-language transmissions. Hindenburg and Ludendorff, the German commanders at Tannenberg, were fêted as heroes, although the fact that they later rose to positions of supreme political as well as military authority in Germany owed perhaps as much to poor Russian wireless security as to their own competence.[16]

Once combatants on both sides appreciated that their communications required due care, more sophisticated techniques were needed and signals intelligence started to become formalized. 'Signals intelligence involved the interception of messages; traffic analysis or the inferences drawn from observation of the procedure of communications circuits; the solution of codes and ciphers; signals security; and signals deception, the endeavour to mislead the enemy about one's own intentions and capabilities. Most of these techniques were only evolved during the Great War itself.'[17] These techniques, developed in the armies of Britain, France, Germany, Austria-Hungary, Italy and the United States, would all mature and play an important part in codebreaking during the Second World War. But, in the First World War, the very immaturity of wireless was one of the reasons why warfare on the western front remained so static. Landlines could be used to connect headquarters to trenches in the very fore of the line, but they were easily disrupted or destroyed by artillery fire. As a result, commanders found themselves completely out of touch with the progress of offensives once they had been launched. Invariably, when attacking troops did manage to advance through the enemy lines, they were unable to signal back for the reserves that could consolidate and exploit their breakthrough.[18] It was effective wireless communications, as much as tanks, and the co-ordinated concentration of mobile armour, infantry and air support, that was to end the days of trench warfare.

In the land war, signals intelligence was but one source of intelligence. In the war at sea, however, it was effectively the only form of intelligence available. The most renowned decryption unit in the First World War was the Royal Navy's codebreaking department, Room 40. The traditional account of Room 40 makes great play of the fact that its creation was almost accidental and, in this respect at least, archetypically British. Some amateur wireless hams who had ignored wartime regulations requiring them to surrender their sets for the duration continued to listen in and picked up enciphered German transmissions, which they then sent on to the Admiralty. And the man in the Admiralty who received these transmissions just happened to have a lunch appointment that same day with a codebreaking enthusiast. Thus, apparently, was Room 40 established.[19] But there is an alternative view.

The British, and in particular Winston Churchill, who was First Lord of the Admiralty [i.e. the Navy Minister] during these events, wanted it believed that their cryptological achievements in World War I were the result of good fortune cleverly exploited by a handful of amateurs. This story would reassure future potential enemies that such fortuitous circumstances were unlikely to happen again, and that there was nothing inherently superior in British Naval Intelligence. Both during and after the war, the Germans refused to believe that the British had a better cryptanalytic service than their own, and attributed British success to better direction finding and sheer blind luck. Lulled by an over-optimistic faith in their own

communications security, they fell into the same trap in World
War Two. Deception served a useful purpose.[20]

The accepted accounts of how British codebreakers came into possession of the three main German naval codebooks are certainly dubious, involving tales of extraordinary acquisitions and long delays. The HVB was seized in Australia in early August, but did not reach Room 40 until the end of October, although the reason for the delay in getting a copy of this vital codebook to London is unknown. The SKM code was captured by the Russians in the Baltic at the end of August, probably from the German warship the *Magdeburg*, and it arrived in Room 40 in mid-October. Historians have cast doubt on many, perhaps most, of the details of this story so that little seems certain other than that it did come via Russia. The claim, for example, that it was found clasped in the arms of a dead German sailor washed up on the Baltic shore is undermined by the fact that the copy of the codebook held in the National Archives in London has clearly never been immersed in salt water. The recovery of the third code, the VB, was attributable to miraculous intervention, even according to British Intelligence accounts. It was claimed it had been dumped at sea by the crew of a sinking German ship in a lead-lined case that was among the fish trawled up in the net of some perplexed British fishermen a few days later. These colourful, yet highly questionable stories may have been designed to mislead observers about the extent to which British naval interception was in operation even before the war began, contrary to the official story. According to the semi-official account of Room 40 by Patrick Beesly, 'certainly few steps were taken to intercept, to pluck from the ether, the increasing flow of wireless messages… or most important of all, to set up an organization to decode any disguised messages that were obtained'.[21] But, contrary to this impression, the wireless messages quoted above from the start of the war, and many more, were intercepted by various naval and Empire wireless stations from as early as March 1914.

Certainly, the Royal Navy had been intimately involved in the development of wireless technology for some time before the war started and it had developed an awareness of the potential for intercepting wireless messages. Experiments within the Royal Navy with attempts to transmit and detect wireless signals had preceded Marconi's practical solution. The service decided, however, to follow Marconi's more promising technical approach and worked closely with his company to develop effective wireless sets for use in ship-to-ship and ship-to-shore communications. By allowing the Marconi Company to test its sets on ships, the Royal Navy gained early experience with the use of wireless as well as ensuring that sets were developed which met its specific requirements. In Germany, on the other hand, the Kaiser's naval commanders took a more high-handed approach and declined to test wireless sets, demanding instead robust, finished products. This slowed down development of the technology by Telefunken and minimized opportunities for the Germany navy to become acquainted with the use of wireless.

One consequence, in part at least, of these different approaches was that the British wireless industry was one of the few electrical sectors in which Britain did not lag behind Germany. Indeed, British wireless companies sold far more wireless sets on international markets than Telefunken did, leading the global industry in the period up to the start of the First World War.[22] Another consequence was that the Royal Navy was much better prepared and more thoroughly versed in the use of wireless than is generally thought. Similarly, just as the extent of Room 40's achievements was down-played, so great emphasis was placed in later British accounts on the importance of direction finding during the First World War – accounts which stressed how the German armed forces were constantly surprised at the accuracy and sensitivity of British direction-finding apparatus. But once again, such stories were intended to hide the truth – that British codebreaking operations were both organized and very effective.

As it was, Room 40 intercepted some 40,000 German naval messages in the course of the war, giving the Royal Navy an unparalleled oversight of German naval operations. There were few encounters between the big ships, although on the one occasion when the British and German battle fleets actually met, at Jutland in 1916, Room 40's intelligence was poorly handled by the Admiralty, thereby denying Jellicoe, the British commander, vital information about his opponent's likely position and heading. But the war at sea was one that involved large numbers of smaller vessels – in particular, minelayers and submarines. And the interception and decryption of the wireless traffic of these smaller vessels was critical to Britain's continued ability to import food and supplies.

Room 40's greatest success, however, was in decoding a diplomatic telegram. In January 1917, the British interception service, eavesdropping on US government telegram messages sent over transatlantic cables, spotted a rather long telegram in what looked like a German diplomatic code mixed in with American traffic. Enquiries showed that it had been sent from the foreign minister in Berlin, Arthur Zimmerman, to the German ambassador in Washington, despite its being sent as if it were standard US diplomatic traffic. This was one of the two routes still open to Germany, since Woodrow Wilson, the then US president, supposed that allowing German communications would help peace talks. (The other route was mixed in with Swedish government traffic, but traffic on this route was also intercepted and recognized.) But, far from promoting peace, this particular message was intended to provoke war against the United States itself.

It took the British codebreakers some time to start unravelling the message hidden within the groups of figures making up the telegram, as it used a slightly different code from the usual German diplomatic code, details of which Room 40 had reconstructed. However, as the process of teasing out the meaning of the coded message advanced, it became clear that the telegram was potentially explosive. It was to be forwarded from Washington to the German minister in Mexico and it instructed him to try to bring Mexico into the war against the USA, offering the Mexican government assistance from Germany 'to regain by conquest her lost territory in Texas, Arizona and New Mexico'. Once the telegram had been handed to the US government and made public, it brought the United States into the conflict Wilson had tried so hard to avoid – and ended any real prospect that Germany could win the war. Indeed, perhaps no other intercepted message has had such a profound effect on the course of history as the Zimmerman telegram.[23]

After the First World War, the Allied codebreaking story was made public by the heads of both the American and the British operations, and, on several occasions, the British government openly used information derived from intercepts to admonish the errant Bolshevik rulers in the Soviet Union. As a result of these public dressings down, the Soviet government adopted a highly secure system of ciphering messages known as one-time pad. One-time pads are difficult, if not always impossible, to break, and their use effectively prevented Britain from peering into Soviet communications. Codebreaking retains its greatest value if the information it provides can be used without giving away the fact that the code has been broken. Britain and America were slow to learn this lesson after the First World War, but, once they did, it became ingrained, particularly in Britain, and would underlie the extraordinarily persistent secrecy that continued to surround Bletchley Park's activities after the Second World War.

The revelations about Britain's First World War codebreaking activities led states other than Russia to look for better means of secreting messages. Wireless was too vital a tool to be discarded. Indeed, technological developments in the 1920s and 1930s meant that wireless sets were coming into use that were light enough to be carried by a person, rather than needing a team of horses or a lorry. 'Few industries, if any, grew so fast in [the inter-war] years as radio, which profited from a peculiarly favourable demand and a rapid flow of technological improvement.'[24] In the next war, every unit in the army would be in wireless contact. Thus, more effective codes and ciphers were needed. The Japanese military and diplomatic corps started to develop cipher machines in the expectation that they could produce an unbreakable means of hiding messages. The machine, stated a Japanese military assessment, was 'the only means which can absolutely withstand scientific attacks'.[25] There was shock in Germany, too, where the significance of the loss of codebooks to the enemy began to be appreciated fully. Looking back, the German armed forces concluded that the technical challenges of introducing wireless into both the navy and the army had occupied too much of their attention. And, as in Japan, a more advanced technical solution – cipher machinery – was adopted, while wireless security and codebreaking were given lesser and, as it transpired, insufficient priority.[26]

Coding or decoding devices were nothing new, but the refinement of manufacturing methods and availability of advanced electrical techniques in the 1910s and 1920s elevated the concept of cipher machines to a much more sophisticated level. In the United States and in Europe, inventors turned to machines based on rotor wheels that were intended to provide so many potential cipher keys that they would be unbreakable.[27] The wheels would have lots of connections and turn at different rates, generating a mass of different combinations of wheel positions. Even if one had access to the design details of the machine and its wheels, it would – or should – remain impossible to work out the meaning of an enciphered message unless one knew the initial settings. The turning wheels would generate the key, and both the design of the wheels and their settings would determine what key value would be generated at each stage of the enciphering process.

The most famous of these machines derives from a patent applied for in 1919 by Dutchman Alexander Koch for his concept of what he called the Geheimschrijfmachine or secret writing machine. In 1927, after failing to exploit his patent by creating any machines based on it, Koch sold the rights to Arthur Scherbius, a German engineer, who then patented his own further ideas and did indeed build a machine, which he called the Enigma. According to a marketing brochure:[28]

> The [First] World War promoted the art of cryptography in a way never known before. New systems have been developed and astonishing things accomplished in the solution of cryptographic systems… Such a [new] cipher system must have, along with security, the property that it can be used quite mechanically and for any text whatsoever. Only a very few systems have this property… [Some think] it would be impossible to construct cipher machines capable of achieving even approximately the cryptographic security which good hand systems are able to provide. In consequence of recent inventions, this point of view has had to be revised entirely. There are today machine methods of encipherment which are far superior to hand systems in cryptographic security… Now this [Enigma] machine affords the possibility of employing 22,000,000,000 different keys… the only chance for the unauthorized decipherer is to find in the traffic, assuming that he has a vast amount of material, two passages which were enciphered at the same point in the same period.[29]

The Enigma machine was widely used commercially and was also adopted by the German armed forces; eventually, many thousands were distributed. But it was clumsy and awkward to use. If the letter to be encrypted is 'H', the first operator presses the key marked 'H' on the keyboard. This opens an electric circuit through the machine, initially via a plugboard where a fixed transposition may take place, then twice through a series of three wheels, before going through the plugboard for a second time. The circuit then lights up the lamp under the letter to which the 'H' is to be transposed – in this example, 'C'. One or more wheels turn after each letter is enciphered, so that the route through them changes unpredictably. Entering a series of identical letters, 'H', 'H', 'H', 'H', 'H', would produce, say, 'C', 'W', 'L', 'Q', 'G' rather than 'C', 'C', 'C', 'C', 'C'. A letter could not be transposed into itself, but was always changed into a different letter.

The letter that was lit up would be written down by a second operator before the message was tapped out using the Morse code and sent over a wireless link by a third operator. At the distant end, a first operator would write down the letters represented by the Morse code he heard, then a second operator would enter them letter by letter into the decrypted version. The rotor wheels had to be placed in the same initial settings as those of the sending machine, then each letter would be turned back, one after another, into the plain message by depressing the key – 'C' – and the third operator writing down the letter indicated on the lampboard to see the plain-language original, 'H'.

The main technical point about Enigma is that it works by having so many different potential routes through the machine's wiring of each wheel and all the connections between the different wheels, as well as the extra transpositions possible via the plugboard. There were, in fact, several layers of complexity. First, there were five – or, in the German navy version, eight – rotor wheels from which three in the machine itself were chosen for any particular day. Each wheel had different wiring arrangements. Second, there was the possibility of sliding the external ring on each wheel so that each character took a different path through that wheel. Third, there were the initial positions, or settings, of each wheel – these were varied for every message. Finally, a further layer of complexity was added, at the German navy's request, in the form of the plugboard, which allowed pairs of characters to be transformed.

According to Heinz Bonatz, a German intelligence officer and later a military historian, Enigma was officially adopted by the

German navy in the mid-1920s, though the service was aware of its limitations. The navy required some changes which brought 'considerable improvements', such as the addition of the plugboard, which it thought were essential 'to ensure security of the key, [even] if a machine should fall into enemy hands'.[30] Indeed, having an Enigma machine would in itself be no use in trying to decrypt messages: it was essential to know which wheels had been used, the outer ring positions and the initial wheel settings for messages.

During the war, tens of thousands of Enigma machines were distributed among the armed services for use – although hand ciphers were also widely used at lower levels – and it was Enigma that carried the orders and reports transmitted within German army groups and other armed forces. Yet it remained an inefficient system. Using Enigma to encipher a message and transmit it according to regulations required three operators, and another three to decipher it. (Obviously, if necessary, two operators could work the system at each end, or even one, but, naturally, using three reduced errors.) Each letter had to be written down several times and the whole process was decidedly time-consuming, providing many opportunities for mistakes. It may have been suitable for the operational units of the armed forces, but the administrative units – the general staff, army headquarters, intelligence, quartermasters, weapons-production organizations, transportation authorities, and so on – produced vast volumes of printed material. It soon proved to be impractical to encipher even a fraction of that material by the Enigma process. A totally different, and very secret, cipher machine was needed.

chapter two

Codes and Ciphers

The logbook of the Royal Navy frigate *Imperieuse* as she sailed along the coasts of France and Spain during the Napoleonic Wars contains several laconic entries, such as that for 18 August 1808: 'Boats sent out to destroy signal post. Boats returned and completely destroyed [the post] without opposition.' The next day another telegraph-signal station was destroyed. On 22 August there was a less successful operation as the boats 'had to be recalled when [it was] observed that the fort was being reinforced with a number of troops'.[1] In September, the attacks started again, this time with help from another British boat, the *Spartan*, commanded by Captain Brenton, who reported to Admiral Collingwood how on 'the 8th a party from the ships landed and blew up a signal house and Telegraph in the bay'. Four days later another raiding party did more damage and, according to Brenton's report, 'carried off their books'.[2]

These 'books' were the codebooks which explained the meaning of the signals displayed on the French semaphore or visual telegraph stations. But the Scottish captain of the *Imperieuse*, Thomas Cochrane, did not just spirit the codebooks away. Although Cochrane was something of a swashbuckler and later played an important role in the revolutions of Greece, Chile and Peru after his fiery temper had ruffled the sensitivities of staid British admirals and forced him from the navy, he was essentially a thoroughly professional and modern naval officer, and, as such, he recognized the true value of the codebooks. On one raid, he deliberately left behind a few partly burned but clearly recognizable shreds of the codebooks near the fire that had been started to destroy the telegraph-relay station. He hoped these remains would be seen and lead the French to conclude that the codebooks had been burned rather than stolen.[3]

The telegraph stations were part of a large network of visual telegraph lines that spread out to most of the capitals of the Napoleonic Empire, even reaching Vienna and across the Alps to Italy. The visual telegraph was a development of the French revolution, but reached its zenith in Napoleon's imperial service. As one military historian puts it, 'An Imperial order uttered in Paris late one evening would have drums booming across Venice barrack yards six hours later, with the garrison under arms and ready to march.'[4] Nothing like this had been possible before, and the visual telegraph brought modern telecommunications to the world. Other nations adopted similar technologies, which lasted in service until the invention of the electric telegraph displaced its less sophisticated forerunner.[5]

Cochrane sent the captured codebooks on to Admiral Collingwood, who made use of them to read the signals being transmitted from one telegraph station to another along the coast – simply by observing the fluttering arms of the relay stations with the help of a telescope from a British ship off the coast, just out of artillery range. As Collingwood reported to the Admiralty, 'Yesterday the French Signal Post telegraphed that a Fleet of Transports were anchored to the southward of Port Especcia and Transports landed – the Ships of War standing into the Bay.'[6] British naval attacks in the Bay of Naples followed, based on this unusual but highly reliable source of intelligence. While Napoleon was well served by the most sophisticated communications network the world had seen, its security was breached by a simple, cunning ruse.

Living as we do in an age of instant electronic communication from desktop computer to the global internet, with text messages sent over mobile-phone links, and hundreds of television channels beamed down the telephone line to our homes, even the electric telegraph age might strike us as desperately archaic. When hundreds of different waves of light, each carrying thousands of millions of bits of data, can travel though a single optical fibre across the Atlantic or the Pacific, then the days when a few bits per second – pulses representing the dots and dashes of the Morse code – flowed through chunky electric cables seem a technological eon away. The visual telegraph seems even more quaint and antiquated – constrained as it was by fog and the onset of night. However, many of the characteristics of the codes underlying the invention of Colossus, and indeed of modern computer codes, are the same as the codes of the visual telegraphs of the Napoleonic era. One very simple British Admiralty code used six shutters, each of which can be either open or closed – giving a total of sixty-four possible combinations. It was set up during the Napoleonic Wars, copying the French invention. Each letter of the alphabet and each numeral was allocated to one combination, with the remaining combinations allocated to some short, commonly used phrase or signal (such as 'To the Admiral of the Fleet' or 'Court-martial sentence to be carried out'). The only exception was the 'all shutters open' combination, which was not used for the simple reason that it was difficult to see.

A second example is a code used on the original French Chappe telegraphs – named after their inventor, Claude Chappe. Each signal represents an arbitrary number between 1 and 95 which refers either to a codebook or to an entry in one of the codebooks. Signals were sent in groups of three. The first signal could be either '1', '2' or '3' and represented one of three codebooks. The second signal represented the page number in the book, and the third signal represented the code entry on that page. So, '2, 38, 67' would signify 'codebook 2, page 38, entry 67'. Each codebook had 8,464 possible entries (ninety-two pages times the ninety-two entries on each page), giving a total of around 25,000 'messages', any one of which could be sent with just three signals. This slightly more complex system enabled long messages to be sent much more quickly than if they had to be spelled out letter by letter, as on the Admiralty shutter system. The important point to note about this particular Chappe code is that a signal can have more than one meaning, depending in this case on the signals that precede it. In the second signal of a group of three, '38' means 'page 38' in 'codebook 1', 'codebook 2' or 'codebook 3', depending on whether the first signal is a '1', '2' or '3'.

Cochrane took great care not to let the French know that he had captured the codebook for the visual telegraph. If they had realized the codebook had been taken, it would have been easy for the meanings to be changed – though the system's signals would have remained the same. Code assignations can be changed at will by issuing a new codebook, thus the actual assignations are arbitrary. With the invention of the electric telegraph towards the end of the 1830s, scores of new coding systems were introduced, some secret and some public (they could also be used to cut the cost of sending telegrams by keeping them very short, for example). One of the most common was the Morse code and it became very widely used, as it is relatively easy to pick up and, given application and ability, experienced operators can achieve a high speed. Until recently, the knowledge of Morse was so popular and so widespread that it was applied to all sorts of communication systems in addition to cable and wireless, including semaphore flags, reflected lights and Verey signals.[7] As the actual assigning of code meaning to signal is arbitrary, the inventor of the code, Samuel Morse, was thus at liberty to distribute the alphabet and other characters as he wanted. He worked out a highly practical assignment of character to signal, giving the most commonly used letters of the English language to the shorter dot-and-dash combinations. The most common letter is 'E' and in the Morse code it is a single dot; the next most common letter, 'T', is signalled by a single dash. The modern version of the International Morse Code requires about 940 dot-units (a measure of Morse traffic) to send a message of 100 English letters; a random distribution would need about 1,160 dot-units, nearly 25 per cent more.[8]

The reason for the popularity of the Morse code is that, in the jargon of modern technological theory, it is a 'people-centred' technology. Its dots and dashes are easily distinguished by the human ear.[9] However, while the different-length dots and dashes are suited to human beings, they are not always the most efficient way of exploiting the capacity of a transmission channel, whether cable or wireless. At the time, it was thought that the greatest throughput could be achieved by keeping signals as short as possible – which also meant that the signals should be of equal length.[10] Furthermore, as telegraph traffic exploded in the late nineteenth century, network-operating companies looked for ways of increasing the capacity of their cables by the greater use of fast machines rather than slow and expensive human telegraphy. One such method interleaved several different messages and this required fixed-length signals. The variable signals that accounted for Morse code's popularity was not the best way to exploit machine telegraphy.

Emile Baudot was an 'untrained and unassuming official' in the French Telegraph Administration who 'succeeded in making one improvement after another, until by the end of the [nineteenth] century, he came to be acknowledged and honoured as one of the great pioneers' of telecommunications.[11] The unit of the rate of change of a signal was later named in his honour as the Baud, giving us the still occasionally used term Baud rate, a measure of data transfer speed for modems.[12] The particular invention of Baudot that is of relevance to the Colossus story is his code for use with telegraphic printing machines. Adopted by the French telegraph service in 1877, this eventually became an international standard following two conferences of telegraph administrations in Berlin in 1929 and 1931.

The Baudot code is quite straightforward (though with one slightly confusing aspect owing to its shift function, as will be seen below). In each Morse code assignation, there can be a variable number of dots/dashes (one dot/dash each for 'E' and 'T', three each for 'S' and 'O', and so on). In the Baudot code, however, there is a fixed number of units for every signal. Essentially it is the same as the Admiralty shutter system except that it has five signal units rather than six. Each of the five units in a single signal can be in one of two states. The Admiralty system, with its six units with open or closed states, had sixty-four possible signals, whereas the Baudot code, with its five units which, in the telegraphic terminology of the time, could be either a mark or a space, had just half that number – that is, thirty-two possible signals.[13] The marks and spaces of the code could be punched on a five-channel paper tape, with a hole representing a mark and the absence of a hole representing a space, with up to five holes across the tape representing one character. The paper tape could then be read by a machine and transmitted at a steady, precise pace. In general, the all-spaces combination, that is '00000', was not used, just as the Admiralty all-open combination was avoided. The mark and space names are arbitrary, but there is of course another meaning to the word – the space between two words on a printed page. This type I will call a SPACE to distinguish it from a space in the telegraphic sense. A printing machine had to be instructed to print a SPACE, so it had to have a signal in the Baudot code and was represented by '00100'. Indeed, the SPACE was one of the most commonly occurring 'characters' in telegraphic printing-machine language – as will become apparent later in the story of Colossus.

By the 1920s, printing telegraph machines had evolved to what became known in German as the Fernschreiber and in English as the teleprinter (or teletype in American English). The teleprinter is essentially an electric typewriter with a transmitter/receiver connected to a cable or a wireless link. Two teleprinter operators could literally chat to each other using the keyboard, with characters typed at one end appearing on the other teleprinter at the distant end of the connection.[14] When a key was depressed, the sending teleprinter would generate the appropriate Baudot combination and transmit the five units over the link. At the other end, the Baudot code combination would cause the receiving teleprinter to print the appropriate character (or 'SPACE', 'line feed' and so on). Alternatively, a message could be pre-punched, or perforated, on to a five-hole paper tape and transmitted later using a tape reader attached to the teleprinter.

A shift system was introduced with teleprinters – very much like that used on typewriters and modern computer keyboards – to nearly double the number of meanings that could be signalled by the thirty-two Baudot code combinations. There were two shift levels, letters and numerals – which can be compared to the three Chappe codebooks. Two code combinations were reserved for letters-shift and figures-shift commands. The remaining thirty signals were given a letters and a numerals meaning (though in some cases – namely 'SPACE', 'carriage return' and 'line feed' – the meaning is the same in both shift levels). The system thus had fifty-five possible signals. Where it was possible for a signal to have two meanings, the actual meaning was determined by whether the last preceding shift signal was letters-shift or figures-shift. Thus, following a letters-shift signal, all subsequent signals signified the letters meaning until a figures-shift signal was sent, when all subsequent signals represented their figures meaning.[15] The Baudot code as used on teleprinters is shown in Appendix A.

There is one slight complexity. Although it was actually introduced to make things easier, the basic teleprinter code can initially seem confusing. The signals transmitted between two teleprinters contain a stream of Baudot units, each group of five units representing one of two possible meanings, some meaning letters, others figures and so on. The operators working on the teleprinter at each end of the link did not see any of this. They typed in (or perforated on to paper tape) the plain-language message consisting of letters, numerals and punctuation, plus the necessary shift commands. The sending teleprinter converted the keyed message to the appropriate commands, and at the distant end the receiving teleprinter reacted to the signals and printed out the appropriate letters or numbers and punctuation marks, carriage returns and so on.

However, if the transmission was intercepted in mid-stream, the message would consist of a stream of Baudot units including the teleprinter-instruction signals. If the eavesdroppers wanted to study the intercepted message, they could print it on the teleprinter and get rid of the shift and other instructions. But, for reasons to do with the cipher technique, the codebreakers needed to analyse the mid-transmission character stream. They could have printed out the string of marks and spaces and worked out what each one meant, but an easier way was to allocate each five-unit signal a single character as an 'identifier' and print that instead. This was called the basic teleprinter code. The eavesdroppers would find it much easier to work with a stream of single characters than with a stream of marks and spaces or ones and zeros. The left-hand of the three columns to the right of the Baudot code in Appendix A shows the basic teleprinter code which serves this purpose.

The important point is that the meaning of a signal is dependent on the last transmitted shift signal. So that, following a letters-shift signal, all 'Q' signals represent the letter 'Q', but, following a figures-shift signal, any 'Q' signals represent the figure '1'. 'M' in the basic teleprinter code means the letter 'M' in letters-shift and 'full stop' in figures-shift and so on. Thus, the intercepted message, printed out in the basic teleprinter code, would show sequences such as '5M89' interspersed between readable words. '5M89' means: '5' – figures-shift; 'M' – full stop; '8' – letters-shift; and '9' – 'SPACE'. The sequence '8QWERT' would mean: '8' – figures-shift; 'Q' – 1; 'W' – 2; 'E' – 3; 'R' – 4; and 'T' – 5 (i.e. '12345'). Sequences such as '5M89' were to be vital to the later story of Colossus. What all this does mean is that the so-called 'plain language' of intercepted messages is often anything but that, especially for messages containing lots of abbreviations and so on, as is clearly illustrated in the full text of an example of an intercepted message reproduced in Appendix O – Whiting decode, 5 February 1945. The interplay of shift and message was to play an important part in the later cracking of the cipher technique used for teleprinter messages.

Another apparently trivial workaday aspect of telecommunications codes is worth noting, for it also contributed to the later codebreaking effort at Bletchley Park. When Samuel Morse first invented his code, he gave the shortest code combinations to the most common characters. Baudot also thought about how to assign code combination to character and allocated the easiest finger movements to the most common characters on the five-hole punch he invented for perforating five-hole paper tape. Later on, in the 1920s, when the typewriter-style alphabetic keyboard was adapted for use on the teleprinter (some early telegraphic printing machines used piano-style keyboards), concern for the operators' finger movements on a five-key keyboard was not a consideration. A new assignment, proposed by telecommunications engineer Donald Murray, aimed to minimize and to equalize wear and tear on the machine parts (in fact, it is Murray's assignment that is now called the Baudot code, not Baudot's original distribution).[16] In it, the more common characters were, generally, given the combinations with more spaces than marks. This was to minimize maintenance, as the paper tape used a hole to indicate a mark and the absence of a hole to indicate a space – with the result that spaces did not add to wear and tear of the wire brush making contact with the metal plate behind the paper tape and thus reduced the amount of maintenance needed over long periods of service. This prosaic motivation for assigning code combination to character was to underlie the later statistical codebreaking work performed by Colossus.

*   *   *

Although codebooks may change, codes represent a *fixed* assignment of a unit of meaning (letter, word, phrase, etc.) to a unit of the code. Patterns will appear in coded traffic because certain entries will appear frequently, giving codebreakers points of weakness which they can attack. Knowledge of the coincidence of certain code numbers with particular events, for example, could offer a way into divining the meaning of code signals. The need for secrecy demanded a more complex means of hiding the meaning of messages – a method that changed the assignment of message to code/signal with every message. This meant the refinement of another concept in cryptology, that of the cipher.[17]

Ciphers began to appear from the beginning of the fifteenth century, but were really hybrids, combining elements of both a code and a cipher, often more the former than the latter. The invention of the electric telegraph, and the vast amount of traffic it could carry, created the demand for complex ciphers – ones that could withstand all efforts to break them. Charles Wheatstone, a key figure in the invention and commercialization of the electric telegraph, also invented a technique known as the Playfair cipher. Rather than having a codebook with lots of specific entries, the Playfair cipher allowed two or more people who both knew a keyword to write down, using a simple rule, a table of up to twenty-six letters. The table would then be used to convert pairs of letters in any plain message to pairs of ciphered letters by following some further simple rules. The recipient would know the keyword and make an identical table of letters, then use a reverse set of rules to work out the plain message. Here are the central concepts underlying the modern use of the term cipher – the key, that could be changed as often as practicable, and the set of rules, or the process. With the Playfair cipher, and other similar ciphers of the time, the process was carried out by hand, using pen and paper, taking the plain message, the keyword and writing out the table, then another piece of paper to write down the enciphered result. A keyword could be a single word, or a string of random letters or numbers. To encipher and to decipher, the keyword had to be known at both ends. It could be changed as often as was liked, provided a system existed for informing users at both ends of the new key. Even if someone knew about the cipher system in use – that is, they knew the process, the rules – they would still not be able to decipher any particular message without access to the specific key used for enciphering it. The purpose of a key-based cipher is to avoid the problem of repeated use of the same transposition, so it was important that keys were not reused often, if at all.

The Playfair cipher was just one key-based cipher of the many that were proposed during the nineteenth century. When General Lord Raglan was sent out to be British commander during the Crimean War, he was given a cipher by the Foreign Secretary, Lord Newcastle. Newcastle was aware that the telegraph line then in use passed through several European countries where foreign governments could read messages sent over it – it was this awareness that led to the development after the Crimean War of the British-owned cable to India, a cornerstone of what became the All-Red Network. Newcastle told Raglan that Foreign Office experts, a Mr Hammond and a Colonel Murphy, had concluded that 'the cypher approved by your Lordship, though perfectly suitable for correspondence by mail or messenger, is not calculated for Telegraphic Messages'.[18] Raglan was given the only copy of a special Foreign Office cipher book and was asked to return it as soon as possible after making his own copy of it. He was recommended, 'In cases, therefore, when it may appear to you expedient to resort to the Telegraph as well as a cypher, you would do well I think to make use of the Foreign Office Cypher, which from a peculiarity of its composition, is, I am assured, singularly well-adapted for telegraphic communications.'

Wheatstone's friend, the mechanical computer pioneer Charles Babbage, was also keenly interested in ciphers. It has recently been established from his papers that Babbage managed to crack the then most commonly used form of cipher, the Vigenère cipher. The most recent account of Babbage, *The Cogwheel Brain*, by Doron

Swade, goes as far as to suggest that the Victorian polymath did not publicize his achievement so that the British government could intercept and decrypt the telegrams of the Russian government during the Crimean War.[19] (Swade was for a long time the keeper of the history of the computer department at the Science Museum in London, where the Babbage papers are kept and thus had unrivalled access to the previously hidden details of Babbage's extraordinary career.) The examples of both Cochrane and Babbage indicate that the codebreakers of Room 40 and Bletchley Park come from a long British tradition in the cryptanalytic craft – a craft which Bletchley Park was to turn into a mechanized industry.

As no one knew of Babbage's breach of its security, the Vigenère cipher remained in use and was considered unbreakable. It was especially popular with military users because of that perceived security. However, in 1863 a retired Prussian army major published a work, *Die Geheimschriften und die Dechiffrir-kunst* ('Secret scripts and the art of decipherment'), which included a solution to the Vigenère cipher. Its use ceased virtually overnight, leaving cipher departments in armies and diplomatic offices across Europe searching for a secure new solution. David Kahn, the historian of codebreaking, identifies this period as marking the birth of the modern cryptologic arms race with the constant development of new codes and ciphers, followed by systematic attempts to find ways to break them.[20] The eagerness of the search varied from country to country, but was pursued most conscientiously of all in France, where a Dutch-born scholar turned French citizen – the rather grandly named Jean-Guillaume-Hubert-Victor-Francois-Alexandre-Auguste Kerckhoffs van Nieuwenhof – published a seminal work, *La Cryptographie Militaire*, in 1883. Better known simply as Auguste Kerckhoffs, he argued that to have secure ciphers it was necessary to devote a large effort to cipher-breaking activities. This was the only way to become aware of the weaknesses of ciphers and the methods of their use, and to make them secure in both construction and daily use. Kerckhoffs's message was greeted enthusiastically in France, where many still smarted from the military defeat that had been suffered at the hands of the Prussians in 1870–71. Thus, interest in deciphering German messages started well before the First World War and gave the French military a useful headstart in interception and decryption when that war started. Britain also entered the First World War with a more rigorous outlook on codebreaking, leading to the success in particular of Room 40. In Germany, however, there was less emphasis on decryption. According to Kahn, with its military prowess well demonstrated, there was less perceived need in Prussia to think about decryption as an essential part of modern warfare. And, in the aftermath of the war, it was hand ciphers themselves that were seen to be breakable, rather than the way a cipher was designed and used. Germany and Japan drew the lesson that stronger ciphers were needed and looked to the use of cipher machines. But there was less appreciation on their part that codebreaking expertise was also a prerequisite for effective cipher security.[21]

It would be wrong, however, to give the impression that only Germany and Japan sought security in machine ciphers. After the United States joined the war, there was intense interest there in machine ciphers. Gilbert S Vernam, an American telecommunications research engineer employed in the research department of the US telegraph company AT&T, was working with his colleagues on developing machine cipher techniques. As telegraphy was increasingly using the Baudot rather than the Morse code, the twenty-seven-year-old Vernam devised a way of using electric circuits to combine a stream of Baudot code signals representing a plain-language message with another stream of Baudot code signals representing a random stream of characters – a key – to create a stream of enciphered characters. This is now known as the Vernam cipher. Unlike Baudot, the American engineer was not untrained, and his scientific background was central to his inventive abilities. For example, he was familiar with the ideas of a tight-laced nineteenth-century Anglo-Irish logician, George Boole, who had formalized various logical techniques. Indeed, Vernam employed one set of Boole's logical tables for the rules used in his cipher to manipulate underlying Baudot code units. There is, though, an important distinction here. The Enigma machine works on the plain-language character, not on the Morse code itself, whereas the Vernam cipher operates on the individual Baudot code units (see Appendix B). The key would be a stream of random characters encoded in the Baudot code, whether on paper tape or generated by the rotor wheels of a machine. The process would be determined by the rules for processing the code representing the plain-language characters and the code representing the key characters. This simple process – using a set of four rules – needs to be studied first.

The technique depended on four rules for modifying the original units depending on an input key. Two '1's or two '0's combine to result in '0'; one '0' and one '1' combine to produce '1' – or, put another way, if both units are the same (both '1's or both '0's), the output is a '0'; if the input units are different the output unit is a '1' ('1' and '0', or '0' and '1'). The five units of each character are independent of each other (there is no carry as in standard binary arithmetic). These rules specify how two characters were combined (according to the Vernam cipher rules) to produce an enciphered text. This was a relatively easy routine to implement in machinery using telecommunications switching devices known as relays, where a control circuit can be used to open or close another circuit depending on the presence or absence of current in the control circuit. But there was another, extraordinarily practical consequence of the rules. Deciphering was exactly the same process as enciphering. The same key was combined with the encrypted characters, using the same rules, to decipher an enciphered message, as illustrated in the example in Appendix B. This reversibility, which is actually inherent in the limited possibilities offered by the two-state binary units and the way the Vernam cipher rules operate, had enormous operational advantages, both in terms of the machine design and ease of use.

To understand why this occurs, it is worth looking at some of the results the rules produce. First, combining a character with itself produces all spaces ('00000') because, when a character is combined with itself, the value of each pair of units will always be the same. And the rules state that, if both input and key units are the same (i.e. both '1's or both '0's), the output is a space ('0'). This is also why the second combination of the key stream in the decryption operation wipes out the effect of the first, enciphering combination, revealing the plain-language original. The second combination of the key is the same as combining it with itself, thus turning it into all spaces ('00000') and allowing the units representing the original plain-language character to be revealed. This effect was central to the working of the technique – and also to its later breaking at Bletchley Park. Second, it is worth noting that, if the key stream contains the all-spaces character ('00000'), then none of the plain-language units is changed, so the plain-language character itself does not change and is copied directly into the ciphered text. (Unlike the Enigma machine, therefore, the Vernam cipher does allow a character to be enciphered as itself.) This effect was also to prove to be crucial to the breaking of the cipher, for the all-spaces combination was not normally used in plain language, but it would have appeared as frequently as any other combination in a random key and in the enciphered text.

Vernam's idea was simple but pregnant with potential. According to the historian of ciphers, David Kahn, Vernam had conceived of a means of automating ciphers, and his patent was 'perhaps the most important in the history of cryptology'.[22] But there were practical issues. It would be fairly straightforward to build devices that could implement the combination of the two streams using paper tapes containing characters in the Baudot code. The drawback was creating sufficient random key tapes. The key stream had to be as long as the message to be enciphered and it had to be purely random. And a completely different random key stream had to be used for each different message. Keys had to be, in the jargon, for one-time use. However, it was just not practical to develop a method of punching random characters into paper tapes in the quantities that were needed, even in the comparatively staid days for the telegraph industry after the First World War. In any subsequent war, there would be millions of messages and it would be utterly impossible to generate sufficient one-time keys

A trial held in 1918 using linked printing telegraph machines in three different US cities proved successful. But it became harder and harder to produce keys on paper tapes of sufficient length. The test network was only capable of handling approximately 135 messages a day, and producing the tens of thousands of different random keys needed during a war was beyond the bounds of practicality. Furthermore, when attempts were made to automate the production of key tapes, they inevitably produced patterns which decryption experts in the US army easily picked up. L Morehouse, a colleague of Vernam, tried creating keys using two paper loops each of different length, which together would produce a considerably longer cycle, and in 1931 Colonel Parker Hitt, a retired US army officer working for the ITT Corporation, developed a machine using two sets of rotor wheels to implement the Morehouse technique. The length of the key cycle was 10.4 to 10 to the power of 19, an impressive-sounding figure, but it was regular and thus broken fairly easily.[23] The Vernam cipher seemed like a good idea, but had a practical flaw and was rejected by the military. In the cipher, as security is entirely dependent on the security of the key, if keys could not be produced in sufficient number, and with adequate security, the idea was of no use. After the First World War ended, AT&T had also tried to interest the telegraph administrations of other countries in the system for their own networks, but none was interested, and it was as much a commercial failure as a military one.

Yet, Vernam's cipher was not completely forgotten. As part of its marketing programme, AT&T had organized a demonstration of the technique for overseas telegraph administrations in New York, including delegates from Germany. The German visitors made no hint of wanting to buy the patent rights to use the technique, but it was quietly noted and taken back for further secret development by electrical firms in Germany in conjunction with the newly security-conscious armed forces. In the 1930s, the Vernam cipher was applied by two German telecommunications companies, Siemens & Halske and Lorenz to develop various different versions of what were known generically as the Geheimschreiber – the secret writer. The machines they devised used rotor wheels instead of paper tapes for the stream of characters in the key – though the rotor wheels were used in a wholly different way to the Enigma machine. And, unlike Parker Hitt's machine, they did not have regular patterns in the keys, or at least not patterns that were easy to identify.

In the Enigma machine, the rotor wheels perform the transposition by complex wiring arrangements within the wheel entry and exit points. The wheels used for the various German Geheimschreiber machines had no internal wiring, but instead had a number of pins (or cams) around the circumference of each wheel that could either be raised (projecting out from the rim of the wheel) or lowered (flush with the wheel). A raised pin would represent a mark (or a '1') and a flush pin a space (or a '0'). The pattern of raised and flush pins on a combination of wheels, grouped in sets of five wheels, would produce the key stream as they passed the active position. The wheels could be removed from the machine and the pattern of raised and flush pins could be changed. The wheels might or might not turn between each character. Alternatively, some wheels might turn one position every character and others intermittently. The complexity of the Geheimschreiber depended on a number of factors – the way the different wheels were used in conjunction with each other; how the wheels turned between each character; how many pin positions there were on each wheel; the pattern of raised/flush pins on each wheel at any one time; and the wheel starting positions used for each individual message. The way different wheels were combined, how many pin positions they had and how they turned were part of the basic machine design, but the raised/flush pin patterns and the wheel-starting points were set by the users and could be changed as often as was deemed necessary.

Obviously, if the wheels were not to be impractical in size, they had to be fairly small, so they eventually would have to repeat themselves. The intricacy of the Geheimschreiber, therefore, lay in the way the wheels were interconnected and designed to run in conjunction with each other to hide the wheel repetitions. The Siemens & Halske engineers conceived of the enciphering device as an integral part of a teleprinter. The first German patent was issued in July 1930 to two Siemens engineers, August Jipp and Erhard Rossberg. (A more advanced version was patented in the US by Siemens engineers in 1933.) Some machines were sold commercially, but the German navy was the main customer for the first of the Siemens and Halske T52 series of machines.[24] A later version was also adopted for use by the Luftwaffe. The Germany army turned as well to Lorenz, a much smaller manufacturer of telephone, wireless and teleprinter equipment, and in 1938 Lorenz started to develop an alternative solution, also using rotor wheels and the Vernam cipher, which was known as the SZ40 and was first released in 1940 (a later version released in 1942 was known as the SZ42) – SZ standing for Schluesselzusatzgeraet, cipher attachment.[25] Unlike the Siemens machine, which was an integrated cipher machine and teleprinter, the Lorenz SZ40 was a 'stand-alone' device that could be attached to any standard teleprinter, thus giving more flexibility in its use.

A point about terminology is necessary here. Neither the T52 nor the SZ40/42 was initially called the Geheimschreiber – rather this is a name that seems to have been adopted informally for the class of machines. The SZ40/42 was sometimes referred to as the G-Zusatz, the Geheimzusatz (secret attachment).[26] However, Geheimschreiber became established as a generic name used by the German military for the Siemens and Halske T52, the Siemens T42 and the Lorenz SZ40/42 – as was revealed to British code-breakers by intercepted messages. Henceforth, the word will be used for the class of machine generally.

The Geheimschreiber would be connected to a teleprinter – as an integral part of the machine or as an external attachment depending on the manufacturer – either before the transmitter or immediately after the receiver. The operator would type a message on the keyboard or feed it from a perforated paper tape. The teleprinter would pass the message to the cipher machine, the enciphered output then going off to either a landline or wireless transmitter. At the receiving end, the enciphered message would be picked up by the receiver and fed into a cable going into another identical Geheimschreiber, which would decipher the message and pass it to a teleprinter for printing in plain language. Neither operator would see the enciphered text and both had only to ensure that their wheels' pin patterns were the same and that they had the same initial wheel positions, or settings. The enciphered text existed only in the transmission – and would be seen only by someone who intercepted it.

This points to another important difference from the Enigma machine which employed a manual process involving pen and paper as well as a mechanical one in the enciphering and deciphering process. The Geheimschreiber did its work automatically on the stream of code combinations emitted by the sending teleprinter. At the receiving end, the automatic process took place between the landline or wireless receiver and the teleprinter again did its job automatically. Nowadays, this would be called an on-line process, while the Enigma did its work off-line.[27] Clearly, the Geheimschreiber was a much more efficient concept, requiring no action from the teleprinter operators other than to set up the wheels in the same way and with the same starting point – the setting – and to switch the cipher machine into the line. The Geheimschreiber then did its work without further intervention – and without the need for a row of operators writing down one character after another. In contrast, the Enigma machine could only encipher the letters of the alphabet, so numbers had to be spelled out in words, a time-consuming and error-prone process. It was common practice for the teleprinter operators to punch or perforate the message on to paper tape before transmission so that the message could be fed in automatically at the appropriate time to enable any messages to be sent at high speed for the shortest time possible – for economic reasons and to minimize the chances of interception.

The Geheimschreiber had the capability of handling large volumes of traffic – far more than could be transmitted by operators using manual Morse to send messages. The different Geheimschreiber versions produced for the German military varied in the way the wheels were integrated – or in their architecture to borrow a modern term. The task of the German codemakers was to ensure that the wheel patterns remained hidden; that of the British codebreakers was to uncover them. The ensuing battle was to be fought out by telecommunication engineers and mathematicians on both sides.

chapter three

Between the Wars

The head of giant German electrical and engineering company Siemens & Halske, Carl Friedrich von Siemens, was put out but not greatly surprised when, at the end of the First World War, the newly established Bolshevik government nationalized the company's establishments in Russia without compensation. 'Thus assets of about 50 million gold Roubles, the result of nearly sixty years' enterprise in Russia, were lost to the House of Siemens for ever.'[1] But it was not just the dedicated enemies of capitalism who confiscated private property. Siemens's branches in Belgium, France, Italy and Britain were also taken away from the company. 'Expropriation of the Capitalist without compensation was one of the main points in the Bolshevist creed… What took place in England, however, and in consequence of the English example, in other countries of the enemy coalition, was basically something much worse.' During the war, all German-owned Siemens property in Britain had been sequestrated by the state, before eventually being sold to British competitors of the German company, and ending up in the hands of the English Electric Company (with complex arrangements made for partly British-owned assets such as Siemens Brothers).

Again, all that remained to be done in Berlin was to write off the whole of Siemens property in Great Britain. What the Siemens brothers resented most, was the fact that the sequestrated Firm continued to be run under the old name. For this purpose, therefore, the German name was good enough… Carl Friedrich von Siemens in particular, for six years Chief of the English House, with many English friends and a certain predilection for the English way of life, was unable to overcome the shock of these events as long as he lived. 'They have even stolen our name', he was wont to say with bitterness.[2]

To make matters worse, the war had damaged Siemens's international markets and encouraged the growth of competitors. And Siemens had not wanted the war in the first place.

As international trading concerns with wide markets, the companies making up the German electrical industry had been none too pleased at being involved in a war which would close sources of raw materials and outlets for products. Production at Siemens was diverted from domestic and commercial goods to military ones. And the demand for ever more bodies for the fronts led to skilled and general labour shortages. There were, however, some products which were suddenly in great demand: field cable, for use at the front, and long-distance telegraph cable were used in enormous quantities by the military, and a new Siemens high-speed telegraph machine was widely used. But the redirection of manufacturing plant to war products distorted the company's structure, as field cable had only one sizeable customer – the army – and high-speed telegraphy was soon to be obsolescent. Shortly before the war started, Siemens had built the world's first long-distance telephone link. This exciting development had to be shelved for war work – leaving the field open for the new challenger to Germany's dominance in electrical industries, the United States, whose electrical and telecommunications companies were quick to move into the void left by Siemens's isolation from world markets. So the victorious Allies not only purloined Siemens's companies and its brand name, but they also ensured that their own companies could take over its markets. It was the most difficult period in Siemens's history as a company.

Yet the company's troubles did not constrain it excessively. Indeed, it was in the inter-war period that the German communications industry started to outpace its British counterpart. The 1920s and 1930s were to be years of constant rapid advance in telecommunications, especially wireless and telephone technologies. This technological turmoil would play to Siemens's strengths in the research and the development of innovative products. Many significant advances, especially in electronic technologies, were to come out of Siemens laboratories in the 1920s, 1930s and early 1940s (including some shipped off to the United States at the end of the Second World War that were instrumental in the subsequent development there of the transistor). Despite the economic constraints on European economies in general and, with its heavy burden of reparations, the German economy in particular, Siemens in the communications and electrical industry, as with I G Farben in the chemical sector and Vereinigte Stahlwerk in steel, was one of the 'spectacular groupings' which dominated investment and rationalization of productive capacity in Germany in the late 1920s.[3] In retrospect, it seems clear that the British industry suffered from the protectionist policies adopted by war and post-war governments, which saw it as preferable for industry to depend less on free trade and more on imperial preferences – but which in reality meant trade within the Empire at the expense of world markets. An illustration of how Britain determined to 'go it alone' comes from an International Telegraph Union conference in the 1930s where every other telegraph administration adopted negatively charged signalling for a new timing technique for telegraphic printing machines, while Britain adopted positively charged signalling for itself and the Empire. While this approach certainly had the advantage of keeping other countries' companies out of the Empire, it also meant that British products excluded themselves from new and expanding markets.

Immediately after the end of the First World War, there was a dramatic decline in the level of telegram traffic in Europe and the United States. The telegraph seemed to represent the past in tele-communications, whereas the telephone and wireless symbolized the future. Yet manufacturers and operators, such as Siemens in Germany and Western Union in the United States, had big invest-ments in telegraphy. Engineers in both countries worked towards the integration of decades of work on telegraphic printing machines and in the early 1920s developed the teleprinter. Unlike previous machines, the teleprinter was placed in the users' offices, not the telegraph company's premises. Anyone who could type could learn to use a teleprinter. And, because it could use the same transmission and switching technologies as the tele-phone, it was possible to conceive of a network with thousands of teleprinter users, where any one machine could be connected to any other. Connections could be made at manual or automated exchanges, just like the telephone. The teleprinter, and the network it would need, could rescue the telegraph industry. But, owing to a general lack of funds for investment, Siemens had no luck in the 1920s and early 1930s in persuading the German Post Office to set up a teleprinter network with automatic exchanges.[4]

Then, wrote Georg Siemens,

Shortly afterwards, with the advent of National Socialism, other people succeeded to the leading positions in the Reich Post Office who in financial matters were rather more generous than their predecessors had been. [Siemens] found a hearing for their proposal to be allowed to install and operate, at their own expense, teleprinter exchanges in Berlin and Hamburg which would enable direct communication to take place between the two cities. After sufficient subscribers had been won over and the system had proved to be reliable, the two exchanges were taken over by the Postal Authorities. This network was soon extended and the neighbouring countries – particularly [the Netherlands] – were encouraged to install similar systems, in order to build up an international teleprinter network. Above all the various State departments in the new Germany installed their own networks for internal traffic. The Army, engaged in a process of rapid expansion, installed a teleprinter network which connected all important centres of operations with their central command, and placed orders for large quantities of mobile equipment. The Air Force, for which no luxury was too extravagant, followed suit on a much grander scale, and the Navy did not lag behind either. The SA and the SS, the Workers Ministry of Public Enlightenment and Propaganda, whose numerous branch offices throughout the country served to keep a check on public opinion and to steer it in the required direction, were soon equipped with the new communications systems, the latter customer making by far the most use of the service. One of the largest of these networks belonged to the Police. It will suffice to mention that the police stations of one single German city were equipped with a total of nearly one hundred teleprinters. In this way the Totalitarian State spread its tentacles out over the entire country like some fabulous millipede, equipped as it was with a communications system that only a few years earlier would have been decried as the product of wildest fantasy. The teleprinter was particularly suitable as far as one special characteristic of National Socialism was concerned: all orders had to be laid down in writing, even the most secret matters, on dictation from the highest command. It was now possible to connect up all these networks in such a way that all machines connected would simultaneously receive the text dictated by a central command. The ideal type of 'yes-man' was furthered by the teleprinter in a way hitherto undreamt of. Over the telephone it was still possible to register doubt or protest, but not on the teleprinter.[5]

The settlement imposed on Germany when it conceded defeat in 1918 was vengeful and left a legacy of discontent which in no small way helped direct Germany down the road to renewed war. That Germany's own settlement imposed on Russia, when it withdrew from the war following the Bolshevik revolution in November 1917, was much more vicious did nothing to minimize the discontent. Radical nationalists exploited the bitterness felt at all levels of German society as the reparations impoverished a Germany left exhausted and in social chaos by the war. The settlement was, in the view of one such rising leader of the right, Adolf Hitler, the 'greatest infamy'. By 1933, Hitler's Nazi party was popular enough for Hindenburg, then president, to appoint Hitler to the post of Chancellor, believing as he did that power would force the uncouth Hitler to compromise or show up his lack of abilities. But, in the meantime, he would serve a useful purpose by physically crushing the Communists. In the event, Hitler proved Hindenburg's strategy to be misguided. By 1936, he had gained complete power and he held on to it until 1945, taking Germany deliberately into ruin with him.

The Versailles Treaty that followed the First World War was particularly strict in regulating the size of Germany's armed forces. As a result, the German generals and admirals paid close attention to the military use of communications and cipher technologies. Good, secure communications would allow the concentration of the small number of forces permitted at a decisive point, thus multiplying their effectiveness.[6] The German Nachrichtentruppe, signals corps, was thus accorded a vital role. Once Hitler was in power, the armed forces were rapidly expanded. The role of the signals corps did not diminish, however, but, in fact, grew in importance, becoming integral to the structure of the mobile armoured forces which Hitler was establishing. The German army and air force were to be dependent on the use of the latest technical developments in both cable and wireless communications. A German army signals corps officer recorded that 'It was expected that when the war began it would demand wide-ranging operations which hadn't been seen before in history. The management of such operations would be unthinkable without appropriate communications technologies.'[7]

German tanks or panzers were fitted out with a wireless set in each tank well before the war started. The tank commander Heinz Guderian claimed in his post-war memoirs that he had argued from the 1920s for wireless control to be extended to every tank. But it 'took a considerable time before our requirements in wireless... – which it must be admitted, were technically very advanced – could be filled. However, I have never regretted my insistence at that time on our tanks being equipped with first-class... [wireless] command facilities... [W]e were at all times superior to our enemies and this was to compensate for many subsequent inferiorities that necessarily arose.'[8] According to a history of the German army signals corps, Guderian wanted to prevent 'splintered, individual fights... [B]esides the greater speed, flexibility and armoured defences, many of the German panzer successes can be attributed to their wireless equipment.'[9] Unsurprisingly, Guderian worked very closely with the head of the army signals corps, General Erich Fellgiebel, to achieve this end.

According to military historian Martin van Creveld,

Although [JFC] Fuller and [Basil] Liddell Hart are widely given credit for the invention of armoured warfare, there is very little in their writings to indicate that they paid close attention to these problems [of command, communication and co-ordination]; the same, with less justification, is true for many subsequent studies of the Blitzkrieg. Thus the credit for recognizing the question, for the first successful attempts at its solution, and for the first brilliant demonstration of how armoured command ought to operate belongs essentially to two men: Heinz Guderian – himself, not accidentally, an ex-signals officer who entered World War I as a lieutenant in charge of a wireless station – and General Fellgiebel, commanding officer, Signals Service, German Wehrmacht during most of the Nazi era. Between them these two men developed the principles of wireless-based command that, in somewhat modified and technically infinitely more complex form, are still very much in use today.[10]

Fellgiebel's engineers developed many other communications technologies, including a landline system that could be erected quickly in newly occupied territory. It looked old-fashioned, using bare or open unshielded wires strung between telegraph posts, but was designed to carry multiple channels of telegraph and telephone traffic, providing the invading armies with all the facilities they needed for communications with the general staff at a distant war headquarters. It was known to the German signals troops as Drehkreuzachse. The term is difficult to translate precisely (drehkreuz = turnstile; drehachse = axis of rotation) and, indeed, its meaning escaped the experts at Bletchley Park until late in the Second World War. In fact, the technique had long been known in Britain at the time as transposition, but there was nothing in the German name to suggest this and no other information in decodes and plain-language intercepts to point to it.[11] The open wires effectively twisted around one another, though without touching, by attaching to a different position on the cross-bars on each telegraph pole. This twisting reduced 'crosstalk' when using the high frequencies needed for sending multiple telephone and teleprinter communications through a single wire at the same time. Commercial technology at that time was concentrated on improving cable technology, such as co-axial cables, which could be laid underground. The Drehkreuzachse had little or no prospect as a commercial product and was only suitable for military use.

Wireless communications were also essential to the air support that accompanied the armoured assault of the panzers. A post-war British intelligence survey concluded,

> No small part of the success of the German Air Force in the early campaigns of the war was due to the high degree of organization of the Signals Service, which formed an integral part of the Air Force... Like the rest of the Air Force ground organization, the signals regiments were organized for mobile warfare. Those attached to the operational commands had the duty of laying out communications networks as soon as newly occupied territory was taken over, as well as the erection of wireless and visual beacons... Taken as a whole, the Luftwaffe signals organization on the eve of the European war was very competent to deal with most aspects of modern air warfare.[12]

In August 1943, there were 305,000 signals staff in the German air force, out of a total strength of 2.3 million – thus an impressive 13 per cent of the full strength was engaged in signals work (including the interception of enemy wireless transmissions).[13]

The application of telecommunications to military purposes also encompassed the German civil and commercial telecommunications networks. Shortly after the Nazis came to power, the domestic and military networks, plus a number of other networks such as those belonging to the railways and some ministries, were meshed into a single network, with priority for military and government use. This process, known as Vermaschung, was followed by an expansion of the combined network in a very dense manner right up to the borders of France, Belgium and Poland in particular.[14] High-capacity cables far beyond that for any likely commercial traffic were laid in specially constructed, concealed underground ducts as far as the Polish frontier. The work had to be hidden from Germany's neighbours, for it could clearly serve only one purpose – to provide for the level of communications traffic that would only be generated by a war.[15] In addition, special communications facilities were developed near the borders from where an invasion would be launched, providing what was called an Aufmarschnetz – mobilization point network.[16]

Twenty years after the 'greatest infamy' of Versailles, Hitler's armed forces had harnessed the most advanced communications technologies to the arsenals they had developed for a new war. Hitler's first military adventures – the reoccupation of the Rhineland in 1936 and annexation of Austria in 1938 – were achieved without a military response from France or Britain. The appeasement proffered by Chamberlain and Daladier at Munich encouraged Hitler to take over Czechoslovakia; however, the same process of appeasement had the important effect of convincing significant parts of the French and British electorates, as well as the ruling elites (which in Britain were also motivated by concerns for the Empire), that war with Germany was inevitable. When Hitler thought he could build on his successes by invading Poland, he found, to his surprise, that Britain and France both fulfilled their undertakings to go to war in the country's defence.

One of the technologies in which British wireless engineers had excelled in the First World War was wireless direction finding. Harold Kenworthy, a young engineer, worked on developing and using direction-finding equipment in Gibraltar, a key location for detecting German and Austrian U-boats entering and leaving the Mediterranean. As well as searching for enemy submarine traffic, Kenworthy and his colleagues also intercepted Spanish government wireless traffic to ascertain whether the Spaniards were deliberately jamming British, French and Italian wireless traffic carrying reports of U-boat sightings. By 1917, the supply of information about German and Austrian submarines was significantly greater than in previous years thanks to improved direction finding, and interception and decoding of U-boat communications improved until eventually the threat to Allied shipping in the Mediterranean was overcome.

When the First World War ended, Kenworthy joined the leading British wireless manufacturer, the Marconi Wireless Telegraph Company. In 1923, he was 'loaned' to the Metropolitan Police at Scotland Yard to investigate the potential of wireless to help with police work. One possible use was wireless communication by the police. The other potential interest was tapping into wireless transmissions to look for illegal users and this soon became Kenworthy's chief concern. The Post Office was responsible for tracking down people who transmitted wireless messages without the appropriate licence, but the Met might find it interesting to know what any illicit users were up to – particularly if it were to involve subversion or espionage. So, while the Post Office wanted to shut down illegal transmitters, Kenworthy's team at the Met wanted the transmissions to continue so that their contents could be intercepted and, if necessary, decoded or deciphered. When Kenworthy was initially loaned to Scotland Yard, he had to start the wireless unit from scratch. He discovered that several ex-service telegraphists had joined the Met as policemen after the war. These officers were soon taken off the beat and put back to working wireless interception sets in a double-lined, silence cabinet, which was built inside Scotland Yard, based on a design developed by the Royal Navy during the war, to minimize interference with inter-cepted signals from electric currents within the building. 'The training these men had had during the 1914/1918 war stood the new [wireless telegraphy] branch in good stead as it was possible to build up a service based on Naval lines,' recalled Kenworthy.[17]

Kenworthy ensured that his wireless telegraphy branch was what nowadays might be called pro-active. He did not simply acquire a few receiving sets and listen in, but from the very beginning developed new equipment, such as aerials and direction-finding gear. He created much more than a listening post, laying the foundations for the core of a sophisticated interception operation that was capable of picking up signals sent by the most advanced wireless techniques of the day. Between 1920 and 1939, wireless technology was in a state of constant, dramatic development, so Kenworthy was faced with an unrelenting technological challenge, and especially with the rapid progress in the transmission and reception of wireless signals by machines rather than by human operators. As Kenworthy recalled,

> During the years 1923 to 1926 a certain amount of interest was taken in the use of short-wave (100 metres and below) and out of petty cash an experimental transmitter and one or two receivers were gradually constructed... Opportunity was [also] taken to procure some useful apparatus from [Marconi Wireless Telegraph Company] (without Home Office authority) on the strength of a promise by Assistant Commissioner to pay out of Police Secret Funds. Later he repudiated this arrangement but although there was a certain amount of trouble... we gained a long-wave set, a short-wave set, an undulator and recording bridge.

The undulator was essentially a rather simple device, though it needed to perform its job with great accuracy. Basically, it consisted of a needle that was deflected by electro-magnets, which were in turn activated by the electric field generated by received wireless waves. The signals caused the needle to deflect to one side or the other. The needle was inked and drew a line on a strip of paper representing the received signal, giving a permanent visual record of the signal on the undulator 'slip'.[18] While engineers wanted to receive the transmitted signals directly on a printing machine, this was a technically challenging task. It could be tough enough technically for the authorized user, even with all the information to hand about the technical parameters in use. But for the unofficial interceptor the task was all the harder. The undulator at least provided a good back-up, ensuring a precise permanent record of the signals for later analysis. As it was, this early experience with the humble undulator was to pay dividends during 1941 and 1942, when the equipment to intercept German machine wireless teleprinter signals was lacking and it was essential to record every signal accurately if they were to be of any use in decrypting the messages contained in the transmissions.

There was a flurry of excitement when, during the 1926 General Strike, Kenworthy's crew picked up illicit signals and suspected that they had uncovered some subversives. But, when they raided the location of the transmissions, they found an employee of the *Daily Mail* newspaper. Fearing that Post Office workers would join the strike, interrupting the paper's news supply, the newspaper had set up a secret wireless station to be brought into use if necessary. Kenworthy later reported, 'As a matter of high policy, nothing was ever published of this exploit.' For Kenworthy the encounter was a setback, but one he turned into an opportunity. The affair had left the interceptors without the prize catch they had eagerly expected and which would have established their reputation within government. Instead, they now had to look for alternative work, including the interception of commercial wireless transmissions.

Immediately after the Strike things in the [wireless telegraphy] branch went flat but our appetite for interception had been whetted. During the course of using our short-wave and long-wave sets some samples of Commercial stations had been taken. It was suggested to the [Assistant Commissioner] Special Branch[19] that it might be a good plan to search for [wireless] stations and report any that did not appear to have [approved international] 'Berne List' status... It should be noted at this juncture that ordinary Police Experimental work was going on very slowly as very little interest could be roused. The only items of interest were mainly functions like the Derby [horseraces] when experimental Traffic control by wireless was

undertaken. It was considered that some extra work would be
beneficial for the morale of the staff.

At the request of the Secret Intelligence Service (better known
as MI6, the foreign espionage section of the Foreign Office),
Kenworthy's work-hungry operators were told to listen into Italian
wireless stations – Mussolini's interest in expanding Italy's empire
in Northern and Eastern Africa was attracting the worried attention
of Britain's own guardians of Empire at the Foreign Office. Somehow, the Italian Foreign Ministry discovered or suspected that its
wireless traffic was being tapped and a representative asked to visit
and inspect the Met's interception unit. For the day of the visit, the
operators retuned their sets and appeared to be searching for other
traffic, leaving the Italians apparently reassured. No more was heard
and the operators once again tuned into Italian stations. But the
British interceptors had learned an important lesson about the
need for absolute secrecy.

   In the mid-1930s, Kenworthy's team was asked to build a
machine to help in decoding Japanese wireless traffic. A Japanese
cipher machine had been broken by the British government's own
codebreaking organization, the Government Code and Cipher
School or GC&CS. (GC&CS had been set up at the end of the First
World War by merging Room 40 and the army's codebreaking
unit.) What was needed was an 'analogue' machine – one designed
to perform the same functions as the cipher machine, but using a
different technology, such as switches rather than wheels. The
original Japanese machine was entirely mechanical and was
'powered' by the operator turning a handle that moved gear
wheels. The codebreakers had discovered how the machine
worked and its key cycle; they now wanted to mechanize the
decoding of intercepted messages. Kenworthy had effectively
become the technical consultant for GC&CS and he was
approached about the problem. He decided that it would be
possible to build an analogue using electro-magnetic switching

components, known as relays, used widely in telecommunications networks for opening and closing circuits. Kenworthy's analogue would be used to decode an intercepted message in exactly the same way as the legitimate user would do with the original machine. This would, however, require the interceptor to know the cipher machine's starting conditions, the key. This was fairly easy as the key was reused on a ten-day cycle, so it was soon spotted.[20] The importance of using machines in codebreaking was thus another early lesson for the British.

In 1932, Kenworthy described how commercial stations had been closely studied and that all round the world they were being converted to handle 'high-speed, auto Morse' using new transmission and reception techniques – reaching speeds of 250 words per minute. He reported that, 'I believe it can be stated that only commercial stations have these facilities [at the moment, but] that in a time of emergency groups of these transmitters would be employed by their respective governments.'[21] In other words, interception of commercial stations was essential in peacetime so that the interception operators could cope with these new techniques if war threatened. But Kenworthy was fairly optimistic. The use of the undulator and careful attention to the development of the best aerials and other equipment meant that British government wireless interception 'stations should be capable of doing even better than the best commercial stations'. He insisted, however, that when acquiring equipment they should buy the best. 'It is not policy to purchase cheap substitutes as these invariably require much attention and possible loss of important "wanted" traffic.'[22]

With the expansion of the service, it became necessary for at least some of the operators to work more than their basic hours to satisfy Kenworthy. 'During the next few years it was customary for interested operators to take signals at their homes as extra work. I myself had a long-wave set, short-wave set and undulator at home. To supplement output further, I arranged to tune in a long-wave station before leaving for the office and my wife looked after the tape, winding it and changing rolls as necessary.' One day in mid-1935, Kenworthy's wife telephoned him at work to say that there appeared to be something wrong. He asked her to describe the line drawn on the paper slip by the undulator needle and he diagnosed the 'long lines and little bumps' that she told him about as a new form of signal for idle transmission (i.e. when the transmission channel is held open between messages, and a holding pattern is transmitted to keep the machines in contact). But, later that evening, when he studied the undulator slip for himself, Kenworthy realized that it was actually something quite different. The intercepted station usually transmitted high-speed, auto-Morse traffic between Berlin and Moscow. But on that day it had stopped using the Morse code and instead was being used to send messages in the Baudot code. This development caused quite a stir. The Baudot code was hardly new and was widely used on landlines, but what caused the commotion, when the discovery was reported, was that the Baudot code was now being used on wireless links, rather than landlines. This posed a new technical challenge to Kenworthy's interception service, which had in the meantime increasingly come to serve the Foreign Office rather than the Metropolitan Police.

In fact, the unit had moved from Scotland Yard to Camberwell Yard, Denmark Hill, in South London, where the double-lined chamber was relocated in a shed in the grounds of the Metropolitan Police nursing home. Now there would be fewer questions from disgruntled senior Met officers about the civilian from a commercial company who ordered around a group of police officers – officers, indeed, who flatly refused to discuss any details of their work. Even with the move, senior managers at the Metropolitan Police still did not want a unit on their patch that was not under their control and tried for several years to get the Foreign Office to take over the interception unit. In the early 1920s, the Foreign Office had assumed responsibility for both the GC&CS and its sister organisation the 'Y' Service, which managed the wireless interception stations, as none of the armed services had wanted to supervise activities outside its own area of direct interest. But following the unwelcome publicity over Room 40 and Bolshevik Russia, codebreaking had become an increasingly secretive area and one for which funds had to be concealed. The problem was that the arrangement with the Met, which had a 'secret fund' it could use without Parliamentary oversight, was useful for maintaining secrecy. If the interception unit had been funded through the Foreign Office, then at least the Members of Parliament on the Public Accounts Committee would have had to be informed, and not all could be relied on to keep a secret.[23]

A Foreign Office official wrote to the permanent secretary,

> We must strongly resist any idea of taking over these policemen... It would be relatively easy to explain the matter to the [Public Accounts Committee] and the Chairman could always be asked not to include the explanation in the published short-hand note. [But] any discussion of 'cabinets noirs' ['Black Chambers', as secret governmental codebreaking departments were widely labelled] in the H. of C. [House of Commons] would on the contrary be disastrous. I feel confident that neither the S. of S. [Secretary of State] nor Lord Cranbourne would relish it all. If the Receiver of the Metropolitan Police has been able to carry these men on his vote [i.e. allocation of funds from government] for something like fifteen years, he surely can go on for now.

The permanent secretary annotated the memo in handwriting, 'I quite agree.'[24] So the arrangement persisted and Kenworthy's unit continued to develop in a hidden interstice of the state.

The new site at Denmark Hill was not sufficient for a man of Kenworthy's dedication to his work. To meet the challenge of the highly secret Baudot, or non-Morse, transmissions a different site was needed to avoid interference – of both the electro-magnetic and the human variety. A meeting was arranged with a discreet official from the Post Office and 'private wires were run down to the house where I was living in Croydon. Special dispensation was obtained from The Commissioner to allow two PC Telegraphists... to report in plain clothes each day to my home in Croydon'. The arrangement lasted ten months and Kenworthy and his colleague from the Post Office, N Heil, gathered a quantity of obsolescent Baudot apparatus to help them understand how they could effectively intercept transmissions in the Baudot code. The Post Office engineers at the Central Telegraph Office also experimented with non-Morse wireless interception, co-operating with Kenworthy, but, when the war began and the importance of non-Morse became evident, Kenworthy's organization pushed the Central Telegraph Office out of the picture entirely and their role has been all but written out of the reports.

While this pre-war work on auto Morse and non-Morse transmission was going on, Kenworthy also became involved in another affair involving illicit wireless traffic – and this time it was indeed the feared Communist subversives. A wireless station based in Wimbledon was sending and receiving encoded Morse messages from Moscow, probably from a Comintern transmitter (the Comintern, or Communist International, had become Stalin's tool for controlling and exploiting foreign Communist Parties). Rather than shut down the transmitter and imprison the operator, it was decided to allow transmissions to continue. John Tiltman, another key player in the later Geheimschreiber story at Bletchley Park, also became involved. A veteran codebreaker, he cracked the code used for the Comintern's traffic that Kenworthy's team had intercepted. Kenworthy recorded that 'Later the station moved to North London, but with our experience, was not long before being located. The successful conclusion of this work brought up the subject of illicit stations generally.' Some time later, Kenworthy took out a 'secret patent' on a portable wireless direction-finding device he invented in the search for the Comintern's London station. Devices known as 'snifters' developed from this patent were widely used in the Second World War.

In the mid-1930s, several European powers set up illicit overseas wireless stations as war beckoned. Italy, Germany and Britain all opened secret stations, with their numbers peaking during the Spanish Civil War. As the general European war drew nearer, the armed services started to put more effort into their own interception services, and the Foreign Office prompted the Post Office to set up several new interception stations for commercial and diplomatic traffic, the first being at Sandridge, near St Albans. By October 1937, the developing international crisis meant that the Foreign Office funds for this type of work were no longer a potentially embarrassing issue. It was time to transfer the interception unit at Denmark Hill to GC&CS. The Foreign Office wrote to the Receiver of the Metropolitan Police that 'Since our last talk there has been an important development of the matter in that the authorities here are now agreed with the Director of the Code and Cypher School that there is no need to maintain the view that it would be impossible in the interests of security, to explain to the Public Accounts Committee the particular duties of these Constables... are employed.'[25] From 1938, the expanding code-breaking section of GC&CS started to be transferred from London to Bletchley Park, a country house located at a central point between London, Cambridge and Oxford and near a main telephone trunk route for easy communications. It was where mathematicians, classicists and linguists began to gather, having been recruited from universities as war drew increasingly near.

Kenworthy, too, was transferred to the Foreign Office and GC&CS, though he was concerned to ensure that he did not lose out financially by the change of employer. He wrote to the deputy director of the GC&CS, Edward Travis,

Before agreeing to this it is only right that I should know how this will affect me... I think it can be assumed that if my services are essential to the F.O. then some additional financial consideration should be made to cover the very much increased responsibility... It would [also] be a distinct advantage to the position you are hoping I shall take up if it were possible to be given a temp[orary] commission say in the RNVR [Royal Navy Volunteer Reserve]. I held the rank of Sub Lt [Sub Lieutenant] during the last war but the nature of this work which I think is very important indicates a higher rank, say that of Lt Cn [Lieutenant Commander]. As explained to you it is becoming more evident each day that the work for your department is growing and that it requires all the expert help available.[26]

Kenworthy got his pay increase, but he was not given that commission and the rank he felt he deserved, and in memos between the Foreign Office and GC&CS he is always referred to as 'Mr. Kenworthy'.

During the first years of the war, the vast bulk of German wireless traffic was transmitted using the Morse code and all of the efforts of Bletchley Park and the intercept stations of the 'Y' Service were dedicated to picking up as much German Morse traffic as possible. Most of this was 'hand'-tapped Morse; however, a watch was kept for different transmissions types such as auto Morse and other codes. In mid-1940, two German stations were intercepted transmitting non-Morse. These transmissions were apparently in the Baudot code, but, when printed, they produced nothing but a jumble of meaningless characters and were thus assumed to be enciphered. As Kenworthy later recalled, 'It did not make much sense and, owing to a shortage of cryptographers, was put aside. Observation was kept on these two stations but after a time they ceased operation. They had apparently been testing.'[27] That summer Bletchley Park was enjoying its early breaks into the Enigma machine used to encipher messages before they were sent in Morse code over the airwaves. Everything was concentrated on building on that fragile success and the non-Morse transmissions were at that stage merely a curiosity, not an urgent priority.

chapter four

Wireless War Two

Hitler's first 'Blitzkrieg' or lightning war was unleashed on Poland in September 1939. Britain and France, which had both offered support to Poland, declared war on Germany, thus widening the conflict into a general European war. Count Galleazzo Ciano, Mussolini's son-in-law and the Italian foreign minister, recorded his forebodings in his diary at the time: 'I do not know how the war will develop, but I know one thing – it will develop and it will be long, uncertain and relentless. The participation of England makes this certain. England has made this declaration to Hitler. The war can only end with Hitler's elimination or the defeat of Britain.'[1] But immediately it was Poland that was eliminated as an independent nation, going on to suffer nearly six years of unrelenting horror. Poles Marian Rejewski, Jerzy Rozycki and Henryk Zygalski wisely chose not to remain in Poland and made their escape to France, which was soon to prove crucial to Britain's initial codebreaking success once the war was under way. While, in the run-up to the war, Britain's codebreakers at Bletchley Park had had no success in cracking the Enigma machine, the Poles had succeeded in breaking open the secrets of the machine cipher – geographical proximity to Nazi Germany had given them a more urgent need than Britain's codebreakers.

The information about the Enigma machine that the escaped

Poles provided when they reached France gave the British code-breakers crucial details about the internal wiring of the German cipher machine. It involved the way in which the keys were wired to the first set of connections – and depended on whether that wiring was ordered or arbitrary. In fact, key 'A' went to the first connection, 'B' to the second and so on. The codebreakers at Bletchley Park had not even bothered to try this out, having assumed that it must be some more complex method, and their failure to work out the details of this wiring had held up Bletchley Park's small codebreaking team working on the Enigma. The Polish information changed the situation completely and set GC&CS down its track towards the industrial-scale mechanized code-breaking.

At first Bletchley Park managed to decode messages using a Polish technique, but within a few months new German security measures in the use of the Enigma machine prevented that method from working, although not before some hundreds of messages had been broken. One of the academics asked to join Bletchley Park was Alan Turing, now probably the GC&CS's most renowned code-breaker. Turing approached the problem from a fresh angle and devised a machine that could help. He won over both Gordon Welchman, another recent recruit, who had also been assigned to work on the Enigma problem, and Edward Travis, the deputy director of GC&CS. Travis managed to get the massive sum of £100,000 to turn Turing's idea into reality and have several 'Bombes' built by the 'British Tabulating Machinery Company' (BTM) at Letchworth. The Bombe's function was to work out the wheel settings by trying out lots of different settings and looking for one that matched a 'crib' – a likely phrase in the plain-language message. The core concept behind the idea, however, was to find ways of reducing the number of settings that needed to be checked, from the theoretical twenty-two thousand billion to a few hundred, making it practical to look at those possibilities on the machine.

When, or if, the Bombe identified a possible valid setting the codebreakers would try the those settings on an 'Enigma analogue' – a machine built, like Kenworthy's earlier analogue of the Japanese cipher machine, to perform the same function as the Enigma, but electrically rather than mechanically. It could be set up to decode the message and convert it from a jumble of meaningless characters into 'plain' German (or, more accurately, plain German military language, full of abbreviations, military jargon, technical terms and so on). One point, though, needs to be emphasized. The Bombe was electro-mechanical and was *not* the forerunner of the computer, as is often claimed. However, it was a cryptographic antecedent of Colossus, which was developed later on to tackle the keys of the wholly different cipher machine, the Geheimschreiber. It was Colossus that was a forerunner of the computer. The Bombe was a 'cribbing' machine, using likely words to break into a message, while Colossus was invented to mechanize a 'statistical' method, essentially based on counting the frequency of characters in messages. So, while the Bombe was a cryptographic antecedent of Colossus in the idea of using machines to perform codebreaking tasks, they were fundamentally different as concepts and as physical devices.

Through their analysis of Enigma traffic, the codebreakers identified various keys used by different German wireless networks belonging to different parts of the armed forces. A key would specify which wheels were to be used and in which position, and also the outer ring position (though the operator would choose the initial wheel settings for each message), and it would be used by all the Enigma users on one network. These different keys were named by the codebreakers after different colours. In early April 1940, Bletchley Park had for the first time read an Enigma message within twenty-four hours of it being transmitted by the Germans. A month later, in May 1940, a German air force Enigma key, codenamed Red, was broken almost currently – that is, with little delay. The Red key remained readable, except for the odd short period, until the end of the war and provided much useful information about both the German air force and the German army (as it was used by air force liaison officers stationed with army units). The same month, Germany repeated its lightning attacks, invading the Netherlands, Belgium and much of France, demolishing the opposing armies in weeks, and chasing the British Expeditionary Force from the Continent at Dunkirk in a sobering defeat.

In mid-1940, Britain was 'alone' (in that peculiarly British sense of the word, as British troops were supplemented by both those from the dominions – Australia, Canada and New Zealand – and from the colonies – most notably from India). The British army had taken a serious battering, exposing inadequacies at all levels from command to planning, training and execution. After Dunkirk, the country stood braced for an invasion. It was the point at which Hitler came closest to winning the war, as a strong current of parliamentary and establishment opinion wanted to make peace with the German dictator. Churchill, who became prime minister after the German invasions of Norway and Denmark, only secured sufficient support within the War Cabinet and among senior politicians to carry on with the war at the end of May, and, according to historian John Lukacs, 'Then and there he saved Britain, and Europe, and Western Civilization.'[2]

The cracking of the Enigma Red cipher was thus most timely. The codebreakers found themselves uncovering apparently uninformative snippets of information – a reply to a memo or an order which was meaningless without the original order or memo; a message ordering a piece of aircraft equipment to be sent to a place no one had ever heard of; or an instruction to an addressee named only as an abbreviation to report on some incomprehensible German military term. At first, it was like trying to reconstruct an entire forest from just a few tiny fragments of bark. However, with time and dedication, the disjointed items of information began to form a picture. Churchill immediately took an interest in Enigma decrypts and demanded to see the raw translations daily. He nurtured what he realised would be a useful tool, or weapon, in the struggle to defeat the threat to Western democracy.

Once the Nazi war machine had occupied a country, its armed forces and its police services – including the Gestapo – moved very quickly to assert their authority. Communications networks played an important role in controlling, administering and exploiting the territories of the expanding Reich. As a British intelligence assessment reported, 'The characteristic rhythm in the flow of [intercept-derived intelligence] was visible from the start. It was due to the German dislike of using wireless telegraphy when other means of communication were available. At the beginning of a campaign, wireless telegraphy had to be used and continued to be used as long as the campaign was in progress. Once the situation was stabilized – in these early days by the Germans reaching their objective – landlines were installed and the volume of wireless telegraphy fell off.'[3]

A British 'secret history', written at Bletchley Park at the end of the war but only recently made public, records that:

> Apart from Poland, the first German landline networks outside Germany were, of course, those set up in Denmark and Holland in the spring of 1940... by the spring of 1941, the Germans had established an efficient teleprinter service between Norway, Denmark and North Germany. By extensive use of this service for non-operational and administrative messages, the bulk of traffic in naval ciphers decreased appreciably... [But the] Germans experienced general difficulty in setting up their landline networks in France because of the extensive destruction of communications facilities they found there. They had, moreover, to take special security precautions for their landline traffic in France, whereas in Germany, at least in the early years of the war, they felt relatively sanguine

about the security of their teleprinter communications... [The German military] gradually extended their cable connections throughout Italy and the Mediterranean Islands, the Aegean, where Athens was a great communications centre, and the Adriatic. Furthermore, they had adapted and expanded the existing landline network in Bulgaria, Rumania and Hungary. In Russia, they do not appear to have made much use of landline teleprinters, but it is known that there were landline connections with the Crimea. Sofia was the main centre for teleprinter connections with the Eastern Front.[4]

This assessment is incorrect only in the assumption that little use was made of 'landline teleprinters' in Russia. In fact, the Drehkreuzachse open-wire landline system (see Chapter three) was used extensively to carry teleprinter communications in occupied Russia. But the overall judgement is valid – the Nazi telecommunications links across the occupied territories, concluded Bletchley Park, 'at the height of German expansion in Europe, formed a vast network'.[5] There was, thus, somewhat less wireless traffic in this period than while the invasions were under way. This reticence about using wireless was most marked in the German army. However, the Luftwaffe, under control of Hermann Goering rather than the general staff, was much more prolific in the use of wireless as a means of communication. Indeed, it was also rather careless, for example, using high-power transmissions which were easy for the British to intercept. Thus, once the German invasions of Poland and north-west Europe were complete, while wireless transmissions generated by the army declined, those of the Luftwaffe did not. This was fortunate for Britain as its immediate challenge was to face an onslaught by the Luftwaffe preparatory to a cross-Channel invasion, 'Operation Sealion', planned by Hitler to build on his success in France and elsewhere.

In the wake of Dunkirk, the level of fear was such that coaches were kept on standby at Bletchley Park so that its staff could rapidly be bussed to Liverpool, where they would board a ship bound for the United States in the event of an invasion. Some of the earliest Enigma decrypts underlined the extent of German preparations. An order to Luftwaffe pilots not to bomb England's Channel ports was interpreted as a measure to ensure that the ports were kept in working order for disembarking German soldiers. But Hitler knew that he could not undertake an invasion without winning air superiority, something the Luftwaffe had failed to achieve in the summer of 1940. Indeed, as one recent account of the Battle of Britain points out, the 'illusion… [that] the British were terribly unprepared and just muddled through, showing their national genius for improvisation… is complete nonsense. Within the RAF… Fighter Command was the best prepared fighter force in the world, by a considerable margin. In 1940 it was given the opportunity of fighting almost precisely the battle it had planned for since 1936. It did not need to improvise, there was very little muddle, and it all worked out much as expected.'[6] Indeed, one historian has pointed out that the Royal Air Force 'emerged with a fighter strength actually larger than had existed when the battle begun'. In July the RAF's fighter strength was 871 fighter planes, with 644 serviceable aeroplanes. In September its full strength had risen to 1,048, with 732 serviceable.[7]

A vital factor in the outcome of the Battle of Britain was an offshoot of wireless telecommunications technology – radar. It allowed an economical use of defensive force, which led to an unsustainable rate of attrition for the attackers, but without seriously stretching the defenders. This was not necessarily due to British foresight, but was more likely a reflection of circumstance. Continental European countries were naturally concerned with the threat of land war. Britain, perforce, gave greater attention to naval and air war. Germany developed aircraft to support the army's armoured assault strategy and the appropriate technologies, such as radio communications between tank commanders and aircraft. In contrast, Britain developed an effective defensive radar system, a broad range of aircraft capabilities, and a well-organized industrial codebreaking effort to exploit the German armed forces' reliance on wireless communications. Before the war, shadow factories had been set up in which aircraft production could start as soon as hostilities broke out – another part of the reason why, at the end of the Battle of Britain, the RAF had more aircraft than when it had started. Pre-war planning had also uncovered the disturbing fact that production of electronic valves – essential for wireless equipment – was concentrated around London, the traditional centre of the telecommunications and electrical industries, so shadow factories were also set up for the production of electronics in the north of the country, out of the effective range of German bombers.[8]

In the summer of 1940, Enigma decrypts were far less important than radar, but they did provide advance warning of the coming battle for Britain's skies and they uncovered the German order of battle, which military units were to be involved and, sometimes, where they were based. A British intelligence report concluded that, 'the opening of the offensive on this country must be anticipated from 1 July onwards'.[9] Enigma intercepts also allowed the first realistic assessment of the size of Germany's air force, which proved to have substantially fewer aircraft than had been feared. As the intelligence was derived from the Luftwaffe's own internal communications traffic, it was considered to be 'apparently sure', enabling the British air staff to 'view the situation much more confidently than was possible a month ago'. Of particular import-ance for air warfare was the strength of reserves (to replace the aircraft lost in daily battles). Here Enigma intercepts showed that the German air force reserves numbered not, as previously believed, 5,000, but the much lower figure of 1,000 aeroplanes. Such intelligence was 'heaven-sent'.[10] And, if the British had over-estimated the size of the Luftwaffe's threat, the German intelligence service made the opposite mistake and underestimated the numerical strength of the RAF.[11] The pattern was set whereby Enigma decrypts provided strategic rather than tactical intelligence.[12]

The collapse of German plans to invade Britain was Hitler's first military setback, which was due both to the Channel, which very effectively prevented the German army from demolishing its British counterpart - as it surely would have done - and Britain's air defences. Britain thus won the time to draw on its reserves of human, industrial and technological potential to fight a long war. Indeed, this would become a war of attrition, where the victor was likely to be the country that could mobilize its economic and technological resources most effectively. Hitler had already begun economic mobilization,[13] and, as Britain did not possess better technology or significantly better technicians, it would have to use its technocrats much more effectively.

Following its failure to win the Battle of Britain, the Luftwaffe changed tactics to bombing British cities and ports. However, as Enigma did not reveal Hitler's change of mind about the invasion until well into October, during September the fevered preparations to meet the invasion continued, until decryption of, for example, instructions to step down German armed forces units specifically established for the invasion. One threat may have lifted, but another was coming to the fore - the attack on Britain's vital supplies by aircraft, surface ships and, increasingly, U-boats. Bletchley Park was putting a lot of effort into German naval Enigma keys, but they were proving to be a much tougher nut to crack than those of the Luftwaffe. For a start, although the German naval Enigma machine used just three rotor wheels at any time, these could be selected from a set of eight wheels compared with five for the Luftwaffe machines. Details of these additional three wheels were unknown to Bletchley Park. In addition, the navy used codebooks to specify the wheel starting-position indicators before the message was enciphered. Without access to the extra wheels (so that their wiring arrangements could be assessed) or the indicator codebooks there was little chance of progress. Hugh Sebag-Montefiore's book *Enigma: the Battle for the Code* describes the brave - and sometimes fatal – attempts of British naval officers and ratings to capture these wheels and codebooks from U-boats and German Atlantic weather ships. But, once these prizes had found their way back to Bletchley Park, the codebreakers were finally able to crack the German naval Enigma codes in June 1941. Their success was turned to immediate effect and reduced the effectiveness of the U-boats, ending the first of what the German submariners called their 'happy times'.

What is important to recognize here is that, from early in the war, Britain managed to establish a strong position in codebreaking. The cracking of the Enigma machine gave GC&CS the impetus to intensify its efforts and the time to get itself reasonably well organized. Historian and Bletchley Park veteran Ralph Bennett later summed up the luck and the achievements of the first years of the war: 'Providence or Hitler's stupidity granted the two further years required to organize an adequate intelligence system as well as to manufacture new weapons; most remarkable of all, within that period it was possible to develop and exploit a new and un-precedented intelligence source: the German Enigma cipher [machine], which revealed the enemy's dispositions, his state of readiness for battle, and even his strategic intentions, thus giving the Allied commanders an advantage enjoyed by none of their pre-decessors.'[14] According to Bennett, this grace period was crucial for the British intelligence service to learn what intelligence could be derived from Enigma and to set up the means for disseminating it.[15]

But it was a close-run thing. Although by mid-1941 the Bombe had fully proved its worth, the growing amount of intercepted German wireless traffic was threatening to overwhelm GC&CS. Whether it was the number of interception sets and operators, or the availability of clerical and other staff for Bletchley Park, there were severe shortages in every part of the operation. A rapid expansion was necessary, which in turn meant a substantial increase in resources had to be wrung out of an always reluctant Treasury.

GC&CS, in fact, needed to employ intelligent staff even for quite repetitive tasks at both Bletchley Park and the intercept stations. For security reasons, it also needed reasonably contented workers, who wanted to stay put and do a good job. Yet it found it hard to compete for the available supply of labour. In part, this was because it was constrained from telling anyone why it needed intelligent, capable young staff, and, in part, because the repetitive work was deemed to be of low status and thus low pay. There was, for example, in mid-1941, an 'acute shortage' of Grade III clerks in the Machine Section, where much of the work was mind-numbingly dull but demanding of skill and concentration. Bletchley Park wanted to promote clerks to the higher Grade II, which offered better pay rates. But this plan upset the Treasury. Initially, it ignored the pleas and simply did not reply to GC&CS's first letter. A reminder from Bletchley Park finally elicited a response, and a negative one at that. The Treasury had consulted its experts, who provided a powerful reason for rejecting the suggestion: 'We refused to allow Temporary Clerk II below twenty-one… because it is prima facie unlikely that girls below twenty-one can possess the qualifications required.'[16] Meanwhile, the staffing problems only got worse. The director of GC&CS, Alastair Denniston, for all his strengths, was not the person to win the bureaucratic wars of Whitehall. So Bletchley Park, despite the successes it was demonstrably having, was being snowed under.

Churchill, however, was well aware of the importance of the intelligence offered. He had a long-held interest in intelligence and appreciated its value.[17] He visited Bletchley Park in the early autumn of 1941 and praised the staff for their efforts. Later that year, four of the leading codebreakers – Alan Turing, Gordon Welchman, Hugh Alexander and Stuart Milner-Barry, all civilian recruits – broke with the honoured conventions of the Civil Service and went straight to Churchill, delivering a letter to him by hand at Number 10 Downing Street. Their letter read in part,

You will have seen that, thanks largely to the energy and foresight of [the deputy director] Commander Travis, we have been well supplied with the Bombes for the breaking of the German Enigma codes. We think, however, that you ought to know that this work is being held up, and in some cases not done at all, principally because we cannot get sufficient staff... we have done everything that we possibly can through the normal channels, and we... despair of an early improvement without your intervention... We realize that there is a tremendous demand for labour of all kinds and that its allocation is a matter of priorities. The trouble is that, as we are a very small section with numerically trivial requirements, it is very difficult to bring home to the authorities finally responsible either the importance of what is being done here or the urgent necessity of dealing promptly with our requests.

Churchill, never one to be bound by rules himself, was unperturbed by this shocking breach of bureaucratic protocol. He waged his own regular battles with what he termed the 'ministry of bellyaching' in many departments of Whitehall. After reading the letter, he gave the following instructions to General Ismay, Chief of the Imperial General Staff, 'Make sure they have all they want on extreme priority and report to me that this has been done. WSC.' The instruction, dated 22 October 1941, was written on a slip of paper marked: 'Action this day'.[18] Denniston was soon moved to a post in London, while Edward Travis, who, according to Welchman, was 'definitely of the bulldog breed', became director at Bletchley Park, and extra staff and resources started to become available.[19] The scene was finally set for the expansion of GC&CS's activities.

The bureaucrats did not give up trying to limit the growth of GC&CS, but their efforts were increasingly irrelevant as authority now came from on high for whatever GC&CS wanted. One frustrated pen-pusher wrote to Travis pointing out that other departments had agreed to a Treasury request to co-operate with liaison officers sent out to anyone requesting extra staff 'to try and persuade departments to meet their problems other than by increasing their staff'. But, for security reasons, GC&CS turned down the offer of Treasury management experts studying their operations. To the dismay of the Treasury, the 'Code and Cipher School meanwhile continue their non-stop recruitment irrespective of whether their authorized complement is exceeded or not... Have you any idea when you will have all the staff you want, or is it a fact that there is no limit to the staff you are likely to want?' Travis responded that the extra staff he was recruiting were needed to undertake new tasks he had been set. 'I hope,' he wrote, 'that you will feel able to accept my assurance that the increase in staff is justified' – and if he did not feel so able, then, suggested Travis, the Treasury should contact the Chief of the Imperial General Staff.[20] Bletchley Park would still struggle to maintain the rate of expansion it needed to achieve, but the constraints on it were significantly relaxed.[21]

One of the new tasks that had been set was the investigation of non-Morse transmissions. These had started to appear again from early 1941, and one particular new non-Morse link which opened in mid-1941 seemed to be of interest to the British codebreaking operation. It appeared that it was being used by the German army. The early successes at Bletchley Park with the Enigma machine had, of course, been with Luftwaffe and navy keys. Initially, the German army made comparatively less frequent use of the Enigma machine and wireless transmission than the navy and Luftwaffe, and it possessed much better security measures, thereby making its keys harder to break. But now, as Hitler turned his immediate sights away from Britain in 1941 and sent his troops, first, into the Balkans, and then into the limitless horizons of the Soviet Union, the German army began to take to the airwaves in a way that could be exploited by GC&CS.

chapter five

A Window on a War

In 1870 and 1871 Prussia and its German allies soundly defeated France in one of the first modern wars on European soil. Paris was besieged and French military prestige, buoyant since Napoleon's adventures, sank to its lowest point. Prussian success on the battlefield led to German unification and a long-lasting and over-powerful role for the military in the new state. The bloody battles of the Franco-Prussian War were fought with modern rifles and field artillery but, most notably on the French side, with tactics from Napoleon's days. Helmut von Moltke, the great military strategist, who was the chief of the Prussian army staff, directed his war, with more or less skill, by telegraph, ordering generals in command of the field armies where and when to attack, thereby concentrating the massive firepower of modern rifles and artillery. Until then, soldiers had, by and large, fought standing up, bunched together in a column or line, and dressed in brightly coloured uniforms. But now they lay down or crouched to take cover, dug in, spread out and wore uniforms that helped them blend into the background. This meant that a given force covered a much greater field of battle than before. Along with the rapid growth in the size of armies – armies that could now be delivered in massive numbers to the front by railway – it also caused the battlefield itself to spread out over many miles. In effect, the forces involved became so big that they could only be mobilized and directed from afar.[1]

Moltke was renowned for his coolness, never getting upset at the news the telegraph brought. This remained true even when, as happened quite often, the generals ignored his telegraphed orders and went off in the wrong direction or marched across the path of another Prussian army, causing chaos. The telegraph may have been necessary to marshal the armies of the late nineteenth century, but the military caste had not yet fully adapted to the new technology. In that sense, the Franco-Prussian War was also one of the last of the traditional wars in Europe, with generals determining their own tactics. And Sedan, one of the greatest battles of the war, was also one of the last outings of Europe's aristocracy, off to war for fun, for all the world as if on a day's hunting.

Sedan was a disaster for the French, their army being destroyed, but a great victory for the Prussians. As Michael Howard has written, 'It was now a superb day, and Moltke's staff had found for the [Prussian] King a vantage-point from which a view of the battle could be obtained such as no commander of an army in Western Europe was ever to see again. In a clearing on the wooded hills above Frenois, south of the Meuse, there gathered a glittering concourse of uniformed notabilities more suitable to an opera-house or a race-course than to a climactic battle which was to decide the destinies of Europe and perhaps the world.' The Prussian King, the Prussian Chancellor, Bismarck, Moltke and the army's top brass, leading Prussian officials and civil servants, Colonel Walker from the British army, General Kutusov from Russia and the British war correspondent of fame from the Crimean War, William Howard Russell of *The Times* all looked on, as did 'a whole crowd of German princelings – Leopold of Bavaria and William of Wuerttemburg, Duke Frederick of Schleswig-Holstein and Duke of Saxe-Coburg, the Grand Duke of Saxe-Weimar, and the Grand Duke of Mecklenburg-Strelitz and half-a-dozen others – watching the remains of their independence dwindling by the hour as the Prussian, Saxon and Bavarian guns decimated the French army around Sedan.'[2]

Although no army commander was ever again able to directly observe a European battle in such a direct way, some six decades later the interception of Hitler's strategic communications during the Second World War, and the decryption of the messages they contained, certainly gave the British and the Americans an unparalleled view of their war, one which spread across the globe, affecting all continents. The communications that flowed between Hitler and his armies were intended to give the commander-in-chief the information he needed to control Germany's war machine. Hitler tried to be a new Moltke, but, instead of the inflexible electric telegraph and hand ciphers, he had at his disposal advanced teleprinter and wireless technology and machine ciphers. No commander had ever been able to direct so much armed force at such distances. But even in this strength there was weakness – not so much in the Enigma machine, which was used mainly to transmit messages within army units, but in the Geheimschreiber, which was used for communications between the high command and the commanders of army groups, as well as army commanders and other organizations of the Reich in distant occupied lands.

The decryption of the Geheimschreiber messages was to provide an utterly unique running commentary on, and insight into, the detail of the strategic and operational thinking and planning of the German high command, first in the Balkans, then the Russian, North African and Italian theatres, and later in north-west Europe before, during and after the landings in Normandy and in the final battles for Germany's borders. Germany would end up shorn forever of East Prussia, with virtually all the German-speaking populations forcibly removed from east of the Oder, for the first time in 800 years. For the next forty years, Germany would also be disunited, divided into two, the work of Bismarck and Moltke seemingly undone. And Britain's codebreakers watched it all happen from their vantage point in an ugly old mansion house some fifty miles north of London.

* * *

The great Prussian victories, in 1866 over Austria and 1870–71 over France, were based on the strategy of Kesselschlacht (encirclement or pincer battle) and fixed the German army's perspective on how to fight wars. They 'suggested Prussia/Germany could extend its influence and make vast annexations against any rival if only it struck fast and hard enough. This thinking, which originated with Claustwitz and Moltke, would be the basis of Prusso-German strategy' in 1914, 1939 and, most spectacularly of all, in June 1941, with the attack on Russia.[3] According to a British official internal history of the Second World War, written shortly after the war but kept secret until recently (the files at the National Archive containing this account are based on the intelligence information available to Britain and the Allies from intercepted Axis wireless transmissions): 'In a directive dated 18 December 1940 and entitled 'Contingency Barbarossa', Hitler made the fatal plunge: "The German Wehrmacht", he ordered, "must be prepared, even before the end of the war against England, to overthrow Soviet Russia in a swift campaign."'[4] After the lightning defeats of Poland and the Western European states, Hitler looked to the biggest Kesselschlacht of all, the surrounding and annihilation of both the Russian army and Soviet state.

The German radio and teleprinter cipher technology which was ultimately to lead to the conception of Colossus was first deployed between the end of the Battle of Britain in autumn 1940 and the launch of Operation Barbarossa in June 1941. The location was the Balkans. The British secret history continues:

> there was another problem [apart from Romania] which made it essential for the Germans to deal with the Balkans before they attacked Russia; for in October 1940, their allies the Italians had attacked Greece. After an initial setback, the Greeks had recovered, and by December had expelled the invaders from Greece and were fighting well in Italian-occupied Albania... [It] was obviously impossible for the Germans to

leave wide open this back-door to the continent of Europe while they attacked Russia... Therefore Greece had to be conquered... The new campaign did mean that forces had to be employed in Yugoslavia which would otherwise have been moving into position for the Russian campaign while the attack on Greece was still in progress. Other things being equal, it is probably correct to say that the Balkan campaign as it eventually took place delayed the invasion of Russia by a month. And it is arguable that one month of good weather would have made all the difference to the Germans and would have tipped the balance between failure and success in Russia.[5]

Later in the war, Hitler adopted the Balkan diversion as one excuse for why his assault on Russia stalled before Moscow in December 1941. 'If we had attacked Russia already from May 15 onwards... we would have been in a position to conclude the eastern campaign before the onset of winter,' he said in early 1945.[6] In fact, today few historians would agree with this explanation of the eventual failure of Barbarossa. It is unlikely either that the invasion of Russia could have happened according to the original schedule or, more important, that Germany could have knocked the Soviet Union out of the war before the onset of winter as specified in the planning for Barbarossa, even with an extra month.[7] But, as the fighting in the Balkans and Greece dragged on and intensified, Hitler was forced to divert experienced troops that would have been useful on the eastern front – this was one item of information revealed at the time by intercepts to the British.[8]

The Polish campaign had already demonstrated the vulnerability of landlines. The submarine cable section of the landline that linked East Prussia and Danzig to Germany proper was cut by Feindein-wirkung (enemy action) as soon as the war started, and a radio link had been necessary to communicate with the army command in East Prussia. On land, a basic one-wire field telegraph cable – used close to the front – could be put out of action by the simple expedient of creating a short-circuit by pushing a pin through the wire. The high-tech, high-capacity open wires on poles, the Drehkreuzachse were just as susceptible to a pair of wire-cutters. The problems were considerably greater in the Balkans. The area provided a quite different theatre of war for the German army, which had thus far experienced little persistent opposition. At first, things went well for the Germans, and the cities were quickly taken. However, the mountainous terrain aided the development of an ever more brutal guerrilla, or partisan, campaign that tied down Axis troops in policing operations. The mountains that sheltered the partisan groups severely limited the use of landlines – which meant that wireless communications became ever more important. When the Germans occupied Greece, they had to control and communicate with scores of islands, again boosting the need for wireless communications.

Wireless messages within German army and air force units relied on the Enigma machine and, nearer the front, hand ciphers to encode communications before broadcasting them to the ether. It was inevitable that such tactical communications would be transmitted by wireless, especially in the midst of an invasion, but higher-level communications – between the commanders in the field and staff headquarters back in Germany – had previously been carried over more secure landlines. Now, as Germany's armed forces started campaigning a long way from home and in a hostile landscape, some of that high-level information also had to be transmitted over the airwaves. The Balkan campaign provided an immediate need, as well as a suitable testing place, for the technologies that were being developed for this very purpose. The issue of communications links between, on the one hand, Hitler and the high command and, on the other hand, the army group or army commands in the field had been recognized as a problem before the war. Landlines were easy to cut, and amplifier stations were needed at regular intervals. These stations were vulnerable to partisan raids and required additional troops and patrols to guard them and the amplifying equipment. All these pressures pointed away from reliance on landlines for these major backhaul links.[9]

The German army Nachrichtentruppe (signals corps) considered that the Enigma cipher system was not sufficiently secure to protect the flow of information between army headquarters units, such as those in the Balkans, and the high command back in Berlin. Nor was it efficient enough – enciphering and deciphering with the Enigma machine was time-consuming and demanding in terms of personnel. Organization of the war involved literally tens of thousands of messages sent out on teleprinter links each month; indeed, the entire German administrative and military systems were built around intensive use of the teleprinter. The Enigma system would not have been able to cope. But, in 1937, Erich Fellgiebel, the general in charge of the Nachrichtentruppe, had been treated to a demonstration of a new development in radio technology, a 'directional' transmitter that had been developed by the signals corps research unit, WaPruef7. It was provided with a particularly powerful transmitter, which enabled high-speed auto-Morse. The directional transmissions would severely limit, though not entirely exclude, the potential for inter-ception and meant that a wireless link could be treated as if it were a landline. Fellgiebel's response had been to point out that that the amount of enciphering and deciphering that would have to be done to make the high-capacity system worthwhile meant that 'it would turn every soldier into a signals soldier'.[10] Yet, the needs of war meant that the German high command was increasingly confronted by a communications crisis. The official conclusion on the Polish campaign was that the German army would have to 'reckon with faster movement and wider distances. The management of high-level as well as minor links using only wireless transmission *must* be ensured' (italics added).[11] So, whatever the misgivings of the head of the army signals corps, development of high-speed radio trans-mission technologies carried on to meet the requirements of modern warfare and those of the commander-in-chief.

Several short- and medium-range directional wireless systems were developed capable of carrying Morse, non-Morse and telephone calls simultaneously on different channels and were widely used by the army and air force in occupied Europe. But, in general, these links – codenamed 'Michael', 'Krabbe' and 'Stuttgart' by the German signals engineers – were hard to pick up in Britain as they used low power for the transmissions over 20 to 150 kilometres. But, once high-powered transmissions came into use, it became possible to intercept the last fading remnants of the signals even as far away as Britain, provided that sensitive enough aerials and receivers could be developed. The first German wireless teleprinter system was deployed in the Balkans to provide the communications between the German occupying army headquarters in Athens and Vienna, near where Hitler was temporarily based in his special train (in a tunnel for protection from air raids). The link was used to send teleprinter transmissions which had been enciphered on a Geheimschreiber machine developed by the Lorenz company. The Lorenz SZ40 was first distributed within the army commands when the German armed forces were reorganized after the Polish campaign.[12] These cipher machines were initially used on landlines and submarine cables to provide protection from interception within German-occupied territory and by neutral neighbours – for example, on the cable to occupied Norway, which passed through unoccupied Sweden. But now in the Balkans teleprinter messages enciphered by the Geheimschreiber were to be sent by wireless transmissions too. The Geheimschreiber, according to a German assessment, 'guaranteed a virtually complete protection for the cipher'.[13] General Fellgiebel briefed Hitler and the high command on 15 April 1941 on how he proposed to address the communications problems that the Balkans – and Russia – would pose. As one British military historian later wrote, Hitler was 'persuaded that radio and teleprinter had abolished for him the disadvantages of distance from the front'.[14] But Hitler was predisposed to such persuasion, and privately the man whose job it was to do the persuading, Fellgiebel himself, remained sceptical. 'Who will guarantee me that the enemy can't pick up these signals?' he asked his colleagues who had developed the wireless systems, as he was well aware that a virtual guarantee is no guarantee at all. But his reservations were overridden by the need for Hitler and the army high command to keep in constant touch with the armies on the front. The objective seemed both worthy and attainable. In the words of a German signals officer, 'It would be the first time in history that the command of an army was based entirely on wireless links.'

'The Germans have not stuck to Morse for their communications', Bletchley Park reported in an account given to American codebreakers after the US had entered the war in December 1941. The report continued:

> They have gone in for various unusual types [of transmission codes] and they have, in Occupied Europe, a very intricate system of wireless [teleprinter links] which is giving us a bit of a headache to intercept. We have a special organization which is run for us by the Foreign Office and in connection with that we have started an inter-service bureau which we call, for want of a better name, the Noise Investigation Bureau. We were getting from all our interceptor stations reports in their logs of signals heard like a cow mooing or the bleating of sheep and things of that sort. Some of these things were rather disturbing as we didn't know what they were. But we have now got this small bureau which collects all these reports and has, as a rule, been able to tell us what they are.[15, 16]

In April 1941, a Research Section was established which reported to the head of the Military Section of GC&CS, Colonel John Tiltman, who was by now a veteran codebreaker. Its job was to study 'unknown systems' and to improve codebreaking techniques generally – including mechanized solutions – building on the success of the Bombes. Tiltman's wide experience made him the best person to take on a variety of new projects, casting a fresh look at what the interception stations were starting to gather. Initially, at least, Tiltman would have only a few people available to staff the new section, although, whoever they were, they had to be the very best. The head of the Research Section was to be Major Gerry Morgan, who joined in May, and Tiltman hoped that 'three or four of the best students' could be selected from the intake of university students at the end of term to join him.[17] He estimated that he needed six clerical assistants, although that number would increase to twenty over the next few months. He emphasized that, whatever the number, what was most important was 'the very careful selection of the nucleus of clerical staff', and all had to be 'university graduates or linguists'.[18] Morgan was well chosen. He had been working on the Italian Hagelin cipher machine and had previously published a paper on 'letter subtractor' cipher systems – which was the theoretical category of Vernam-type ciphers.[19]

Within a couple of months, the Research Section was up and running. In June 1941 Tiltman was able to report that it had tackled the Hagelin cipher machine used by the Italian armed forces and would be ready to hand over the technique for its regular breaking, 'as a going concern', by mid-July. The list of ciphers that the section was studying was already quite impressive: Japanese military ciphers; a German diplomatic code known at Bletchley Park as 'Floradora'; high-grade Vichy; French diplomatic; Finnish; Japanese naval attaché; some 'unknown material' (probably either German or Russian secret services); Hungarian diplomatic; Irish diplomatic; Polish and Czech diplomatic; Vatican; Free French; 'American Book'; Spanish; and Comintern. Tiltman's small team certainly had its work cut out for it.[20] But others were swelling its ranks. One of the young students who joined the Research Section straight from the end of the term at Cambridge university was a bright and unassuming chemistry student, William (Bill) Tutte, who was to play the key role in cracking the Geheimschreiber. Yet, when it was initially set up, the Research Section's work list did not include mention of what would become its major single task and its most significant achievement – the interception and cracking of the Geheim-schreiber-enciphered messages of the German high command.

During the spring of 1941, several British intercept stations started to pick up new types of transmission of various sorts – high-speed auto-Morse and some non-Morse: Baudot (commonly just called teleprinter) and a special hybrid teleprinter/facsimile system known commercially as the Hellschreiber (see Chapter seven) which was used on the German army links as well as standard Baudot teleprinter transmission techniques. The interception service also picked up transmissions and operator chat about new directional wireless systems that would be used to replace point-to-point landline links. Some of these transmissions were in the decimetre wavelength range; others were of even higher frequencies. 'If the Germans think that they are safe in using [directional] communication instead of landlines, we may expect some interesting results,' concluded one report in May 1941.[21]

When investigations suggested that some of these transmissions were being used for the communications of the German army high command, the codebreakers started to pay serious attention, although the initial stages remain unclear. The first report on the non-Morse traffic to go to senior officers at Bletchley Park was, in fact, Kenworthy's third report, and the copy held in the Public Record Office has a note attached to it from his deputy, addressed to the director, Edward Travis, observing that, 'I have never seen his first two reports… The Foreign Office gave Kenworthy responsibility for this non-Morse investigation and he appears to be taking his duties seriously… Tiltman has suggested that he should include in the Research Section a man capable of assisting Kenworthy in this task.' Thus did Tiltman's research team first become involved with the Geheimschreiber.

Some of the early non-Morse signals were picked up at a naval intercept station, at Capel, South Foreland, near Dover. Kenworthy spent several days there and at Hawkinge, another nearby intercept station, which had also heard the new signals. Kenworthy took with him an undulator, which provided a continuous record of the received wireless signals on a strip of paper, known as a slip. The German signals operators would have received the transmissions for direct printing of the message on a teleprinter (or on a special Hellschreiber printer). The transmitter and receiver would almost certainly have been designed and built by the same company and to the same specifications so they would be compatible. But the British intercept operators would not have known any of the technical details of the transmission – the complex set of technical choices available for transmitting a signal – except those that could be deduced once the transmission had been intercepted. One fact was given, though: the transmissions were much too fast for human operators to listen and transcribe the characters represented by the code-signalling units, as was possible with transmissions of hand-Morse. Instead, they had to be, in the technical jargon of the times, 'taken mechanically'. British interception stations would have to use whatever equipment was to hand from British suppliers or could be developed in the small Metropolitan Police Wireless Workshop at West Wickham. So it was, initially at least, very difficult for the British intercept teams to receive the transmissions directly for printing by a teleprinter or on the special Hellschreiber printer (British versions of the commercially available Hellschreiber were too slow to cope with the high-speed transmissions used by the German army). Therefore, they had to rely on the humble but dependable undulator, which left a permanent record of the transmission. The message could then be typed or perforated on to five-hole paper tape for the codebreakers to work on.

None of the operators at either station, accustomed to taking Morse transmissions, had any experience with an undulator or of how to 'slip-read' the images recorded by the needle, and

Kenworthy spent much his visit teaching the operators how to use and interpret this vital piece of equipment. The undulator, he said, 'is of the utmost importance when dealing with non-Morse transmissions intended to be taken mechanically'.[22] Much effort was devoted to preventing interference and to tuning in the aerials very precisely, as a lot of other signals were found on similar frequencies, including 'harmonics' of commercial transmissions from places such as Madrid, and even German radio-telephone traffic from the Russian front. Electronic noise, generated by the electric and electronic components of the receiving set, was also thought to be interfering with the intercepted signal. So Kenworthy had to devise new techniques of reducing 'set noise' to a minimum. It was, he reported, going to take the best equipment and precise techniques to pluck these transmissions from the airwaves successfully. He organized the operators at Capel and Hawkinge, as well as at a station on Beachy Head, further to the south-west along the coast, to take direction-finding readings on the non-Morse transmissions. But they got conflicting results, perhaps because there was, in fact, more than one station transmitting on the same frequency.

At the time it seemed to have been a frustrating trip: 'We returned to London on Wednesday afternoon after a short watch in the morning... The attempt to print signals up to the present have been disappointing considering the hours spent at Hawkinge and South Foreland. Very few signals have been received in spite of the first-class receivers now available. Signals are often badly mutilated by passing traffic, which points to the necessity for carefully choosing sites for VHF [very high-frequency] work... It is considered that every possible effort must be made to secure the maximum number of signals in order to fully analyze each transmission.'[23] There was no capacity to take on the interception of the non-Morse signals at Capel, so Kenworthy's unit at Denmark Hill was given the task, aided by another Admiralty intercept station, Abbotscliffe, near Dover. The Admiralty, Royal Air Force and the army each supplied two operators to work receiving sets.

Kenworthy later recorded, 'The early days of non-Morse investigations were beset with many difficulties. The specialized type of transmissions means different training; the reading of undulator slip was far more difficult and tedious than Morse, coupled with the fact that no sets could be spared without a sacrifice of other – at the time – more wanted traffic.' However, it was not all bad news. Two Hellschreiber receivers were acquired or found. Though they were designed to an older standard than the ones used by the German army and could not cope with the high transmission speeds, Kenworthy and his colleagues set about upgrading them to take direct signals alongside the undulator slip record.[24] Gradually, as technique and technology were improved, the intercept operators began to pick up more and more of the transmissions.

Soon some small amounts of information were gleaned. The Research Section later reported that 'On 17 June 1941 a… [wireless link] working between Berlin and Athens introduced teleprinter transmissions… A large number of messages, upwards of 300 weekly, are sent by automatic methods between Berlin and Athens. The link appears to be a military one; a message was sent on 30/8/41 from an Attaché with the General Staff of the army to the German [military attaché] at Athens.'[25] There were hints too that the traffic included 'some messages of the highest order of secrecy. The only message rendered completely legible was a general progress report on the fighting on the Russian front issued at midday on 29/8/41 to the German Military Attaché in Athens for his information. Messages are frequently of great length – some have extended to as much as 15,000 symbols [characters] sent continuously in cipher.'[26]

This high number of characters in a transmission contrasted with the Enigma machine where each transmission was limited to 500 letters. Although the link clearly carried important operational traffic, it was also apparent that the German operators and signals corps were having technical difficulties of their own. 'Apparently reception is not perfect, since messages are constantly repeated, some as many as twenty times.' And, as will be seen, it was precisely this repetition of enciphered messages that was to give Bletchley Park the initial means of understanding the workings of the cipher system.

While Kenworthy was making his trip to Dover, the world was being turned upside down. On the morning of 21 June 1941, Hitler unleashed Operation Barbarossa, his assault on Soviet Russia. Britain was no longer alone; it now had Russia as an ally. However, initially at least, it seemed as if that ally might not survive for very long. In his account of the Second World War, written in the late 1940s and early 1950s, Winston Churchill recorded that it 'was with relief and excitement that towards the end of March 1941 I read an Intelligence report from one of our most trusted sources of the movement and counter-movement of German armour on the railway from Bucharest to Cracow... This shuffling and reversal of about sixty trains could not be concealed from our agents on the spot.' Churchill recalled how the realization that Hitler intended to attack the Soviet Union greatly eased the pressure Britain was under at that time with daily bombing of its cities, industrial centres and ports. 'That Germany should at this stage, and before clearing the Balkan scene, open another major war with Russia seemed to me to be too good to be true.'[27]

With the postponement of the invasion of Britain, Hitler had turned his attention to the east. He needed to expand eastwards to acquire the economic resources that would be demanded by a prolonged war of attrition against Britain, and in any case he 'expected the war for Lebensraum [living space] in the east to establish Germany as a great world power'. Hitler also justified his switch of target to his generals by insisting that, when Russia was defeated, it 'will force England to make peace'.[28] The Nazis and the German armed forces convinced themselves that the Soviet Union was a house of cards, ready to be toppled at the first blow. A few days before Barbarossa, Count Galleazzo Ciano, the Italian foreign minister, asked his German counterpart, Joachim von Ribbentrop, about rumours he had heard of an attack on Russia. Ribbentrop dropped a heavy hint to his Italian colleague: 'I cannot tell you anything as yet. Every decision is locked in the impenetrable breast of the Fuehrer. However, one thing is certain: if we attack them, the Russia of Stalin will be erased from the map within eight weeks.'[29] In actuality, the invasion plans were widely known despite German attempts to hide them from even their closest allies.

Churchill's explanations of how he knew of Hitler's intentions are deliberately misleading. His references to 'one of our most trusted sources' and 'one of our agents on the spot' hide the fact that the source was Enigma intercepts, not the doughty spies his words imply. In fact, it had taken quite some time before British policy-makers had come to accept that Hitler intended to attack Russia: they had initially interpreted the Enigma evidence as indicating a German assault towards Britain's oil supplies in the Middle East. When the true objective became apparent, the decision was taken to warn Stalin. But Stalin treated Churchill's warning as just another British attempt to get Russia into the war with Germany. His ideological outlook led him to expect that Britain and Germany – exemplars of capitalism and fascism – would engage in a battle of mutual devastation, one so awful that it would lead to the proletarian revolution breaking out across Europe, and this suggested that he should do anything to avoid being dragged in. As it was, Stalin had much better intelligence about German plans than the British, with agents at all levels of the German military and state apparatus. However, he still believed he could negotiate a political solution with Hitler and that any attack would be preceded by 'incidents' and an ultimatum. He also feared that any hint that Russia was preparing for war would give Hitler the excuse to attack Russia. 'The sense among the Russians that one false move, a military provocation or a diplomatic blunder, might begin a war now led to prudence bordering on paranoia.'[30]

Stalin's refusal to do anything that would provoke an invasion was one reason why Barbarossa was initially as successful as Hitler had predicted, with the Soviet army collapsing before the advancing Germans. Hitler watched events unfold from the famous Wolfschanze (Wolf's Lair), his command centre built in a dank wood a few miles inland from Koenigsberg in East Prussia, where he would spend most of the following three and a half years. A short distance away was the Mauerwald camp, at Angerburg, where the Oberkommandos des Heeres or OKH (German army staff) was located. Part of this site was occupied by what the German signals corps believed was the world's most advanced telecommunications centre, codenamed Amtes Anna. Here was where the landline and radio circuits carrying telephone and teleprinter traffic terminated and Amtes Anna formed the centre of the web of communications links that kept Hitler and his generals in touch with the Russian front, with Germany itself, and with the other theatres of war in which Germany was engaged. A third, separate site at another location was used to house the all-important amplifiers and other transmission equipment. The three sites were connected to each other, and the wider networks, by double ring circuits so that several cables would need to be severed if all three sites were to be cut off from the outside world. When Mussolini visited Hitler at the Wolfschanze shortly after the launch of Barbarossa, he was taken around the communications centre to impress on him the comprehensive technological effort that was being put into the attack on Russia. Hitler showed Mussolini the tools with which he would conduct his war from afar, controlling the impending events on the thousand-mile-long front. It was a kind of war which would have been impossible without these extensive communications links.

Troops of the German Nachrichtentruppe followed closely behind the invading armies uncoiling the high-capacity Drehkreuzachse open-wire landline to create the backhaul communications links from the front to Amtes Anna at Mauerwald and so on to Hitler. Landline connections to Minsk, using two different routes, were in operation just three days after the German army took the city. The Germany newspapers announced that the 'last remnants of the Red Army were now trapped in two steel vices, tightened day by day by German forces; their destruction... was assured'.[31] But, as early as July, German commanders realized that everything was not proving to be as easy as they had imagined. Despite the hundreds of thousands of captured Soviet soldiers, ever more appeared in defence and they were well armed. German casualties mounted, and they suffered a high rate of loss of tanks and other equipment. Hitler 'admitted that there were at present not sufficient weapons to counter the heavy Russian panzers. Where they kept producing them from was a mystery... [and] currently the most serious concern of the front.'[32] Both a lack of reserves and a high casualty rate began to take their toll on a German army that also found it was simply insufficiently motor-ized, having to depend on some 600,000 horses in its Ostfeldzug (eastern campaign), and so infantry lagged too far behind the panzers. Logistics were also overstretched, partly owing to wholly inadequate planning, and there was strategic indecision over which objective on which to concentrate forces – Moscow or the Ukraine and Leningrad.[33]

Most critical of all, however, was that Russian resistance was found to be much stronger than expected. As had been the case with British air strength and capability in the air, German intelligence was disastrously wrong about the size and stamina of the enemy it would face in Russia. The Red Army began to organize even as it was retreating hundreds of miles before the German onslaught.[34] In December 1941, the Red Army launched a major counter-attack before Moscow, which finally put paid to Hitler's assault and his chances of achieving a knockout blow. The counter-attack could be mounted because troops had been brought from the far east of Russia's vast empire, where Japan's clear transfer of attention towards the United States relieved Soviet fears of a

Japanese intervention. According to Hitler's chief of staff, Franz Halder, 'Regarding the situation, it stands out more and more clearly that we underestimated the colossus Russia, which prepared itself consciously for the war with the complete unscrupulousness that is typical of totalitarian states.'[35]

Henceforth, the vast space, considerable population and enormous resources of Soviet Russia would start to wreak havoc with Hitler's plans. The outcome of the battle for Moscow left him feeling devastated. 'The victory of the Red Army before Moscow was certainly a watershed in the entire war... Thereafter, Hitler could only attempt for as long as possible somehow to bring the Soviet Union to its knees by mounting attack after attack.'[36] Hitler's response to the crisis was to increase his direct control of the armies, reducing the role of the high command, the OKH, almost to that of a secretariat passing on his orders. Hitler ignored Moltke's view of the role of the commander-in-chief. 'Headquarters, Moltke believed, had no business other than to deploy a field army wisely and direct it to its strategic objectives, where field commanders would plan and fight its battles to their conclusion.'[37] A German army signals corps officer noted that 'Prior to the winter catastrophe before Moscow the army group commands were "requested" to do something, after they were "ordered" to do it.' Exactly the same change in tone was noted at Bletchley Park in Enigma decrypts (see Appendix P – Hitler as seen by Source). If, as many historians believe, the battle for Moscow in the autumn of 1941 was a key turning point in the war, it was also the occasion after which Hitler became determined to set tactical objectives as well as the strategic.

Hitler and his closest collaborators knew that this was a war they could not afford to lose. They 'were only too aware of the Rubicon that had been crossed with the descent into the barbaric treatment of the Poles' and then the peoples of the Soviet Union.[38] Decrypts of Enigma-enciphered wireless traffic of the German police in the east linked Hitler to the mass killing programme unleashed by the Nazi special forces, the SS Einsatztruppen, and the German army in Russia in 1941. And, since the war, historians have established that it was around September 1941, as his plan to smash Russia started to go awry, that Hitler gave his approval for the Final Solution. It meant that the Nazi leaders and their followers would have no choice but to fight on, in the hope that the next summer would bring an opportunity to weaken the Red Army before it recovered. The German high command feared that the war was taking on a life of its own - and that they were being drawn into a chasm of distance, stretching lines of supply and communication, and leaving hostile elements behind the German frontline. As early as July 1941, Army Group South advanced so far that it was not practicable to connect it directly back to the general staff, and it had to have its communications forwarded via Army Group Middle. 'The issue in Russia depended less on strategy and tactics than on space, logistics and mechanics,' observed military historian Basil Liddel Hart.[39]

Stalin's generals had also made thorough preparations for partisan warfare in the event of an invasion. This aspect of Soviet strategy has received far less attention than it deserves, and its contribution to Soviet victory has been greatly underestimated. Many of the soldiers and civilians marooned behind the initial German advances joined the partisan forces which survived in forests and marshes in the endless rolling landscape. One significant stronghold was the great Pripet marshes, which have traditionally been a major barrier to east–west movement in the region where Russia and Poland collide. The impassable marshes have forced invaders, whether heading west or east, to travel south or north. The heirs of Genghis Khan went to the south, Napoleon to the north. Hitler's armies went both ways, as did their communications networks. Islands of resistance developed in these and other marshes and many densely wooded areas, from where partisan units sallied forth and, among other things, made a habit of destroying German cables and their supporting poles.[40]

Indeed, the destruction of communications and supply lines was one of the prime objectives of partisan bands. Instructions issued by the Russian North-Western Military Front in July 1941 specified that the partisans should organize themselves into two types of unit, large combat groups for attacks on enemy troops, and 'diversionary groups' for attacks on communications and other facilities. The directive instructed that 'To destroy communications lines, the poles should be sawn down'. But, for a more discreet method that would be harder to trace, it suggested the following: 'A good means of interference is tying wires together. This is achieved by joining all the wires on a pole by a thin unobtrusive wire, the end of which leads down the pole and is buried.' Another favourite technique was to loosen a length of rail on a railway track, preferably towards the bottom of a slope, and then cut down nearby telegraph wires. The wires were then tied to the loosened rail in several places. The partisans simply waited until a train was almost at the loosened rail and then tugged on the wires, thereby pulling the rail out from underneath the locomotive. One historian of the partisan movement has observed that 'When summing up the impact of German anti-partisan operations conducted in 1943 in the occupied territory, it is clear that, in most cases, the Germans inflicted heavy losses on the partisans and those in the population who supported them, and they temporarily dispersed the most important formations. However, usually the bulk of the partisan fighters, including their commanders and commissars, managed to evade capture and simply moved to another region where they reassembled and prepared to conduct further operations.'[41] Partisans would continue to harry the German armed forces, and their communications links, until the invaders were defeated.

Hitler's renewed campaign in 1942 took him further into the vast spaces of Russia – as far as the Caucasian mountains. It was during these advances that the high-powered radio technique, previously deployed in the Balkans, began to be heard by British wireless operators. The new links were used to transmit enciphered tele-printer messages on the Russian front, supporting the communications link for Army Group South as it pushed towards the southern limits of the Soviet empire, connecting it with Hitler as he moved his headquarters, for three months, to near Vinnitsa in the Ukraine. These new wireless teleprinter links, which came on line in mid to late 1942 demonstrated that the Balkans had been a testing ground for the new enciphered teleprinter transmission system. Within a few months, there were five links on the eastern front, in addition to the original Balkan link, and shortly after that another link was opened, this time connecting Rome to Tunis, replacing a submarine cable link that had been cut by the Allies. Throughout this time, at Denmark Hill and other intercept stations, an increasing number of wireless receiving sets was being made available for intercepting the new non-Morse links. As Travis reported in April 1942, 'The increasing use of non-Morse by the Germans in the last three months has made it necessary for us to take rapid action on a bigger scale than has hitherto been contemplated.'[42]

chapter six

NoMo

At much the same time as Thomas Cochrane was stealing the French visual telegraph codebooks used by the Napoleonic army, Captain George Scovell, a professional British army officer, was penetrating another of Napoleon's communications networks. The visual telegraph provided good communications within safe territory, but in Spain the French army faced a vicious guerrilla campaign (guerrilla actually means little war in Spanish), as well as a more conventional series of encounters with the British army led by Wellington. Apart from stretches of the coast, where the French were able to exercise effective control, the isolated relay stations of the visual telegraph network were too vulnerable to guerrilla attack. Napoleon's armies, which had been divided and needed good communications to know when and where to concentrate for battle, had to rely on couriers who could carry written messages back and forth. The couriers, too, were vulnerable and several had to be sent with each message, given the likelihood of the capture (and subsequent painful death) of at least some. So, to protect the content of the messages, Napoleon used a grande chiffre or grand cipher, actually a hybrid code/cipher. The situation here has parallels with that faced by Hitler. He, too, could rely on landlines in secure territory, but, in geographically challenging theatres such as Russia and Yugoslavia, landlines were vulnerable. The courier, like the wireless, provided a practical solution, but one that was vulnerable to interception, and so the French had to rely upon ciphers they hoped were secure. Scovell, however, worked out how to crack Napoleon's ciphers and his decodes gave Wellington a useful military advantage in defeating the French armies one by one before they could link up and overwhelm his more modest forces. Wellington, whether for security reasons or because he felt disdain towards the non-aristocratic Scovell, saw to it that the story of the breaking of Napoleon's ciphers remained a secret. Nevertheless, a century and a half later, Scovell's latter-day counterparts set about the interception and decryption of the wireless teleprinter transmissions that Hitler needed to exercise control over his armies in distant guerrilla-ridden theatres of war.[1]

In May 1942, a report was made to a meeting of the 'Y' Board, which co-ordinated wireless interception operations, on the emerging use of non-Morse transmission techniques by the German armed forces.

Members of the 'Y' Board will wish to know that the Germans are rapidly building up a wireless communications network throughout Europe, using teleprinters. In the system the signal in the ether is of a non-Morse character and requires a different interception technique from that used for Morse signalling. At the same time the signal is highly beamed, which makes the interception problem more difficult. It is thought that the Germans are developing this method of signalling, first to curtail the need for training Morse operators, and secondly, to make it more difficult for our 'Y' Services to intercept this traffic. So far this technique is confined to fixed services, but there is no technical reason why the method should not be extended in time to mobile stations. The new development is being carefully watched by the FO [Foreign Office] station and suitable apparatus is being designed to keep pace with progress.[2]

Telecommunications traffic analysis, which is the use of any information that is not part of the contents of the message, can yield a significant amount of data, without actually reading, or listening to, the contents. Thucydides, in his epic account of the conflict between ancient Athens and Sparta, tells the story of one city tyrant who conspired with his proclaimed enemies. He sent his secret communications by courier, each message instructing the recipient to kill the messenger in order to ensure secrecy. Near the climax of his planned treachery, he used a well-established member of his household slave force as a courier. But the observant slave had noticed that none of the previous couriers had returned and so, shortly after setting out with the message, he opened it to confirm his suspicions of what it contained.

Traffic analysis is best at producing information about the users of the network. Today, for example, the police and security services use sophisticated computer software packages to analyse telephone-call traffic, without tapping in and listening to the conversations or reading the emails. They claim to be able to identify criminal gang structures from the analysis of telecommunications traffic, tracing the patterns of who calls whom, reconstructing the links between different parts of a criminal organization, establishing its hierarchy, its geographical coverage, its organizational structure and the rhythms of its activities. The idea is not new. In the early days of the First World War, it quickly became apparent that traffic analysis was often the only way of discovering the enemy's order of battle. Even if a message could not be decrypted, it might be possible to watch its passage from headquarters to different divisions, then down through different units and on to the front. When enough traffic routes had been accumulated, patterns would emerge. Traffic on particular routes, for example, between infantry and artillery units, might presage an attack. Indeed, the relationship between the interception of a particular set of wireless traffic, followed by artillery bombardment and a subsequent infantry advance, would first identify those sending the traffic as artillery and infantry. Each wireless user had a call-sign which could be logged and later, when those units had been moved elsewhere on the front, would be recalled as infantry or artillery when they reappeared. From punctilious attention to all the detail of traffic, a picture emerges of the enemy's communications and its overall organization and even of its immediate intentions.[3]

One important source of information for the British traffic analysts about the new non-Morse links came from chat between teleprinter operators and telecommunications engineers setting up the links and testing them. While Tiltman and the Research Section at Bletchley Park would be working out the mechanical structure of the Geheimschreiber (see Chapter nine), the wireless interception operators were trying to build up a picture of the expanding wireless teleprinter network. Clearly, the Balkan link had been experimental, and now the German armed forces were able to exploit the fruits of that experimentation. By the spring of 1942, the traffic analysts had identified five non-Morse 'groups' using different types of cipher machine and/or different transmission techniques. NoMo1 was the name assigned by Bletchley Park to the Balkan link, an army link between Germany and Greece. NoMo2 was a German air force link, initially between Berlin and Koenigsberg. 'This link was investigated and produced plenty of information on the system being used and their own difficulties of reception, etc.' It gave the traffic analysts a lot of information because messages sent on it were also transmitted over a parallel Enigma link, 'much to the exasperation of the teleprinter operators who were aware of this'.[4] NoMo2 was to become the technical template for later German air force wireless teleprinter transmissions.

The Enigma link paralleling NoMo2 provided the titbit of information that one of the wireless transmitter systems used for teleprinter transmissions was known to the Germans as Saegefisch (sawfish) after the shape of the image on the undulator slip.[5] An Enigma message gave the transmission bearing of 171 degrees between 'Robinson' (the German codename for the special train belonging to the head of the air force, Hermann Goering) and the location of Fliegerkorps X (Air Corps X).

> This angle, in fact, gives a bearing on Athens from the probable location of Robinson at that time. This message bore the reference 'Saegefischtrupp'. Later evidence makes it appear that this message concerns the inauguration of the group known as NoMo1… On [17 April 1942] Saegefisch was mentioned in a corrupt plain-language message on NoMo2. On [18 April] a further reference to this group appeared; Saegefisch, it appeared, was 'not the easiest thing to handle'… The hypothesis was propounded that Saegefisch was the code-name used to indicate non-Morse (teleprinter) transmissions. This hypothesis has since proved to be correct.[6]

In fact, the German signals troops used the term Saegefisch to refer to the high-power wireless transmitter system, not the cipher machine. The 'Saegefischetrupp' (sawfish troop) turned out to be a reference to the unit that set up the wireless links and operated them in the experimental phase before handing over to a signals unit. The interception service became quite familiar with these units, charting their activities across Europe and North Africa as they installed Saegefisch transmitters. Indeed, this German codename was borrowed to provide the overall codename used at Bletchley Park for anything to do with the non-Morse transmissions and the Geheimschreiber – 'Fish'.[7] NoMo1 was later named Codfish.

NoMo3 was an experimental link used by the army between Germany and Romania, but later reappeared as a full operational link and was codenamed Octopus. NoMo4 was identified from intercepted plain-language chat and radio direction-finding techniques as linking Varna in Bulgaria and Koenigsberg. Towards the end of 1942, it also reappeared as an operational link. NoMo5 turned out to be a training system based near Paris. The French capital was identified as a key location for research and development work on non-Morse technology by both German army and air force units. Intercepts confirmed 'the picture of Paris as a showroom-cum-training centre', for example, revealing that on 14 September 1942 there were fifty-five teleprinter operators, twenty-one telegraph engineers (Wechselstrom Telegrafie, alternating current telegraphy in English technical jargon), sixty-seven T/F personnel (wireless telegraphy engineers), nineteen telephonists, eight cable personnel, and eighty-eight telephone engineers, a total of 258 people.[8]

Identification of each link, or group as Bletchley Park named them at this time, was based on the collation of information from direction-finding tests on the intercepted wireless beams, analysis of the transmission characteristics and of the call-signs and the data revealed in plain-language messages about the system. There was no fixed relationship between the NoMo group and location. NoMo2, for example, was tested for about two months between Berlin and Koenigsberg before it disappeared; then, in April 1942, five or six transmitters of the same type started operating and passing coded traffic for about eighteen hours a day. Bearings located these transmitters at different times in Germany, France, Italy and North Africa. Each link or group started as a testing phase, setting up the radio transmission system. 'When a group makes its first appearance, it passes largely plain-language traffic consisting of test phrases, series of letters (RY etc.) and chat between operators concerning reception conditions, operating schedules, technical information and requests for information, and personal messages.' Once the testing phase was complete, there was much less plain-language traffic, and it was important for links to be identified as early as possible so that the technical data could be gleaned before the link became used mainly for coded traffic.[9]

A report from traffic analysts in February 1942 on NoMo4 illustrates the way in which snippets of information, some of an apparently quite banal nature, were logged, collated and analysed.

On 3/2 there was a reference to a [teleprinter] message from the Funktrupp [wireless unit] in Varna. On the same day a corrupt fragment stated, 'We are transmitting with a directional transmitter (Schraegstrahler) 45 degrees 25 minutes... in the direction of Varna'. Unfortunately, the figures in the bearing were not thoroughly reliable in the text. (A back bearing of 225 degrees from Varna gives a line through Africa...) On 4/2 there was a further reference to Funktrupp Varna, and on the same day an operator recounted that 'the mother of an unnamed person wanted to know where a certain letter came from, as she thought that he (the operator) had recently come from Varna'. On the same day the postal address of one station on the link was Field Post number 34437 W, which is known to be near Varna. Two personalities known to source from Chaffinch [Enigma] material have also been mentioned on NoMo4. It appeared from operators' chat that on 3/2 [officers] Oberst Karn and Oberstleutnant Hennigst were expected, probably at the Berlin station. Karn, on 19/9/41, was with Wapruef (Arms Testing Department) and was due to go to Africa in October. On 3/10/41 he was at Cyrene and was to decide about the Italian participation in experimental [wireless telegraphy] transmissions. On 25/9/41 an OberstLtn Hennigst was known to be with Ida Gans III, thought to be at Rome or Berlin, and to be connected with experimental wireless transmission. Both these officers were at this time (Autumn 1941) concerned with a wireless experiment, whose nature is not known; the scene of the experiment was in Africa, where there was an experimental [wireless telegraphy] station at Tripoli and a house south of Cyrene where 'Anna Sued' was located. From isolated references to Army formations and authorities (e.g. German Military Mission Rumania, and AOK 12), and also to the two above-mentioned officers, it is plain that this group is under Army control.[10]

On information such as this, an understanding of the Fish network was painstakingly pieced together.

Although the links at Berlin and Koenigsberg were housed in permanent exchanges, at the field headquarters end, the equipment was held in two or more trucks. One truck, the Betriebswagen, held the teleprinter, cipher attachment, paper-tape-feeder and hand-punch for pre-perforating the tape, and the other, the Sendungs-wagen, held the transmission gear and the wireless transmitter. The wireless receiver was located some distance from the transmitting aerial to avoid interference.[11] Although the system was indeed mobile, it was much less so than an Enigma set-up, which needed just one small vehicle for the cipher machine, Morse key and wireless transmission gear. So the interception engineers found that, once a non-Morse link had gone through its experimental phase, it tended to be fairly static and this remained the case until the final years of the war when moves became quite frequent. The radio link was often only one leg in a longer transmission link, involving landlines and occasionally submarine cables. 'It appears probable from the frequencies used and the distance to be covered that retransmission takes place automatically at some intermediate point.'[12]

As well as the different transmission technologies, it became clear from both plain-language snippets and analysis of intercepted messages that there were also different cipher machines in use. The air force link NoMo2 provided references to the Geheimschreiber: 'References (as on 27/1/42) to Geheimschreiber provided an indication that the secret teleprinter was used for these trans-missions. It was also apparent that a simple scrambling switch was in use for going to "secret" from "normal" and vice versa… On 18/3, the Fliegfuehrer reported that his Geheimschreiber was out of order, though a standby machine could be used. On 25/3 a second Geheimschreiber arrived, and the Fliegfuehrer requested per-mission to retain it.'[13] Bletchley Park was already aware of the Geheimschreiber. A German military telephone directory for

occupied France that had come into the possession of British Intelligence had aroused interest: 'From the arrangement (the Geheimschreiber subscribers are interspersed in the main list of teleprinter subscribers) it looks as if the Geheimschreiber is a special type of apparatus in the subscriber's office which can only be used with a similar machine at the other end, but that between the ends communication can be over the ordinary lines and exchanges (analogous to scrambler phone).'[14] This British intelligence assessment is referring to the use of the Geheimschreiber on landlines rather than wireless. When the same name appeared in NoMo2 chat between operators, it confirmed that it was now being used on wireless teleprinter links as well as landlines.

Clearly, the German armed forces were investing a lot of technical effort in the cipher machines and the wireless transmission techniques. Bletchley Park concluded in May 1942 that 'There is little question in view of recent developments that experiments with this new type of transmission over a period of about six months have convinced the Germans of its practicability. The original group has been working for about nine months, and, since the end of March, NoMo2 has definitely been used for messages of high intelligence value. It is expected that when experiments are finally completed, a high percentage of traffic may pass by this method between higher commands.'[15] Tackling the non-Morse transmissions and cipher was becoming a matter of some importance at Bletchley Park.

chapter seven

'If the Wind Meets It'

The *Mabinogion*, that collection of ancient British legends written down in the early eleventh century in the language that became Welsh, includes a tale about Lludd and Llefelys, two of Beli's four sons. Lludd, the eldest, inherited the kingship of Britain and, according to mythical tradition, gave London its name, while Llefelys married the daughter of the king of France and later became king there. After many good years, three plagues affected Lludd's people, one of which was the arrival of a troublesome tribe called the Coroniaid about whom it was said that 'There was no discourse over the face of the Island, however low it might be spoken, that they did not know about it if the wind meets it'.[1] Lludd arranged to meet Llefelys at sea to talk about the troubles affecting his kingdom and they looked for a way of talking whereby 'the wind might not catch their discourse, lest the Coroniaid should know what they were saying'. Llefelys arranged for a long bronze horn to be made which the two could use to talk in confidence. But, when they first used it, 'whatever words they said to one to the other through the horn, it came to each of them as nothing but hateful contrariety. And when Llefelys perceived that, and how there was a demon making mischief through the horn, he had wine poured into the horn, and had it washed, and by virtue of the wine had the demon driven out of the horn. And their talk was unhindered.'

Transmitting teleprinter messages over the airwaves was a technically demanding task, pushing at the boundary of telecommunications technologies of the 1930s and early 1940s. It was all too easy for transmissions to become hopelessly garbled – appearing as 'nothing but hateful contrariety'. Repeated experimentation was necessary before reasonably satisfactory techniques were developed, with much trial and error needed to finally wash the demons and bugs from this 'bronze horn' in the ether. Great efforts were made to ensure that the cipher system was highly secure, but considerable attention was also devoted to making it as hard as possible even to intercept the wireless messages themselves by adopting innovative techniques. Yet, once it became clear that there were important messages passing through this new channel of communications, Britain's interception and codebreaking experts switched their focus to finding ways of detecting the merest hint of a breeze carrying those secret conversations.

The Vernam cipher (see Chapter two) is based on a form of two-state, or binary, logic (which is slightly different from standard 'binary arithmetic' which uses a different set of rules for combining the units). The Baudot code also features a binary form of coding. The wireless transmission system thus had to transmit binary, digital signals.[2] The basic technique was to transmit one of two different types of tone – or electric current at a specific frequency – for a short duration. Tone A would signal a 'mark' and tone B would signal a 'space', although this is a simplification and, in fact, there were several different tone techniques used. The NoMo groups listed in Chapter six to which Bletchley Park consigned a link were in part determined by the tone transmission technique used (and in part by the type of cipher machine used). Some NoMo groups used one tone for a mark and an absence of any tone for a space. Others used two tones each for a mark and a space (tones A and B for mark, and tones C and D for space). This was a more secure system, because it was less liable to corruption if noise in the airwaves overwhelmed one tone, as the receiver could still detect the second tone, but it was also more complex and expensive.

The ability of the receiver to detect incoming tones determines how long a tone has to be signalled for it to be recognized, and thus the signalling rate. The slower the signal speed, the easier it is to detect the individual signals. A single signalling unit is known as a Baud, in honour of Emile Baudot (see Chapter two). In the inter-war period, a commonly used standard for teleprinter trans-missions was 50 Baud. This simply means that fifty mark/space units were signalled in one second, or 50 bits per second, as we would say today. This works out at ten characters per second (ten characters each of five units = fifty).[3] If the signals were all marks, one would hear a continuous tone. Similarly, if they were all spaces, there would be a continuous, though different, tone. Most transmissions would be a mix of space and mark and thus of the two tones used, most commonly with groups of one, two or three marks or spaces, and occasionally longer sequences of the same unit. This changing pattern gives a characteristic semi-regular howling sound as the tones veer back and forth, at one moment representing one, two, three or more marks, then one or more spaces and so on.

However, it was, in fact, found necessary in practice to have some timing information and to sacrifice the theoretical desire for signals of equal length, the most efficient technique for machine telegraphy. So the transmitter automatically added two extra units – a 'start' unit (a space) at the beginning of each character and a 'stop' unit (a mark) at the end. The stop unit is the only one that is of different length – it is usually about one and a half times as long as the other six signals. A typical system would be based on signal times of twenty milliseconds (thousandths of a second) for each for the five units of the character and the start unit, and thirty milli-seconds for the stop unit. The receiving equipment has to be able to recognize the stop unit before the sending device begins to transmit the next character or a timing mismatch will occur and the machines will get out of step. The addition of these start and stop units for transmission reduced the traffic throughput or characters per second rate, which worked out at just seven characters per second, at a Baud rate of just over fifty signals per second.

This all worked reasonably well with landlines, but it was a different matter when it came to wireless transmission. The 'propagation' or transmission of wireless signals is considerably more difficult than sending signals through a cable. Even now, the many variables of wireless or radio propagation are far from fully understood and trial and error remains a key development technique for the wireless engineer. A cable provides a relatively well-protected environment, and thus also a predictable one, where the causes of interference are well understood. The manufacturing process ensures that decay of the signal is kept well within an acceptable level. In wireless transmission, it is much more difficult to control the environment. Wireless conditions are eminently variable, from minute to minute, from day to night, from season to season, and from one place to another.

As the British interception service observed, 'It was obvious that [the Germans are] combining voice frequency landline with wireless telegraphy, but whereas landlines are easily controlled, wireless telegraphy has many pitfalls where machine printing is the goal. Atmospherics, jamming, R/F and selective fading all combine to make the task more difficult.'[4] This is a particular problem for binary transmissions where the state of a unit is easily lost or corrupted. In modern digital communications systems, and indeed within computer systems, streams of binary numbers are surrounded by palisades of 'check digits' that can be used to perform a 'check sum' to work out if any particular bit has been corrupted – and errors can even be corrected. But these techniques were only being developed in the early 1940s and were not widely used.

The Baudot code is a so-called lean code. Every unit matters. The corruption of a single unit would result in a corrupt character just as if all five of the units in that character were corrupt. If enough units in enough characters were corrupted, then the whole message could be unintelligible. Every one of the thirty-two combinations is used to signify a character (with the exception, in some usage, of the all-spaces combination). There is no waste, no redundancy at all, no unused combinations of the five units. However, the very leanness and efficiency of the Baudot code was also what made it prone to corruption. The Hellschreiber non-Morse transmission and printing system, named after its German inventor, Dr Rudolf Hell, employed an ingenious technique to circumvent this problem. The Hellschreiber was a hybrid digital/analogue system (sometimes described as a form of facsimile or fax). Hell used lots of 'redundancy' in the form of a rather obese code in which the message could survive quite severe corruption. It needed eighty-four units to represent one character – providing lots of unused, or redundant, code combinations which had the effect of minimizing the effects of corruption. The concept of redundancy in communications systems is comparable with using a bucket to carry water. If the bucket is filled to the very brim and then carried up a couple of flights of stairs, there is bound to be some spillage. However, if a bigger bucket is used to carry the same amount of liquid, so that, say, it is only three-quarters full, it may well be possible to avoid spillage altogether. The spare capacity in the bucket (or the transmission bandwidth in the tele-communications jargon) provides security against spillage (or corruption). The German Hellschreiber system was, reported Bletchley Park, 'capable of operating satisfactorily under adverse wireless propagation conditions. The wireless receiving equip-ment is not elaborate and the printer is simple and easy to maintain.'[5] It was the redundancy Hell built into his system that allowed this.

The precise details of how this worked are not essential to the story (it translated the marks and spaces into a set of printed 'mosaics' representing the character) but the Hellschreiber did play an important part in helping the British wireless intercept engineers improve their skill at intercepting German non-Morse wireless transmissions. It was a familiar commercial product, although in Britain the available machines worked at slower speeds than the German versions and used a slightly different printing mosaic, these were both problems that could be overcome fairly easily. It is a measure of the difficulty that the German signals engineers had in receiving standard Baudot code transmissions that they needed to use the Hellschreiber. But, as the British wireless engineers would always have less technical knowledge of the transmission technical parameters than the German engineers, they had even more difficulty than their German counterparts in intercepting transmissions without corruption, so the corruption-tolerant Hellschreiber gave them a useful start in learning about the German systems and techniques before pure teleprinter-to-teleprinter transmission was made standard. The British Hells-chreiber devices were adapted to create a Universal Hellschreiber Receiver. The British interception service reported in the spring of 1942 that 'Many thousands of groups of Hellschreiber [were] read up [manually] before we designed and made a satisfactory universal Hellschreiber machine' – one which used a special printer to print the messages on paper tape in enciphered form.[6]

This underlines the limitation of the Hellschreiber. The incoming transmission was sent directly to a special Hellschreiber printing device that worked only with the special Hellschreiber signalling code. It was not possible to send the incoming signals automatically to a Geheimschreiber to decipher the message before printing. Instead, the Hellschreiber printed the message in its cipher version. This meant adding a further, deciphering stage, requiring the printed cipher text to be typed into a teleprinter with a Geheim-schreiber attachment. The Hellschreiber was a short-term solution, an intermediate stage on the way to direct teleprinter-to-teleprinter working. It was an interesting but not overly important hybrid analogue/digital system. Nonetheless, its pioneering role should not be overlooked in the development of the digital wireless communications techniques of the ubiquitous mobile telephone of modern times.

We tend to think of the transition to digital machines as being a phenomenon of the post-Second World War years. In fact, the telecommunications industry was pioneering digital techniques in the decades before the war. There was no single straightforward and seemingly direct route from analogue to digital techniques, and there were several backward steps from digital to analogue techniques along the way. Electric telegraphy started out in the 1830s using digital signalling by pulses of direct current, but in the 1920s and 1930s telegraph traffic was increasingly sent using analogue transmission techniques, so that it could share telephone cables. This technology allowed several simultaneous voice telephone calls or telegraph transmissions on a single cable. The details of how it worked are not important here – except to note that the original signal frequency is converted to a different frequency at the transmitting end and converted back again at the end, so this is essentially an automatic re-encoding and de-coding task performed by electric machinery and wires. Indeed, telecommunications systems essentially consist of encoders/transmitters, transmission media (wire, wireless, optical fibre, and so on), receivers/decoders and switching nodes.

In this transitional period, the advantages of, first, digital techniques and, second, binary digital began to be appreciated in an increasing number of uses. Binary digital techniques were used much more frequently in telecommunications research and operational applications. But in most cases, it was not digital, let alone binary, as such that was adopted. Rather, it was that various techniques were developed to solve particular problems which later turned out to be performed at a basic technological level in ways that we now identify as digital or binary. The topic of binary arithmetic appears hardly at all in the mathematical histories and textbooks of the first half of the twentieth century. In the 1920s, 1930s and 1940s a mere handful of people were becoming more aware of what the industry was alighting upon. Just as Baudot worked out that the most efficient way to send teleprinter signals was a five-unit, two-state code, so telecommunications theorists began to realize that all signal/coding information could be broken down and recorded as such binary units and others that machines could theoretically perform complex logical processes.[7] But these visions took time to develop and to integrate. The telecommunications industry edged through practical discovery towards binary digital technology at various times and points with the different technologies employed in telegraph and telephone networks. The theory, the understanding that these were, in fact, binary digital techniques, came later.

Two factors which helped drive the trend towards use of binary digital techniques were the increasing automation within the telecommunications networks and the growing use of electronics. The automatic telephone exchange (known as the telephone central in continental Europe or switch in the United States) was invented in 1890 by Almon Strowger, an American funeral undertaker, who feared that the local manual operator was switching calls from prospective customers to a competitor. This momentous invention generated an ever-growing need for control circuitry. Initially, electro-magnetic relays were used as switches in the control circuits of automated telephone networks. The simplest relays are two-state devices. These and more complex devices can be wired into sophisticated arrangements – to perform, for example, the combination of two Baudot code streams following the set of rules specified by Vernam or to perform standard binary arithmetic using a different set of rules. The rules are translated into electrical circuits and automatically carried out by the wiring and the relays. Massively complex relay circuits were used to control the routing of telephone or teleprinter calls through the automatic telephone and teleprinter networks. Tens of thousands of relays were used for a vast variety of technical functions within networks.

From the 1930s, electronic valves also started to be used, especially in the research establishments maintained by all the major telecommunications companies, whether network operating companies or equipment suppliers. The first use of electronic valves in communications was as analogue amplifiers for wireless signals and then for voice telephony. They were also used in scientific research laboratories for very fast 'electronic counters', which were needed for experiments in the then emerging field of nuclear physics. A few pioneers appreciated they could also be used as switching devices, replacing the much slower relays. One of the engineers who used electronics for switching purposes was Tom Flowers, a British Post Office engineer, who was later to use his knowledge of valves in the building of Colossus. Another pioneer of electronics was Godfrey Wynn Williams, who developed a digital telephone exchange while at the Cavendish Laboratory in Cambridge in the 1930s. This exchange was probably mainly electro-magnetic but retained some use of electronic valves for counting purposes.[8] Wynn Williams later worked on radar and then became an expert on electronics and digital circuits at Bletchley Park, leading a small team developing machines for the code-breakers. However, whether electro-magnetic or electronic technology is used, such control circuitry rapidly gets very complex, and designing and maintaining it is a formidable undertaking. A theory of switching and control circuits was needed so that standardized design techniques could be established. Thus, in the late 1930s and 1940s, the theory started to catch up with the practice. A short diversion will shed some light on the process, with a brief look at three of the major contributors to the theories that underpinned the adoption of digital techniques.[9]

In the 1930s, Alan Turing, then a precocious Cambridge

mathematician, developed a concept of a theoretical machine to address some important outstanding problems about the provability of mathematical theorems. By conceiving of a conceptual machine which could handle any mathematical algorithm, or set of mathematical processes, Turing showed that the result could only be known once the processes had been completed – and thus that a result could not be proved by some overarching theoretical short cut. But, in the late 1930s, this was such a rarefied theory that few engineers, not even those with a strong theoretical bent such as Flowers, were aware of it. More practically, in 1937, Turing spent some time in the United States at Princeton University. While there, he designed a binary multiplier using electro-mechanical relays. The Vernam code could use combinations of relays to perform the rules of his cipher. A binary multiplier uses a slightly different set of rules to perform repeated binary additions rather than the Vernam cipher's combinations to achieve the multiplication of numbers. It was implemented by a more complex set of wires and relays than that required to perform the binary combination of the Vernam cipher, as in Turing's multiplier, there was a need to wire in the ability to carry from one unit to another, and to re-circulate the units for the next step in the multiplication. As Turing's biographer, Andrew Hodges, has observed, 'Mathematically, this project was not advanced, for it used only multiplication. But although it used no advanced theory, it involved applications of "dull and elementary" mathematics which were by no means well known in 1937.'[10] Turing, however, was aware of theories of mathematical logic and binary, and the concordance between them. Several projects were under way in the United States developing electro-magnetic calculating machines and some of them would have employed the sort of circuits that Turing was making.

Another important pioneer of digital techniques in telecommunications was Alec Reeves, a British engineer, who conceived of a technique for digitalizing voice transmissions known as pulse code modulation. The details of Reeves's technique are not important here, but it is worth noting that, as the name suggests, it encodes an analogue voice signal in binary, digital pulses. In one sense pulse code modulation is rather similar to a Vernam cipher machine, except that it encodes/decodes rather than enciphers/deciphers, and indeed it initially used a five-unit binary code, although later this was extended to eight units. Although the technique only really became practicable after the war with the development of the transistor, by the end of twentieth century, it had become the standard digital telephony transmission technique used in most modern telecommunications networks. Only then did it face a potential challenge from a different technique of digitalized voice transmission, such as 'packetized' voice using the 'Internet Protocol'.[11] A version of pulse code modulation was used during the Second World War to develop a form of voice scrambling, but it required rooms full of electronic valves and was rather fragile. Reeves's work performed in the 1930s and 1940s paved the way for the practical post-war digitalization of telecommunications.

Reeves, like Turing, was not cast in a conventional scientist mould. During an experiment off the coast at Dover in the early 1930s, he recorded the reflection of microwave wireless transmissions from the vertical chalk cliff face. This, he was convinced, was communication from beings in other universes. Their signals, which would be in some form of code, he thought, could perhaps be converted into a different code that could be understood on Earth, such as the Morse code. Reeves also took part in séances, where he conversed with such departed souls as Michael Faraday, the nineteenth-century pioneer of electricity. Reeves certainly took such activities seriously: 'Having been told that dealing with the paranormal entailed risks and that some protection could be obtained from gold and steel in water, he later kept at the back of his recorder a glass of water containing a half-inch drill and the OBE awarded for his war work.'[12] His ideas also made him repelled by violence. His colleague Professor Cattermole later recalled that Reeves 'expressed his belief in a better era "with a much saner set of values, based on truth so far as seen, combining science with direct intuitive knowledge"'.[13] Reeves had been working in France in the late 1930s when he developed the concept of pulse code modulation and had to flee the invading German forces in the summer of 1940. On returning to Britain, he was initially resistant to the idea of working on weapons. Eventually, and after much agonizing, he decided he could work on a radar system, Oboe, which would reduce the number of lives lost through the then notoriously inaccurate bombing by making it somewhat more precise. As part of Oboe, he developed an electrical timing device that was accurate to one-thousandth of a second. This device was later also used in the weapons that destroyed airborne V1 rockets, and for distinguishing between Allied forces and German coastal batteries and defences during the landings in Normandy in 1944.

Another great pioneer of telecommunications, who was also active in the 1940s and later had a significant role in promoting post-war digital technology in telecommunications networks, was American Claude Shannon. He is not remembered for any particular piece of telecommunications technology but for putting modern communications on to a sound theoretical footing. His work on information theory is heavily mathematical and philosophically abstruse. Perhaps his most important conclusion was that all such information could be expressed in binary units. The theories he developed 'also established important relationships between [logic] and the design of switching networks'.[14] The logician's algebra, borrowed from George Boole, offered a way of expressing the different types of binary processes and thus Shannon's work, originating in telecommunications switching and control circuitry theory, established the basis for the later design of digital, binary circuits for computers. 'It was not well known in 1937 that the logical properties of combinations of switches could be represented by [logical] algebra, or by binary,' wrote Turing's biographer, and, while this would have been 'not hard for a logician', such as Turing or Shannon, to appreciate, many others adopted binary techniques without realizing that they were doing so.

Shannon and Turing met during the war when Turing visited the United States on behalf of GC&CS. As with that of Reeves, however, Shannon's work only came to the fore after the war. It is significant that Shannon called his ideas 'information theory' rather than 'communications theory'. His analysis is anchored in the concept of the intelligibility of the message, of the signal in the face of the inevitable corruptions or noise generated by the transmission medium, giving rise to the important idea of the signal-to-noise ratio. He also provided a theoretical explanation of why the more redundancy there is in telecommunications bandwidth, the less liable the signal is to be corrupted – something Rudolf Hell had, in fact, implemented in a practical system before any precise theoretical explanation was advanced.

But to return from the realm of distant universes – whether those of Turing's at once sublime and prosaic conceptual machines, Shannon's rarefied mathematics or Reeves's spiritual other worlds – to the harsh practical realities of communicating a teleprinter transmission consisting of on/off, space/mark signals. It all seems quite simple. The two different states can be represented by different tones or sounds transmitted at different frequencies. The problem is equally simple to state – as the speed of signalling increases, it gets harder for the equipment to distinguish one signalling unit from another, and harder for the machines to keep in step, with slight timing mismatches soon building up into distortion. A report written by an American wireless expert who visited Britain in 1942 to look at the organization of the British wireless interception service recorded that the Germans had taken considerable precautions against interception: 'Every possible device is used to confuse and mislead the interception operator and to prevent him from securing reliable information concerning the identity of the transmitting station, its position, the formation to which it is attached, etc.... Specialized intercommunication systems, or nets, such as the Netz [network], the Kreis [ring], the Stern [star], etc. [are] designed to defeat interception and confuse radio direction-finding... Technical developments, both mechanical and electrical, such as flick frequency changes and Non-Morse forms of transmission' were also intended to frustrate the eavesdroppers.[15]

The Hellschreiber was an intermediate step, as what the German army signals engineers really wanted was to be able to use the tone transmission of the Baudot code for direct teleprinter-to-teleprinter communication – thus eliminating the need to manually type in the ciphered text to get a plain-language version. As the German signals corps transmission techniques improved and there were fewer corrupted signals in a transmission, less use was made of the Hellschreiber. British interception engineers then had to develop techniques to intercept those Baudot signals, as well as the Hellschreiber code transmissions. The challenge facing the 'Y' Service was, in effect, to develop the equipment it needed to detect and record the transmissions. 'Before this type of transmission can be recorded special equipment must be designed and manufactured,' observed Harold Kenworthy from the Metropolitan Police/Foreign Office wireless interception unit. 'The methods used by the Germans preclude the use of standard machines... The undulator was the obvious line of attack. It was found that no recording gear existed which would give the necessary well-shaped signals and therefore work was put into the design of suitable gear.'[16]

Indeed, all Kenworthy's experience with the undulator in the inter-war years was about to pay off. Yet, despite initial appearances, reading the signal marked on the paper roll or slip produced by the undulator was a highly skilled task with just a handful of practitioners at the Post Office and Cable & Wireless. 'The Foreign Office, so far as is known, has only five operators capable of analysing, recording and then reading up the slip obtained... To get the best out from these transmissions, it takes a really keen and efficient operator,' Kenworthy reported.[17]

In April 1942 it was reported that

Non-Morse is at present being watched at Dover (Abbotscliffe) where there are one set, one filter and one recording gear. Three operators [have been] lent from the Admiralty to Mr Kenworthy for this purpose but if UHF [ultra-high-frequency traffic] crops up, they have to drop their work on non-Morse. Otherwise they keep a continuous watch on non-Morse. In the hut at Denmark Hill there is one set with poor recording gear which is used for checking generally and there is no continuous watch. Mr Mason has also one experimental set in his house at West Wickham. The following are immediately required: 8 sets; 8 bridges; 8 undulators; 16 filters; 8 separate aerials and about 30 operators and 12 slip-readers. Furthermore, if a German experimental channel which is now working is to be properly watched, a further 12 sets are required to record these simultaneous transmissions. It is obvious that a drive must be made to get the necessary gear manufactured for recording non-Morse. The increasing use of non-Morse by the Germans in the last three months has made it necessary for us to take rapid action on a bigger scale than has hitherto been contemplated.[18]

A request was made for twenty operators 'to be delivered to Denmark Hill for immediate training or slip-reading and teleprinter interception operating… [T]raining will take about six weeks… [Also,] the moment traffic is obtained at least twenty slip-readers will have to be employed.' And there was bad news about the availability of the gear needed to detect and record the signals. 'Equipment is virtually non-existent except [that some] experimental gear is available. Five sets of recording gear could be collected at the expense of other commitments. Fifteen are on order – delivery doubtful within six weeks… [and there is] no satisfaction on the delivery of condensers.'[19] In July 1942,

Kenworthy reported that 'During the last month, two new types of teleprinter transmission have been located and investigated. One is… active for about twelve hours a day. One man has been kept on this station continuously to record all possible traffic. The amount of traffic per day is colossal. It is going to take a long time to read up all the slip with the present number of slip-readers but they are gradually being added to and delays will eventually be cut down.'[20]

Increasingly, it became clear that the interception of the Fish traffic was a considerable technical challenge in itself, far more complex than the lower-frequency transmissions used to carry Morse signals with Enigma-enciphered messages. The engineers would have to develop their own techniques, and, indeed, they would have to be much better than the techniques developed by the Germans, who, of course, would be doing their utmost to minimize interception. The British engineers would have to develop systems capable of picking up even tiny lingering traces of the original signals, doing so with the utmost accuracy. This challenge was huge: it could not be met by the 'Y' Service, the existing intercept section of GC&CS, but demanded a wholly new and effectively independent organization that could concentrate, in total secrecy, on developing the equipment and the training operators needed to capture the teleprinter signals.

chapter eight

Knockholt

The White Cliffs of Dover were one of Britain's great national wartime symbols, immortalized in an immensely popular song of that name. The cliffs acquire their colour from the great depths of chalk which underlie much of southern England. The cliff face is nearly vertical because the chalk, made up of the shells of billions of small creatures, is porous and thus dry, so the rock maintains its mechanical strength. Long after the chalk was laid down, great mountain-building forces to the east sent shudders through the chalk, causing it to fold and crack, eventually leaving an undulating landscape of ridges with steep scarp and gentle dip slopes, intersected by dry, riverless valleys. These whale-backed ridges create one of England's classic landscapes – the Downs. Actually, Downs is a rather misleading name, for really they are ups, forming distinct lines of hills that rise sharply, and most noticeably on the scarp face and the sea cliffs. The name, in fact, derives from the older English word that nowadays survives as 'dunes' with a somewhat different meaning.

The cliffs at Dover form the truncated eastern end of a long ridge known as the North Downs. The ridge runs inland through Kent to skirt south of London towards the Salisbury Plain – home of Stonehenge and many other prehistoric sites – where it merges with two other long fingers of chalk. The South Downs start dramatically with those other great white cliffs, Beachy Head, and run west along the coast to Brighton before moving inland towards the Salisbury Plain. The third ridge, the Chilterns, rises gently, almost imperceptibly, to the north-east of London, rising in height and tending to the south-west until it too joins the great chalk plain. The height of the ridges was important, as it provided many potentially suitable locations for wireless intercept stations. Accordingly, some of the initial non-Morse transmissions were intercepted at Dover and direction-finding readings performed near Beachy Head, while the Post Office/Foreign Office interception station at Sandridge near St Albans, which helped with non-Morse interception, stood on one of the wide summits of the Chilterns, with vast open skies and long views (and the area is still used for wireless masts today). With the growth in the number of Fish links, and the technical difficulties of intercepting them, GC&CS decided that a dedicated interception station should be opened for Fish traffic. A site well above sea level was needed and the North Downs provided a good place to start looking.

Intercepting teleprinter non-Morse transmissions was going to be an entirely different technical challenge from the interception of Enigma messages in Morse code, and a much tougher one, requiring new equipment, special techniques and highly skilled staff. It was decided by April 1942 that Harold Kenworthy should be moved from the intercept station at Denmark Hill to take charge at a new site of at least fifteen acres, allowing room for directional antennas and other equipment. A location was needed that was some 200 metres above sea level, offered easy access for operators and was close to long-distance telephone cables.[1] After a site in Surrey was rejected, Ivy Farm at Knockholt on the North Downs, not far from the affluent town of Sevenoaks in rural Kent, was chosen for the new non-Morse interception centre. It was, as Kenworthy later recalled, 'a converted farm house… [which was] requisitioned with upwards of 30 acres of land – subsequently extended to about 160 acres in July 1942.'[2] And, on a broad summit plateau, at 240 metres above sea level, the site was almost the highest point on any of the great chalk ridges.

One problem that constantly held up progress in opening the new centre was the need for absolute secrecy. That the project deserved priority could be stressed, but not the reason why. The result was predictable. No sooner had the ideal site been identified than the farmer started ploughing up the land. An appeal to the Ministry of War had no effect and the ploughing continued. A second letter to the Ministry elicited the response that it could do nothing until it had heard from War Lands, another part of the government, which was not under its control. War Lands' permission came at the end of August, but, despite that, by October, there were still appeals going up from Kenworthy for workmen to build the huts. This time the Ministry replied that it was waiting for contracts to be signed and insisted that no work was to be started until it gave the go-ahead. Having been told to expect approval in five days, eight days later Kenworthy was still waiting. He reported that they had 'made our own enquiries and located a horse and cart. The Labour, however, is not forthcoming. Enquiries of the Ministry of Works, Tunbridge Wells, elicit the statement that no Labour can be supplied as this is not a priority job... In fact Sevenoaks [Labour Exchange is] sending 48 men away on Saturday to other parts of the country... Unless something drastic is done, there seems no prospect of this vital work being completed for several months, as we may expect bad weather and of course shortening days.'[3] Eventually the wheels of bureaucracy wound on and the station went into full operation early in 1943, although interception started well before then. In the meantime, slip-reading had to be done in part at Aldford House, a Post Office establishment in London, with the help of radio operators on loan from the army. There was concern at Bletchley Park that these operators could come to learn what their work was about and, after Knockholt took over fully, 'they could become "wise men" and subsequently returned to the army to tell all they know when they are in their cups'.[4]

At first, it was estimated that about eight interception sets would be needed (plus items such as filters that prevented interference being interpreted as a valid tone), although this soon jumped to twenty-five sets to be delivered 'as soon as possible', with the likelihood of another seventy-five being needed shortly after that. Some of the equipment could be bought in Britain. Marconi supplied some undulators, although they were not the most appropriate type and the company would be unable to complete the full order for nine months, so more had to be ordered from the United States. 'It was found that no [existing] recording gear existed which would give the necessary well-shaped signals and therefore much work was put into the design of suitable gear. The result has been a satisfactory bridge which works well with the [Marconi] UG6A undulator.' This bridge, later called the Kenworthy bridge, and filters had to be designed from scratch and prototypes were made at the Metropolitan Police Workshop at West Wickham. The best receivers were ones imported from the United States. Masts for the antennas were also urgently required. 'It is obvious that a drive must be made to get the necessary gear manufactured for recording non-Morse,' reported Kenworthy.[5]

The rapid growth in the demand for equipment put a lot of strain on the relationship with the Metropolitan Police Workshop. The Police Engineer had taken on a contract to supply the RAF with automatic Beacon transmitters and wanted to expand it to mass-production levels. According to Kenworthy, 'Although our "Y" work was very important, no special priorities had been allocated by the Production Boards and that meant that materials were very difficult to get. At one time, it was almost impossible to get small transformers made. The matter was brought to a head in early 1943 when the Police Engineer accepted an extension of the Beacon contract and practically squeezed Foreign Office production out.'[6] Edward Travis, the director of GC&CS, decided that the best solution was to set up an internal equipment research and development operation, and 'authority was obtained at a high level to build and equip a suitable Laboratory and Workshop at Knockholt entirely under Foreign Office control'. This unit, later known as the Foreign Office Research and Development Establishment (FORDE), took three months to set up. Kenworthy, ever conscious of the need for secrecy, noted, 'The value of this Establishment cannot be over-estimated as added security to our operation was possible.'

The engineers put much effort into acquiring the best receivers, then into isolating them as much as possible to reduce any inter-ference. But most important of all were the aerials, which were designed to pick up the smallest traces of distant radio trans-missions. 'We wanted the best and the latest aerials, therefore all possible data was gathered together from all sources regarding aerials, aerial amplifiers, feeder lines and so on. Where improve-ments were possible, they were made. By this method the station was very soon equipped with a number of "Rhombic" aerials and special wide-band amplifiers to cover the very wide range of frequencies used by the Germans.' These Rhombic or diamond-shaped aerials were enormous – as much as 1,000 feet (approx-imately 300 metres) across the major axis. One niggling little problem was the damage caused by grazing cattle to the masts that supported the aerials and these masts had to be protected by metal picket fences instead of wood. However, electro-magnetic interference was a more persistent concern than the local ruminants. 'Everything possible was done to screen the receivers from "pick up" [of electro-magnetic noise] from the undulator and teleprinter motors and any other local disturbance,' noted Kenworthy. Each receiver had its own co-axial cable direct from the aerial amplifier. This was an expensive solution: at other British wireless intercept stations, 'feeder' cables brought aerial signals to a switching point where the operator switched his or her set into the aerial they wanted. But 'no amount of screening can make up for the single coaxial cable direct to the set. The result justified the decision to do this as no trouble has been experienced as the station gradually grew and not only teleprinters but reperforators and relays were added to each receiving position.'

Knockholt initially found it a tough task to keep up with the constant German changes and to get precise transcripts of the transmissions. Although the accuracy of interception improved enormously over the months, it remained a nagging issue until the end of the war. There were never enough slip-readers to handle all the traffic that could have been intercepted, and there were always inexperienced staff at work at some point or other, limiting throughput and reducing quality. And with the deliberate complexities designed into the directional wireless transmission system by the Germans, not to mention the vagaries of the atmosphere and radio-wave propagation, it is a wonder that any interceptions were read accurately. Conditions varied rapidly for technical and atmospheric reasons. Bletchley Park reported in 1942:

> To date this month [October 1942] a very large proportion of all [teleprinter] traffic on this group has been printed. On the first instance very little was printable owing to traffic being passed at a speed higher than usual. On 8th, 9th, 10th instant wireless conditions were very poor and again on 21st and 22nd conditions were poor... figures show (excluding October 1st) 896 messages of which 696 were printed – 77.6 per cent... When wireless conditions are good the signals are normally quite legible [and] can be read without difficulty, but immediately there is a deterioration of signal strength, a very variable signal is recorded which cannot be read with any degree of accuracy.[7]

Interference during fades or pauses could be mistaken for signals, especially when the German operators were hand-sending in chat mode, using the keyboard rather than pre-punched paper tapes. In chat mode, pauses between letters and words became common and 'interference makes the signals very largely unreadable or at best unreliable'.[8] 'Absolute continuity of the cipher is essential,' implored Captain Tester who had charge of the decryption effort.[9]

There were serious problems in achieving the level of quality needed to pick up the very weak signals from the Continent. The problems of interception were often a complex mix of technical and human issues, difficult to pin down to specific causes, and led to some friction between Bletchley Park, Knockholt and the Post Office. 'We deplore the acrimonious tone which has crept into this controversy and has almost reached the "pistols for two and coffee for one" stage', reported one Bletchley Park witness about one dispute which erupted between Kenworthy defending Knockholt's precision of transcription and Post Office engineers at Sandridge and at Aldford House in London.[10] Kenworthy was highly sensitive to what he saw as encroachments on his territory and indeed interpreted any complaints as personal criticism. Experts Mr Hunt and Mr Saunders, who were sent from St Albans to advise on improving reception, received short shrift. As a letter of complaint from St Albans to Colonel Sayer, who was in charge of the interception operations of GC&CS, put it: 'Every attempt made by Mr Hunt and Mr Saunders to put forward suggestions to improve conditions is rebuffed... an attitude which would be merely childish if everything at the Station were at the highest point of efficiency, but alarming when this is not so... It must be remembered that Mr Saunders and Mr Hunt have both several years' experience as operators with Cable & Wireless Ltd., on reading signals from slip, and they do know what they are talking about.'[11]

Hunt himself wrote to Colonel Sayer of GC&CS in an angry tone: 'I have been most upset personally at my reception [at Knockholt]. I have now been employed – with the exception of 1936–1939 – for fourteen years upon operating wireless reception and have had to wait until now to be told I do not know my job.'[12]

However, Kenworthy responded in kind, penning stinging replies defending his team's work, although he was obliged to admit problems did exist. Hunt he dismissed with the words that he clearly found the most damning of all: he 'is not a wireless operator', and 'if [Hunt's] instructions had been carried out it would have put him in charge of the wireless side'.[13] That would upset the natural order of things. Kenworthy referred to his own long years of experience of listening to illicit transmissions, which the senders did not want intercepted, contrasting this with the much easier task facing Post Office and Cable & Wireless engineers, whose job was simply to make connections work well. Clearly, in Kenworthy's estimation, they were not up to doing his job and should mind their own business.

Behind the row there lay a power struggle as the Post Office tried to find a role in non-Morse interception, while Kenworthy wanted to keep it as his exclusive domain.[14] On reading the reports, held today in the files at the National Archives, submitted by the two sides sixty years ago, it seems clear that the differences in interception quality were mainly to do with different generations of equipment used by the two stations, and differing conditions for receiving the radio signals at each site. In fact, the two stations tended to complement each other in that, when Knockholt failed to record the message accurately, St Albans was successful, and vice versa. The equipment at Knockholt, for example, recorded only one tone – the mark – and assumed space if there was no mark tone. But at St Albans the equipment detected both tones, giving a better idea of the real level of missed signals.[15] This meant that no clear comparison could be made or conclusions drawn, and so the dispute became personal and prolonged.[16]

If nothing else, the row did clearly focus everyone's attention on addressing the problems of accurate interception and, in this respect, it helped hone the interception operation. As he fought to prove to his critics, and his superiors, the quality of his team's interceptions, Kenworthy came to appreciate that the delicate interception gear was more prone to failure than ordinary wireless kit. It had to be maintained carefully, with the sets and the undulators requiring regular and frequent attention, as well as substantial stocks of spare parts. This improved maintenance produced better results. It also demanded better-trained staff and a lot more checking and attention to quality. Diversity reception was developed where two aerials were tuned in to each frequency that was being intercepted and the two received signals merged to give a better result when one aerial could not pick up the signal. The two aerials were at different places on the site and differently angled to cover as wide a range of potential signals as possible. More kit and more maintenance, more staff and more resources: needs grew relentlessly. And it became clear that Kenworthy and his colleagues were all on a technological mystery tour as the German signals engineers tried new techniques to make it even more difficult to pick up stray signals. '[The] task of recording this form of transmission is one for highly qualified wireless experts, equipped with special apparatus, which will from time to time have to be modified,' said Kenworthy.[17]

The Post Office staff at Sandridge wanted a bigger part of the operation, sensing both its technological interest and the military/strategic significance of the information it imparted. They recommended that all signals be intercepted at two centres for accurate coverage. Their case, however, was undermined when a leak occurred in the Sandridge station's internal staff newsletter.[18] An item implied that the station was involved in interception of German non-Morse transmissions. An investigation was launched and the appropriate people warned in no uncertain terms, but it damaged the Post Office's case to have had a wagging tongue among its staff. Kenworthy would never make that sort of mistake. He had been trained for years in the importance of absolute secrecy, and knew full well that it would not matter a jot how good or bad the various stations were at interception if the German armed forces picked up any inkling of what the British were doing with their non-Morse transmissions.

Moreover, the Post Office staff at Sandridge were pitted against the Foreign Office's own. And the Foreign Office was the responsible ministry for GC&CS. Furthermore, Kenworthy or, to be more precise, his wife had been the first to intercept teleprinter signals, the first to draw attention to these strange sounds in the ether. They were his baby. When St Albans had been used in 1941 to pick up NoMo1 signals – Codfish, as the link was later codenamed – it had been done without his knowledge and since then he had 'regarded St Albans as a competitor' that wanted to take over from him. Kenworthy won his bureaucratic war, and non-Morse interception was stopped at St Albans and concentrated at Knockholt, although he had to ensure greater accuracy of output at Knockholt. As the quality of interception improved, the code-breakers started to have more success. New Fish links, such as Octopus in southern Russia, were being broken within weeks of their going on line. The very fact that this was done is the best measure of the efficacy of Kenworthy's interception service, whatever the opinions of the experts from the Post Office and Cable & Wireless.

part two – decryption

chapter nine

'HQIBPEXEZMUG'

Peter Wohlrab was German by birth, but in 1923, when he was seven, his family moved to Switzerland, where he was still resident when war broke out in 1939. By then Wohlrab was working as a publisher's representative. He was, he later claimed, an anti-Nazi and had no desire to serve in the German armed forces. He hoped to sit out the war in Switzerland, but was forced in May 1940 to return to Germany, where he was conscripted into the army. He served in a variety of posts before eventually working as an interpreter in North Africa, where he flew as passenger in German aircraft, listening in to British fighter pilots communicating with each other and their base by 'radio-telephone', before returning the information gleaned to intelligence officers in the Luftwaffe and the German army. It was during his eighteenth sortie, in April 1942, that the aircraft in which he was flying was shot down by a British pilot and Wohlrab was taken prisoner.

His British interrogators acknowledged that he seemed to be 'a genuine anti-Nazi'. He certainly gave them a lot of information about what he had seen during his service – in total, his testimony filled twelve densely typed pages. He had initially 'joined the R/T [radio-telephone] listening station', before going to Paris to work for a German codebreaking unit, W-10. 'Wohlrab there joined the Karthotek [the card library]. He stated that entries went back to

1932 and he formed the idea that it was in 1932 that the Germans had seriously begun to attack Russian ciphers... [he] thought that the German cryptographic effort at W-10 was very successful and that there was not much that was not read.' Wohlrab, however, had not enjoyed the work and asked if he could again be employed as an interpreter. It was then that he had been sent to North Africa.[1]

One subject was of particular interest to GC&CS. Wohlrab was asked nonchalantly if he knew about something called the Geheim-schreiber. It was vital to do this without giving him any hint that the interrogators knew much about the subject themselves or that it especially interested them. Wohlrab could have been a Nazi spy or could later talk to other prisoners about the subjects on which he had been questioned. Unfortunately, Wohlrab's lack of interest in codebreaking limited what he could recount. He had certainly seen and heard of the Geheimschreiber and described a machine

> about 3 ft high, 2 ft wide and 3 ft long. The operator behaves just as if he was sitting at an ordinary teleprinter, and the scrambling is done by the machine. It is all done by key manipulation. He does not know how many wheels there were. Said it was very secret, and quite impossible to take it to bits on the premises. Wohlrab believes that there is an explosive charge in the secret teleprinter, so that if anybody were to take it to bits who was not entitled to it would blow up. When one is operating a secret teleprinter, a tape runs out of the side, on which a copy of the message appears in clear. Wohlrab has never seen a secret teleprinter receiving. Wohlrab knows nothing about the way in which the keys are made up, or the way in which they are changed.

There is no evidence to suggest that the devices were booby-trapped, as Wohlrab suggested. Indeed, this was probably a scare tactic used to discourage the curious among German troops from prying into the machines. It had, of course, no such restraining effect on the codebreakers at Bletchley Park who, having no access to a physical machine, would have to open it up conceptually, in order to ascertain its principle of working.

In January 1942 – a few months before Wohlrab was interrogated – Colonel John Tiltman, head of the Military Section at Bletchley Park,[2] had reported to the director, Edward Travis, that 'It is thought improbable that any considerable further step in reconstruction of the [Geheimschreiber] machine will be made without some independent evidence of the details, dimensions, etc. of the parts of the machine.'[3] But, contrary to this prediction, by the time Wohlrab had been squeezed dry, the machine had, in fact, been fully diagnosed – its design had been divined and its processes had been understood. The task was achieved without any sight of the machine or information about its innards: it had been a purely 'logical' process.

A year later, at the beginning of 1943, in a review of achievements in the previous year, Travis was able to report,

> Turning now to the general work of the Research Section, probably its most sensational feat has been the elucidation and re-construction of the German Secret Teleprinter starting from scratch. The problem was analogous to the other machine ciphers about as analogous as a Maori and an Eskimo. In tackling all other machine cyphers, some basic knowledge was possessed of the mechanical and the electrical construction of the machine beforehand. In the case of the Secret Teleprinter nothing whatever was known and the machine has been reconstructed on the basis of pure cryptography.[4]

It was a combination of errors – in the use of the system and in its design – that gave Colonel Tiltman and his colleagues a way into breaking the cipher machine. The only information they had to go on was the intercepted, enciphered messages; their resource was codebreaking experience and expertise.

Tiltman was a veteran codebreaker and, early in the Second World War, had made a major contribution to cracking the Enigma system used by the German railway authorities. He was the obvious person to put in to oversee the Research Section when it was set up in mid-April 1941. An exceptionally talented man, Tiltman was not easily diverted from his task – for example, he had taught himself enough of the Japanese language to tackle Japanese ciphers. As the war intensified, there was an urgent need for more people with some knowledge of the notoriously difficult language to satisfy the codebreaking effort in the Pacific and Asia. Tiltman knew that not everyone could manage to learn Japanese through self-study as he had done. He visited the School of Oriental and African Studies (SOAS) based in London's fashionable Bloomsbury district. He explained that he had learned as much Japanese as he needed in six months and asked the School to organize a course of similar length. The august academics demurred, explaining that it normally took five years for a diplomat to reach an adequate standard. By cutting corners, that could perhaps be squeezed down to a minimum of two years, but six months was quite impractical. Tiltman refused to accept this denial of his own experience, so he set up his own training centre. The six-month course focused rigidly on the task in hand. One student recalls that when his course was finished, he knew the Japanese for 'submarine', but not for 'I' and 'you'. But it successfully trained several codebreakers – despite being based at the rather less impressive location of a former gas appliances showroom in Bedford. Indeed, the courses were so successful that SOAS was shamed into setting up its own parallel lessons.[5]

Tiltman was a professional soldier who had been decorated in the First World War. But he was no typical military man. He treated his staff as individuals and spoke with them on first-name terms, whatever their rank – something that would generally have been unthinkable in the British military. Perhaps Tiltman had been in GC&CS for too long and had forgotten the behaviour expected of an officer, having been assigned to signals work only by chance in the early 1920s. Alternatively, perhaps it was Tiltman who helped set the tone for GC&CS – a tone that stuck when it expanded rapidly during the war – for his style did indeed become common-place despite its upsetting more tradition-bound officers and unsettling some of the 'other ranks'. Private William Filby, who became a cryptanalyst, recalled his first meeting with Tiltman on reporting for duty. As normal, Filby saluted, stamping his boots down noisily on the wooden floor, and followed this up with another loud stamp as he came to attention. Tiltman turned, looked at his feet and said, 'I say, old boy, must you wear those damned boots?'[6] From then on, Filby was allowed to wear plimsolls instead of boots. The problem facing Tiltman certainly demanded quiet concentration, and he preferred to work on his feet at a special high desk where he stood for hours on end, preferring this self-discipline to sitting at a more conventional desk.

The first step in understanding how Tiltman and his team approached their task is to switch terminology. While tele-communications engineers talked of marks and spaces, the cryptanalysts used the terms 'cross' and 'dot'. However, as before, the examples will continue to use the notation of '1' and '0'. It makes no real difference, 'mark', 'cross' and '1' are different names for the same thing as are 'space', 'dot' and '0'. The terminological shift represents the progress from practical solutions in telecom-munications (mark/space), via cryptanalytic work (cross/dot), to our modern understanding of the role of binary (1/0). The cryptographers also spoke about code 'impulses' rather than units, but this is a misleading term and so will not be used.

The first interceptions of experimental non-Morse transmissions were soon identified at Bletchley Park as the output of a teleprinter in the Baudot code. By analysis of corrupt messages, Tiltman worked out that it was indeed the standard international Baudot teleprinter code that was being used, rather than a special secret version of the code, as could have been the case. Having identified the Baudot code, Tiltman turned to the cipher. As a practised codebreaker, Tiltman was aware of the Vernam cipher and that seemed to be a good starting point for his investigation of the machine. After the war, Tiltman wrote, 'The next advance to be made was the demonstration that the cipher machine was a letter-subtractor cipher and the determination of the laws of addition used. This was made possible by the occurrence of a number of "depths".'[7] A 'depth' is two, or possibly more, messages enciphered with exactly the same key, and a 'near depth' is two or more messages enciphered with very similar keys. Every enciphered teleprinter transmission sent by the German army operators at this stage was preceded by a serial number and another character sequence 'in clear' or plain language, this was known as the 'indicator' and was twelve characters long. If two intercepted messages had the same twelve-character indicator at the start of each message, Tiltman guessed that they were likely to be in depth. This usually happened with two consecutive messages – a concurrence which strengthened the assumption that they were dealing with a repeated message, perhaps owing to the first transmission being received in corrupted form.

Tiltman looked closely at the workings of the Vernam cipher and thought that he saw a potential way in. He drew on a paper about letter-subtractor ciphers written before the war by Gerry Morgan, the head of his Research Section, and realized that, if two intercepted messages had indeed been enciphered with the same key, then there was theoretically a way of stripping the key out. The way to do this was to combine the two enciphered messages together using the same rules as the Vernam cipher. Tiltman reasoned that combining the two cipher texts would be the equivalent of combining the two plain-language messages and the key stream twice, thus wiping out the effects of the key and leaving a single string of characters which would represent the combination of the two original plain-language messages. The reason for this is that the second combination of a key wipes out the effect of a first combination. The second combining has this effect even when dealing with a pair of ciphered messages. (This is illustrated in an example in Appendix C – 'The First Break' technique. This appendix also expresses the cipher workings in some simple formulae which the reader may find useful when looking at some of the decryption techniques that led to the conception of Colossus in later chapters.)

Whether this would achieve anything in terms of breaking the cipher was another matter. The combined text of two plain-language messages would still be a jumble of meaningless characters. There was little way of knowing what two sets of plain-language characters were represented in the combined stream. Trial and error may perhaps have produced sensible results, but there would be no way of knowing if those results were right without some way of getting started. But at least testing a few intercepted messages might confirm the assumptions Tiltman had made. When Tiltman combined the character streams of several pairs of messages thought to be in depth, he 'noticed that some pairs of them began with same sequence of five or six letters. This was regarded as a proof of the assumptions that had been made, namely that the cipher was a letter subtractor, and that the law of addition had been inferred correctly.' This was precisely the effect that would have been expected if all the encrypted messages began in some stereotypical way. The group of letters '++ZZZ' appeared in clear before many messages.[8] Tiltman guessed that this group of characters might well also appear at the start of the ciphered section of a message (note that the character '+' was sometimes used as an alternative to '5' to indicate the figures-shift code combination). According to Tiltman, the 'proof was completed when about fifteen letters of one of the depths were decoded. When a group "++ZZZ88", which had appeared occasionally in clear preambles was tried as the clear of one message, the clear of the other message came out as the first letters of the word

SPRUCHNUMMER' – the German for serial number (see Appendix C – 'The First Break' steps 3 and 5). This was a truly significant advance. The remote possibility that random events should have unveiled the word 'SPRUCHNUMMER' was ruled out. Instead, the result seemed to confirm the assumptions that had been made and gave Tiltman the impetus to persevere. Yet, to go further, Tiltman now needed a long depth but with minor differences between the two messages.

Tiltman realized that there was one possible way of prising open the character stream produced from combining two messages with the same key. If an operator sent the same message twice, using the same key, but with a few minor changes in the content – corrected spelling mistakes, extra or fewer spaces, an abbreviation in place of a fully spelled-out word and so on – then it might be possible to start identifying the real characters in both messages. If the two messages were identical, it would be impossible – combining together two identical plain and key streams would result in a stream consisting entirely of zeros. But, if a few small differences appeared in the two plain texts, what was revealed in the shorter version of the message would help determine how to strip the two texts hidden in the combined text further on, as the character that was likely to appear could be deduced.

In the extended example in Appendix C – 'The First Break', the word 'oberkommando', revealed in the shorter message (M2) immediately after the serial number, would suggest that the same word is likely to appear after the *spruchnummer* and serial number in the longer message (M1). Rather like a treasure hunt, each clue that was uncovered would point to the next. This situation, of two messages with the same basic content but with minor differences in spacing and so forth, would probably only arise if a message was sent by an operator typing it directly on to the keyboard. If the operator had pre-punched the message on paper tape, it would indeed be identical in every 'dot and cross' when re-sent. But if, having failed to punch a message on to paper tape, an operator had to type a long message out again by hand, he might well have cut some corners the second time around, producing a few small differences in the message, although the contents as a whole would be almost identical. Fortune in this conflict favoured the mathematically astute, for one German operator came to Tiltman's rescue and delivered just what he needed – a long depth.

According to a history of the codebreaking effort written shortly after the war but released to public view in the late 1990s,

> The first attempts to reconstruct long key-sequences from depths… were failures. Depth-breakers then had no previous experience of the traffic, and so depth-breaking was much slower and much more difficult than it was in later years. Apart from this, there was one very serious obstacle… it cannot be done by the depth-breaking process alone, without independent evidence… It is not surprising, therefore, that for some time little progress was made with the Tunny cipher. The construction of long pieces of key was very difficult, and even when it was possible the results were not unique.

But, then, 'on 30 August 1941, the German cipher operators came to the rescue' and provided that much-desired long depth. The two messages shared the same twelve letter indicator: 'HQIBPEXEZMUG'. When the long depth was broken into,

> [I]t was found that the messages were essentially the same, but the spacing, the mis-spellings and the corrections were different. Evidently the same message had been typed out twice, by hand. As a result, the two versions, at the same number of letters from the beginning, would be at slightly different places in the true text of the message. This divergence increased slowly, until at the 3,976th letter, where the shorter message came to an end, it had increased to more

than one hundred letters. This depth was much easier to read than the earlier depths had been, for at any stage the next letter of clear language in the less advanced [i.e. the longer] message could be predicted from the clear language already derived for the other. The messages were, in fact, decoded over the entire length of the shorter message, so that the ambiguity in the key was resolved... From this depth a [length of] key of 3,976 letters was reconstructed... during the remaining months of the year 1941 the Research Section were engaged in attempts to analyse this key, and so discover the nature of the machine which had produced it.

At this point Tiltman moved away from the work on the Geheimschreiber cipher, having achieved the first successful glimpse into it. He had other responsibilities – in particular, Japanese codes – and had been ignoring them to concentrate on the Geheimschreiber. In December 1941, Travis had been urged to put Tiltman back on to Japanese codes, 'when the time is right'. Work on these codes 'was set back by [the] Japanese changing code [on] December first' (shortly before the attack on the American Pacific fleet at Pearl Harbor) and Tiltman's help was needed urgently.[9] As Tiltman explained to an American colleague in May 1942, 'The Geheimschreiber... is a great worry to us. We have had difficulty in finding staff to service it. As it is, the whole of my Research Section has had to be turned on to it, to the consequent detriment of the Japanese military investigation.'[10] Now that Tiltman had achieved a breakthrough into the Geheimschreiber, he could once again address the Japanese codes. When the war ended, he stayed on with GC&CS's successor, GCHQ, the Cold War codebreaking centre at Cheltenham. He carried on working there until he was seventy, and even then he refused to retire, moving to the United States, where he continued cryptanalytical work for another few years.

Tiltman's was the first major insight into the Geheimschreiber, and many writers have said that it was his greatest single codebreaking achievement. Certainly, as will be seen in later chapters, the breaking of the teleprinter cipher machine was, in its contribution to the war effort, of the utmost importance. However, it is important to emphasize that the achievement, at this stage, lay not in decoding two identical messages for the information they held. What was of use to Bletchley Park's codebreakers was the long run of the key stream that they extracted as a result of Tiltman's efforts. The next stage in prising open the secrets of the Geheimschreiber would come from close analysis of that stream of key characters at the binary level – working out what patterns could be distinguished, and what those patterns could tell the cryptographers about the structure of the machine and the wheels that generated the key stream. Tiltman's breakthrough in providing a run of the key stream sufficient for an incisive reckoning of the innards of the Geheimschreiber (formerly known as NoMo1) was, perhaps, made just in time. As he later recorded, the 'Germans may have noticed [the] breach of security. For the traffic stopped for a few days, and no more true depths are on record for the remainder of 1941.'

The problem of extracting something useful out of the stretch of key produced by Tiltman's break into the long depth involved the entire Research Section, including one new recruit, Bill Tutte, a modest young chemistry student from Cambridge university. Their challenge was to understand the structure of the cipher machine purely from that single key stream of somewhat less than 4,000 characters. According to Shaun Wylie, another Bletchley Park veteran, 'It was months before they had a smell of a feature, and the final diagnosis did not emerge until January 1942.'[11] It was Tutte who made the breakthrough, and his achievement was later described by Nigel de Grey, deputy director at Bletchley Park, as 'one of the outstanding successes of the war'.[12]

After the war, Tutte himself recalled that he was only brought in after the other members of Gerry Morgan's team had spent three months getting nowhere with the results of Tiltman's insight. Morgan came to Tutte, 'gave me a copy of the key and said, "See what you can do with that."'[13] It was likely that the machine was based on rotor wheels, so the task focused on teasing out information about the design of, and interconnection between, those wheels. Given that the wheels must be a reasonably practical size, there was a good chance that repetition of their patterns might be observable. It was also assumed that there would be more than just five wheels. With five wheels, and with each wheel generating one unit, only one key character would be combined with the plain character, so the wheel patterns could be easily traced. It was thus assumed that two or more characters would be combined in turn (or combined with each other, then combined with the plain character – it makes no difference in which order it is done) so there could well be ten or more wheels. An official account recorded that 'For a long time, no progress was made in the analysis of the subtractor key of the [long] depth. This was due to concentration on a hypothesis now known to be wrong.' The problem was that it was assumed that each unit 'in the key was the sum of two or more periodic [i.e. regular] components, the periods being small... The first success in the analysis of the key was obtained towards the end of January 1942 when [Tutte] found almost accidentally that many [groups of] repeats occurred in the first [unit] of the key at intervals which were multiples of 41. This suggested that this first [unit] was the sum of a periodic sequence (of period 41) and of an aperiodic but non-random sequence rather than two periodic sequences.' Although this made the task harder, it was this realization that gave Tutte the means to make further progress.

'At my pre-Bletchley cryptographic school in London [after call-up] I had learned that you can sometimes get results by writing out a cipher text on a period and looking for repeats,' recalled Tutte. Working with information given to him by other cryptographers,

Tutte deduced that there seemed to be some relevance to the numbers 23 and 25, and so he decided to use the result of their multiplication – 575 – as the period with which to start, although with little expectation of achieving anything. 'I can't say that I had much faith in this procedure but I thought it best to look busy... [when he tried seven rows of lengths 575, he] looked for repeats of start patterns of dots and crosses, vertical repeats from row to row. As expected, there were not significantly many. But then I noticed a lot of repeats on a diagonal. It seemed that I would have got better results on a period of 574.' When he tried this, he got 'pleasingly many repeats of dot/cross patterns of length five or six'.[14] When he tried again, with a length of 41 (choosing this number as it was relatively prime to 574 and prime numbers would most certainly be used in the machine design, he got even better results suggesting a wheel for the 1st unit with 41 pins. The analysis also revealed a second pattern on the 1st unit, an extended pattern of 43 that turned in a non-periodic fashion. The periodic wheel clearly turned once between every character to be enciphered, while the non-periodic stream was 'evidently generated by a wheel of period 43 which sometimes moved one place, and sometimes stayed still when the cipher machine moved' from one character to the next. What Tutte had discovered was that, for the first unit at least, there were actually two key streams involved, not one. The first stream, the periodic one, he called the Chi-stream (pronounced 'kigh'); the second stream, the non-periodic one, he called the Psi-stream (pronounced 'sigh'). These are the names of the Greek characters χ and ψ. There is no significance in these names, except that statisticians often use Greek letters in their equations. They could just as well be called the A-stream and the B-stream, but, as they are extended into longer appellations later in the story of the breaking of the Geheimschreiber, it makes sense to employ to the names that were used at Bletchley Park.

'At this stage the whole of the Research Section joined in to analyse' the other four streams, and soon they found that each had a Chi wheel and a Psi wheel, with the former in all cases being periodic and the latter non-periodic.[15] Eventually it was worked out that, in all, there were twelve wheels – grouped into two sets of five, as well as two 'motor wheels', as they were dubbed. (For consistency's sake, the cryptographers occasionally referred to these as the μ wheels [pronounced 'mew'], after the Greek character for 'M'. However, except in mathematical/statistical formulae, they were usually referred to as the motor wheels.)

The first set of five wheels, the Chi wheels, turned regularly – in periods of 41, 31, 29, 26 and 23. All these wheels turned in step, once for every character to be encrypted. However, the Chi wheels formed only the first stage. A second set of five wheels produced five more units for a second key character to be applied to the character produced by the first enciphering operation. These were the Psi wheels (Appendix D).[16] The motion of this second set of five wheels was determined by the remaining two motor wheels, and the Psi wheels did not necessarily turn for every character. The Psi wheels, it was calculated, had 'lengths' of 43, 47, 51, 53 and 59, and were turned irregularly, depending on the state of pins on the motor wheels, which had lengths of 37 and 61. The motor wheels increased the number of possible combinations, and contributed to the apparent 'random' nature of the key character stream produced by the other wheels. The Psi wheels either all turned one step together, or else they all stayed still. They would all move if the active pin on the first motor wheel, with 37 pins, was a cross ('1'), and would stand still if it was a dot ('0'). This first motor wheel was in turn driven by the second motor wheel, with 61 pins. The first motor wheel moved one position if the active position on the second wheel was a cross ('1'), and it stayed still if the position was a dot ('0').

This was highly significant. The motor wheels prolonged the pattern of the Psi wheels and gave them an apparently non-periodic action. But there was a consequence of this attempt to strengthen the security of the machine. If the Psi wheels did not move between two characters, then the same character was used twice in the Psi stream to perform the enciphering operation thus extending it. The Psi wheels, it might be said, 'stuttered'. The pin patterns on the Psi wheels would, if they had turned every character, generate a stream, say, L8QTC93N5HP4XEAKU. But the Psi stream that was actually used in the encipherment operation would have a significant number of such stutters, where the wheels had not been turned by the motor wheels. Thus, double, and even triple or more, repeats of characters were common, converting the initial Psi stream to something such as L8QTTC993N5HHHP44XEAKUU (where the underlining indicates a stutter). This stream was to be particularly important in the codebreaking process and was called the extended Psi stream. Depending on the way the pins were set on the two motor wheels, between 20 per cent and 40 per cent of the extended Psi stream consisted of repeats.

Such was the Geheimschreiber's attempt to hide patterns and to generate a pseudo-random key stream. The two streams of key characters generated by the Chi and the Psi, together with the non-periodic effect induced in the Psi wheels by the motor wheels, were intended to create an apparently random key stream. The later unravelling of Geheimschreiber keys by Colossus involved identifying and removing the periodic Chi stream from an encrypted message, whereupon the 'stutter' was exploited to give a statistical glimpse of the plain language. Although they were intended to provide extra security, the two streams, in fact, gave the codebreakers a way of getting into the cipher.

Tutte had worked out the number of wheels and the different periodic and non-periodic rotations of each for the long depth from August 1941. This was without doubt a stupendous intellectual achievement by the young student, who, from a single strip of key of less than 4,000 characters, had diagnosed how the machine worked and the layout of its wheels. Tutte's achievement was perhaps even more impressive for his having been studying chemistry, rather than mathematics. Indeed, if he had made the same sort of advance in work which was not secret, his academic reputation would have been firmly established for life. Some hint of what he had achieved obviously did reach some of his seniors at Trinity College, Cambridge, and Nigel de Grey, the deputy director of GC&CS, received a letter from the College, asking

> to whom I should write in order to obtain a confidential report this autumn on the work of Mr W T Tutte, who is candidate at the Fellowship Election of Trinity College, Cambridge, without submitting a thesis, but competing on the evidence of confidential reports from those under whom he is working. I am also writing to W G Welchman and M H A Newman [who supervised Tutte's work at Bletchley Park, respectively on Enigma and on Fish] for reports on his powers and promise… Generally speaking, the competition is severe, and a very high standard is required on any candidate. Before he has a chance of success, it must be possible to establish by reports in support of his candidature that he is of outstanding promise for a man of his age.[17]

Somehow or other, however, Tutte's qualities were conveyed to Trinity, and Tutte was successful, despite the secrecy that necessarily surrounded the details of his 'outstanding promise'.

As for the Geheimschreiber's wheel structure, as far as was known at the time, it applied only to the key used for those two particular messages which had been sent in depth. So would the same structure hold good for other keys, or could the wheel size and order be changed? Could the wheels be changed around and put into different positions, as was possible with the Enigma machine? Or were the wheels used in the same place all the time? After that question had been answered, the next step would be to work out how often the distribution of raised and flush pins on each of the wheels changed. Without knowing the answers to these questions, it was not possible to know whether the structure of the machine so carefully identified by Tiltman and Tutte would ever be applicable again.

As was later reported:

> The cryptographic problem presented by the depth had now been completely solved. The next problem was to find out what changes were made in the machine between the encipherment of different messages... The first attack on this problem was made by attempting to set messages of 30 August 1941 and other dates close to this, on the set of wheels found for [the original break of the long depth]... But these attempts at message setting all failed. An attempt was then made to set a depth of 3 July... Now that a good knowledge of the type of plain language used in the traffic had been obtained... and now it was known that keys could be broken, depth-breaking became a much more rapid and successful process than it had been in July and August 1941. Two passages of depth were read, one about 500 letters long, and the other about 300 letters long, and two possible subtractor keys were obtained from each passage.

When these keys were analysed, Tutte was able to conclude that 'the order of the wheels was fixed... It could now be assumed that one reason why the attempts to set messages not in depth had failed was that the wrong motor wheel patterns had been assumed. The attempts were now reassumed, but no assumptions were made about the motor patterns. Messages intermediate in time between [the first depth] and [the latest] were taken, so that there could be no serious doubt about the pattern' of the various wheels in the machine they were dealing with. After several other depths were analysed, it was concluded that, first, the order of the wheels was fixed; second, the Chi and Psi patterns remained unchanged over periods which could exceed one month; and, third, the patterns of the motor wheels were changed comparatively frequently.

Thus, the overall wheel structure worked out by Tutte seemed to hold good for all the messages that could at this stage be deciphered, and it could be assumed to be a fixed structure. The machine and its inner workings had been understood. All that remained now was to work out how to decipher the messages it encrypted day in, day out. To go any further would mean devising a way of working out which patterns of raised and lowered pins were used on wheels to send messages (a process known as wheel-breaking), and then what was the start position of each wheel for each message (wheel-setting). Tiltman and Tutte had 'broken' the machine, but that still left the job of wheel-breaking to be done every time the pins were changed and then the task of wheel-setting for each individual message.

The Geheimschreiber had been cracked open in the virtual sense, to use a modern term. It could be described and understood through logical analysis, even if it had not been seen in reality. Yet merely knowing how the machine worked could be compared to a mountaineer having purchased a map of a peak he intends to climb. A practical route to the summit still had to be identified out of a vast number of theoretically possible routes, and the mountain still had to be climbed. Similarly, although Bletchley Park understood the logical mechanism of the Geheimschreiber, it nonetheless had to identify routes and climb new peaks in order to earn the view of the contents of the enciphered messages. Identifying the route or the pin positions – which pins were raised to represent a 'cross' and flush to represent a 'dot' – involved making the right selection from an utterly vast number. Such was the challenge of wheel-breaking.

As there are 501 'pins' on the complete set of 12 wheels and each of them can be placed in either of two states, the number of possibilities is 2 to the power of 501 = 10 to the power of 151.

In the words of a modern mathematician, 'This is the "breaking work factor" and it is so large that if every particle in the Universe was a computer and had been assigned full time ever since the "Big Bang" to trying out all the possibilities the solution would still not have been found.'[18] As will be seen, the task was achieved largely by employing Tiltman and Tutte's technique of combining two (or more) messages sent in depth – that is, with the same key – to strip out the key. The codebreakers would then painstakingly strip out the two plain-language messages by hand. This would leave a stretch of key which could be analysed to reveal which pins were raised and which were flush. The revealed pin positions tended to remain valid for all messages for a month, but each individual message was sent with different wheel-starting positions. The settings used for a month or other period were often called at Bletchley Park a 'key'. But, before any other message sent with that key could be decoded, the message starting positions still had to be identified. The amount of effort needed to identify the starting positions for one message – known as wheel-setting – was far less than that demanded by wheel-breaking. But, the Geheimschreiber was still a formidable opponent. The number of possible wheel settings is: 23 x 26 x 29 x 31 x 37 x 41 x 43 x 47 x 51 x 53 x 59 x 61 or about 1.6 x 10 to the power of 19 – or 160,000,000,000,000,000,000. Though much smaller than that involved in the wheel-breaking effort, it still could not be solved by brute-force calculation. These tasks became the daily upward slog of the work on the Geheimschreiber decryption operation that led to the 'ascent' of Colossus. But initially no one was thinking of such a machine. Rather, they had to rely on the German operators' bad habits in sending messages in depth – two or more messages sent using the same key or initial wheel settings. Messages that were not depths could not be decrypted, and so regular decoding of messages would require methods that were not dependent on depths.

chapter ten

Fishing the Depths

The story of Colossus begins with a coincidence – the breaking of the Geheimschreiber in two places at roughly the same time. In Stockholm, the capital of neutral Sweden, and two years before Bletchley Park, Arne Beurling, a Swedish codebreaker, working alone, had already cracked the secrets of another version of the Geheimschreiber, the Siemens T52. In 1940 Germany had raced to invade Norway before British troops arrived. Vital raw materials for Germany's continental war were safeguarded by the installation of the Quisling regime, and 'with Norway and Denmark now absorbed into the New Order and garrisoned with German troops, with the German navy patrolling the waters off Sweden's shores and with the Luftwaffe unchallenged in the air, Sweden found itself isolated and weak. During the years 1940–43, the Germans were firmly in the saddle and extracted significant concessions over a whole range of activities… But in the background, a secret war was being quietly waged.'[1]

That hidden war was fought, in part, using interception and code-breaking. German communications with occupied Norway were carried on cables that passed through Sweden, where the secret services listened in, picking up telephone traffic and enciphered teleprinter transmissions. As the transmissions were tapped physically from the cables at a Swedish telephone exchange, the interception engineers had none of the problems with radio interception that faced the British interception engineers (later in the war, when the German army used wireless transmission, Swedish engineers gave up trying to intercept the transmissions, finding it too difficult a task). The Geheimschreiber machine used, initially at least, on the Scandinavian cables, the Siemens T52, was quite different to the Lorenz SZ40. The wheels in the Lorenz were arranged in two fixed sets of five, plus the two motor wheels, each set of five wheels combining to one key character. In the Siemens machine, each of the wheels could be put in any position in the machine to form two sets of five wheels. The first set of five wheels was used to perform a Vernam cipher combination action, while the second set of five wheels was used to control a 'permutation', or sorting, of the five units.

Once the machine had been analysed, the Swedish codebreakers developed a method of cracking individual messages by working out the daily wheel-settings – aided by poor security which produced substantial numbers of messages in depth. For quite a time, the Swedish cryptographers were liberally showered with message after message sent in depth. By the end of the war they had intercepted some 500,000 messages, of which 350,000 were decrypted. A machine was designed to decode the messages once the codebreakers had worked out the daily wheel settings by hand. The apparatus, or The App as it was known, was constructed by local telephone equipment company Ericsson. Ericsson built thirty-three of these electro-mechanical devices that produced plain-language output when provided with the ciphered message and the key. They were analogues of the T52, performing the same task, but using telecommunications switches rather than rotor wheels.

Arne Beurling, who first broke the Siemens T52 machine in May 1940, kept his method secret, and modern accounts of how he managed to diagnose the nature of the Geheimschreiber machine are at best guesses. According to some accounts, he did hint that his technique depended on the occurrence of the combinations of units that were represented in the basic teleprinter code as '3' and '5' – the basic teleprinter code identifiers used in Sweden for letters-shift and figures-shift. Beurling's background was as a mathematician and he knew nothing of teleprinters or telegraphy, yet in a few weeks he was able to diagnose the machine, something that took a team several months at Bletchley Park, albeit a different version. When he was asked in 1976 how he had managed the feat, Beurling responded, 'An illusionist does not disclose his tricks.'[2] But mathematicians generally do, and Beurling was an academic mathematician who held senior posts in the USA as well as Sweden after the war. Yet precisely how he did achieve the breakthrough remains a mystery as he kept his secret until his death in 1986.

Unlike Beurling himself, the Swedes were unable to keep the secret of their breaking the Geheimschreiber, and the Russians, the Germans and the British all learned, from various sources, that the messages were being deciphered on Swedish soil. The Germans became aware of what was happening sometime in mid-1942 and implemented changes in the way the machine was used to improve security. However, these initial changes contained some further flaws, and so it was not until further measures were introduced in 1943 that the flow of deciphered messages was stemmed. By mid-1943, the T52 was virtually unbreakable and no serious attempts were made to crack the Lorenz SZ40, as the Swedish engineers were unable to develop effective wireless interception equipment. The British had heard about the Swedish success in 1941, a year before the Germans. Roscher Lund, the Norwegian chief of intelligence, who fled to London via Stockholm, met a representative of GC&CS and offered information to the British on intelligence and codebreaking activities in Scandinavia. A paper in one of the preserved GC&CS files now at the National Archives, dated 15 November 1941, records the following: 'Lund said that the Germans were sending masses of messages to their troops in the north of Norway by teleprinter and that the [Swedish] telephone manufacturing company of L M Ericsson had built a machine which deciphered these machines which dealt mainly with personnel and administration.'³

It is not clear whether he provided any further information that may have helped Bletchley Park achieve its own breakthrough, but in any case it seems unlikely that Lund could have provided solid information about the practicalities of unravelling the Geheimschreiber. If Beurling did not inform even his colleagues of his technique, details of it could not have been passed on to London. But the news arrived at a point when any information would have been useful, coming as it did when Tutte was building on the result of Tiltman's work to describe the workings of the Geheimschreiber. Even if there was no hard technical information to pass on, the fact that the Swedes had cracked a version of the machine was a decidedly reassuring confirmation to Tutte and his colleagues that their quest might be attainable. And shortly after Bletchley Park had been informed of the Swedish breakthrough, the British managed to drag their own solution, based on the work of Tiltman and Tutte, out of German messages sent in depth.

The extent to which Bletchley Park was prepared to go for any hard information about the Geheimschreiber is indicated in a telex from Bletchley Park to the British Military Mission in Moscow dated 11 December 1941. This records that 'Tiltman... [would be] glad [for] any information at all about German secret teleprinter (Geheimschreiber). We are prepared if necessary [to] disclose details of rather small amount of progress made in its investigation.' Tiltman's draft for the telex noted that the '[m]achine has been largely used over [wireless telegraphy] chiefly on frequencies 6490 and 6530 for past five months between Germany and Balkans. Material first transmitted by Hellschreiber but lately more usually in form of [teleprinter tone] signals.'⁴ There is no indication that any exchange of information actually took place, but the telex does indicate that Bletchley Park was willing to consider letting the Russians know at least something about its work on the Geheimschreiber. The Russians, of course, already knew that the

Swedish codebreakers had cracked one version of the machine. Indeed, a later decrypt of a Russian message shows that, as early as April 1941, the Soviet Union knew that British codebreakers had broken the Enigma machine – yet it seems clear from the lack of German counter-measures that no hint of this was ever passed to the Germans, even in the period when Stalin was desperately trying to avoid war with Germany and deeply mistrusted British motives.[5]

Beurling's breakthrough certainly helped minimize the in-securities of Sweden's perilous wartime position. But Bletchley Park helped speed the end of the war and, in the process, invented the electronic computer. And, unlike what had happened in Sweden, new security measures introduced from mid-1943 did not keep the British out for long – although the new techniques introduced by the German signals corps were eventually serious enough to require a production line of Colossus machines to establish a system to identify the wheel settings. In addition, the British wireless interception engineers stayed on top of the technical challenges they faced. Throughout the war, Bletchley Park maintained its ability to crack the Lorenz version of the Geheimschreiber. The British also broke the Siemens T52 machine, but decided not to exploit that achievement, concentrating instead on breaking messages enciphered on the Lorenz version of the Geheimschreiber. (See Chapter seventeen and Appendix K – Sturgeon and Thrasher.)

It should be emphasized that, at this stage, Colossus had not been conceived of. The Geheimschreiber machine had been diagnosed by hand, by writing the characters and the units on paper and manipulating them, looking for patterns. It was assumed that working out the pin positions (wheel-breaking) and wheel-starting positions (wheel-setting) would also be done by hand, initially at least. Only when the German signals engineers introduced security measures that prevented the use of hand methods or restricted their usefulness that a need for decryption machines become apparent. 'The theory of message setting which was attempted in

March 1942, after the breaking of the first three depths, is simple. It had been observed that from these, and from depths that had only [been] decoded for a few letters, that most messages contained the group "SPRUCH9++" or "SPRUCHNUMMER9++" either right at the beginning or else preceded only by such groups as... "++ZZZ889". In most attempts at message setting therefore, the groups "SPRUCHNUMMER9++" or "+++ZZZ889SPRUCH" were assumed as the clear language in some position near to the beginning of the message.[6] These common phrases were thus used as cribs to test whether the enciphered message might contain the phrases. This process gave the codebreakers key strings of about fifteen characters long.

Once this had been done, the codebreakers would look closely at each unit stream in turn to see if they could produce patterns that would give an indication as to the Chi and Psi settings. 'Usually there were two or three sequences which could be interpreted as extended parts of the Psi pattern.' This was done for all five units, then

the results were compared to see if the same motor key could be fitted to five of the possibilities... If so, a possible setting of the Chi and the Psi wheels had been obtained. It was finally tested by an attempt to decode more of the message... The message can [thus] be decoded letter by letter, the motor key being built up sign by sign at the same time... For a long time the would-be setters had no success, but at last came the great day when the first single message was set and decoded. By the end of April several other messages had been set, and the Research Section was in a position to attack the July indicator system. But then some messages were broken which were only about a month old. The message setters thereupon forgot all about July 1941 and concentrated on March 1942.[7]

The prize was near to being won – current intelligence from the Geheimschreiber links.

Donald Michie, a young student, just eighteen years old, found himself on a cryptography course, rather than the Japanese course he had expected when, on the advice of his father, he reported to a 'mysterious establishment at Bedford'. Here the field codebreakers, who would accompany armies and other services in the theatres of war, learned the tricks of their trade. But the most accomplished were recruited by Bletchley Park. The industrious Michie, who studied in the evenings in the absence of any other diversions, was among those who were selected. On arrival at Bletchley Park, he was assigned to a new section which was being set up to exploit the break into the Geheimschreiber. Initially, Michie was charged with learning by heart the Baudot code. Then he was put in a newly constructed hut, occupied by some forty or so uniformed men, all apparently non-commissioned officers. He was told to supervise the soldiers whose job was to take a crib, or likely phrase, and to try and locate the phrase in the text of an intercepted depth (i.e. two different messages sent on the same key). Their mind-numbing task was to try the crib in position one, perform the necessary calculations, then try position two, and so on all the way through the message looking for a likely fit. If one was found, then the message was handed over to a cryptographer to work on further. The NCOs were truly being used to undertake a brute-force approach, 'dragging' the crib through an entire message.

It seemed like a good idea, using Intelligence Corps clerks to perform a mindless task, and reserving scarce cryptographic expertise for worthwhile messages. Michie, however, soon concluded that, in fact, the process was not a productive one. 'The flaw lay in the non-decomposability of a task once talent and much practice had melded into a fluent unity… The dogged endeavours of my well-drilled force of crib-draggers in due course generated sufficient documentation for me to report that the "human wave" assault was unlikely to contribute effectively and was best disbanded.'[8] Michie was convinced that the crib-dragger had to be closer to the practical details of the task in hand, understanding what he was doing, with a knowledge of German and the ability to see the job in its entirety. Breaking the job into two types of work – one perfunctory, the other incisive – was a mistake and better results were to be obtained by unifying them. However, later in the war, two electronic machines were designed precisely in order to perform the dragging of cribs though an intercepted message (see Chapter twenty-one).

Another of the young codebreakers was Peter Hilton, a twenty-one-year-old mathematics student from Oxford University who had some knowledge of the German language. He also worked on depths, prising out the real meaning of two intertwined plain-language messages. As he later recalled, 'There is this enormous excitement in codebreaking, that what appears to be utter gibberish really makes sense if only you have the key and I could do that sort of thing for thirty hours at a stretch and never feel tired… [when we had a depth] you were trying to tear this thing apart to make the two pieces of text. And it's absolutely a marvellous process.' He would guess a word, say 'Abwehr' (German military intelligence) and combine it with the depth text to see the result. That might show 'Flug' (flight) in the second message, and so then, guessing it would be the start of 'Flugzeug' (aircraft) he could work out the first characters of the word following 'Abwehr' in the first message, and thus slowly, carefully on. 'So you keep extending and going backwards as well. You break in different places and try to join up but then you're not sure if top goes with top, or top goes with bottom… for me the real excitement was this business of getting two texts out of one sequence of gibberish. It was marvellous. I never met anything quite so exciting, especially since you knew that these were vital messages.'[9]

There was even a depth of three – three different messages all sent on the same key – on 25 March 1942.[10] This created much excitement and the entire section was diverted to unravelling it, and a length of key just under 1,000 characters long was soon produced. But this key defied analysis. The German signals engineers, it seemed to the codebreakers, had taken steps to eliminate traces of the non-random characteristics of the Psi patterns. This made it impossible to use the technique Tutte had developed to analyse the wheel settings. Work on the depth of three had to be abandoned despite the enthusiasm which accompanied its arrival. In fact, the key produced by the depth of three was not analysed until later, when a break into a near depth (two messages sent with some, but not all, of the same initial wheel settings) yielded information about important changes in the Chi, Psi and motor-wheel patterns then being used by the German signals engineers.

Close analysis of a possible key produced by that near depth showed that there had indeed been some significant developments. The number of raised/flush pins on the two motor wheels were now arranged so that there was almost an even balance of dots/crosses across the two wheels. The second motor wheel had to have a large number of dots ('0's) to allow the stutter when the PSI stream was extended. And thus the first motor wheel had to have a predominance of crosses ('1's) to create the balance across the two wheels. An imbalance in their combined pin patterns had allowed the techniques used on the earlier breaks to succeed. Tutte's analysis, it seemed, had only been possible because of a surplus of dots in the two wheels. If this had not been the case, the long repeats in the units spotted by Tutte would not have appeared. When the codebreakers looked back, they discovered that there had indeed been more dots than crosses in the unit streams of the two motor wheels in the early messages. Now that the German signals engineers started to take great care to ensure that there was a balance, it became that much harder to break messages. Indeed, the codebreakers drew the chilling conclusion that the SZ40 'machine would probably never have been broken if there had been no stretch of key susceptible to the single [unit] analysis', thanks to the excess of dots.[11]

Yet as one door closed, it seems that another one opened. The near depth, which had revealed to Bletchley Park the change in the dot/cross balance, also allowed the codebreakers to confirm how the preamble indicators were now used to pass information about the wheel settings. 'The first five letters of the indicator corresponded to the five Psi wheels, in order, and the last five letters corresponded to the Chi wheels, in order. The obvious assumption that the same indicator letter in the same place for two messages meant that the corresponding wheel had the same setting in both messages was also made... The process of message setting was very successful, and with each success it became more powerful, since the meanings of more indicator letters were known.'[12] Bill Tutte recalled how the wheel patterns for a whole month could be broken from the indicators alone by exploiting stereotyped beginnings. 'I remember trying this method myself, getting some initial success, but soon losing control. Then Captain J M Wyllie tried. In civil life, he edited the *Oxford Latin Dictionary*. "This is just the job for a lexicographer," quoth he. And he broke the wheel-patterns for a past month, hitherto untouched.'[13] But this was only possible when there were many messages that could be used.

As one anonymous codebreaker wrote at the end of the war, 'It is impossible to fully describe the subtleties of exploitation used by the expert breaker with his great familiarity with plain language and [cipher] forms and his faculty of instantaneous teleprint addition.'[14]

Some of the people who worked on the hand solution of Geheimschreiber messages went on to become famous for other reasons after the war. One of them, Peter Benenson, founded Amnesty International. The best known was Second Lieutenant Roy Jenkins, later a politician, statesman, academic and biographer of, among others, Winston Churchill. In fact, Jenkins went on to become Home Secretary (where he was responsible for significant social reforms), Chancellor of the Exchequer, President of the European Commission and, later, Chancellor of Oxford University.

Michie recalls that one of his early tasks was to teach the Baudot code to the 'uniformed and exquisitely charming' new recruit. Jenkins later wrote, 'From an early stage of the war, Bletchley Park's decrypts played a vital role. According to some commentators, they more or less won the war. Perhaps partly because I spent the last fifteen months before VE [Victory in Europe] day endeavouring to break the daily traffic between Berlin and the principal commanders in the field, I put the results a little more cautiously. But they were certainly substantial.'[15]

Of his own work, trying to break open depths, Jenkins said, 'We had to operate on a semi-intuitive basis and sometimes your intuition worked and sometimes it didn't. It was a curious life. It could be very wearing, particularly if you didn't succeed. You could spend nights in which you got nowhere at all. You didn't get a single break, you just tried, played around through this bleak long night with total frustration and your brain was literally raw. I remember one night when I made thirteen breaks. But there were an awful lot of nights when I was lucky to make one. So it was exhausting.'[16]

Peter Hilton, who worked with Jenkins, recalled that they were aided by operator error. At the start of a message, the operator transmitted by hand a short run of text in cipher. The distant operator would reply whether the message was being clearly received or not. If reception was fine, the sending operator would then switch from hand transmission to automatic. 'Some of the German operators began to reveal their own personalities by referring to their own conditions and circumstances. I remember one message which the operator began, "Moerderische Hitze" – murderous heat. Well, once I'd broken the first few letters to guess he was talking about "Moerderische" and it was quite likely, because that's a sort of natural German expression of an ordinary German when something is terribly bad. What could be so bad? He was writing from southern Italy, so it was very likely it would not be the food. It was probably the heat. So you got to know people.'[17]

The success of the Research Section in working out the keys

used in messages meant that an analogue of the German Tunny machine was needed. Once the codebreakers had worked out the wheel settings, an equivalent of the Geheimschreiber was required to perform the deciphering of individual messages. This analogue did not need to work with rotor wheels – any technological solution would do, as long as it could reproduce the function performed by the Geheimschreiber. The British telecommunications engineers naturally chose to build it using the familiar electromagnetic relays, and the first analogue was ordered in April 1942 and delivered in June. The 'machine hours' for which the analogue machine was available became the limiting factor in the amount of decodes that could be produced so four more machines were ordered in June. In fact decodes could be produced with remarkable speed.'Decodes were being produced, when [the pin positions for] a month had been broken, a very few hours after investigation – a position never again reached in the history of Fish'.[18]

But, while the understanding of the significance of the indicators represented a real advance, it remained the case that 'no way of breaking a length of key, without independent information, was known'. One idea was to study the patterns of a large number of enciphered messages to look for information that might give an idea of the indicator values. This technique was called the 'Indicator Method' and was used to decode traffic during June and July 1942. In the same month, Alan Turing was asked to look at the problems and he found a way round the impasse that had been reached on decoding depths because the Germans were now employing an even balance of dots/crosses in the motor wheels. Also, it was decided that the Research Section had done all it could. The Fish system was in growing use and the messages that were decoded revealed that the links were used by the German army high command, enabling Bletchley Park to tap into its strategic communications. The problem of breaking the Geheimschreiber was just within grasp, but would obviously prove to be a constant search for new methods and techniques. Fish needed its own section. The Research Section, which had effectively put all its resources into the Fish problem, could now get back to its original function of looking at other ciphers.[19]

The Fish Section, usually known as the Testery, saw as a priority the search for independent ways of breaking the machine which did not rely on depths or indicator information. The Testery was named after its officer in charge, Captain Ralph Tester, and was not charged with testing machines or techniques. Tester was a thirty-nine-year-old accountant who had worked for many years in Germany, developing a close acquaintance with the language, the people and the country. He was assigned to the BBC monitoring station at the outbreak of the war, to listen in to German-language broadcasts, then moved to Bletchley Park where initially he worked with Tiltman on German police ciphers. Donald Michie said, 'Tester had the sense of purpose and personal humility of an outstanding leader.' But he was even more impressed by his physical presence: 'I recall his mesmeric impact on female spectators in the lunch break as he leapt, daemonic and glowing, about the tennis court with an animality that I had only ever envisaged as radiating from the great god Pan.'[20]

The engineers of the German army signals corps introduced two changes shortly before the Codfish and Octopus links came into use in the autumn of 1942, thus marking the start of the expansion of the Fish network. One significant development was that they stopped using the twelve-letter indicator system, and instead introduced what was called a QSN number, later known as QEP. This number referred to a codebook or listing of wheel settings so that the information about the settings was no longer passed in the message. Bletchley Park had no way of gaining access to that information (unless a codebook could be captured, but this was not going to be very practical, there being no isolated submarines or weather ships that could be raided as happened in the breaking of the Naval Enigma cipher keys). Depths could be recognized from having the same QEP number, but near depths could no longer be distinguished.

However, messages were being sent in great numbers and there were lots of depths among them, so breaks could still be managed using Turing's recently developed technique. 'Fortunately, the German operators began to send depths in great profusion, and so on many links it was still possible to read a fairly large fraction of the traffic. The link to the Balkans, Codfish, (by this time the British codebreakers had allocated a Fish-related name to each new wireless link) was one which gave a large proportion of depths – indeed, depths of more than a dozen messages in a single day were sent on this link. On the well-used link to southern Russia, dubbed Octopus, depths were much rarer.'[21] As it was, the codebreakers learned how they could create their own artificial depths. It was not uncommon for messages transmitted on the Fish links to be as long as 10,000 characters. At this sort of length, the key patterns repeated themselves several times, so a very long message could be treated as a depth of two or three messages.[22] But the codebreakers had to overcome this reliance on depths, as it left them vulnerable to potential new security measures which might prevent the operators sending messages in depth. 'The Germans could not be relied upon to continue to send such a proportion of depths, and in any case the single messages presented an urgent problem. The wheel patterns for a link could only be obtained from the depths, but there seemed to be no way by which single messages could be set on those patterns.'[23]

Another change came in August 1942 when the use of standard-ized message openings was replaced with what the Germans called 'Quatsch' – nonsense words – and padding words so that messages started with meaningless jumbles of words of unpredictable length. They also started using lots of padding words in the message itself, thus making it extremely difficult to use cribs to peel open messages sent in depth. Yet, over time, the Quatsch developed its non-random patterns, QWE and ABC, for example – as did the padding words, which mutated into popular phrases or nursery rhymes, or more immediate mottoes, such as 'Nieder mit den Englander' (Down with the British) and the inevitable, in this respect at least, 'Heil Hitler'. All these provided potential cribs, likely words or phrases, for use with future messages on the same link. Over the next year or so, thanks to the hand methods, decodes from these various links provided much very useful information, but it was clear that the codebreakers were only skimming the surface. New links were coming into use – Herring to North Africa and Bream to Rome, as well as new links on the eastern front – and traffic was increasing.

But by the beginning of 1943 the number of successful decodes started to fall off again because of the problems of breaking non-depths. The number of shifts worked was reduced from three to two. Between first of February 1943 and the twentieth of the same month 305 messages were intercepted on Codfish, of which 35 per cent were decoded, on Herring a 'small' number of the 220 interceptions was decoded, and on Octopus, none out of 105 interceptions was decoded.[24] An anonymous report from August 1943 described the limited success the Testery was having. It succeeded in breaking only a small percentage of the total number of settings. And, for the settings that were broken, often only a few of the other messages with the same wheel-pin positions, but different wheel-starting positions were also decoded. 'Only Herring, Codfish (ex-Tunny) and Bream have ever been broken regularly. During the hey-day of Herring not only were the individual "days" broken punctually: the vast majority of the actual signals of those days were decoded. The cryptographers say, however, that Herring, after threatening to defy the angler's art completely was in the end served up on a plate. Bream and Codfish (with its predecessor, Tunny [the name given to NoMo1 before it was renamed Codfish; Tunny then became the codename for the SZ40/42 versions of the Geheimschreiber]) have been broken regularly; but it is estimated that we have rarely decoded more than a quarter of the signals of the "days" broken. Squid and Octopus are rarely broken; when "days" are broken only a fraction of the signals are successfully decoded.'[25]

When the introduction of Quatsch and padding words, along with the QEP system, made it harder to decode any messages, extra attention was paid to the search for an alternative solution. 'Sometimes a fairly reliable crib for a link would be found, but the position of the crib in the message was then so variable that the method was still not practicable. *The only hope left was that it might be possible to set messages by using the statistical properties of the plain language or extended Psi stream*' (italics added).[26] A few attempts were then made to develop statistical methods, but they only looked possible if that crucial balance of dots and crosses in the two motor wheels was not fifty-fifty. The real step forward only came when Tutte realized of the powerful implications of using a technique known as the difference or delta method. This made the statistical approach possible, even with the fifty-fifty balance. The idea of mechanizing Tutte's statistical method was the brainchild of Max Newman, a Cambridge mathematician who had joined the Testery. This technique is looked at in detail in Chapter thirteen, as it underlies the processes performed by Colossus. Here it is only necessary to note that 'when two or three messages had been set by [hand, using the] statistical method, it was seen that new machinery, and a new section to operate it was needed, for the methods took far too long to be of much practical use. Mr Newman was put in charge of [machine] developments and his section came into being later in the year.'[27] Max Newman was the first to suggest that Tutte's mathematical technique could be mechanized, and to that end he was appointed head of the newly created Machine Section in 1942. This need for a machine led to the development of, first, the Robinson and, later, Colossus.

One further point needs to be made about the Testery. There is at least one document on the methods employed by the Testery which remains closed to the public, the so-called *Testery Report*. I did ask the Foreign Office and GCHQ for access to the file during the writing of this book (see A Note on Sources), but this was declined on the grounds that the file would reveal information about the methods of codebreaking still in use today. However, Donald Michie, who worked in the Testery for some time during the war and was one of the authors of the *Testery Report*, was given access to the file in 2001 to 'refresh' his memory for a memoir he was preparing on his wartime work. In the memoir Michie wrote, 'I also received guidance from GCHQ's Chief Mathematician as to which details in it cannot yet be disclosed. [However,] A good deal of knowledge of these hand procedures is directly inferrable from such sources as the *General Report on Tunny*'. This latter report forms the basis of the account given in this chapter of the hand methods used by the Testery. According to Michie, the information in the still secret *Testery Report* only 'amplifies this knowledge'.[28] It is thus a moot question as to whether the full Testery story is still too secret to reveal, or whether, in fact, we already know most of what is worth knowing.

chapter eleven

Herring and the Cat's Whiskers

The Allies achieved two significant victories in North Africa in the second half of 1942, shortly before the stunning Russian recovery at Stalingrad at the end of the year. First, at Alam Halfa, the headlong advance of the Axis forces was halted not far from Cairo – not much more, in fact, than the distance the panzers could cover in a couple of days. Second, a few months later, at El Alamein, the Allies went on the offensive, pushing the German and Italian forces into retreat. Soon after El Alamein, American troops landed further west in Algiers and Morocco, advancing on Axis forces from the rear. By the summer of 1943 Axis forces had been pushed out of North Africa entirely and the effective use of Ultra intelligence – the rubric generally taken to be synonymous with Enigma actually also covers Geheimschreiber decrypts – played a significant part in that turnabout.

The fighting in North Africa had started once Italy joined the war, and it was inevitable given the presence of both British and Italian forces in that region. When the Italian troops gave way in the face of an Allied advance, Hitler was forced to send reinforcements to prevent a rout. In June 1942, General Erwin Rommel's forces took Tobruk and drove the Allied forces back towards Cairo, before eventually coming to a halt at El Alamein, a minor railway station. An Axis breakthrough would threaten Britain's essential oil supplies. At no time in the war, even after Dunkirk, did the Allies' position look more fragile. Rommel's advance spread panic and pessimism and all the faults of the British army were relentlessly exposed – its resistance to change and modernization, the resolutely amateur outlook of its officer class, and the difficulties it experienced as it tried to integrate troops from the Dominions and Empire and from France, Poland and Greece. The German approach in mid-1942 to Cairo – and to Britain's oil supplies in the Middle East – was matched by the Axis advance south through the Soviet Union to the Caucasus and Grozny – with the objective of capturing Russia's oil fields. If either advance, or both, were to succeed, the balance of forces could have swung sharply towards the Axis. And with Rommel's panzers so near to Cairo, it looked as if that might indeed happen. Morale in the British forces was at rock bottom. Intelligence from Enigma intercepts was available to the commanders, but it seemed they did not know how to use it effectively. Major Bill Williams, an intelligence officer who received Ultra decrypts for passing on to the British army command in North Africa, later recalled, 'You had this feeling that we kept producing stuff that was out of this world in terms of the amount of information we were getting about the enemy, and somehow it never seemed to get put to any purpose.'[1]

Churchill, in deep despair at the performance of his generals, sacked the commander, General Claude Auchinleck, but his replacement was killed in an air crash. As a result, another appointment was made, one Churchill had avoided making until circumstance forced it on him – General Bernard Law Montgomery. Montgomery went on to mastermind the victories at Alam Halfa and El Alamein. His biographer controversially concluded, 'In the small wars of empire, the use of regular army units had obviated or masked these old-fashioned democratic problems in the field; but against the better co-ordinated, more professional, classless forces of Nazi Germany and her allies, British performance had [so far] been abysmal, leading inexorably from Norway and Dunkirk to the surrenders of Singapore and Tobruk.'[2] As Montgomery's biographer puts it, 'out of the chaos of modern Blitzkrieg warfare, a small, beaky-faced misfit had extrapolated the essentials for success in battle.'[3]

In the mid- and late 1930s, Montgomery had expounded his vision of how modern armoured wars would be fought and the demands that would place on modern armies and air forces. He also acknowledged the vital role of training and intelligence: modern war planning needed to be 'well thought out and well rehearsed using [the] latest intelligence information'.[4] But, while Montgomery was an astute professional soldier, his self-confidence and demanding approach made him as unpopular with his fellow senior officers as he was popular with the troops.

Unlike his predecessors, Montgomery understood not just how to use armoured forces, but also how to integrate intelligence into planning and into deception of the enemy. Even before Auchinleck had handed over command, Montgomery issued orders to prepare for Rommel's next advance by developing a defensive trap at Alam Halfa based on his assumption that Rommel would launch his attack to the south. Enigma intercepts, which arrived after Montgomery had planned his tactics, confirmed his reading of German intentions, but offered little help in the battle itself, given the time delay involved in decrypting the messages. Yet, the successful defence of Cairo boosted Allied morale and allowed Montgomery time to train the army to take the initiative a few intensive weeks later. Enigma intercepts did play a role in the successful assault on the Axis forces at El Alamein in October 1942, as did a plan to deceive Rommel into expecting an attack in the south rather than the north, which involved dummy tanks and the generation of deliberately misleading wireless traffic. From that time on, the Axis forces started their long retreat towards Tunis, and during this retreat came the news about the Russian turnaround at Stalingrad. The fighting in North Africa was on a wholly different scale to that on the eastern front. One sobering statistic serves to illustrate the order of difference: at El Alamein, 'the full tally of men on the Axis side was no more than a fifth of the German casualties in the battles in the Kursk salient' in 1943.[5]

Perhaps the most important contribution of Enigma intercepts to the war in North Africa was in disrupting Rommel's supply line across the Mediterranean. In the desert landscape, war was as much about supply as about fighting and it was here that Rommel was seriously weakened. Enigma intercepts allowed Allied planes to sink much of the oil and other supplies essential to Rommel's war-fighting capabilities. In October 1942, the month of the battle of El Alamein, half of Axis supply ships were either sunk or forced to turn back.[6] The growing numerical dominance of the Allies in North Africa and the disruption of his supplies left Rommel with little choice but to retreat. Another set of important intercepts were the regular tank returns sent over an Enigma link. These gave the Allies detailed information about the number of German tanks, their state of readiness for action, their crews and their fuel supplies. The Allies were slowly building up superiority in numbers of troops, tanks and aircraft, but these decoded tank returns allowed them to concentrate their dominance to even greater effect.

Montgomery was a rather different commander from Rommel, with his rapid and risky dashes forward. Monty had been moulded in a well-established British military tradition developed in the Crimean, Boer and First World Wars and less familiar smaller wars (the hundreds of policing conflicts conducted in defining the limits of the Empire).[7] Inadequate preparation would lead to a military defeat, which would prompt a drawing together of whatever resources necessary to reverse the defeat. The richest industrial and commercial economy in the world, and its Empire, usually had little trouble summoning sufficient resources to ensure victory, however long it took. British generals needed to be experts in the build-up of military and material superiority, and in applying it in overwhelming force. There was little place for the imaginative, dashing generalship of a Rommel or a Guderian. Even Wellington, the hero of the turn of the eighteenth and nineteenth century, fitted the tradition. He was, as one historian points out, 'strategically... a past master in the organization of marches and supplies... because that was his view of generalship'.[8] Kitchener, the military idol of the turn of the nineteenth and twentieth centuries, fitted the pattern, too. It was not until ten years after General Gordon had been killed in Khartoum that the British government decided to send Kitchener and the army to the Sudan to avenge his death. Then Kitchener took a full two years to advance along the Nile, building railway and telegraph lines to ensure his supplies, and enabling him to inflict a crushing blow by the use of modern arms on relatively poorly armed opponents at Omdurman, one of the largest battles of Britain's colonial wars.[9] Montgomery's methods for the rest of the Second World War, in North Africa, Sicily, Italy and north-west Europe, aped those of Kitchener, not Rommel. He would only attack when fully supplied and reasonably sure of victory. Thus did he attract much criticism, from American commanders in particular, but also from plenty of British officers (and since the war from military historians too), for his ponderous, cautious rate of advance. Whether the criticisms are fair or not, the apparently incongruous Montgomery was very much a product of a tradition of the army in which he served.

As it was, Montgomery was well served with intelligence and he used it effectively in planning his moves, determined to seek victory at minimum cost in lives. A new Fish link, codenamed Herring at Bletchley Park, first appeared in December 1942, between Tunisia and Rome, and it was broken in January 1943.[10] The intelligence it offered up helped in the final clearing up of Axis forces in North Africa in 1943. The Rome end of the link was stationed in the teleprinter office of the panzer army staff in Rome, while in North Africa it was located with the 5th Panzer army headquarters in Tunis. The wireless link replaced a submarine cable, which had been put permanently out of action by the Allies, and so, once again, the German high command was forced to put its strategic communications on to the airwaves. Herring allowed the codebreakers to observe the Axis retreat based on at least some of the same information that was available to the German high command. The regular tank returns sent over an Enigma link were also transferred to the Fish link and, when the wheels had been broken, could once again often be read. In March the Germans introduced a new technique to the Lorenz Geheimschreiber, known as a 'limitation' (see Chapter eighteen), which meant that 'depths were no longer readable and work was almost at a standstill'.[11] But, while limitations remained a problem on other links, on Herring it soon disappeared again. As the Axis forces continued their withdrawal they let security slip on the Fish link between Tunisia and Rome.

At first, Hitler and Mussolini refused to allow reinforcements to be sent to North Africa to help the Axis troops which were penned up in the broad peninsula on which the city of Tunis stands. The demands of the eastern front, with standstill at Stalingrad turning into the shock of defeat, were too pressing. As Montgomery's troops advanced from the east and more Allied armies from the west, the Axis forces faced a serious crisis. To avoid a devastating defeat, the two dictators finally started to pour large numbers of troops into the defensive area around Tunis. Hitler charged General Albert Kesselring, Oberbefehlshaber Sued, ObS, commander-in-chief south, in Rome with throwing the Allies back into the sea by expanding the Tunis beachhead. Kesselring sent orders to field commanders detailing the tactics they should follow, thus unwittingly revealing his intentions to the Allies. The troops that Rommel had been denied when they were needed were now made available – but it was too late and simply added to the total number of Axis soldiers taken prisoner. According to the official history of British intelligence, the information provided by the Herring link meant that Allied strategy was developed with 'the knowledge that the enemy's supply position was deteriorating but that he nevertheless intended to prolong his resistance'.[12] The seriousness of the problems facing the Axis forces became fully evident to the British codebreakers when they realized that frequent changes of location of the wireless transmitter were leading to operating difficulties for the Germans. In April the distribution system for informing the operators in North Africa of the new pin settings must have broken down for from then until the end of the campaign in North Africa, the limitation techniques were abandoned, 'security measures were thrown to the winds and the last messages from Tunisia were all sent on the same setting'.[13] For several weeks right up to the final Allied assault Herring revealed substantial amounts of information thanks to the large number of messages sent on the same settings.

Although the final defeat of the Axis in North Africa was put off until the summer of 1943 by Kesselring's desperate defence, it came with a sudden and audacious armoured attack against the defensive Axis line some thirty miles south of Tunis. The break-through was exploited to thrust forward to Tunis the same day, and it left 250,000 stunned Axis soldiers to be taken prisoner by Allied troops. So fast and unexpected was the advance that the head-quarters of the Hermann Goering division was captured, along with eighty staff officers. War correspondent Alan Moorehead was not far behind the head of the advance and reported that the German army collapsed and surrendered because its command and communica-tions structure was destroyed by the sudden drive forward. It was, he said, 'An extraordinary scene of havoc and confusion... The sheer depth and swiftness of the thrust entirely disorganized [the German] command [and it was] put to flight... There were a dozen other factors in the Tunisian victory, like our dominance of the air and sea, but this question of the breakdown of the German system seems to me to be the governing one.'[14] On the morning of 12 May, General Dieter von Arnim ordered all German wireless installations attached to his headquarters to be destroyed. Before his instruc-tions could be fully implemented, von Arnim was captured but, rather ridiculously, refused to surrender on the grounds that he had lost contact with his subordinate units. The last of these units ceased resistance the next day, and at 1.15 p.m. of 13 May 1943, the British 'Y' Service intercepted a message sent from German Radio Control Station in Rome to the general staff of the armed forces, OKW, in Berlin, reporting that Radio Station XIII had 'closed down at 1312 hours. Radio Control Rome is no longer in radio communication with Africa'.[15]

Moorehead reported how, at one airfield, he saw smashed planes lying about and 'communications machines of every possible sort'. Later he saw, among the detritus abandoned by an imploding army, an 'abandoned signals vehicle under camouflage' with the 'teleprinters still working'. He even admitted that he was 'keen to do a little looting', although he added that he knew he would have to hand anything over to the military police later.[16] It appears that someone, although most certainly not Moorehead, did do some looting and it looks as if, among the trophies taken or destroyed, there was at least one Geheimschreiber machine.

Accounts of the breaking of Fish by Bletchley Park veterans state that no physical Geheimschreiber machine reached Bletchley Park before the end of the war and all the decryption work was based on a mathematical model of what the machine did from analysis of enciphered transmissions. However, one of the first books on the overall British codebreaking effort in the Second World War, *Ultra Goes to War: The Secret Story*, by Ronald Lewin, published in 1978, states that, 'During the fighting in North Africa the 8th Army captured two models of the Geheimschreiber.' This reported capture is not recorded in the official multi-volume *British Intelligence in the Second World War*, published between 1979 and 1984, and which, according to its lead author, Sir Harry Hinsley, another Bletchley Park veteran, was based on unfettered access to official files. In the preface Hinsley states, 'No considered account of the relationship between intelligence and strategic and operational decisions has hitherto been possible, for no such account could be drawn up except by authors having unrestricted access to intelligence records as well as to other archives. In relation to the British records for the Second World War and the inter-war years, we have been granted this freedom as a special measure... As for the archives, we set out to see all; and if any have escaped our scrutiny we are satisfied that over-sight on our part is the sole explanation.'[17]

The first British publication about the Enigma and Ultra was Fred Winterbotham's revelatory account, *The Ultra Secret*, in 1974. It was based on personal memories and perspectives, and gave a somewhat distorted account of the role of Enigma intelligence. Lewin, who reported the capture of the two Geheimschreibers in North Africa, was a historian, however, and a wartime intelligence officer. His book was thus the first attempt to provide an overall account of the role of decrypt intelligence during the war. He recognized the need for a more coherent approach, but, because no documents were then available, he still had to rely on the memories of veterans. But he approached the work with great thoroughness, gathering a wide range of interviews, evaluating the evidence in trying to draw an overview. Unfortunately, he was unable to provide anything like adequate references to the sources of his information. Thus, we have no indication of the source of his suggestion that two Geheimschreiber machines were captured.

Lewin gave an accurate account of the Geheimschreiber as a teleprinter cipher device, and he was aware that the Geheimschreiber carried 'information at the highest level of command – long-term strategical plans, for example, or diplomatic evaluations – [which] remained valid for much longer than a signal' transmitted at the levels that used the Enigma. Lewin also knew that Siemens had produced the Geheimschreiber, but he did not mention Lorenz. He did record that Arne Beurling in Sweden had broken the Siemens machine. Clearly, Lewin had some idea of the real Geheimschreiber story and did the best he could with the information to hand. But a mystery remains over his statement about the capture of the machines. Lewin knew that the information he had was extremely limited. He concluded, 'No information has yet been released about the content of the signals transmitted by the Geheimschreiber, nor is it clear whether they were first enciphered on an Enigma machine before being fed through the [teleprinter]. What is certain is that the Germans continued to use the Enigma ciphers until the end of the war, and until specific evidence is produced we must rest on the assumption that the Geheimschreiber's main purpose was to achieve additional speed and security for top priority signals by the extremely high rate of its transmissions. In that sense, Colossus extended Ultra's scope and range.'

In recent years, more evidence has been made available – evidence which shows that Lewin's account of the capture of a Geheimschreiber is correct, even though the details remain confusing. The relevant documents are quoted below in the original language of the memos, and they use an abrupt, often punctuation-free, style of language common in the days of teleprinter communications. The first document, held at the National Archives in London (formerly the Public Record Office), dated 25 May 1943, states that a 'tele-typex' machine was indeed captured. 'Teletype' is the American name for a teleprinter and Typex is the Allied name for its cipher machine, a teleprinter equipped with a cipher machine (though using a similar cipher technique as the Enigma rather than that of the Geheimschreiber). The memo is to Colonel Sayer of GC&CS, from an unidentified person with the codename Barker Charlie, presumably one of Bletchley Park's liaison officers in North Africa. The telex says,

Important ((Sayer from Barker Charlie OLSU/TZ 37 of 25/5)) While at Bizerta a captured German quote tele-typex machine was handed to me. I showed it to De Laszlo [a senior Bletchley Park official on a liaison visit in North Africa] who supplied the above general description. The machine is capable of sending non-Morse impulses either by line [i.e. landline] or by William Tare [i.e. wireless telegraphy]. Only slight damage has been done to one motor otherwise perfect. The inscription on the maker's plate is as follows. Begins Siemens Halske Type Tare Dash Typ 52B, DO 34388, Clokal 2Z60 Victor 220, Alpha 32, 50£5BZ£BD AUSFG 1941 ENDS. Have arranged to transport machine to Algiers and suggest you send authority for extra weight for de Laszlo to bring it back to Uncle King [United Kingdom] with him. Hope it proves interesting.[18]

The following day Sayer replied to the memo:'Kitten your OLSU/TZ three seven of twenty fifth May definitely cats whiskers… Since machine required here urgently yoke ['Y' Service] committee unwilling await de Laszlo's… departure and are wiring Lonnon [sic]… details of urgent priority air passage. Please inform him of this and ensure apparatus well packed. Most valuable for use is encoding attachment or component on the keys.'[19] Sayer also informed Kenworthy of the capture of the machine, telling him that it 'has been captured almost intact'.[20]

However, on 16 August 1943 another memo from Bizerta was sent to Sayer. It said, 'Wreford Brown asks if I have received Gen 224. Ought I to have[?] At present conducting tricky three cornered discussion, self Bizerta, de Laszlo Algiers, W[reford] B[rown] Cairo. I have no files here but WB coming here next few days only fear is he will cross Laszlo going to Cairo.' A handwritten note on telex version of the memo says, 'Gen 224 was the wire from Pritchard about D in ciphers? No copy sent to us but Sawyer [sic] is having an extra one typed out for us. Looks like the usual circular balls-up.'[21]

Then, a few days later, the following appears in a memo dealing with a number of issues mainly about codebreaking in North Africa and Sicily: 'Part three – Being a specialist on W/T [wireless telegraphy] equipment, he fully realizes importance of documents. Same difficulties, lack of transport and army. (Comment: he found the apparatus with ten to twelve drums, see previous OLSU)… Looting. Without exception all persons interviewed complained of extensive looting. Details later. Fact that apparatus is smashed and documents destroyed by our troops, again underlines vital need for (able) briefing... at highest.'[22] It seems that the cipher machine, or machines, captured in North Africa were stolen, damaged or destroyed during a bout of looting by Allied soldiers sometime after their capture. And it appears too that cipher documents may have been destroyed, and not just in North Africa. A telex suggests that similar destruction took place in Sicily as well. 'Telex from TOO. Part one – Sicily. Saw Wiseman... has been worried about documents for some time. Fully realizes value two kinds: tactical, that is at once useable by forward units and strategical, that is high grade and Welchman's type. He considers that special pool of trained intelligence officers is essential, with their own transport these... to have high level authority to go whenever places of interest are taken.'[23]

If this was all true, the disappointment at Bletchley Park must have been intense. However, a few pieces of evidence also suggest that at least one Geheimschreiber machine was returned to Britain, despite later claims that no such machine was seen. First, not all communications equipment captured in Tunisia was damaged. Harold Kenworthy, who was in charge of the non-Morse inter-ception operations in Britain, wrote an account of his activities at the end of the war. In it he recalled how 'Decimetre aerial gear captured in Tunisia and sent to Knockholt was repaired' before it was sent out to a British army field unit for use – 'and proved to a very valuable asset'.[24] Second, there is some clear evidence in files at the National Archives that at least some cipher-related German documents were indeed captured in North Africa. One report from 1943 notes, 'Documents captured in Libya and Russia have now made it possible to build up a fairly complete picture of the wire-less communications system of the German Army.'[25] And another British report on German Luftwaffe wireless networks states that a German report on the directional radio techniques used by the Luftwaffe was also captured 'during the retreat of the German army' in Tunis.[26]

Even more pertinent is a comment from a recent release from the United States National Archives. In one of a series of dense technical reports in June 1944 from American codebreakers about Fish decryption, Captain Walter J Fried comments, 'The actual [Geheimschreiber] machine is believed to have a zeroing mechanism and is probably similar to a captured machine (apparently of an earlier design) which Lt Col Rowlett and I saw on a recent trip to Knockholt [the non-Morse interception station]. He is planning to take some photographs of this model.'[27] From the context of the rest of the report it is clear that he is talking about a Siemens and Halske T52 machine, not the Lorenz SZ40 machine which was the one broken at Bletchley Park.

So what conclusions can be drawn from all these snippets? Clearly, Lewin was right. One or more T52 machines were captured and, even if damaged, were shipped back to Britain and the archives indicate that other machines were captured later in the war. For whatever reason, the authors of the official history of British Intelligence would undoubtedly have seen the documents quoted above (with the possible exception of the American memo), but chose not to mention the incident and to allow to continue uncorrected the story that no Geheimschreiber was seen until the end of the war. Perhaps they saw it as a minor, and irrelevant, issue; it was the Lorenz version which had been broken, not the Siemens T52, so the capture of the latter would only be confusing and difficult to explain. And, indeed, whatever happened, the affair in itself is not particularly important. The breaking of the Lorenz Geheimschreiber had been achieved by the time of the docu-mented capture, so the overall story of Fish decryption is not altered by the revelation of this incident. But what it does serve to remind us that we still do not know the full story of Bletchley Park in general and of the Fish story in particular. The effects of the absolute secrecy erected around the role of Bletchley Park cannot be discounted even today, and the details of how much success GC&CS had during the war at breaking diplomatic ciphers, of enemy, ally and neutral governments, remain unknown. Although many documents about Bletchley Park were indeed destroyed at the end of the war, many were retained and were still being released by the post-war interception and decryption organization, GCHQ in Cheltenham, even as late as mid- 2004 while work was in progress on this book. And the public files are littered with slips stating that papers within the file are still being withheld. In addition, it reminds us that the multi-volume official history *British Intelligence in the Second World War*, despite its impressive density and detailed account, is not the complete picture, and in its currently published version is the story as approved at the date of publication. The editors of that vast work instruct readers that, with regard to files then closed, the 'text must be accepted as being the only evidence of their contents that can be made public'.[28] However, there is no need to go along with that injunction to accept the official text uncritically – indeed, it is the duty of historians to do just the opposite.

But why did the official historians omit this particular detail of the story? Perhaps the misbehaviour of those Allied troops responsible for the looting in North Africa was too embarrassing to recall even all those decades later. Or perhaps we can read between the lines in the documents and perceive what in fact happened. The actual or feared loss of the captured machines caused GC&CS to think more carefully about what to do in future when the Allies had the opportunity to capture German cipher material. The war was entering a new phase with the German army on the retreat in Russia and Sicily, where the Allies had landed after defeating the Axis forces in North Africa. If the Allies continued to beat the German army in battle, then there would be more opportunities for capturing cipher machines and documents. The secret about what happened in North Africa is likely to have been the result of an evolving policy of absolute silence about 'signals intelligence' – Sigint, as it was beginning to be called. Clearly, the events in North Africa and Sicily had shown that the army was not sufficiently aware of the importance of capturing intact cipher material.

In the midst of the correspondence quoted above, a memo was sent from Military Intelligence to Bletchley Park pointing out that Intelligence Assault Units had been set up, 'for the express purpose of carrying out, during raids on the enemy coastline or in a theatre of land operations, such tactics as the Intelligence Service may require'. The targets would include wireless telegraph stations as well as Gestapo and Abwehr (German military intelligence) sites. 'It is thought that the opportunity may well occur for them to obtain material which would be of value to GC&CS and we would like to know whether you would like to avail yourself of the opportunity of instructing selected members of the Units in the recognition of material which would be of interest to you.'[29]

Whether or not this coincidental solicitation of GC&CS's interest was prompted by what happened to the captured machine or machines is unclear, but what is evident is that the incidents in North Africa and Sicily led to a more careful policy which would ensure the capture of as much cipher machinery and documentation as possible. The objective was not so much in furtherance of decryption (though this and other intelligence-gathering was important, too) as in minimizing any chance of anyone asking awkward questions. The intelligence commando units would attack enemy headquarters posts at the very head of an offensive – this was a tactic which had been learned from the German army – storming them for intelligence material before the enemy commanders realized it might be necessary to destroy it. Cipher material was to be removed from the field before the fog of war had lifted so that no one would notice that anything had disappeared. The search for, and capture of, Axis cipher material came high up on the list of priorities for the advancing Allied troops in Italy and later in north-west Europe, with specialist commando squads – advancing as far forward as possible, seizing all the cipher material they could find. The campaigns in North Africa and Sicily taught the Allies much about the capture of cipher material, and were instrumental in creating the post-war policy of secrecy surrounding the codebreakers' achievements. The incident did not make its way into the official history for the simple reason that it pointed to a subject which officialdom did not want aired, even four decades after the war – the preparations for post-war interception and decryption operations.

In any event, what mattered with the Geheimschreiber was that its interception and decryption was possible even without seeing the machine. It was the intelligence it offered that was important, not the appearance of the machine or the quality of its manufacture. The early Fish messages that were decrypted had been obtained from links on the eastern front and the Balkans, both theatres where British and American forces were not directly involved. Codfish briefed the Allies about the Balkans, Octopus (to a less detailed extent) about the eastern front. In North Africa, Enigma decryptions had played an important part in Montgomery's success against Rommel at Alam Halfa and El Alamein in 1942, and the Herring link to North Africa was broken in January 1943. It was the first time wireless teleprinter transmissions had been used by German forces fighting the British and Americans. Then, when the Allies crossed into Sicily and Italy, Fish decrypts, from the link between Rome and Berlin, started to provide an exceptional level of strategic intelligence to back up Allied operations in the 'long, hard grind' up the Italian peninsula. And during that time, far from the Fish business being just an extension of 'Ultra's scope and range', as Lewin incorrectly guessed, it in fact turned out to be its most important source – more important even than Enigma.

chapter twelve

'Hier ist so traurig'

The initial Balkan link between Vienna and Athens was closed down at the end of October 1942. Although experimental in terms of wireless transmission techniques, it had carried plenty of enciphered operational traffic, much of which was deciphered using hand techniques. But it was only a preparatory link, operated by wireless development engineers, and was replaced by a new link, maintained by an army signals unit. The new link connected the headquarters of the general staff of the armed forces, OKW, near Berlin, with Athens and Salonika, where the Oberbefehlshaber Sued-Ost, ObSO, Commander-in-Chief South-East, was based. The experimental link was at first known as NoMo1 by the British but, on adoption of the Fish theme, became Tunny (tuna). The air force NoMo2 group became known as Sturgeon. When the codebreakers realized that different cipher machines were used in these two NoMo groups and that they were employed respectively on army or air force links, these codenames were applied to the different machines. The Lorenz SZ40 became known as Tunny and the Siemens T52 as Sturgeon. Then individual links acquired their own codename (to add further confusion, Tunny later acquired another use, as the name of analogue machines built to decipher Fish messages after the settings had been worked out). The new Balkan link was given the codename of Codfish.

Other Fish links quickly followed. In October 1942, the first of the many wireless tentacles that were to spread out across the Soviet Union was intercepted at Knockholt. The first such link, between the army high command, OKH, at Koenigsberg in East Prussia, and the German army in the Crimea, was codenamed Octopus.[1] It was 'a very active group, using auto and hand-speed... probably Army... [as it] uses Tunny Army call-signs'. Another route opened in Russia the same month was codenamed Salmon, while a plain-language group passing press reports between Berlin and Bucharest 'has not yet been named'.[2] In December, a Saegefisch link to the surrounded German forces at Stalingrad was opened, but it appears that this link was not intercepted or known about at Bletchley Park. In the same month, in a different theatre of the war, a link between Rome and Tunisia came on the air, and was broken in January 1943. Codenamed Herring, it quickly played an important role in the final months of the war in North Africa. 'Herring has become most interesting,' according to a report in January 1943, and extra interception operators were needed to ensure full cover.

By the autumn of 1943 there were fourteen links in operation, creating a high-level 'backbone' network supporting not just army commanders, but all sorts of German military and administrative organizations as well.[3] All the early Fish links were broken fairly soon after they appeared – although only a few of the total number of intercepted messages could be decrypted. As more links were broken, the codebreakers became aware of the extent of the network into which they had begun to make inroads. Most importantly, the decodes provided Britain and the United States with an insight into German strategic thinking about North Africa (where they were engaged) and also about the Balkans and the eastern front (where they were not directly involved). Immediately, the Fish links to the Russian front enabled Britain and America to watch the development of German plans and the progress of battles from information that flowed within the German army high commands. Stalin gave his allies little information about the war on the eastern front, and their main source of information about the fighting in the east remained intercepts of German wireless traffic.

Codfish was one of the most productive of the early Fish links, so a few examples from it in early 1943 will illustrate the breadth of material produced by a Fish link.[4] As the link was between Berlin and Athens, much of the information concerned the Balkans and the Mediterranean, but not all. On 27 February 1943, a detailed German army report described the massing of various Communist divisions facing the German army and SS formations in Serbia. On 3 March 1943, a message from ObSO to OKH asked for the rapid provision of supply troops for the Jaeger (Hunter) division, which was engaged in Croatia in 'lengthy mobile operations under extremely difficult conditions. Fully competent supply troops are urgently necessary and should be brought up with all speed.' On the same day, a message sent from the OKH Quartermaster's office in Berlin to ObSO gave details of an ammunition allocation for Crete (including 23,000 grenades, 22,000 7.5mm shells and 15,000 mines) and announced to whom it would be sent and how. However, not all the messages were about the practical details of military operations. Administrative and economic organizations also used the link: a message dated 9 February 1943 requested the German Bank to increase the limit on a letter of credit at the National Bank of Greece by 252,000 Reichmarks to pay for 3,000 tons of coal sent from Upper Silesia. And messages could also provide information about the widening war. On 11 February, Inter-Service Reports were sent from OKW Operations Staff to ObSO and copied to officers commanding German forces in Ortland, Ukraine, Norway and the Netherlands; Liaison Staff North; Lapland Army A; German generals at headquarters of Italian armed forces; Planning Staff Paris (at the Hotel Claridge); and ObW (C-in-C West). The message gave situation reports on the eastern front, Army Group A, Army Group B, Army Group Don, the Luftwaffe in Russia, North Africa, the Western and 'Home' areas. A truly astounding treasure trove had been opened.

Some of the decrypts revealed information that was even closer to home for British Intelligence, so that Codfish occasionally offered a mirror as much as a window. On 11 February a message sent to the War Maps and Survey Department of the army high command, OKH, from the Military Geographical Group, South Greece, requested 'immediate dispatch of "England", Folio C, Volume 7, and the description of the Atlantic Coast already requested'. On 3 March, a message gave a German military intelligence assessment of the wireless telegraphy situation in England and the United States, an appreciation of the abortive Allied landings at Dieppe in 1942, and a report on the British map grid system – all this on a wireless link between Berlin and Greece. The very range and variety of message types carried on wireless teleprinter links must have surprised the codebreakers at Bletchley Park.

For the advance into southern Russia in 1942, Hitler moved his headquarters to Vinnitsa in the Ukraine. A Geheimschreiber and Saegefisch operator and maintenance engineer in Vinnitsa at the time recalled that the teleprinter room was fitted out with eight Lorenz Geheimschreiber machines.[5] The operators were kept constantly busy with sending and receiving traffic. And as pin position and other changes were made overnight, the night duty often had this unpopular task to perform. Early on, the operators used to type out messages on the keyboard but, as they developed routines, they increasingly turned to pre-perforated tape. The German advance took troops on one arm to the Caucasus and on the other to the Volga, where increasingly fierce but static fighting developed around the city of Stalingrad. The headquarters of Army Group A, which struck far south into the Caucasus, was at Stalino near the Sea of Azov, while that of Army Group B, which was responsible for the attack on Stalingrad, was based at Poltava. This was an inauspicious location, for it was here in 1709 that the previously invincible Swedish army of the overconfident Charles XII was annihilated after being drawn too deeply into Russian territory. The battle marked the end of Sweden's run as a major European power, and the dramatic arrival of Russia in its place. Just as Charles XII had ignored his senior officers and insisted on an offensive battle in unfavourable conditions, so Hitler dismissed several of his generals, assumed more power for himself and promoted General Erich von Manstein, one of his favourites. One of the German army's most competent field commanders, Manstein took charge of the Army Group Don (formerly Army Group B) in November, just as the disaster at Stalingrad was about to occur, and, once the wireless teleprinter link was in place, he regularly sent Hitler long messages detailing his views about the fighting on the eastern front.[6] Soon the codebreakers at Bletchley Park would be reading the appreciations of Hitler's commanders about the precarious situations in which he had put them.

Hitler's forces were stretched very thinly indeed. Many of them were non-German soldiers from Germany's more or less reluctant allies in central and southern Europe. They were needed to protect a frontline that stretched well over a thousand miles. Eventually, after an epic battle in the ruins of Stalingrad, the German line cracked in the winter of 1942 in the face of an overwhelming Russian counter-attack, resulting in the capture of the German Sixth Army in a Russian pincer movement. Hitler withdrew from his temporary headquarters near Vinnitsa in the Ukraine back to the Wolf's Lair in East Prussia. Goering promised that the Luftwaffe would supply those cooped up in the Stalingrad Kessel (or encirclement), but his bravado only led to the whittling away of even more German aircraft. One item that was successfully flown in was a new long-distance radio transmitter, codenamed Saegefisch. This enabled the unfolding tragedy to be followed in detail by the OKH, though they were unable to help avoid the loss of about a quarter of a million men once Hitler had refused permission for them to withdraw. However, it seems that this Saegefisch link was not intercepted in Britain.

The Russian success at the Germans' trademark encirclement battle dealt a devastating blow to the Nazi leadership. 'Even before Stalingrad, Germany's meagre remaining economic and manpower resources made ultimate victory in the East very unlikely. The defeat on the southern wing of the front merely removed any lingering hopes of final triumph in the East.'[7] It did not mean that Germany would inevitably be defeated and its army destroyed, but it did show the world that Hitler's great army was not invincible, especially as it followed hard on the defeat at El Alamein in North Africa. Goebbels, the propaganda minister, tried to cover up the impending loss of the Sixth Army and the damage it would do to German military prestige and morale on the home front. He had broadcast on German public radio service a Christmas Eve choral programme that was supposed to have been recorded in Stalingrad, yet had, in fact, been taped in Germany. Later, he had the postcards which had been sent home by the soldiers who surrendered intercepted and withheld from the addressees.[8] But the secret was already leaking out and many Germans learned the truth of what had happened to their army.[9] And in the weeks after the surrender of the Sixth Army, interception by the German security services of letters written home by slave labourers in Germany showed that they not only knew about Stalingrad, but that, in fact, their entire mood had changed. They now saw that Germany might well lose the war. The tragedy of the Sixth Army signalled hope to Hitler's enemies at home and abroad.

The big German gains in the south had to be abandoned under the Soviet counter-attack following the disaster at Stalingrad. However, as had happened the year before outside Moscow, Stalin ordered the attack to continue beyond the ability of the Russian army to sustain it and the advance fizzled out, forcing the Russians to cede some of the territory they had just recovered. But the high tide mark of Nazi expansion had been passed. The following summer, 1943, Hitler remained convinced that he must remain on the attack, so the German army planned to launch its third massive armoured attack, on the Soviet army in the region around Kursk, where the front formed a massive bulge into the German-occupied territory.

The German codename Zitadelle (Citadel) had appeared in some Luftwaffe Enigma intercepts, but it was not clear to what it referred. However, all became clear when one of the first decoded Geheim-schreiber messages on the link codenamed Squid between Army Group South and the army command, OKH, was read in April 1943. It was, in the assessment of the official history of British intelligence in the Second World War, the 'earliest example of the great addition to operational intelligence of the highest importance about the eastern front that the non-Morse decrypts were to make for the rest of the war'.[10] On 25 April, a 'Comprehensive Appreciation for Zitadelle' sent by Generalfeldmarschall (Field Marshal) Maximilian Maria Joseph von Weichs zur Glon – von Weichs for short – Commander-in-Chief of Army Group South, to the Operations and Intelligence Sections of Foreign Armies East, OKH, in Koenigsberg, was intercepted and decrypted. The appreciation repeated previous views (which Bletchley Park had not seen) about Russian troop movements on the northern flank of Army Group South's frontline, and concluded,

> At present, however, it is not apparent whether the object of this concentration is offensive or defensive... In the event of Zitadelle, there are at present approximately ninety enemy formations west of the line Byelgorod-Kursk-Malo-Arkhangelsk. The [planned] attack of the Army Group [South] will encounter stubborn enemy resistance in a deeply echeloned and well-developed main defence zone (with numerous dug-in tanks, strong artillery and local reserves)... In addition strong counter-attacks by the strategic reserves from east and south-east are to be expected. It is impossible to forecast whether the enemy will attempt to withdraw from a threatened encirclement by retiring eastwards, as soon as the key pillars [Eckpfeiler] of

Kursk salient front line... have been broken through... Summarizing, it can be stated that the balance of evidence still points to a defensive attitude on the part of the enemy... [bringing up more troops may indicate an offensive, but even in that event] it is improbable that the enemy can even then forestall our execution of Zitadelle.[11]

Details of what was learned of the Zitadelle plan were passed to the Soviet Union, with suitable measures to ensure that the source was kept secret. As it was, Stalin's agents high in the Nazi administration and military had already presented him with the full plans for Zitadelle, allowing the Russian generals to prepare an effective counter-strategy.

Although von Weichs concluded that the Russian attitude was 'defensive', it was, in fact, the very opposite. The Soviet aim was to build a strong defence works and to soak up the anticipated German assault on the inner corners of the salient until the attack ran out of steam.[12] When the German attack in July 1943 duly petered out, the Russian army was ready to move against its exhausted opponents. For the first time it would be a counter-offensive, not just a counter-attack, launched in summer weather and aimed at pushing the invader out of Russian territory. Forty combined-arms and five tank armies on ten fronts – each front roughly equivalent to an army group – advanced on a 2,000-kilometre-wide line.[13] The scales were indeed tipping. The Russian army advanced far enough that year to recover Kiev and the Dneiper – the historic home of the first 'Rus' civilization in the tenth and eleventh centuries, before the era of Mongol domination and the rise to pre-eminence of Muscovy.

The ferocious combat in the fields and woods around Kursk put the German army on to the defensive. It could now only look forward to fielding diminishing numbers of troops: increased casualties as the fighting intensified and there were demands for garrison troops across occupied Europe, as well as growing labour shortages at home. In Russia, on the other hand, recovery was getting under way after the dislocations caused by Barbarossa. In 1941, literally thousands of factories (many of them small or medium-sized workshops) had been dismantled and shifted eastwards, together with their workers, and dumped on the frozen ground east of the Urals. By 1943, these factories were back in operation, producing guns, tanks and aircraft in vast numbers, comprehensively outnumbering German production, and this supply of heavy material was supplemented by lighter goods – trucks, vehicles and food – from the Allies. The German signals corps had planned to be able to support frequent changes of location of army commands, but only in a war of advance. The technology they developed proved mainly to be of use in a war of retreat. The British codebreakers picked up hints of the changing mood. One Fish operator was recorded as chatting with his colleague near Koenigsberg. The operator serving in the Germany army's horrific siege of Leningrad tapped out the phrase 'Ich bin so einsam' – 'I'm so lonely'. The following day he said, 'Hier ist so traurig' – 'It's so sad here'.[14] The misery inflicted on central and eastern Europe had begun to encompass its instigators as well as its victims.

Five Fish links which were intercepted in Britain after they had been opened, connecting the eastern front with Hitler's Wolf-schanze for the planned summer offensive of 1943, centred on Operation Zitadelle and the attack on the Kursk salient. The links were Squid to Army Group South, Octopus to Army Group A and the 17th Army, Tarpon to the Luftwaffe mission in Romania, Trout to the German authorities in Memel and, from August 1943, Perch to Army Group Centre. In October 1943, Octopus was replaced by Stickleback, which was broken in February 1944, the month Colossus went into service at Bletchley Park. Octopus was then reopened from a station in the Crimea, as Hitler insisted that his generals fight to retain what he saw as an aircraft carrier that threatened the Balkans; it would be a constant threat to his oil supplies in Romania if Russia re-took the peninsula. The opening of more Fish links meant that Fish decodes started to rival the role of the Enigma in providing intelligence about the eastern front. According to the official history of British Intelligence, these Fish links 'produced a steady rise in the volume of Sigint, and they yielded a high proportion of decrypts of long-term significance that more than made up for the fact that GC&CS had no success at this stage against the army Enigma keys on the eastern front and broke few of the German Air Force Enigma keys'.[15]

Communications had to be maintained at all costs. Every day, three times a day, each German unit was required to submit a situation report upwards to its commanding unit. In turn, the reports would be collated and a wider report drawn up for higher commands within each army, all collected by landline or Enigma wireless link. Each army headquarters staff would then compile its own report for onward transmission by teleprinter – over landline or wireless link – to the army high command at Koenigsberg or Berlin. The reports would then be forwarded to Hitler's head-quarters to form the basis for the commander-in-chief's thrice-daily military briefings. 'Modern warfare is too complex to depend on [direct communication]… it generates far more information than people can keep in their heads. Therefore the Germans created a carefully organized system of reporting.'[16]

This organization had its structural limits. Information had to be reported according to a carefully controlled timetable of wireless transmissions, arranged to make best use of available wireless network capacity and to avoid congestion in the airwaves. In 1939, for the invasion of Poland, 80,000 wireless sets had to share 4,000 usable transmission frequencies.[17] So each unit would have to wait its turn to report events. Subordinate units were instructed to minimize use of wireless by relying on telegraph or telephone landlines, but they also became congested with traffic. This strict system meant that, even during military operations, when the system worked well it still took between five and seven hours for information from units actually fighting on the front to reach Hitler's war headquarters and the same time for orders work their way back out again. Telephone links could be used to circumvent the delays in an emergency, but the teleprinter network remained essential for most communications.

One interesting example serves to illustrate that Britain was not alone in its eavesdropping activities. A report from mid-1943, now in the files of the National Archives, provides a detailed analysis, over a dozen closely typed pages, distilling everything that Enigma and Fish intercepts had revealed about German interception of Russian wireless signals on the eastern front. It listed the successes and the limitations of the structure, operations and technology of the German 'Y' Service, the German appreciation of Russian tele-communications networks, German decryption of Russian ciphers and the ability of the Germans to determine the Russian order of battle without decryption by using traffic analysis and direction finding. The decodes of German messages also revealed that 'There were at the beginning of 1943 indications that (possibly through capture of German Army Staff documents) the Russians were becoming aware of the leakage.'[18] There is, however, another possible explanation of how the Soviet Union became aware of its poor radio and cipher security. John Cairncross, who worked at Bletchley Park in assessing intelligence, was also a Soviet agent and took copies of intelligence reports which he copied and passed to his contact. Presumably he did not pass on details of the breaking of the Geheimschreiber – or, if he did, then it seems not to have leaked back to the Germans. He would have known, of course, as would the Russians, that the intelligence came from decrypted wireless messages. But, in all likelihood, Cairncross would not have been personally aware of the difference between the Enigma and the Geheimschreiber machines – he was in a section that dealt with the translated intelligence, probably with all indications of its source removed.

There was a sort of circle, where everyone was both watcher and watched, and which comprised allies spying on each other as well as on enemies – Britain watching Germany watching Russia watching Britain. The Russian advance, which began in 1943, was observed in Britain and America in a sort of negative image through Enigma and Fish intercepts detailing what the German army intended to do in response to Russia's attacks. And, as early as 1943, the Allies, and no doubt Stalin, too, were already thinking about the post-war world, and about the role interception and codebreaking would play in it. Ultra decodes – from Enigma and Geheimschreiber transmissions – became a part of the opening moves of the Cold War.

When the Crimean War, between Russia on one side and Britain and France on the other, broke out in 1854, the overland electric telegraph cable only reached as far as Belgrade. The British and French governments, unusually allies rather than enemies on this occasion, found themselves trying to make decisions based on out-of-date information and so a submarine cable was rapidly laid across the Black Sea from the Romanian coast to Balaklava on the Crimean peninsula. A direct link back to London and Paris was eventually opened at the end of April 1855, thus reducing the time taken for messages to get from the war zone to London and to Paris from some three weeks to twenty-four hours. A twentieth-century British admiral concluded that 'it cannot be claimed', in terms of the outcome of the war, that the reach of the telegraph cable to the commanders in the field 'made very much difference. No great strategic move was achieved by its existence and its influence on plans was marginal... [However] It is probable that in administrative matters and logistics it paid greater dividends.'[19] For example, the telegraph allowed communication between ports so that the required transport ships and supplies could be ordered from, say, Marseille, in hours rather than weeks – or a reply could be sent reporting that not all the supplies could be acquired and thus some needed to be ordered from elsewhere. The telegraph reduced the opportunity for confusion and mistakes in such fields. It allowed the British government to demand a daily report from the commander in situ, Lord Raglan, keeping them up to date with events. But the French leader, Napoleon III, went further and used the telegraph to give direct orders to his commanders, for example, on when to launch an assault on Sevastapol, forcing his commander to ask to be allowed to resign from the 'sometimes paralysing [effect] of the electric wire'.[20]

Ninety years later, Hitler was also to intervene with paralysing effect in his war on the eastern front. British Intelligence assessments on one episode from the months following the Russian success at Kursk – the issue of whether Germany would withdraw from the Crimea in southern Russia following the Russian counter-offensive at Kursk – illustrate the level of information gained from Fish intercepts on the eastern front. In early September 1943, decrypts showed that the German army had estimated that evacuation from the narrow-necked peninsula would take about four weeks, should it prove necessary. In the meantime, it started the process of thinning out (Auflockerung) and dismantling installations. In addition, the headquarters of Army Group A and Luftwaffe Fliegerkorps (Roman) I were moved from the Crimea to near Nikolaev. The thinning out continued until 20 October when a 'serious deterioration on the Eastern front' led to the issuing of the order for the full evacuation to begin. But, on 26 October, the OKH instructed local commanders to stop the evacuation, 'since the Fuehrer has ordered the Crimea to be held'. The general movement out of the Crimea ceased, but further thinning out ensued, while the army commanders organized holding operations against Russian attacks. However, throughout November, the supply position deteriorated rapidly, so the 'possibility of evacuation had soon to be faced again', reported a British Intelligence assessment. 'There is, however, every indication that Hitler's order is still in force.'[21] Indeed, as is now known, Hitler told his generals, 'We're obliged, if it's even possible, to defend this second Stalingrad – if it can be done. We can't just dismiss it coldly… we have to consider that the men here are lost... We could say: higher purposes. Maybe we could reach a higher purpose without it. But something else could happen.'[22] To make sure his orders were enforced – while waiting for his higher purpose or something else to develop – a direct wireless teleprinter link, between Hitler's high command and the commander of the 17 Army in the Crimea, was needed alongside the link from 17 Army to its superior Army Group headquarters, the normal chain of command.

Georg Gluender was a wireless and teleprinter engineer on the eastern front, involved in setting up and maintaining Saegefisch and Geheimschreiber stations. On 1 November 1943, his unit was flown into the Crimea to open up two wireless links from the 17 Army in the peninsula to Army Group A in the Ukraine and to OKH near Koenigsberg. His unit took with them two Geheimschreibers, three teleprinters, two tape perforators, five receivers and two transmitters, plus a stock of spare parts. The first job was to construct an enormous aerial complex, which was needed to achieve good transmission over long distances. It required eight masts, each over twenty metres tall. Following many calculations, and much use of a compass, as they decided where to place the masts, Gluender and a colleague faced a rather gruesome task in getting everything ready on the ground. The site was a flat piece of land that not long before had been a battlefield and it was littered with unburied skeletons. As they continued their calculations and surveying, they piled up bones to mark the spots where the masts would need to be placed.

Gluender recalled, 'At the end of the job, I had earned such a reputation of being good at antenna construction and in my off-duty hours I was sent up on to a lot of roofs [to fix aerials for colleagues]. I don't know whether my clients always limited their listening with my antennas strictly to broadcasts from Germany. We certainly didn't with our military receivers. But woe to the one caught listening to enemy broadcasts: the disciplinary company was his certain destination and this was usually a death sentence.'[23]

Some other illicit eavesdropping also took place. One function the wireless station served was to relay messages from the headquarters of Army Group 'A' in the Ukraine to the OKH near Koenigsberg. Wireless transmission between the Ukraine and East Prussia was actually more difficult than between the more distant Crimea and the Baltic shore (an indication of why the transmissions could be received in Britain). The operators were instructed not to retransmit these transit messages using different keys (i.e. different pin positions and wheel starting positions), but they soon began to ignore this fundamental rule – at least until Gluender set up an automatic relay system. This transit traffic provided an opportunity for more eavesdropping – this time on exchanges of the messages between their superior Army Group headquarters and the high command and Hitler. As any important items of news were made known to the general on the spot, the practice was tolerated. Gluender also recalled that 'I did my utmost to lighten [the operators'] work by utilizing little technical tricks', such as a 'rotor-setting recovery key' to reset the wheels for a retransmission. He realized that these tricks were against the rules, but seems not to have given any thought to the fact this may have been helping the British break the cipher.

For the first five months of Gluender's time in the Crimea, it was peaceful enough. But, when pressure increased from the Russian army in mid-1944, Gluender and his unit were among the first to be evacuated. It was vital that no cipher equipment or troops be captured by the Russians. After an initial retreat to a new site, a temporary station was set up for a month near Sevastopol, maintaining communications, but most of the unit were killed by shelling. As the Russians drew closer, Gluender was ordered to destroy the Geheimschreiber machines. A few days later, he and the three remaining members of his unit boarded an evacuation ship, led by their NCO using his pistol to force a way past the wounded and the fleeing. Saegefisch communications between the Crimea and Koenigsberg ceased, and Bletchley Park now had to learn about progress on the eastern front from other surviving links.

The intercepts had provided an intimate insight into the German command process – and into Hitler's policy of not pulling back from occupied territory even if it made good military sense to retrench. German commanders wanted to withdraw, as the troops in the Crimea were needed to shore up the main front. Understanding how Hitler would react was important for the Allies in their strategic planning, as there was a danger that they would assume that Hitler would react in the same way as they would in allowing withdrawals to more easily defensible positions. With the help of Fish decrypts, they were to learn that they had to resist such conclusions (see Appendix P – 'Hitler as seen by Source'). Hitler's concept of war and statehood was derived in part from his economic outlook, which can perhaps best be summed up as autarkic, in that he believed that Germany had to acquire and control its own empire, one which would supply it with all its economic needs in terms of resources, especially rare resources such as minerals and oil, as well as providing living space and agricultural produce. Much of his strategy (though more often he reacted tactically to opportunities than to a developed strategic plan) can probably be understood through his concepts of economics: Norway was essential for iron ore; Serbia, Macedonia and Bulgaria for copper; Transylvania, Dalmatia, Phokis, in northwest Greece, and the island of Naxos for bauxite; and northern Albania, northern Greece and eastern Bosnia for chrome. Similarly, Hitler's preferred emphasis in the invasion of Russia in 1941 and 1942 was towards what he saw as economic targets (Leningrad, the Ukraine and Caucasus) instead of the military targets picked out by his generals. The understanding that Hitler intended to maintain his hold on these captured regions, for what he considered to be essential economic reasons, was to inform the development of Allied strategy. The decrypts supported those who argued that Hitler could be persuaded to spread his forces, weakening their grip in particular places, a process which could then ease an Allied invasion of mainland Europe. The more land Hitler occupied, the greater the strategic disadvantage he faced in working out where to place his troops.[24] The knowledge that Hitler would divert troops to hold on to valued economic resources was worth several army divisions in the field. It is often difficult to ascertain exactly how intelligence was used to influence decisions – whether tactically or strategically – but it is clear that the information produced by Fish links was exactly what was needed to help the highest policy-makers, who were privy to decodes, to come to well-informed strategic decisions. The strategic importance of Fish decodes was, as quotes from wartime documents above and in succeeding chapters demonstrate, of vital importance, and, indeed, far more so than Enigma decodes.

Hitler's increasing refusal to concede the reality of the situation slowly became evident to British intelligence from the Fish decodes. One German historian has written, 'It was plain to everyone that the summer of 1943 had brought the great turning point in the war. Until then the over-extension of forces had been hidden or drowned by propaganda… When, in the autumn of 1943, the War Economy Office submitted a memorandum about the Soviet Union's exceptionally large reserves, Hitler was outraged for weeks on end. Eventually, he simply forbade the Wehrmacht High Command [OKW] to prepare such analyses. Much the same happened some time later to a study of Allied armaments capacities produced by Speer's planning office; and soon afterwards Hitler altogether prohibited information on the enemy's war industry to be passed through official channels.'[25] In early October 1943, a British intelligence assessment had difficulty defining what seemed to be a confused German strategy. With the failure of Zitadelle, 'the Germans have lost their initiative; and they have given little sign of definite planning since', but, plans for withdrawal from the Crimea then in place, 'the real answer may well be that the lessons of Stalingrad and Tunis have sunk in'.[26] Hitler's decision to hold on to the Crimea came just a fortnight after this assessment was issued, forcing a re-assessment. Understanding Hitler's decision meant that it was, in fact, British Intelligence who learned the lessons of Stalingrad. Or, to be more precise, the lessons of Hitler's reactions to Stalingrad.

A file held at the National Archives in Kew contains a 'résumé of the Fish Talks delivered May 17th to 24th [1943]'. Unfortunately, there is no indication as to who gave the talks and to whom, but they were probably given within the Testery or Hut 3 (which translated and annotated Enigma and Geheimschreiber decrypts). Whoever they were, the information imparted was strikingly important. 'Dependent on our ability to break the Fish keys, fishing will become, increasingly, our main concern.'[27] The speaker trawled the fish metaphor deeply:

Who are the Fishes? The Fishes are the catch resulting from purposeful angling in the gaps – that is, the [wireless] beam stages – in the German Armed Forces networks. Our successes have so far been confined to the beams controlled by German Army Signals. These are the most efficient available to the Germans: German Air Force and German Navy make extensive use of them. Our angling produces, however – this is a point which I have evidently not succeeded always in bringing home – any signal however or wherever originated for which for some good reason was passed by the signals authority on one of the beams... The signals system is extremely efficient, hence the Fishes carry longer and fuller routine reports than were ever passed on Enigma. The Germans deem it highly secure, hence the Fishes may contain signals of the greatest secrecy.

The growing number of links broken by the Testery's hand methods also gave the traffic analysts a much better view of the network with which they were dealing. The breakthrough came in Hut 3 when it was discovered that a significant part of the enciphered messages included vital information about the structure of the organizations using the network and of their teleprinter traffic. Hut 3 thus became involved in traffic analysis of Fish messages, supplementing the traffic analysis performed by the intercept operators who did not see the decodes. What Hut 3 found was that the links were not just between general staff headquarters and army headquarters, but connected Fernschreibstelle (teleprinter offices) that provided a service for the armed forces and the Reich's administrative organizations in the area. Each morning, the office would receive messages, via regional or local wireless and landline links, from these organizations and collect them together for later enciphering and transmission in one long message at a specified time each day. The Fernschreibstelle at large exchanges near Berlin and Koenigsberg also had a Geheimschreibstube (a secret writing room or cipher room), where messages that were received in plain language were typed into a teleprinter or, if pre-perforated, were fed directly into a Geheimschreiber by operators given special security clearance.

The operator at the sending end would punch all the messages received from different users on to one stretch of paper tape for automatic transmission. At the receiving end, the individual messages would be forwarded on to the various end recipients, either on paper or by teleprinter message on further networks of local landlines and wireless links. Each message contained information about to whom it was addressed, who had sent it and at what time, a serial number, and a call-sign so that the receiving Fernschreibstelle could forward it to the addressee as well as maintain records of when messages were received and forwarded. All this information was within the ciphered part of the messages. Analysis of these call-signs (of which there were over 3,000 and were sometimes reorganised) gave Allied Intelligence a detailed view of the structure of the German armed forces and military administration. The call-signs, which could only be analysed when the messages had been decoded, thus opened up a new source of intelligence not just the German army, but also the armed forces generally and the overall war administration of the Third Reich. The call-signs were, according to an assessment made at Bletchley Park in August 1943, 'rapidly becoming a most important secondary source of intelligence'.[28]

The European-wide teleprinter network on which the German war effort depended for its information flows was known as WANDA-Netz.[29] The traffic analysts also built up a picture of the German network links, determining the origin and destination of messages passed on Fish and other local networks. It became evident that the beamed directional radio link was often only one part of the link between Berlin or Koenigsberg and the army command headquarters in the field. The headquarters of Oberbefehlshaber Suedost, ObSO, Commander-in-Chief South-East, in charge of Army Group E, was based in Salonika and nominally the recipient of wireless teleprinter messages. The teleprinter office was an exchange, managed by the signals corps, where messages could be transferred by local landline or radio link to other German army locations in the region.

A British Intelligence report from June 1943 reported how the Balkan networks were being integrated around the teleprinter office in Saloniki. It reported that, in mid-1943, two new local networks were opened. One of these new networks linked ObSO to four other German army organizations: Deutsche Verbindungstab zum Cdo Superalba (German army signals unit) at Tirana, Albania; Befehlshaber der Deutschen Truppen in Kroatien (Commander-in-Chief German troops in Croatia) at Sarajevo; Kdr und Befehlshaber in Serbien (headquarters of Commander-in-Chief Serbia) at Belgrade; and, probably, XIV Italian Army Corps, in Greece. The second new network linked Saloniki with Athens, Crete and Deutscher Verbindungsstab sum Cdo Superegeo (German army signals unit) on the island of Rhodes in the Dodecannese. ObSO also had a direct wireless telegraphy link with Rome and a large number of minor links – for example, to Organisation Todt (which organized labour for construction and other work) near Mostar and its local sources of bauxite.[30]

This particular link was a civilian one, until Communist partisans started to drive the Germans out of the area. In response, the German army took control of the entire bauxite region and integrated the civilian links into military networks. Daily reports on the operations against the partisans were sent over the link to ObSO at Saloniki, where they were forwarded in overall reports back to Berlin – and interception and decryption by GC&CS in Britain. 'At present the Befehlshaber der Deutschen Truppen in Kroatien is in Sarajevo directing a second Combined operation aimed at destroying both the Communist and the Chetnik forces in the area South-East of the bauxite zone... A feature of the German Army system in the Balkans is the passing of a daily routine report, which is produced by ObSO from reports sent in from the different sectors... The whole message is passed by wireless teleprinter and landline to Berlin' and addressed (i.e. with a teleprinter call-sign) for onward distribution to five different general staff organizations. An extract was also sent to Rome, to Belgrade and Tirana for onward copying to divisional commanders via local networks. 'Apart from the daily report... a Balkans evening report has been observed on the wireless teleprinter and landline link to OKH passing from ObSO to OKH/Abt Fremde Heere Ost [eastern armies Military Intelligence department]. The Todt Organisation also makes use of this channel... This link is a communications channel capable of carrying a very large amount of traffic and is used by a variety of Government services, including commercial and secret service authorities.' No wonder the codebreakers at Bletchley Park were beginning to realize that breaking the Geheimschreiber cipher was going to provide intelligence of a breadth and depth that they had never imagined was possible.

Decodes also showed the extent to which partisan activity was continuing to make the use of landlines difficult – with the result that more and more communications were forced on to the airwaves. The Luftwaffe spent much time and effort developing its own non-Morse wireless teleprinter link from Berlin to Greece because of the congestion on the main army link. Most of the pressure for improved communications came from OKW in Berlin which was frustrated by delays in finding out what was happening on the ground. 'Much emphasis is laid by Berlin on [the new link]. One reason may be to try and relieve the great pressure on landlines which have to pass through largely hostile territory.'[31] In early September 1943, operator chat on the Berlin–Bucharest link revealed that all landlines through Sofia, Budapest and OKW to Belgrade were down, so the army in Bucharest was having to communicate with ObSO in Saloniki via a Luftwaffe link, and the Donan–Belgrade link was overloaded with traffic, leading to delays of three or four hours.[32]

Whether it was at the strategic political and military level, or whether it told the codebreakers what they needed to know about the German communications networks, the interception of the Fish networks was beginning to produce a remarkable oversight of the German army just at the time when the Allies were meeting that army in battle on mainland Europe in Italy. As one anonymous report from August 1943 put it, 'The quality of the intelligence derived from Fish is of the highest order.'[33]

chapter thirteen

Making the Difference

The disagreements at Hitler's headquarters had intensified as it became clear that the German advance in southern Russia in 1942 was not going to achieve its objective. Hitler squabbled with his generals over not just strategy and tactics, but also the apparent trivia of who said what to whom. After one such row, Hitler ordered his officials to organize a team of stenographers to keep a written record of his thrice-daily military briefings so that he could prove whether his generals had followed the orders he gave. By mid-April 1945, the stenographers had accumulated over 100,000 pages of text from the briefings. As Russian troops closed in around Berlin, the stenographers and their transcripts were among the people and papers flown from the Reich's capital to its reputedly impenetrable inner core, near Salzburg. The transcripts were stored in an underground tunnel dug for protection into a mountainside near Obersalzburg, but, as the German war effort began to falter, officials of the Nazi Party broke into the document bunker and attempted to burn the contents. When American troops arrived in the area in May they were led to the site of the bonfire and, on searching through the ashes of the burnt documents, they found remnants of the papers of some fifty of the military conferences which had survived because of their proximity to the corners of the ditch in which the fire had been set. Most of the surviving documents record the whole of a day's briefings and give an invaluable insight into Hitler's running of the war.

The records are detailed discussions about the progress of the war and the placing of German forces. Hitler dominates the proceedings, questioning the generals before sharply asserting his authority, veering abruptly from one theatre to another, from grand strategic issues to ridiculously banal ones. There is one man trying to command in excessive tactical detail several armies on two, then three, fronts, as well as other areas of the war. Needless to say, such meddling ensured that things went from bad to worse. Hitler responded to the failures of his excessive interference with yet more of the same. All this was evident to British Intelligence from Fish and Enigma decodes (see Appendix P - 'Hitler as seen by Source') where increasingly it was noted that orders were being issued on his direct authority. What was not so apparent from 'Source' was Hitler's state of mind or why he made the decisions that he did. However, the transcripts of Hitler's military conferences now allow us to see how well Fish and Enigma decodes performed in providing enough intelligence to develop an understanding of Hitler's likely reaction to events. However fragmentary and partial the information provided by Ultra, it gave enough of a glimpse into Hitler's mind to be able to work out how the dictator could be militarily defeated.

The military conference transcripts also reveal the trivia of how Hitler, as the war went against the German armed forces, not only interfered, but also frequently gave vent to his feelings about subjects that excited him and quite often he simply ranted at his patient staff. His observations were apparently randomly assembled, but, in fact, were highly patterned and repetitive. He had his favourite subjects – 'the evils of smoking, the construction of a motorway system throughout the Eastern territories, the deficiencies of the legal system, the achievements of Stalin as a latter-day Genghis Khan, keeping the standard of living low among the subjugated peoples, the need to remove the last Jews from

German cities' – and the weaknesses, including racial ones, of what he called the plutocracies, especially the United States.[1] One of the surviving fragments of Hitler's wartime military briefings, believed to be from March 1944, unlike the other surviving daily transcripts, is particularly short and reads in full: '... become... If a person is constantly between... of machines, he becomes ill. It's a... to the nerves. By nature a man is intended for... but not for standing between buzzing machines. Life in cities like New York... St Louis is unbearable. That's why the people are also... If it's possible that a radio speaker... reports about Martians landing... in some places a panic breaks out, then... how hysterically the whole population... not... that the Americans also only... can be compared. There is...'[2]

Clearly, this is one of Hitler's rants, immediately identifiable even though it consists only of a few parts of some sentences and fewer than one hundred words in total. The style and the subject are a classic Hitlerian tirade. It can perhaps be compared to listening to a mobile phone call under conditions of very poor reception, but still recognizing the speaker complaining about a familiar subject. The language patterns inherent in one of Hitler's rants remain recognizable, even in a quite discontinuous sample. The principle behind codebreaking, for which Colossus was developed, exploited this aspect of language – the intention was to distinguish statistical evidence of what can be called German military teleprinter language in partially decoded fragments of an intercepted message.

Hand methods had allowed Bletchley Park to break several of the Geheimschreiber links in the Balkans, Russia and North Africa, but this had its limitations. German army security measures threatened to put an end to existing methods of breaking messages. These were, in the words of a Bletchley Park internal history, 'comparatively simple hand methods... [so] more complex methods [were] required when wheels and indicating systems were constructed so as to invalidate the more simple-minded approaches'.[3]

213

What, in fact, was needed was a general method – and preferably one that did not depend on depths – so that individual messages could be deciphered. The value of the intelligence derived from Geheimschreiber messages was becoming clearer, and as the British, Americans and the Western Allies expected to meet the Axis forces in battle in Europe itself, they wanted to ensure that the flow of intelligence would continue.

Following Tutte's breakthrough and the diagnosis of the nature of the Lorenz version of the Geheimschreiber, Bletchley Park watched closely for potential depths and tried to use cribs, likely words or phrases in the message, to see if other messages could be prised open. According to Tutte, 'We were reading only those messages that the German operators were careless enough to send in depth or near-depth. That was too few to satisfy Bletchley's customers. We learned, however, to use known wheel patterns to break messages not in depth. Basically a commonly occurring crib like SPRUCHNUMMER or OBERKOMMANDO9WEHRMACHT would be dragged, that is tried in one position after another until a plausible stretch of key was obtained… In the second half of 1942 with all this progress we thought we were doing well. And so we went on through 1943. It could not last. Eventually the Germans, noticing that the indicators were giving away information that need not be given away, abolished 12-letter indicators.'[4] With the introduction of Quatsch (nonsense and padding text), which ruled out the use of cribs on messages not in depth, things became even more difficult. The codebreakers could still work with depths when they received them, but no longer on single messages. At the moment the Geheimschreiber had been forced to reveal its secrets, the German army closed it up once again. The codebreakers therefore began to look at statistical aspects of the Fish messages to see if there was a way of breaking into the cipher without relying on depths and external information such as indicators.

The objective of the Geheimschreiber, of course, was to remove all the statistical information about the frequency with which the various letters of the alphabet and other characters occur in natural or plain language and create a random string of character frequencies in the enciphered version. The fundamental statistical technique used for codebreaking is the character frequency count. So the fundamental purpose of a cipher must be to hide the plain-language character count and to offer no obvious ways into unravelling the hidden information. The frequency with which characters occur in the plain varies from language to language, so that of English is different from that of German. What is perhaps less obvious is that there was also a 'German military language, which had its own characteristic character count (biased by, for example, frequent military abbreviations), and indeed a teleprinter language, again with its own frequency count. For technical reasons (to do with the interaction of the teleprinter shift function),[5] the most common character in teleprinter language was the basic teleprinter code character 9, which represented SPACE, followed by the letters E and N, then came 5 (shift to figures) and 8 (shift to letters). The result of the combination of the characteristics of teleprinter, standard German and military German can usefully be called German military teleprinter language, even if this was not a term employed by Bletchley Park.

That the Geheimschreiber enciphering technique could quite successfully hide the plain-language patterns can be seen from the figures on the left of table 1 in Appendix E, which shows the frequency of characters in the original plain – German military teleprinter language – of a message intercepted on 10 January 1945 on what was codenamed the Grilse link. The message was 3,200 characters long. In the plain language, there was a highly uneven distribution of the occurrence of each character, with 9 by far the most common character, occurring 544 times, followed by E with 304 occurrences, N 212 occurrences and 5 with 200 occurrences. The least common characters were J and Y, with six and seven occurrences, respectively. This vastly uneven distribution of the character count of occurrences was typical of plain language; the particular pattern of frequencies was typical of German military teleprinter language. The figures on the right of the table show the enciphered text stream, with all characters occurring somewhere between 81 and 124 times – a good random distribution. The recognizable peaks and troughs of the plain-language character count have been substituted by a nondescript, undulating terrain in the cipher. The Geheimschreiber thus successfully produced an enciphered message that appeared random.

The Geheimschreiber key was made up of two stages: the Chi wheels applied one key character, and the Psi wheels a second. While the Chi wheels followed a simple periodic pattern, the Psi wheels followed a more complicated pattern, determined by two other wheels, the motor wheels. The combined effect of the motor and Psi wheels was to create the second key stream with between 20 per cent and 40 per cent of repeated characters, or stutters. This second key stream was called the extended-Psi stream. Each key stream was combined in turn with the plain text (alternatively, the two key streams could be combined together first and then the result combined with the plain). Deciphering was based on the fact that these key streams were reversible. Combining the same pair of key streams with the cipher stream would wipe out the effects of each in turn. It may help to view the full key as consisting of two key layers laid on top of the original plain-language message each hiding the plain. Although the full key was combined with the plain into a single stream, the reversibility inherent in the process essentially meant that the cipher text contained a memory of each key stream. The second application of each key stream wiped out the memory of one layer, turning it transparent so that the original plain could be seen once again

Two points already made about the Vernam cipher are important here. First, the Vernam cipher rules mean that combining a character with itself results in all dots (00000), or the character / in the basic teleprinter code. This is the principle which leads to the wiping out of a key stream on its second application, as the key is effectively combined with itself. Second, whenever a key stream contains the all-dots character, then the plain language (or the partly enciphered character if it has already been combined with one key character) will be unchanged. This means that, unlike the Enigma machine, the Vernam cipher allows a character to be enciphered as itself. It also means that the all-dots character is effectively transparent.[6]

Bill Tutte, who had played a major role in diagnosing the Geheimschreiber, also made the next great breakthrough by combining these facets of the cipher into a potentially practical statistical method of cracking the cipher machine. He saw a possible way of exploiting the cipher rules and the fact that, although the combined key stream (the Chi and the extended-Psi) was random, its two constituent key streams were not and could be manipulated to display statistical anomalies.

Tutte assumed that the wheel pin patterns were known – that is, that the wheels had been broken to determine which pins on each of the twelve wheels were raised and which were flush. This information would have been the result of hand breaking of a depth. These pin patterns would apply to other messages sent in the same period for which those patterns were in use, but each message would use a different starting position for each wheel. The problem Tutte set himself was to develop a method of working out these starting positions, given that the wheel-pin patterns were known – that is, to set the wheels.

Tutte saw that theoretically it was possible to work out every possible starting position for the five Chi wheels, and thus, as the pin positions were known, to generate every possible Chi stream with which an intercepted message could possibly have been enciphered (about 22 million). Each possible stream could be combined in turn with the cipher text stream. When the correct Chi stream was combined with the cipher text, then the Chi stream contained in the cipher text would be stripped out, leaving a combination of the extended-Psi stream and the plain-language text stream. This stream was called the de-Chi stream (i.e. the stream with the Chi removed). Leaving aside for the time being the question of how it was possible to recognize that the correct Chi stream had been combined, this process, called de-Chi'ing, removed one key layer, turning it effectively into a transparent layer consisting entirely of all-dots characters.

The next step involved exploiting that characteristic stutter of the extended-Psi stream. Tutte used a technique to create a new stream which used the stutters, or repeated characters, to create transparent gaps, through which a form of the plain could be seen – rather like seeing the fragments of one of Hitler's rants in English rather than German. The technique was known as the difference or delta and involved combining each character in a stream with the next character in the same stream. For example, the delta of K O M M A N D A NT U R is created by combining K and O, O and M, M and M, M and A, A and N, and so on, and finally combining U and R (the resulting stream is one character shorter than the original as there is no subsequent character to combine with the final one). A key point to note is that repeated characters (such as the M M in Kommandantur) combine to produce the transparent all dots character in the delta stream. This was the feature which Tutte exploited to gain a glimpse of a form of the plain. (See Appendix E for examples of the delta.)

The delta stream of an enciphered text stream is the same as that which would be produced by creating the delta of the plain, the delta of the Chi and the delta of the extended-Psi and then combining them. The delta of an enciphered text can be said to contain the delta of the plain, the delta of the Chi and the delta of the extended-Psi. By the same reasoning, the delta of a de-Chi stream would contain a combination of the delta of the extended-Psi and the delta of the plain. So, wherever there was a repeat in the extended-Psi, it would result in a transparent, all-dots character in the delta-extended-Psi component of the de-Chi, through which the delta of the plain would be visible. As repeats made up as much as 20 to 40 per cent of the extended-Psi stream, the delta-extended-Psi stream would consist of 10 to 20 per cent of transparent characters in the delta-de-Chi. It is important to note that it was the delta of the plain stream that was visible, not the plain itself but a translation of the plain into its delta form. The breakthrough depended on the fact that the average delta-plain stream also had its own characteristic character frequency count, one that reflected the frequency of common pairs of characters in German military teleprinter language. Thus, although the original plain was still indecipherable, it was potentially recognizable statistically. In the example of Hitler's rant, the original German language has been translated into another language, yet the feel of the original is still evident, even if in watered-down form. The character frequency count of the original German and the English translation would be quite different, but both would display their own pattern of non-random effects (even with fewer than a hundred words). The delta was simply a form of re-coding, translating a Baudot code stream into a slightly different version. Different character frequencies would be seen in the plain and in the delta-plain, but the statistical divergence from the average would still be potentially recognizable in translated delta form. The delta process is given in equations in Appendix E.

This was a theoretical breakthrough. The Chi stream could be removed by generating the Chi stream for every possible starting position, combining each in turn with the cipher text. The correct Chi stream would strip itself out, leaving a de-Chi stream which could be converted into a delta-de-Chi stream which would contain a significant number of characters that were identical with the delta of the original plain-language text (in other words, whenever there was a repeat in the extended-Psi causing a / in the delta-extended-Psi within the delta-de-Chi). And, theoretically, the delta-de-Chi should display the statistical profile of the average delta-plain, though again in watered-down form. If that statistical profile could be identified and measured, it would answer the question of how to identify the correct Chi-stream – all non-correct de-Chi streams would display more or less random counts, while the correct one would display a weak form of the statistical bulges of the average delta-plain. This still leaves aside the question of how it would be practically possible to generate every possible Chi stream and then combine them with the cipher stream, work out the character frequencies and identify the non-random one, but it does suggest a way in which the two key streams could be made partly transparent.

The delta of the average plain-language Fish message did indeed display its own, highly uneven character frequency count. The character frequencies in a delta-plain stream are the product of common pairs of characters in the plain. So, for example, in German military teleprinter language, frequently occurring combinations such as EI (which results in a delta stream character U), 5M (also giving U), M8 (giving A) and 89 (giving 5) affect the statistical profile of the character count in the delta-plain. EI is part of the contribution of the German language to the plain; 5M and M8 and 89 are the contribution of teleprinter punctuation (5M89 being figures-shift, full-stop, letters-shift, SPACE). Each such frequently occurring plain-language pair created its own frequently occurring delta character – U, 5 and / for example were particularly common in delta-plain streams – that differed from the underlying plain language but contained a measure of frequently occurring relationships within the plain. So here was a potential way forward, if some means of measuring these statistics could be devised.

In the words of the *General Report on Tunny*, written at the end of the war but kept secret until recently, 'Statistical methods of breaking Tunny are possible because (and only because) cipher, plain, key, Chi, extended-Psi, de-Chi and motor streams can – *with suitable treatment* – be made to exhibit marked characteristics which will distinguish them from a random sequence of letters' (italics added). The suitable treatment was the creation of the delta stream. The non-random character counts of the delta-plain would be visible through the Chi layer and the extended-Psi layer in two steps. First, the correct Chi stream was laid on top, turning the Chi layer to all dots throughout, exposing the extended-Psi and the plain. Alternately, as in fact became the procedure, all possible delta-Chi streams were created and combined in turn with the delta-cipher stream, the application of the correct delta-Chi stream leaving the delta-de-Chi stream. Then parts of the delta-de-Chi stream would be transparent, so that evidence of the delta-plain could be seen through the all-dots characters in the delta-extended-Psi component of the delta-de-Chi. This would only allow small sections of the delta-plain to show through. Table 2 in Appendix E shows the character counts for some messages of the delta-plain, delta-de-Chi and delta-extended-Psi streams, all displaying non-random bulges. The delta-de-Chi in particular displays, in a weaker form, the statistical profile of the delta-plain.

But there were limits to the usefulness of Tutte's insights. There were simply far too many possible Chi starting positions for any serious attempt to generate every possible Chi stream – some 22 million in all. Here a point already made became of almost casual relevance – Donald Murray's reassignment of the Baudot code units to accommodate the engineer's perceived priority of minimizing wear and tear. If the occurrence of frequent pairs of letters in the plain was the determinant of the characters in the delta-plain, it was Murray's assignments which affected the statistics of the underlying units used to represent those common resulting characters. And it was these unit statistics that gave Tutte the chance to scale back the number of Chi wheels that would have to be used to detect the non-random features of the correct Chi stream and to bring the method into the realm of the practicable. Tutte worked out that the sixteen most common characters in the delta-plain were likely to be: /, 9, H, T, O, M, N, 3, which all have dots in units 1 and 2, and A, U, Q, W, 5, 8, K, J, which all have crosses in both units 1 and 2. The likelihood that both units 1 and 2 in a delta-plain stream would be identical (i.e. both dots or both crosses) was thus greater than 50 per cent, the random occurrence. This meant that it was possible that statistical evidence of the correct delta-de-Chi stream could be identified in just the first two units, even in the watered-down form visible through the all-dots characters in the delta-extended-Psi component of the delta-de-Chi stream. This reduced the number of possible delta-de-Chi streams to be tested from some 22 million (41x31x29x26x23) to just 1,271 (41x31). Once the first two wheels had been set, another pair could then be set using appropriate statistics, leaving a fifth wheel to be set last of all.

Tutte also devised a routine to perform a test that would give an indication of a non-random statistical bulge. Given that the more common characters in the delta-plain all have the two identical values in units 1 and 2 (both dots or both crosses), combining units 1 and 2 of any of them produces a dot more than 50 per cent of the time (0 + 0 = 0 and 1 + 1 = 0). Tutte's routine combined units 1 and 2 of a delta-cipher text stream and the delta-Chi stream, and counted the number of times the result equalled a dot. An excess number over the random would be an indication of a valid delta-plain being observed, in fragments, through transparent gaps in the delta-de-Chi. Tutte called it the double-delta. He had identified a method that turned the top layer of the key fully transparent, and the second layer partly transparent. But it would require a lot of combining and counting operations to allow a statistical assessment to be made of the likelihood that a particular delta-Chi stream represented a hit.

Those 1,271 sets of settings would be used to generate all possible delta-Chi streams, combine each stream in turn with the delta-cipher text and perform the test and count positive results for all the resulting delta-de-Chi streams, This meant that the number of states to be tested would be 1,271 times the number of characters in the minimum necessary enciphered text, which could be, say, 2,000 characters for a typical wheel-setting operation. The total number of individual double-delta processes needed was in the order of many millions, even to test the 1,271 possibilities. Each thousand characters would require 1.27 million double-delta operations, each requiring seven Vernam combination processes, a total of nearly 8.9 million operations – or 17.8 million for setting the wheels with a 2,000-character message.[7] Once the settings of these two Chi wheels had been found, the process could be repeated on wheels 4 and 5, followed by 3, because the number of settings to be tested was significantly reduced. So the informal name for the statistical method, brute force, was still apt, despite the reduction in processing levels from 22 million to 1,271.

Tutte recalled how he developed the double-delta test and the reaction when he told his superiors about it.

> I suspected that [delta-Psi-unit-1 combined with delta-Psi-unit-2] would be mostly dot. It is always so when Psi stays still and sometimes so when Chi does not. I calculated that it would be about 70 per cent dot... [Delta-cipher-unit-1 combined with delta-cipher-unit-2], constructed from a military German message, was expected to be about 60 per cent dot or a little more. I calculated that [delta-cipher-unit-1 combined with delta-cipher-unit-2] agreed more often than not with [delta-Chi-unit-1 combined with delta-Chi-unit-2]. In favourable cases there might be as much as 55 per cent agreement... I remember explaining the [double-delta] method to Gerry Morgan and Max Newman. There were rapid developments.[8]

This was in November 1942, just after El Alamein and just before Stalingrad. The developments that flowed from Tutte's insight were to contribute significantly to sweeping Hitler's forces back from their conquests.

chapter fourteen

The Robinson Family

The idea of using a machine to perform a massive statistical analysis as part of wheel-setting first arose towards the end of 1942, when Max Newman, a new recruit to Bletchley Park, suggested that Tutte's process could be mechanized. A special department was set up to research into new machinery. On 1 February 1943, Edward Travis, director of GC&CS, wrote to John Tiltman, Alan Turing, Gordon Welchman (a key figure in the Bombe, who was to become Assistant Director, Mechanization in September 1943[1]) and others who had a special interest in mechanized codebreaking: 'In many cases cyphers are becoming so difficult that solution depends on the provision of specially designed machinery to bring to notice clues upon which a cryptographer can work. It is therefore desirable to centralize research on special machinery, and I have appointed Mr Newman of the Research Section for this work.'[2] While it was Tutte who developed the mathematical technique in November 1942, it was Max Newman who saw that what was involved in exploiting the double-delta technique could be performed by a machine. He suggested that the 41x31 (1,271) comparisons (of delta-Chi-unit-1 and delta-Chi-unit-2 with delta-cipher-unit-1 and delta-cipher-unit-2) could be performed with two loops of perforated paper tape. He proposed that one tape would hold the generated delta-Chi patterns. It was already known which pins were raised and which were flush, so the objective was to determine the starting position of the two wheels for an individual message. The second tape would contain the delta-cipher text. The pin patterns on the delta-Chi tape would need to start one position further on for each run through the delta-cipher tape to step through all possible starting positions for the Chi settings. Some electrics would do the combining and counting. Theoretically, this should allow the correct Chi settings to be determined.

Born in 1897 in Chelsea, London, Maxwell Neumann was the son of a German father and an English mother. Hermann Neumann was a company secretary and his wife, Sarah Pike, a school teacher. Max proved at a young age to be a gifted mathematician, attending leading schools in Dulwich and the City of London, before heading to Cambridge in 1915 after winning an entrance scholarship to St John's College. The following year, he changed his name by deed poll to Newman – no doubt as a result of the xenophobic response of his fellow students to his Germanic name (similarly the Saxe-Coburgs became the Windsors, Battenberg became Mountbatten, and Santa Claus became Father Christmas).[3] The war meant that he had to postpone his studies and perform national service, which he did as a teacher in Yorkshire. However, in February 1918, he was finally called up for military service – and he hoped that his father's origins might actually prove advantageous and help him avoid being sent to the trenches. He wrote to a friend,

> Having received on Feb the 9th a letter asking me, with singular lack of courtesy, to present myself at Cambridge RO [Recruiting Office] on the 22nd inst, after various shufflings I have become a Conchy [conscientious objector], more or less, skilfully welding my objections, as I call them, on to my unfortunate father's place of birth. I am seeking exemption from military service, but am not refusing work of national importance. Among twenty odd soul-searching questions I am at present wrestling with is this: 5b What evidence can you

produce in support of your statement? Please forward written evidence (from persons of standing, if possible) which should be quite definite as to the nature and sincerity of your conscientious ob. Casting round vainly for anything remotely resembling a person of standing among my friends, relations and acquaintances, I was suddenly illumined by the fact that you are a Fellow of an Illustrious College and moreover, may write Doctor before your name and DSc after it according to the degree of sophistication of the person with whom you are dealing. Surely a person who could stand with anybody... [write and] tell him you know I have a rooted objection to taking part in the war. You'd better not say much more on this point or you may put your foot in it, as the system of beliefs I've evolved for this Tribunal is Queer, it only allows its master to work it out. An impression of immense age would be good [and] don't forget to splash a bit around your signature.[4]

His friend's letter of support, his opaque system of beliefs and his father's suspect nationality seemed to have done the trick and Newman avoided having to participate actively in the fighting, although he did serve as a paymaster in the army and also worked for two years as a teacher. He resumed his studies at Cambridge in 1919 after a second year of teaching, presumably because he was not discharged in time to return in 1918. He later developed an interest in the field of combinatorial topology – involving questions such as the theory that on a map it is sufficient to have just four colours to mark each country in a different colour, while no two touching countries have the same colour. He became a Fellow of St John's College – one tutor supporting his election noted that he had 'a mind which is fresh, vigorous and unexhausted'.[5] He spent time studying in Vienna and Princeton in the United States, and developed into a talented musician. He had met Alan Turing in the 1930s, when Turing had attended a now famous course of lectures by Max Newman in the spring of 1935 on the 'Foundations of

Mathematics' in which Newman suggested the application of machines to logical mathematical processes. Turing gave Newman a typescript of his 'Computable Numbers' paper in April 1936 and worked closely with him to get it fit for publication.

As the work at Bletchley Park expanded into the widening array of ciphers used by the German, Italian and Japanese governments and armed forces, as well as those of neutral countries, so the call went out to trusted academics at colleges such as Cambridge to suggest mathematicians and other academics who could fill the vacancies the new work offered. One of the most prominent of these academics was Frank Adcock, Professor of Ancient History and, during the First World War, a codebreaker in Room 40. It was Adcock who was responsible, before the war started, for Alan Turing being recruited to GC&CS. Another key recruiting agent was Patrick Blackett, a physicist at Cambridge and Fellow of King's College. In May 1942, Blackett wrote to Bletchley Park recommending Newman. 'The man I mentioned to you is M H A Newman, FRS [Fellow of the Royal Society], of St John's College, Cambridge. He is about 45, and was born in England, his father being German and his mother English. He is one of the most intelligent persons I know, being a first-class pure mathematician, an able philosopher, and a good chess player and musician.'[6] Adcock also wrote to Newman advising him that 'There is some work at a governmental institution which would I think interest you and which is certainly important for the war. If you are disposed towards it, would you let me know and a meeting will be arranged to talk it over with someone without either party being committed to anything in advance.' And in June he reported, 'I spoke to the Director of Naval Intelligence about the possible job for you at B. He seemed to think that there was plenty of scope, and the work would be very important. I think this is probably the case, and that you would not feel it was uninteresting or not useful.'

It is clear that Newman was concerned whether the work would be sufficiently demanding to hold his interest. There was 'doubt of finding a job big enough to keep [Newman] interested and usefully employed for the duration', according to a colleague. Newman was under no compulsion to join, as he was not being called up. And obviously it was difficult for the codebreakers to give him any details of what the work would involve beyond bland assurances. Nigel de Grey, the deputy director at Bletchley Park, wrote to him in guarded terms: 'The post would certainly be a very important one from the point of view of the war.' And there was a possible sticking point – the nationality of Newman's father. While it may have been useful in the First World War in fending off enlistment, it was possible it would now prove a bar to his being allowed to work at Bletchley Park in the Second World War. De Grey told him, 'I am not certain at the moment what attitude would be taken by the authorities concerned, about your Father's nationality.'[7] Certainly the attitude was simple – no foreigner could be trusted. An order issued in September 1942, signed by Edward Travis, stated that all GC&CS employees should be aware 'no matter what position or grade they hold, that in future marriage with any foreigner is a bar to further employment in GC&CS. Each case is open to examination, but the principle remains. In general, close and continuing association with foreigners, except on duty, will make members of staff concerned liable to transfer to another post' (in fact, GC&CS had almost as much trouble in determining who was a foreigner and who was not as the Nazis in determining who was a Jew and who was not; the strict and apparently clear-cut rule often had to be applied to complex situations – such as the in-laws of people already married to a foreigner).[8]

However, the reticence was finally overcome on both sides, and Newman left Cambridge for Bletchley Park, joining the Testery in October 1942, on the condition that he could leave after one year if the work did not live up to the billing. And, in fact, this came close to happening. Newman found that the linguistic crossword puzzle-type of work in the Testery did not suit his abilities, and he could see that others were much better at it than he was.[9] Some of his colleagues, such as Peter Hilton, could 'see' the teleprinter characters merging in their mind's eye, but not Newman. However, what Newman did have was the ability to see that a machine could theoretically be used to perform Tutte's statistical double-delta method. It was a repetitive task, doing the same simple set of sums over and over again. Effectively, all that Tutte's basic statistical technique needed was a complex combining and counting machine. The challenge for the machine would be to perform myriad numbers of those same few calculations repeatedly at slightly different settings, for each setting performing the test and keeping a count, and to do it in a practical amount of time.

So, instead of leaving, Newman set about persuading Travis that resources should be devoted to developing such machinery. The success of the Bombe helped Newman win backing for his proposal. In December 1942, Newman got the go-ahead and he was given the job of developing machine methods of setting the wheels, that is determining the wheel starting positions for each message.[10] A new section was set up 'to research on special machinery' on 1 February 1943, the Machine Section,[11] which became known as the Newmanry. The aim was to design a machine that could trawl through all possible settings of the Chi wheels looking for statistical glimpses of the right settings for a message. 'The Section was at first regarded by members of Major Tester's section with some amusement.'[12] A variety of machine ideas were proposed and considered. One method contemplated for a time was an optical technique which depended on sliding photographic plates over one another looking for patterns.[13] This technique was later used with mixed success in the USA and a version of this US machine was tested for some two months immediately after the war ended to see how it compared with Colossus.

Newman was soon joined by two young students, Donald Michie, also from the Testery, and Jack Good, who had been working with Turing on Enigma decryption. Michie had been a Classics student and had to learn his mathematics at Bletchley Park.

After the war he became well known as a Professor of Machine Intelligence. Good, on the other hand, was another mathematics student from Cambridge, where he had recently obtained a doctorate. He was also the Cambridgeshire chess champion. At Bletchley Park, Good had initially worked for some eighteen months on the statistics associated with Enigma messages, under Turing's direction, before moving to work on Fish. The important advances in statistical theory that Turing had made for Enigma were applied by Good to the Geheimschreiber messages and were to provide an invaluable tool once Colossus was in operation.

Newman soon came to the conclusion that 'the best machine for the early experimental stages was one which read a "message-tape" and a "wheel-tape" photo-electrically, and combined them electrically before counting [see Appendix F]. Emphasis was laid from the start on the need for flexibility, in order that routines designed [in abstract] might be able to be modified in the light of experience without changing the machine.'[14] Comments such as these, contained in a few preserved documents, give us a small insight to the design process of Newman's first machine. It would need two paper tapes and tape-reading or scanning devices, so that the ciphered message and the Chi-wheel settings could be fed into the machine in delta form (the paper tapes containing the delta streams of the Chi settings and the cipher text would be created on a separate, simple machine); it would also need a way to count the number of times a condition occurred, display the results and move on to the next setting, before repeating the whole process. The pin positions (the wheel-breaking effort to identify which pins were raised and which were flush) had already been worked out, so the machine was needed to identify the correct wheel-settings or starting positions. It was a matter or trying out all 1,271 possible starting positions of wheels (or units) 1 and 2. The loops of paper tape, one a single character longer than the other, provided a simple means of stepping from one position to the next when one round had been completed.

After he had worked out what the machine would need to do mathematically, Newman called on outside help from two establishments outside GC&CS: the Post Office Research Establishment, at Dollis Hill, north London, and the Telecommunications Research Establishment or TRE, based at Malvern. Despite its name, the TRE had nothing to do with the Post Office or even with telecommunications. Indeed, the name had been chosen precisely to mislead anyone who heard of it about its real purpose, which was to develop Britain's radar technology. The reason for recruiting help from the TRE was that it made use of electronics in radar.[15] The machine that Bletchley Park, Dollis Hill and the TRE devised was known as the Robinson.

Dr Godfrey Wynn Williams had gained useful experience working on radar with electronic devices at the TRE during the first years of the war and before that at the Cavendish Laboratory in Cambridge. Experiments in nuclear physics demanded the development of very fast counters that could detect and record events happening at the speed of electronics. Electro-magnetic devices, with their moving parts, operated in milliseconds (thousandths of a second), but electronic activities occurred in microseconds (millionths of a second). In the late 1930s, Wynn Williams developed an electronic counter at the Cavendish Laboratory. This familiarity with electronics led him to be posted to the TRE's predecessor organization at the outbreak of the war, which, in turn, led to his being called to Bletchley Park in late 1941, when he was asked to advise on the potential of electronics for use in the Bombes.[16] He thus became the codebreakers' electronics expert and, when the Fish problem demanded a very fast machine, he was asked to design electronic circuits for the counter and to help perform the double-delta routine to identify the Chi wheels.[17] He later formed a small department at Bletchley Park which worked on developing machines for use in codebreaking.

However, although electronics were essential, the policy at Bletchley Park insisted on minimizing the use of what was seen as a fragile technology. Wherever possible, parts were to be constructed using existing technologies known to be reliable. Frank Morrell of the teleprinter section at the Post Office Research Establishment – which did indeed have much to do with telecommunications – was asked to construct the non-electronic parts of the machine such as the tape readers. Morrell and his team were the obvious choice, as they had the most experience with teleprinter technology. Morrell was also asked to make an analogue of the Lorenz Geheim-schreiber, but using electro-magnetic relays instead of rotor wheels so that messages could be decoded once the key had been identified. These analogue devices were called Tunny machines (originally this codename had been given to the first wireless teleprinter link in the Balkans, then to the Lorenz version of the Geheimschreiber). While the Dollis Hill and TRE engineers got on with developing Robinson, Tom Flowers, another Post Office research engineer, was brought in on the secret. Flowers had previously been to Bletchley Park to build an analogue machine for the Enigma codebreakers and had met Turing. Flowers and Turing, despite being quite different personalities, got on well together – presumably because Flowers could understand Turing's interest in the use of machines for the work at Bletchley Park. He was one of the few people at Bletchley Park who got on with Turing who was notoriously difficult to engage in conversation and they had several meetings together. As it turned out, the Enigma codebreaking machine built by Flowers was not used, but Turing did not forget the man from the Post Office and later recommended to Newman or Welchman that he be brought into the discussions. Flowers was head of the telephone switching department at Dollis Hill and was unaware of Morrell's work at Bletchley Park on the Robinson, and without Turing's recommendation he probably would not have become involved with Fish – and Colossus would never have existed.

Flowers was asked either to help address problems with the paper tapes or to identify problems with the electronic circuitry used in Wynn-Williams's counting unit. But he went further than asked, and instead of a few modifications needed to make the counting unit perform better Flowers proposed a mammoth, wholly electronic machine as the best approach to the brute-force method with its need for lots of calculations in as short a time as possible. But this was thought to be too complex and would take too long to finish. Instead, the 'simple machine with tapes', the Robinson, remained the choice. It would still use a few electronic valves for parts of the logic circuits and parts of the counter, but far fewer than the machine Flowers envisaged. Newman was pleased that Flowers had not been upset when his proposal was turned down and he reported, 'Morrell and Flowers were here this morning. There seems to be no doubt that they are putting the simple machine with tapes first, as we want, and they hope to have their part ready in two months. Wynn-Williams also hopes to have his part (the counting apparatus) done by then, and both parties seem to have a healthy desire not to be finished last. When the operators get the hang of this machine we should set six to eight messages a day. More machines will do more messages, but this means another two or three months wait, I suppose.'[18]

One biographical account of Newman says, 'To use an American term, Newman was a great "facilitator"; he ensured that those who worked in this section had the best possible conditions for success and the greatest possible freedom from interference. He was uncannily good at anticipating future needs, with respect to both equipment and personnel. Unobtrusively but with supreme effectiveness, he ensured that no effort of any member of his team was wasted.'[19] There was no single person in charge of the Fish project. Indeed, the Testery and the Newmanry were in different parts of the Bletchley Park hierarchy. So Newman's organizational skill – identifying what was needed, persuading senior managers to back him, and then carrying the project through – was crucial to the success of his section. However, Newman's skill at dealing with the senior management was not always balanced by tact in his handling of his often young staff who quickly learned that he was not a man to stand contradiction once he had made up his mind. One young cryptographer, Arthur Chamberlain, who joined the Newmanry at the beginning of 1944, later recalled that 'Newman was a good organiser, but had a tendency to be hypercritical. Whereas Turing made few judgments, Newman, one felt, had a poor opinion of those of us who failed to come up to his standards.'[20]

The Robinson consisted of three main functional units. First, a frame on which were mounted holders for the two paper tapes and an optical reading device (sometimes known as the 'scanner'). The tape frames were known as Bedsteads. Second, a metal rack or frame, which held the electronic counters, a lamp output panel for indicating the results and, later, a printer. And, third, the valve rack, which held the logic circuits and jack (socket) field for plugging up the sequence of operations. The valve rack and the Bedstead were both built at Dollis Hill. A suitably misleading cover name was given to the project, Apparatus Telegraph Transmitting.

There were several problems to be overcome during the building of the machine. One annoying issue was the way spurious phase changes were generated in the ring modulator logic that controlled the counters. The problem persisted, and Flowers was asked if he had any ideas of how to control this annoying effect. He recommended changing the electronic frequency at which the valves were operated, which solved the problem. However, to their dismay, neither Flowers nor the engineer working on the problem (Alan Coombs) could understand why this should have successfully prevented the unwanted phase shifts. Another machine ordered at this time was a much more complex version of the Tunny analogue machine used for decoding. This, the Newmanry Tunny, could also produce the perforated delta tapes needed by the Robinson and became what, in the 1970s and 1980s, would have been called a front-end processor to the mainframe Robinson (and, later,

Colossus). Once built, these Newmanry Tunny machines handled many routines for testing and paper tape-making.

By the end of May 1943, the Post Office had reported that a delay in manufacture of their part of the Robinson machine was inevitable, but that they were hoping to be able to deliver six machines within twelve weeks. To avoid any technical delays incurred by having two teams working on different parts of the machine, Newman insisted that the Post Office agree not to make any changes to Wynn-Williams's part of the machine if, when the parts were assembled, they all worked. Any improvements would have to be held over to a second machine. Indeed, one noteworthy aspect of the extraordinary period of machine development at Bletchley Park from 1943 onwards is the extent to which the devices that were constructed were work in progress – designs frozen at some point to get a machine into use. The lessons learned both in construction and in operation would then be used to make changes in the next generation. 'We agreed,' said Newman, 'that the temptation to alter designs to make minor improvements would be fatal to the output which was necessary if were to get the first six machines within twelve weeks.'[21]

On the other hand, 'Emphasis was laid from the start on the need for flexibility, in order that the routines designed in abstract might be able to be modified in the light of experience without changing the machine... [The] Robinson amply satisfied the demands for flexibility, and there can be little doubt that the opportunities it gave for trying new techniques at this crucial stage played a decisive role in the later success of Colossus.'[22] Although the Robinson, and later Colossus, were special-purpose machines, designed primarily for decrypting Fish messages, they were also intended to be capable of fulfilling that purpose in different ways, Colossus even more so than the Robinson. (In fact, the double tape-bed provided for a later version of the Robinson, known as Super-Robinson, gave it a flexibility for certain jobs, such as running depths and cribs, which Colossus lacked.)

The first Robinson to be built – not surprisingly, as it was built in three parts at two different sites for operation at a third – was a something of a lash-up and its name was extended to Heath Robinson, after the ludicrous imaginative machines drawn by the cartoonist of that name. The first versions of both the Robinson and new Tunny analogue machines were delivered in June 1943. When all the parts were finally delivered, wired together and run for the first time, the tension must have been palpable. And there must have been a good deal of satisfaction given what transpired. Newman was able to report to Travis on 18 June 1943, 'The second instalment of the Post Office machinery, the scanning apparatus, arrived on Monday, the 14th. The first adjustments were completed by Tuesday evening. On Wednesday the Chi wheels of a known message were set, the results agreeing with those already obtained by hand.'[23]

However, the following tests were not all quite so successful. 'On attempting to carry the process further (motor-setting, Psi-wheel settings) on Thursday evening and Friday, completely discordant results were obtained. After running some other pairs of Chi wheels I had one of the original pairs run again, and it was found that the results did not agree with the former ones. Which part of the machinery has gone out of adjustment is not yet clear.' In retrospect, it can be seen that, of course, it would be perfectly possible to make machines perform repetitive adding and counting tasks. But that is hindsight which was not available to Newman, Travis and others involved at the time. Certainly, they had faith in the concept. Theoretically, it was possible to get a machine to do masses of calculations in sequence, but could it be done without everything getting out of sequence at high speeds? Was it really practicable to co-ordinate so many circuits and so many technologies? The difficulties of what they were trying to do were all too apparent.

The biggest concern was not the electronic circuits, but the peripherals, in particular the tape-reading or scanning sub-system. This had to be high speed for the calculations to be performed in a practical time, but it had to use fragile technology of paper to get the information to be processed into the machine. Newman reported to Travis,

Such initial troubles are, of course, entirely natural, and I should expect them to go on for some weeks. (The tape-punching machinery has so far given only about one correct tape in three, which slows down our tests a great deal.) But while these troubles give no cause for surprise or alarm, there are strong reasons for not going ahead until it has definitely been shown that they can be cleared up. The whole process is based on the assumption that the mechanical scan, plus count, will be absolutely reliable, with only very occasional lapses. Frequent mistakes would multiply the setting time not by two, but by five or more, since one would have to go round and round testing the counts (not to mention time out for adjustments); and in addition this would have a demoralizing effect on a process entirely based on probabilities. The standard we are asking for is extraordinarily high. For example, on the tape-punching machine, what is now happening is that a single extra character is sometimes punched in a tape 2,000 letters long. This is only discovered at the end, and the tape must then be thrown away. This means that each individual [Chi-]wheel is slipping about once in 5,000 times it moves, a very low error, but fatal for us.[24]

The initial problems made life uncomfortable for Newman. One thing that he 'was very put out about' was that repeated runs with the same tape produced different results – whereas, if the machine worked perfectly, all runs using the same two paper tapes should have produced identical results.[25] Thus, Newman, who had undertaken the enormous amount of work and persuasion necessary to get the project authorized and the machine built, came under considerable pressure to produce results, though he remained determined and confident. 'Somewhat premature attempts were made to use it operationally', but this had to wait until staff in the Newmanry, including the Wrens, worked overtime in the evenings to do the research needed to prepare for the machine to be used effectively. According to Jack Good, one of the key people who worked out the statistics needed to produce good results, these initial problems meant that 'the future of the Newmanry was in jeopardy'.[26]

Although the tests showed up many problems, they also proved the concept. A machine was indeed possible. Newman concluded, 'It is already clear that the general arrangement has been well thought out, and that use of the [partly electronic] counters is easily taught. I am getting the Wren operators to work at once, so that we may get evidence as soon as possible on the approximate setting times, and the number of operators required.'[27] And the need for Fish-decryption capabilities was becoming urgent. The Allies were just about to launch the invasion of Sicily and a new Fish link, Bream, between Berlin and Rome had come into use. The content of messages carried on the link were to play a vital role in the allied invasion of Italy.

There was some disagreement within the Newmanry about how best to use the machine. Before it could be used to best effect, it would be necessary to devote a lot of time to analysing cipher, plain and key texts to amass the statistics needed for working out what would be a statistically significant count. But Newman had to prove that the time and resources invested in his idea would produce decrypts of immediate intelligence value. Donald Michie recorded:

> When the first Robinson became operational, Jack Good and I spent our day shift in frontal assault [amassing statistics], with Max pacing around for positive results to announce. Although he agreed in theory with our argument that pure recon-naissance of the problem should be the first use of the newly operational machine, the need for credibility, with high-ranking

military and others dropping in to see what results were being got, pressed him sorely. Once he had laid it down, Max Newman was not someone that a person in his senses would continue to oppose. From nine to six each day, Jack and I accordingly went through the motions. But many evenings were spent in a clandestine ghost shift, with one or two volunteer Wrens and an engineer... With the aid of Heath Robinson and our volunteer assistants we systematically extracted from Testery decrypts batteries of general rules governing the statistico-logical structure of military German... Armed with these tabulations, statistical summaries and empirical rules we were now in a position to make frontal assaults in earnest. This yielded sufficient operational success for Max Newman to announce feasibility. I doubt if he ever knew of the clandestine operation.[28]

Newman's section was initially small – consisting of Good, Michie, two engineers and sixteen Wrens, all of whom were housed in a one- or two-room hut for several months. After two or three months, however, the machines were helping the Fish section to set two or three messages a week using the statistical determination of the Chi-wheel settings. By the end of the war, there would be twenty-six cryptographers, twenty-eight engineers, 273 Wrens, ten Colossi, three Robinsons, three Tunnies and twenty smaller electronic and electrical machines, setting hundreds of messages a week. But, before that could happen, the modest team had to overcome the problems they faced in using the first Robinson.

Not all the problems were with the actual machine. Later, it was realized that one problem was the high rate of errors in the punched paper tapes. A wide range of testing routines was developed that reduced the troublesome runs (see Chapter nineteen) but initially the need for such checking was overlooked and any errors were blamed on the machine itself rather than the organization of the simpler stages in the process. Another issue was slides – spurious characters in the intercepted cipher text that passed the slip-readers. And there was a high rate of mistakes made by the operators in setting up each run. 'The standard of accuracy needed before there was any possibility of success was very much higher than would ordinarily be required of this kind of apparatus or of operators. A single letter omitted in error in a tape destroyed the value of the run and the ordinary length of a tape was about 3,000 letters… An error which passed undetected through several stages of the work could take hours or even days to track down.'[29] The checks eventually became so comprehensive that, in the machine operations rooms, they constituted about half of the time worked by the operators.

But the biggest headaches came from the machine itself. There were problems affecting all its parts: input, processing and output. The optical reader was found to create corrupted units if it was presented with a long run of either adjacent crosses or dots. This meant that the input tapes had to be manipulated to remove any such long runs. The logic circuits were not always very reliable, giving false counts, so making it difficult to distinguish between the correct setting and incorrect ones. And initially the machine was designed with a lamp panel from which the results had to be read or, more accurately, interpreted by an operator and written down. This proved to be a major cause of error and had to be replaced with a printer, though even this was not very effective.[30]

The major problem was synchronizing the two tapes. They had to run at an extremely high speed if the machine-based technique was to work in any reasonable timescale, otherwise it would simply take too long to do all the calculations. But, in an age when teleprinter tapes were expected to work at no more than a couple of hundred characters a second, it proved to be impossible to keep the two tapes in step at speeds greater than 1,000 characters per second. Yet even that was not anything like fast enough to cope with all the operations that would be needed in a practical machine. At first, the tapes were driven by motors that engaged metal teeth in sprocket holes in the tape, but these ripped the tape to shreds at higher speeds. So then friction drives were tried instead that pulled the tape between rollers. Even so, the tape stretched under pressure and accurate reading was difficult to achieve. The Robinson's weakness was not the high-tech parts, the electronic valves (although there were problems with the counters), but in how the data was to be got into the machine from the two tapes. The fundamental restraining factor lay in trying to make paper-tape technology, which had been designed to work in step with electro-magnetic relays, match the much greater speed of electronic valves.

Nevertheless, the problems did not stop the machine being used to test and discover the Chi settings of intercepted messages: 'Towards the end of 1943, the pressure for a large production by machine methods had grown, for two main reasons. The Tunny network [i.e. the network of links using the Lorenz cipher machine] had grown, the value of the contents had raised the traffic to the highest level, and the tightening up of German precautions against depths had caused production by hand setting to sink almost to zero. The introduction of one new technique at the end of 1943 made depth-reading impossible. Twelve Robinsons were ordered in the late summer of 1943, and the first factory model arrived in November just in time for the move to more adequate quarters in Block F. The original pilot model, which was by this time completely worn out, was thereupon abandoned.'[31]

Two or three months after the Robinson was first delivered, the Newmanry was able to set two or three messages a week. It was a small start, but a start nonetheless. And it was to lead to greater successes. Eventually, in the week ending 31 March 1945, 358 messages on Chi and 151 on motors and Psis were set and twenty-three new sets of wheels were to be broken on Newman's by now vast array of machines.[32]

But in 1943 it was clear that continued progress would depend on constant improvement and adaptability. In August, just as the first Robinson was settling in, the German army extended the use of one security measure, known as a limitation, which complicated the movements of the Psi wheels; another type of limitation affected the turning of the motor wheels. Both demanded extra processing and more machine time. Newman observed that the latter measure in particular 'worked against us. These two features are not enough to keep us out, but they do remove any margin for error.' Even errors by operators in the Newmanry were not sufficient to stop decryption:'Mistakes do not, however, prevent the possible messages from being got out in the end, since the effect of a mistake becomes clear at some later stage.'[33] However, this only happened after much operator effort and scarce machine time had been wasted. It was also taking time both to develop effective working methods and to build up a body of statistics which would offer up new insights. Ineffective working practices caused problems and delays which had to be identified. Something as simple as a paper tape being put on the machine the wrong way round could ruin a run, and so rigorous testing procedures and working routines had to be developed, all of which took valuable time and effort. (Appendix G lists problems identified and recorded during the Heath Robinson period that were not faults with the machine itself, but did stop it doing its job properly.)

The order for extra Robinsons was increased to twenty, although only a few were delivered by the end of the war. Four old Robinsons were delivered at the rate of one a month in late 1943 and early 1944, and two Super-Robinsons were delivered by the end of the war (one of which could handle up to four paper tapes at a time). Nicknamed Peter Robinson and Robinson and Cleaver after two London department stores, these new versions of the Robinson incorporated significant improvements but, even so, it took a painfully long time to break or set the wheels. A post-war review of GC&CS's operations noted that in 1943 the amount of Fish traffic that was intercepted had doubled in volume, while the output of decodes had fallen by 26 per cent. The Fish operation was averaging 330 decodes a month at the beginning of the year, but only an average of 244 by its end.[34] As it was, attention was diverted in late 1943 to the prospect of a different machine that was being developed at the Post Office Research Establishment – where the engineers, led by Flowers, had, in fact, been getting on with that mammoth electronic machine they had originally proposed but had had rejected by Bletchley Park in place of the Robinson.

The first Robinson had proved two things: first, that it would be possible to find the correct Chi settings by focused application of mathematical brute force; and, second, that the current machine techniques were inadequate to the size of the task given the time that was available. According to Max Newman, it was obvious by September 1943 that a faster machine was needed.[35] In October 1943, Newman had his first meeting with Flowers about the alternative machine he was developing. It was fortunate that the engineers at the Post Office had carried on developing their idea, for now the delivery date for that new machine, Colossus, was actually drawing close. And where a Robinson might be able to set one or two messages in a day, a Colossus was expected to set fifteen. Decoding Fish might still become a practical proposition.

chapter fifteen

Inventing the Electronic Computing Machine

According to the French writer Georges Ifrah, the author of a comprehensive study of the world's numbering systems, 'There is no doubt that the advent and growth of the electronic calculator was one of the defining events of the twentieth century.'[1] After many years of secrecy, it is now possible to piece together the circumstances in which that defining technology was first deployed. The world's first large-scale electronic computing machine was invented in 1943 by a British Post Office engineer as an alternative to the Robinson. The limitations of the Robinsons, despite their undoubted usefulness, had presented the Newmanry with a serious crisis. The rapid increase in the number of German wireless links using the Geheimschreiber for encrypting messages, and the extra security measures that were also introduced, placed ever greater demands on the machines. And they simply could not cope. The decision of the Post Office to go ahead with Flowers's proposal for a colossal electronic machine, even though Bletchley Park managers had originally dismissed it as a potential solution, was the saving of the Newmanry.[2]

'Tommy' Flowers was born in 1905, a working-class boy, son of a bricklayer from East Ham, then to the east of London. His interest in, and talent for, science and mechanics soon became apparent. He won a scholarship to a local technical college, and in the early

1920s he came first in an open competition for jobs as trainee telephone engineers. The Post Office was then planning to install automatic switching equipment in the British telephone network and needed to expand its engineering staff. Flowers was quickly identified as a highly talented youngster with a particularly good theoretical understanding – gained at night school in study at home, for, as Flowers recalled in later life, the Post Office failed in its promise to give him theoretical training. His talents led him in 1930 to Dollis Hill, North London, where the Post Office Research Establishment was located.[3] His sound theoretical knowledge and methodical approach to problem solving made him a likely candidate for work on advanced technology. He was assigned to a project that was attempting to overcome a problem then holding back the automatic dialling of telephone calls over long distances. According to Flowers, 'the engineer working on the project wasn't getting anywhere – and that's because he wasn't any good.'[4] After the traditional solution to the problem of an underperformer in a bureaucratic organization – promotion – had cleared his boss out of the way, the rising young engineer set about solving the problem.

The issue was not transmitting the voice signal itself. That could be amplified indefinitely. The trouble lay with the dialled pulses, generated by the dial on the telephone set, that were needed to signal the telephone number being called to the distant exchange equipment. The type of electrical current used for the pulses could not be transmitted more than about forty miles. Flowers solved the problem by introducing electronic valves. He devised a technique whereby the pulses were converted to a current similar to the voice signal, which could then be amplified and re-amplified to cover greater distances. As he himself later pointed out, he was not the first person to conceive of such a solution – engineers in the USA, the Netherlands and Switzerland had already adopted electronic valves for the same application a year or two earlier. But he had been unaware of what had been done elsewhere and he effectively transformed himself into an early pioneer of electronics

245

in telephone applications. This was an application of electronics to telecommunications transmission using valves as amplifiers. Later, in the mid- and late 1930s, Flowers also started working on the use of electronics in telecommunications control and switching circuits deploying valves as switches, a quite new and untested concept. 'From 1935 onward I was exploring the uses of electronics in telephone exchanges. By 1939, I felt able to prove what up to then I could only suspect: that an electronic equivalent could be made of any electro-mechanical switch or data-processing machine. I well remember the elation I felt when I reached that point because it meant that not just parts of a telephone exchange could be electronic – complete exchanges could.'[5]

In his pre-war work developing new techniques and devices for automatic switching, Flowers consciously used theoretical approaches to problem solving. Later, he would compare designing control circuits for automatic telephone switching with modern computing programming: 'Very often when a device under development didn't work properly... it was usually because of the circuit – what is now the program.'[6] In the 1930s, theoreticians and advanced engineers such as Turing, Shannon and Reeves had started to draw upon and formalize the congruence between two-state switching devices, and between logic and binary, advancing both theory and practice. Shannon showed how control and switching circuit design could employ defined sets of relays that, wired together, would produce the desired result – connecting the circuits for a telephone call, for example. The relays and wiring needed for a particular new device would often be made up of standard sets. These standard sets could be specified in a formal shorthand fashion – an algebra – instead of in excessively complex electrical-wiring diagrams. The algebra can then be transformed into physical design in standard ways. This alegbra could, indeed, look very much like post-war scientific computer programming languages. It is in that sense that Flowers rightly compares his practice of structured circuit design with the modern profession of computer programming carried out by software engineers when designing processing systems and using low-level computer languages.[7]

A similar development could also be observed in other areas. Logicians and mathematicians – people such as Kurt Goedel, a brilliant but unbalanced German mathematician whose speculations on 'undecidability' set Alan Turing on the path towards his theoretical specification of a universal machine in the 1930s – were using similar mathematical languages to explore their understanding of their own subject. 'Someone knowledgeable about modern programming languages today looking at Goedel's paper on "undecidability" written in 1930 will see a sequence of forty-five numbered formulas that looks very much like a computer program,' writes a modern professor of computer logic.[8] 'The resemblance is no accident... Goedel had to deal with many of the same issues that those designing computer languages and those writing programs in them would be facing.' Nor was it an accident that Flowers and other telecommunications research engineers were using similar techniques, even if for less cerebral applications.

The problems the Newmanry was encountering with the tapes on the Robinsons called for someone with Flowers's originality and creativeness. Flowers had first come into contact with Bletchley Park perhaps as early as 1939, when Gordon Radley, the director of the Research Establishment at Dollis Hill, asked him to visit Alan Turing. Radley and Flowers were the first Post Office engineers allowed to know the Enigma secret. Flowers was asked to help create an electro-magnetic machine for use with Enigma messages, possibly a machine designed to drag a simple crib, a likely word or phrase, such as EINS through an enciphered message. But the machine became redundant even while Flowers was working on it, and it never went into service. Later in life, Flowers suggested that Bletchley Park wanted a small device, but that he had created a monster, using high-quality telecommunications relays. He had automatically adopted the telecommunications engineer's approach of building a robust machine that worked reliably and non-stop. Despite the fact that the machine was not used, Flowers made an impression on those with whom he came into contact, especially Alan Turing, a leading figure in the development of the Bombe, who even visited Dollis Hill for the occasional meeting. Flowers, however, did not always make a positive impression and certainly not on another key figure, Gordon Welchman.

Another telecommunications engineer, Sidney Broadhurst, was also called into help Flowers develop the Enigma machine. Broadhurst had started his working life as an apprentice on the South-East and Chatham Railway and took a job as a labourer with the Post Office while looking for a 'proper' job as an engineer. Again, his talents were spotted and he was promoted to working on automatic telephone exchanges and then to teaching trainee engineers how to work with this complex new technology. Later, he was sent to the Research Department, joining Flowers's team. He worked on radar for the first eighteen months of the war as well as being brought into the select group who were informed about Bletchley Park.

The work at Bletchley Park had to be kept entirely secret. Flowers normally had little contact with Radley, only reporting to him via a head of division. But this head of division was not brought in on the secret, and from then on Flowers reported directly to Radley. Flowers had already had some experience of the awkward consequences that could arise from the need to keep quiet about war work. Before the war started, Flowers had been involved in various projects, including the development of radar. However, he was also called in to help with the data-handling aspects of a project aimed at building an 'electro-mechanical digital device for anti-aircraft ranging'. The problem was that the device was part of an attempt to develop early-warning systems using massive concrete reflectors on the southern coast of England to detect sound waves generated by approaching aircraft.[9] But because of security restrictions, Flowers could not tell those working on the project that electronic radar was going to make their work redundant.[10]

After the abortive work on the machine for the Enigma decryption work, Flowers was next called upon to help with one of the various solutions being sought to counter the introduction by the German navy of a fourth wheel to the Enigma machines they used, including for communications with U-boats. Towards the end of 1941 Wynn Williams, who later designed the electronic counters for the Robinsons (see previous chapter), had been called in 'as one of the leading experts on high speed work with [electronic] valves' according to a report by Gordon Welchman who played a key role in the development and operation of the Bombes.[11] Wynn Williams conceived of a solution using a standard three-wheel Bombe with two new attachments, a device known as a commutator and an electronic valve 'sensing' unit to simulate a fourth wheel, and he set about developing prototypes in early 1942. This solution was code-named Cobra. Around the same time, BTM, which manufactured the three-wheel Bombes, was also told about the four-wheel Enigma problem and its chief engineer, Harold 'Doc' Keen, soon came up with a design for a fully electro-mechanical solution using slower 'relay sensing', later known as Mammoth. This BTM idea was regarded as a 'second string' in case the preferred option of Wynn Williams's semi-electronic approach failed. However, Welchman soon reported that 'it is now clear that Dr. Wynn Williams was badly let down by his engineering advisers and by the [TRE] workshops in which the first prototype Cobra was built. He [Wynn Williams] was led to believe that the sensing was the key to the problem, whereas all subsequent (and previous) experience has shown that sensing is comparatively trivial, whereas the real difficulties are mechanical.'[12] All the same, GC&CS pushed on with Cobra as well as the BTM's solution, so pressing was the need to address the naval Enigma problem. Production of various sub-systems of thirty-six

Cobras were contracted out. The commutators were to be made by a private company, Mawdsleys, while the obvious place to make the electronic valve sensing units was at Dollis Hill, and the natural choice to take charge was their leading electronics expert, Tom Flowers.

As Welchman later reported, 'Things did not go according to plan.' The TRE's prototype part of the system encountered many difficulties and Wynn Williams was unable to test his full valve-sensing unit, though Welchman later claimed that 'all the tests he was able to do tended to show that it would do its job'. There were problems too with the electric brushes used on the high-speed commutators. But, according to Welchman, it was Flowers who created the greatest difficulty: 'Instead of putting the Wynn Williams valve sensing unit into production, Mr. Flowers of Dollis Hill insisted on producing a design of his own, which was not approved by Dr. Wynn Williams.' This led to a prolonged and rather bitter dispute between Wynn Williams and Welchman on one side, and Flowers and Radley on the other. The row initially centred around whether Wynn Williams's design would have worked, but soon Flowers's redesign became the focus of dissent, before Flowers's predilection for using scarce valves for any and all problems fuelled further disagreement.

The production of the valve-sensing unit was not the main reason for the delay in producing the first Cobra. As Welchman noted, 'By the end of September 1942 I was very seriously concerned, and was inclined to believe that Mawdsleys Cobra would never overcome brush bounce.' Therefore, Welchman considered a hybrid using Wynn Williams's valve-sensing unit and BTM machines (though not, at the time, using Mammoth which was thought likely to be too slow). A month later and Welchman had concluded that 'reliability, adaptability and standardization' were actually more important than raw speed. 'Valves will operate faster than relays, but, apart from this disadvantage, relays are on the whole more suitable than valves for most forms of sensing,' he concluded.[13] This led Welchman to back yet another option: to concentrate on BTM's electro-mechanical monster, Mammoth. Relays were a known, proven technology, whereas electronic valves were risky and un-proven. This decision made redundant both Wynn Williams's original valve-sensing concept and Flowers's suggested revamp of it. Owing to technical difficulties and design-specification changes, the first BTM Mammoth was only delivered in February 1943 – and, in any case, in December 1942 it had been discovered that it was possible to break the Enigma Shark ciphers using a three-wheel Bombe. Nevertheless, there were lots of uses to which a four-wheel Bombe could be put.

Travis, CG&GS's director, agreed with Radley that the Dollis Hill engineers should still go ahead and build their valve-sensing unit in case the relay-sensing unit was inadequate. He also agreed to allocate one of the first Mammoths to be used for a thorough testing of the valve-sensing unit. These tests were to prove detri-mental to Flowers and Welchman's uneasy relationship. The Post Office engineers were accused of tampering with and damaging the Mammoth they had been lent. Personal animosity began to exacerbate the situation, and Welchman chose to back Wynn Williams's skill and expertise over that of Flowers. Accordingly, Welchman saw little need to spare Bombe or Mammoth time to test a valve-sensing unit which he believed would not be used. Welchman conceded that his changing policies about which technical solution to follow had left Flowers and his team in a difficult position where they had 'little to do but wait', but he expected the Post Office engineers to accept this without rancour. Not surprisingly, 'This situation, dragging on as it did for months, was an unhappy one for Mr. Flowers.'[14]

Flowers and Radley were reluctant to see their work ignored, and Radley complained to Travis, while Flowers denounced BTM's high-speed relay-sensing device as inferior to those made by Post Office engineers. Flowers fervently argued the case for using electronics, based on his understanding of the potential of valves to replace the much slower relays as switching devices. It became a matter of technical pride and partisanship. As Welchman reported, 'Mr. Flowers also remarked that Mr. Keen and I were determined to use relays "at all costs".' Later at another meeting, Flowers, according to Welchman, 'said with some heat that Mr. Keen should not have been allowed to "get away with it". (I feel that the use of the phase "get away with it" is significant, as it gives some insight into Mr. Flowers' own attitude to the matter). This was followed by a violent attack on Mr. Keen. The BTM machine was badly designed, Mr. Keen created his own problems, and Mr. Flowers could not understand how anyone could have done the things that Mr. Keen had done. It was a scandal that after 15 months BTM had not got a machine running.'[15]

Unfortunately, there are reports from only one side of this dispute. Yet it seems clear that the Post Office engineers were desperate to play a more significant part in the work of GC&CS, sensing that they had a collective expertise lacked by the other organisations, both governmental, such as the TRE, and private, such as BTM and Mawdsleys. Yet the assertion of their technological superiority clearly upset many people. As Welchman reported, 'Dr. Wynn Williams has found it difficult to get on with the Dollis Hill people, and feels that Mr. Flowers' idea of co-operation is to run things himself… It may be that Mr. Flowers honestly thinks that he is better able than Mr. Keen, Dr. Wynn Williams and myself to direct the policy of Bombe production, but, if so, I am quite sure he is wrong. He is probably very good at his ordinary work, and also at designing apparatus for a definite problem that he can understand, but I have found him very slow at grasping the complications of our work and his mind seems to be altogether too inflexible.' Indeed, Welchman insisted that Flowers was not very good with electronics. He reported that he had spoken to Wynn Williams who said that 'he had had continual difficulties with Dollis Hill and does not approve of Flowers' work on technical grounds. I feel sure that on valve gear Wynn Williams is the better man and I am sorry now that we have not given him more support. He has been proved right and Flowers wrong over several technical matters.'[16]

This was potentially damning enough, but Welchman went further and tried to get Radley and Flowers reprimanded for excessive use of scarce electronic valves. He visited a Mr McLaren of the Admiralty supply division, based at Bath, to gather evidence against the Dollis Hill engineers.

> I also wanted to find out the truth about the valve supply situation, because Mr. Flowers does not seem to mind how many valves he uses, while BTM are being urged by the Admiralty to use as few valves as possible. Mr. McLaren said at once, apart from all other considerations, we should certainly use relays instead of valves if we possibly can because of the serous shortage of valves. He said that Dr. Radley must know this perfectly well. He took a very serious view of the reckless use of valves by Mr. Flowers, and said that the Post Office could be very seriously reprimanded for this offence, if it could be established... He [Radley] might have informed us [Bletchley Park] of the acute shortage of valves instead of encouraging Flowers to squander them... The influence of Dr. Radley and Mr. Flowers must be completely removed.

In retrospect, it is fortunate that Welchman's recommendations were not implemented or Colossus may never have been developed. It is also clear that Welchman's judgement on Flowers's technical skills was wholly inaccurate.

Despite such enemies, Radley and Flowers were re-called, and this time it was to redesign another of Wynn Williams's machines – the electronic counting device used on the Robinson.

Flowers was first made aware of the Geheimschreiber when he was called in to help redesign Wynn Williams's electronic counter on the Robinson.[17] But Flowers saw that there was a bigger problem than just the counter – synchronizing the two tapes. And, just as he had done earlier in his career with the problem of transmitting dialling pulses, Flowers both located the problem and conceived of an audacious solution. Once again, he decided that electronic devices were the answer – but in this case his solution would need a substantial number of closely co-ordinated electronic devices. 'With diminishing prospects of success, some new ideas began to be urgently sought. At this point I realized that my pre-war work pointed to a solution… that was simple in principle although it might be difficult to put into practice. It was not the paper tape that was essential, but the data on the tape. All that the [Chi settings] tape was doing was storing pre-generated data so that they could be read into an electronic process at a much higher speed. An electronic equivalent of the machine that had originally generated the data – and I had no doubt that such an equivalent could be made – could work fast enough to issue the data directly to the processor.'[18]

Flowers would recall that, on the Robinson, '[T]hey could drive the tapes up to 2,000 characters per second, but that was not fast enough – it would take many hours to solve problems. They wanted speeds up to 20,000 characters per second – which was fantastic at that time, it seemed to be impossible, but we did it in the end. I quickly came to the conclusion that Robinson would never be any good and we were wasting our time on it, so I thought up something different. Before the war, I had been working on thermionic valves for switches instead of mechanical relays. I was convinced that we could get up to very high speeds and it would be very reliable. I worked out how to use this technology. Of course, there was no one else in the world using this technology and that's what made it so difficult for me to explain to Bletchley Park because they didn't have any experience to guide them.'[19]

His initial idea was to replace both tapes with electronically generated patterns representing the Chi setting and enciphered text streams that were to be processed. This would eliminate the technical problems caused by the mechanical stage of tape-reading. But it would demand a vast number of electronic valves. No such machine had been envisaged before, and it constituted a major step beyond using electronics in a few logic circuits or to store a few dialled pulses before transmission. It would take control circuitry to a level not previously considered practical. The telecommunication engineers who installed the automatic telephone networks with long-distance dialling considered that they had constructed the world's most complicated machine. But the same telecommunications industry was about to launch a machine of much greater complexity.

The idea of dispensing with both tapes and generating them electronically was rapidly dismissed as impractical, given the time and effort that would be involved in plugging up the machine, 'setting up', for each enciphered message.[20] But the Chi settings would be predictable as they would be applicable for every message using the same pattern of raised/flush pins, so it did make sense to generate them internally. The enciphered text, which differed for every message, would still be read in mechanically. Having only one tape meant that it was no longer necessary to synchronize two tapes, so it would also be possible to avoid using the sprocket-hole drive mechanism which shredded the paper tape. Instead, two drive wheels were to pull the tape past the reader by pressure. This meant that the tape could then be passed through more quickly without being ripped to bits. And the now redundant sprocket holes in the paper tape could be used for timing purposes.

When Flowers put forward his proposal, he was disappointed by Bletchley Park's initial reaction. First, there were concerns about the reliability of electronic valves, which had a reputation for being fragile and failing all too easily. The design for Colossus would call for some 1,500 valves, a massive number compared with the hundred used in the Robinson. Valves were seen as far too difficult to handle in the large numbers that would be needed for Flowers's design. Indeed, the design chosen by Wynn Williams for the electronic combining unit in the Robinsons was dictated by the policy of using the minimum number of valves possible. Newman was supportive of Flowers and his design, but he was overruled, as resources were scarce and senior figures were not convinced that electronics devices were reliable.[21] Welchman had certainly resisted the idea of using electronics instead of high-speed relays for the naval Enigma problem and initially his scepticism was shared by senior managers. Looking back in the mid-1970s, Max Newman wrote, 'Flowers's insistence on massive use of valves in face of incredulity was crucial [to the] decision.'[22] According to Flowers, 'If you had them in a radio set which you carried about and they got knocked about, they don't last long, but if they are kept still and are never switched off, they'll go on for ever. I'd been using large numbers of them in switches and I knew that, but they wouldn't believe it.'[23]

But Flowers failed to convince the decision-makers at Bletchley Park. The dispute over valve sensing for the four-wheel Bombes had clearly soured relations, but not enough for Travis, the director of GC&CS, to sever ties. His opinion of the Dollis Hill engineers must have been more positive than that of Welchman and his colleagues. Clearly he was prepared to place a lot more trust in their capabilities to understand what GC&CS was doing and how machines could help than Welchman. Also Flowers got on well with Turing and his support for Flowers's capabilities – contrary to Welchman's harsh judgement – may well have impressed Travis. But, initially, Flowers failed once again to persuade the powers at GC&CS to back his electronic approach.[24]

Another factor that worked against Flowers's design was the urgency with which the codebreakers needed to tackle the Fish-decryption task, as the number of links increased rapidly in 1943. 'I told them it would take a year to build the first machine. They said "in that time the war could be over and be lost," so they decided to go on with the Robinsons. That was what really put them against it, the idea of the electronic machine, the time it would take to build.

They didn't commission me, they said, if you feel like it, that's up to you. So we said, we'll do it.'[25] The Post Office engineers concluded that the war was not going to be over in such a short time and that they could well finish their machine before the fighting was finished, whatever the intelligence experts at Bletchley Park thought about it.

What happened next was perhaps one of the most courageous and far-sighted decisions to be made within the British information technology and telecommunications industries in the twentieth century. Gordon Radley, the head of the Research Establishment, and his boss, Sir Stanley Angwin, the Engineer in Chief at the Post Office, took the decision to go ahead and create Flowers's concept of an entirely different machine, even without Bletchley Park's formal backing. Their decision meant giving Flowers significant resources in terms of staffing and materials (although this did not stop Flowers having to dip into his own pocket to buy various necessary items). The demands of the war for telecommunications personnel meant that engineers, at both the research and workshop levels, were in desperately short supply. The records in the National Archives from Bletchley Park contain repeated correspondence between the Post Office, Cable & Wireless, GC&CS and the armed services over the allocation of skilled staff. Yet Radley took the decision to divert a significant number of engineers to Flowers's project, with no guarantee that it would work or even that it would ever be used by Bletchley Park, guided only by his faith in Flowers's proven theoretical and practical expertise. By this time, Dollis Hill's entire workload was devoted to the war, as it handled projects for GC&CS and the TRE, the radar establishment, as well as the services and the government. No doubt, senior managers at GC&CS must have concurred with Radley's decision, but it is important to recognize the significance of his backing for Flowers. Immediately after the war, Radley was knighted, while Flowers – much to his annoyance – was only to receive an OBE and that not until the 1990s. Yet, without Radley's decision, Colossus may well not have come into being, and so his was a fundamental contribution to the story of Colossus. Another related point can be made here. Above Max Newman and Gordon Welchman in the Bletchley Park hierarchy there were probably very few who really understood the machines and techniques that Welchman's and Newman's departments were devising. Once again, it was a matter of faith, of the trust which the managers had in their mathematicians and engineers.

Flowers set about the task as quickly as he could, aided by a team of up to fifteen engineers at Dollis Hill and forty-odd technicians from a Post Office factory in Birmingham – the latter having no idea of what sort of machine they were working on. Sidney Broadhurst and William 'Bill' Chandler, another maintenance engineer, played key roles in the overall design and development of Colossus. A colleague recalled that both Broadhurst and Flowers 'were the sort of men who could at the drop of a hat design highly complicated relay circuits to perform any operation required – and to get it right first time.'[26] Allan Coombs joined the project as Colossus was nearing completion and eventually became one of the chief engineers working on Colossus. 'I was enrolled in the Colossus team in about September 1943, having until then been engaged in frustrating the knavish tricks of His Majesty's enemies (as we say in our national anthem) in other and rather less interesting ways.' Initially he was set to work on the Robinson, but soon joined those developing Colossus and eventually ended up in charge of the production and manufacture of the later Colossi. He later wrote, 'The team set out to design and build large machines of a totally novel form in minimal time, inspired by the firm belief that this could be done, that it was the right thing to do, and that by guess or by God we were the right people to do it.'[27]

Flowers continued to work on refining the Robinson alongside his work on Colossus, but increasingly he concentrated on his idea for an electronic machine. He drew a number of square boxes, allocated functions to them, drew lines joining up the boxes to show their connections and then converted the functional outline into the circuitry and other components it all needed. As Appendix H shows, the basic functional divisions of Colossus were similar to those of the Robinson, looking if anything less complex, except for the addition of the box labelled 'Timing and Master Control'. When one begins to peer inside the outline functional boxes, it becomes clear that this was a considerably more complex machine, not least through the addition of that master control sub-system that instructed the various components what to do next. The clock sub-system within the master control unit was essential, sending out signals to the components keeping them all in step. The currents in an electronic computer are in constant flow moving 'bits' from one component to another in a cycle. If all the bits do not get to the right components at exactly the right time, the machine will not work properly, corruption will occur and the output will be meaningless. This concept of clock pulse synchronization was central to the later design of post-war computers, but was first conceived for Colossus. Indeed, Colossus had a feature which later computers lacked – the clock pulses were generated by the redundant sprocket holes in the paper tape. By slowing down the tape, the speed at which Colossus worked was also slowed down, so that an engineer could isolate when and where that a problem occurred in a particular process.

The extra functional complexity of Colossus was needed to marshal the electronic bits through the machine in step with each other and also through the complex wiring and array of other components. According to Coombs, they consciously jettisoned the philosophy of minimizing the use of electronics that had characterized the approach to the Robinson. He pointed out that, in fact, the Robinson's 'switching logic was not performed by the valves at all, but by rectifiers of ring modulator', with the valves being only a part of the circuitry, not the actual switch. 'In theory, the [Robinson

switching logic] circuit was ingenious; in practice it was a night-
mare' and needed careful adjustment.[28] For Colossus, the logic and
the ring counters were redesigned exploiting valves for their
advantages of fast, repeated switching operations and other
functions. As Coombs put it, 'This clearly implied a readiness to
multiply the number of valves, contrary to established practice.'[29]

Flowers also decided that the machine needed flexibility in its
logic unit, and with good reason. The Vernam cipher rules are only
one way in which binary units can be combined. These and other
sets of rules are variations of logical operations. The Vernam rules
are known theoretically as 'exclusive-or'; two other key sets of rules
are known as 'AND' and 'OR'. These alternative sets of rules for
combining units could be used in other routines developed by the
cryptographers later on. They enabled the operator to choose
different combining rules so that far more routines could be performed than merely the straightforward Vernam cipher processes
needed for the standard double-delta test. These logical operations
became the basic building blocks of post-war electronic computers. They effectively gave Colossus a form of basic programming, as the logic system could be set up by the operator to
perform the range of different processing routines developed at
Bletchley Park for statistical decryption of Fish messages in addition
to the standard double-delta test.

An account of Colossus 1 was written in 1975 by D C Horwood, a
Newmanry veteran still employed at GCHQ, the post-war successor
to GC&CS. It followed a letter from Professor Brian Randell of
Newcastle University to the then British prime minister when news
of Colossus first became public. Horwood's report was written in
response to Randell's letter and in the author's words, 'To facilitate
its release it has been written so far as possible in such a way as to
attract the lowest level of [secrecy] classification[30] with no details of
the type of cipher or the decryption technique being included – but
despite that it was held secret until August 2003 when it was finally
released to the public at the National Archives at Kew. It records that

From a technical historical point of view, probably the most interesting thing about Colossus I was the fact that it used hard valves for switching and counting on a large scale. The experience with Robinson had shown the limitations of the gas triodes then available as switching devices. In particular, it was difficult to ensure that they de-ionized in the short time available at high counting speeds and, even when they were de-ionized, some residual ionization appeared to persist, in which state they triggered more readily than was desirable. Circuits using hard valves for switching and counting had been designed prior to the outbreak of the War... [but] these techniques had not been employed previously for any form of computing process on anything like the scale on which they were used in Colossus.[31]

Fortunately, British manufacturer Mullard made a suitable hard valve offering fast switching speed and low heater power, which was important as it could be difficult to disperse the heat generated from such a large number of valves. About 1,000 of the valves to be used in the machine were to be hard valves, while the remaining 500, gas triodes, would be used for the internal bit-stream generator.[32]

This electronic bit-stream generator was at the core of Colossus's conception, and it was used to generate the Chi settings (in delta form) to be tested against the cipher text (also in delta form). These settings had been prepared on paper tape and read on the Robinson in synchronization with the cipher text on a second paper tape. Colossus also read the cipher text from the paper tape on a Bedstead. The sprocket holes in the single remaining paper tape provided the timing signals to Colossus used to generate internal clock pulses, so that everything was always in step with the data being read from the paper tape. The cipher tape also contained 'start' and 'stop' holes, which did indeed start or stop a run. But the Chi settings could now be generated internally, one after another for each character, in response to a timing signal generated by the sprocket hole which indicated that a cipher text character had been read.

The thyraton gas valves were wired into twelve ring circuits – though physically they were stacked in a row, as is shown in photographs of Colossus. There was one ring for each of the five Chi wheels, the five Psi wheels and the two motor wheels, so that a bit pattern for any of the wheels could be generated, and not just for the Chi wheels – another indication of the in-built flexibility of Colossus. (This proved to be a useful design feature, as later on the Newmanry and the Testery later developed ways of using Colossus for tasks other than identifying the Chi settings.) The Chi stream was generated as each valve in a ring was 'struck' in turn and in synchronization with the clock pulse. Whether a valve in the ring would generate a cross or a dot depended on whether it was connected to an output circuit by an external U-link. The operators inserted the appropriate U-links before a run to determine the delta-Chi pin pattern they wanted to generate. As the valves were struck a cross would be generated if a U-link had been inserted for that valve and a dot if no U-link had been inserted, thus creating the pattern of dots and crosses in the delta-Chi string, one character at a time. In the standard double-delta test, only two Chi valve rings (for units 1 and 2) would be used (the other three Chi rings would be used in subsequent tests, and the Psi and motor valve rings in Psi and motor wheel setting or wheel-breaking). As each delta-cipher character was read from the tape, the active valve in each of the two Chi valve rings would all be struck by an electric current generated by the clock pulse sub-system, generating a pair of cross and/or dot depending on whether the operator had inserted U-link or not. This is a considerable simplification of the working of the bit-stream generator and it is actually much more complex than it sounds from this account (and, indeed, it required the invention of some techniques), but this outline view will suffice for an understanding of Colossus. Indeed, much more detailed accounts could be given of all the components and sub-systems of Colossus (see Further Reading). To summarize, the operator would set up the cross/dot pattern to be generated with the U-links and the machine would do the rest, generating the delta-Chi pattern in step with the characters read from the cipher tape.

Flowers and his team also decided that the counters needed a complete redesign. One problem with the Robinson counter had been that there were too many valves packed together in too small a space; another was the difficulty of interconnecting and operating them in a single cycle. Instead, the Post Office team designed a counting system with seven valves in each bank – five representing the units between one and five, and the other two representing fives. Relays were used to decode the meaning of the valves for operators unfamiliar with non-decimal numbering. In devising such techniques of how to use electronic valves, Flowers and his colleagues pioneered techniques that would be reinvented after the war. One technique Flowers invented for this electronic logic of Colossus became known after the war as non-return to zero and was very widely used. Another particular problem at that time with wiring large numbers of electronic valves into a single unit was that the electric current became larger and larger during a machine cycle. The solution Flowers adopted to lower the current during the processing cycle was also later adopted after the war for use in the early valve-based computers. It should be emphasized, however, that, although the bit-stream generator, the counters and the logic-processing unit in Colossus were electronic, a considerable number of electro-magnetic relays were also used 'because they were the quickest and best way' to address a particular function.[33]

The design process took several shortcuts, ignoring the normal practice of spending much time in preparing detailed engineering drawings. 'I remember Flowers having made a rush draft of the projected new machine, then tearing his draft into pieces and sharing out the bits to us with the instruction to get on with it. Once completed, the designs were handed over to other engineers whose function it was to lay out the circuits for assembly on standardized plates.' The technicians who performed these tasks included the grade 'female assistants' – an indication of the shortage of skilled staff in the traditionally resolutely male world of tele-communications engineering. Led by the head of the Post Office's own factory in Birmingham, O G Belcher, eventually as many as seventy engineers and technicians were involved, fifteen of whom later transferred to Bletchley Park as maintenance engineers. Except for those who went to Bletchley, 'all these spent long hours on work of such a nature that its very purpose could not be revealed to most of them'.[34]

The heart of the modern computer lies in its data-processing and -handling capabilities. But these processes are wholly invisible. There is no cover to lift, underneath which wheels or pistons can be seen working. Early computers certainly often had lots of flash-ing lights, as did Colossus, but these were a reflection of the design ideas of the time and soon all but disappeared as more useful means of displaying results were devised. Our image of what makes up the computer is indeed largely determined by those means of display – the computer screen – and the keyboard and mouse that allow us to interact with it. Yet really the wonder of the computer lies in those invisible processes, in its logical design and the use, at the core of the machine, of components that lack moving parts – electronic valves, then transistors and later integrated circuits or chips. The physical form of a modern computer is unimpressive. Not so with Colossus. Its name reflected its physical presence and the effect this had on people. Even today, the reconstruction of Colossus 2 on display at Bletchley Park Museum is an impressive monster. The physical layout of Colossus 1 occupied two large racks two metres (about seven feet) tall and needed several square metres to house it. The later Colossi, using 2,500 valves each, were noticeably larger than Colossus 1. In operation,

Colossus was extremely noisy – the consequence not of its most modern aspects, but of its use of older traditional technologies, such as chattering electro-magnetic relays (some 800 in all, as well as 12 noisy rotary switches used to 'step' the bit-generator ring) and the whirring of the complex paper-tape tensioning system. This system of tape and pulley wheels gives Colossus the look almost of some strange machine from the industrial revolution, redolent of the belts that delivered motive power to individual machines in early factories. Indeed, the speed at which that paper tape could successfully be driven past the reading device would determine whether the data could be delivered to the processing parts of the machine fast enough to allow successful decryption. At the birth of the computer age, the engineers were constrained in what they could achieve by the cohesive strength of paper tape.

At first, said Flowers, 'we could get the speed up to 5,000 characters per second. Then one day we sat down to see how fast it could go. We took the longest tape we had and put it on the machine and then speeded it up – it got faster and faster and eventually it broke, and went all over the place, there was pandemonium, it had reached sixty miles per hour.'[35] He described the results thus: 'The various sections of tape did their best to obey Newton's first law and travel in a straight line in the direction which they happened to be going at on an initial velocity of nearly sixty miles per hour.'[36] No one was hurt, but bits of paper tape were found embedded in all sorts of odd corners throughout the laboratory. Flowers decided they had found the speed limit for a single tape: 'Being good engineers, we had to have a safety factor of two, so we kept the operating limit at 5,000 characters per second.'[37] (Colossus 2 had a form of 'parallel processing' that permitted an equivalent speed of 25,000 characters per second.)

Another physical aspect of Colossus was the external set-up capability. The U-links, which determined whether an individual valve in the bit-stream generator rings would generate a mark or a space, were inserted into external sockets by the operator in a set-up phase. There were facilities, jack fields, for determining which units were to be combined – and according to which logical rules (exclusive-or, AND, etc.). There was also a way of determining the starting position of the bit-stream generators. And it was also possible to set a threshold, or set total in the jargon used by Colossus operators, which had to be met in a count before details of a Chi setting would be printed out as a likely result on the IBM electric typewriter which acted as the output device. It is important to note that these set-up procedures were the way in which Colossus was programmed – that is, instructed what processes to perform, on what units and in what order. The great post-war development in computer technology was to transfer this to internal data, as the stored-program-control computer. But, until that happened, programming was a physical activity, which entailed inserting U-links or plugcords to set up circuits.

It is worth pointing out here that Colossus did not have another key characteristic of later computer systems, 'conditional branching', where the machine itself could decide how to carry on after getting an intermediate result – contrary to the claim made when some details of Colossus were first made public in 1975.[38] With Colossus, the operator had to read and interpret the result and make a decision about how to reprogramme Colossus for the next processing step. As one Colossus operator put it, 'I told the machine to make certain calculations and counts, and after studying the results, told it to do another job. It did not remember the previous result, nor could it have acted upon it if it did.'[39]

Flowers, his colleagues at Dollis Hill and the technicians in Birmingham worked in a frenzy to design, acquire, wire and, where necessary, manufacture components. It was, said Flowers, 'a feat made possible by the absolute priority they were given to command materials and services and the prodigious efforts of the laboratory staff, many of whom did nothing but work, eat and sleep for weeks and months on end except for one half day per week... The US also contributed [valves] and an electric type-writer under the lend-lease arrangements.'⁴⁰ And they duly built the machine within ten months. It was actually first put together in the autumn, but it took some months to be 'tested, de-bugged, and modified to overcome some relatively minor problems', recalled D C Horwood, who joined the team at Dollis Hill in mid-1943.⁴¹ 'We started in February 1943 and on December 8th 1943 we had built the first machine, but it was a prototype machine and wasn't perfect. It had defects but it did work.'⁴² Once the machine had been tested to satisfaction at Dollis Hill, it had to be dismantled, transported to Bletchley Park and reassembled. When put back together again, it would have to be re-tested, and the inevitable faults isolated and cured. When it was first switched on, there were quite a few valve failures, but the number of these decreased just as quickly – clearly a consequence of the valves being disturbed as they were transported by lorry. By mid-January 1944, the time was approaching when Colossus could be handed over and start active service. The birth of the computer age was dawning; the machine had been conceived and built. The anxieties in the minds of those who had built it, and those waiting to use it, were no doubt centred on whether, as with the Robinson, it would serve its purpose, or whether the demands of constant repeated, high-speed switching of circuits in order to perform absolutely precise calculation would be too much to expect of a piece of human-made technology. Newman wrote to Travis on 2 January 1944, the 'most optimistic estimates are arrival ten days from now, setting up another ten days, testing another week; but I would add at least another two weeks to this for unforeseen troubles, and should guess at the middle of February as a reasonably hopeful date for starting serious production. Another problem with which we are faced, owing to [the Newmanry now] having to make all initial break-ins in this section, is finding wheel-patterns at the beginning of each month by machine methods.'[43] The Newmanry was now dependent on the delivery and success of the machine that was the embodiment of Flowers's 'reckless' approach to the use of electronic valves.

chapter sixteen

'Colossus Arrives Today'

The ten long months in 1943 during which Flowers and his colleagues built Colossus were a tantalizing time for Bletchley Park. The codebreakers soon stopped worrying about the reliability of electronics. The Robinsons' performance was not negligible, and there were even some in the Newmanry who did not want to stop work on the Robinson to learn how to use Colossus. But, increasingly, they looked forward to the day of arrival of 'the Flowers machine', as it was known for a short time until being named Colossus shortly before its arrival at Bletchley Park.[1] It had been a tense, tough, but eventually rewarding, period for Bletchley Park on a number of fronts. New security measures introduced by the German armed forces on both the Enigma and Geheimschreiber presented challenges that had to be overcome if decryption was to continue to offer up its secrets.

In fact, this period represents the zenith of wartime code-breaking. In response to a more complex naval Enigma machine, new forms of the Bombe that were capable of doing a lot more processing had to be developed. And, in response to the Geheim-schreiber, first the Robinson, and now Colossus, had been conceived and constructed. In addition, the codebreakers working on the Fish messages also invented several other decryption machines, some electro-mechanical and some electronic, with names such as

Dragon and Proteus. Later in the war, there were to be many more machines at work and an enormous quantity of messages was being decrypted, turning Bletchley Park into a veritable information factory (see Chapters nineteen and twenty). This was the harvest of the extraordinarily intense scientific and technological cultivation that occurred in the middle years of the war when the techniques to break the Geheimschreiber were being developed. A rich array of digital machines was devised and built – machines that brought into being a wholly new technological era.

In retrospect, 1943 can clearly be seen as the year the war turned decisively against Germany, following the shock turnaround at Stalingrad at the end of 1942, and the defeats suffered by the Axis in North Africa, Sicily and Italy. However, at the time, it seemed that German power was as strong as ever. Germany still occupied substantial areas of Russian territory and eastern Europe. Italy and the Balkans remained in the grip of the German armed forces. Similarly, German control of western Europe, from Norway to southern France, was being consolidated behind an Atlantic Wall aimed at preventing an Allied invasion of the Continent. And the Battle of the Atlantic was reaching a critical stage. Right up until the autumn of 1943, it seemed to British policy-makers that they were on the brink of losing this battle.

The problem for the Allies in the naval war in the Atlantic was the addition of that fourth rotor wheel to the naval Enigma machine. A Bletchley Park report of 18 February 1943, written shortly after the wheel was introduced, observed, 'The intro-duction of the fourth wheel for submarine traffic and the consequent necessity of building high-speed machinery to deal with it has resulted in a long blank period.'[2] That lack of Enigma intelligence had had fearful consequences in the Battle of the Atlantic. More and more Allied merchant ships were being sunk and the U-boats were threatening Britain's very ability to feed its people and carry on the war. And the German navy was also reading British naval wireless traffic, successfully breaking British codes up until 1943 when the Admiralty finally recognized its own security failings.

Yet, astonishingly, by the middle of the year, the Battle of the Atlantic had all but been decided in the Allies' favour. The introduction of long-distance air cover for convoys and improved submarine-detection radar, as well as the recovery of the ability to break the Naval Enigma keys, meant that the balance shifted against the U-boats. And machine solutions to the problem of the four-wheel Enigma were now coming to fruition. From then until the end of the war, there were sufficient cribs and Bombes to ensure the keys were broken. Whereas in the worst month, March 1943, losses to U-boats were at their highest of the war with 540,000 tons of merchant shipping sunk, by August the figure was down to 25,000 tons[3] and Doenitz, the German admiral, was forced to withdraw his submarines from the Atlantic. In Russia, where the German offensive at Kursk in the summer had been thwarted, German troops were forced to retreat under the great Soviet counter-offensive. There, as in Italy, the Allies had gained the initiative. And, in the telecommunications and decryption war, the Allies were similarly about to press home their advantage.

When the war in North Africa ended in mid-1943, the Allies prepared to invade Sicily. The fighting in Africa had denuded Italy and Sicily of Axis troops and although the German high command expected an invasion in the Mediterranean, they did not know where it would strike land. On the other hand, the Allies had scant reliable intelligence about the German and Italian forces that they were likely to encounter in Sicily. The amount of Axis wireless traffic, and thus the quantity of Enigma interceptions, fell off dramatically as the fighting in Tunisia drew to an end, and Bletchley Park was concerned that the availability of landlines in continental Europe would deny them the intelligence that had been so useful in North Africa.

However, in early May 1943 – one month before the invasion of Sicily was due to take place – a new Fish link opened between the

German general staff in Berlin and Field Marshal Albert Kesselring, ObS, Commander-in-Chief South in Rome. Previously such traffic had been sent via the Codfish link in Athens and forwarded to Rome by submarine cable. The Rome end of the link was based in the teleprinter office of the 5th Panzer Army, and it served various units of the armed forces based in Italy and the Mediterranean under Kesselring's command. The link was codenamed Bream at Bletchley Park and was to prove one of the most rewarding of all the Fish links. It was first broken by the end of May and from then on was to provide a regular stream of information about the state of the German armed forces in Italy and their plans. It would also provide information on other theatres of the war. In the assessment of the official history of British Intelligence, 'as was to be the case throughout the Italian campaign, the traffic on this link furnished from the outset *a more comprehensive guide to the enemy's dispositions and intentions than did any of the Enigma keys*' [italics added].[4]

Kesselring was required by the command in Berlin to submit regular detailed situation reports covering the whole Italian area and daily reports from the fighting fronts. He also had to report his intentions and appreciations of events, as well as details of casualties and reinforcements. The Bream link was also used for supply returns, recording the number and condition of tanks, ammunition and fuel dumps. The tank returns, in particular, played an important role in Allied assessment of the German army's order of battle. German army wireless intelligence reports were also sent over the link and allowed the Allies to view the German assessment of the Allies' own order of battle, which turned out to be a very useful tool in testing the effectiveness of deception plans in the campaign later in Italy aimed at throwing the German defences off balance. The teleprinter exchange near Rome was the central communications node for all the German armed forces based in and around Italy. Two wireless networks carried traffic to and from subordinate units: a low-power fixed network for units near Rome and a set of longer-distance links to army and other commands at or near the front and to Sardinia. A Bletchley Park intelligence assessment reported, 'Considerable communication takes place within the two [wireless networks]. A great number of messages pass between the Army authorities in Sardinia and Naples, one of their supply points; a greater number travel between the German division in Sardinia... and the Armed Forces Supply office at Olbia. The remarkable feature about this latter is that they show no direct communication exists between these two authorities. Messages are therefore sent to Rome for retransmission and very often have to be re-encoded in the process.'[5] The German secret services also used the Bream link to communicate information about airfields, harbours and shipping movements. Additionally, there were several administrative and supply organizations communicating with Berlin. In return, Kesselring received orders from Hitler and the general staff of the armed forces, the OKW, as well as appreciations of the situation on the other fronts, from Norway to Russia. Indeed, this single link gave access to important strategic and operational information on the German armed forces in Italy, which was just what had been lacking until then.

The outstanding strategic value of the information can be seen in the fact that it usually took a week or so to decrypt Fish messages, whereas Enigma messages could be decrypted in as little as three or four hours at best, and more commonly in six hours or so. But the information carried on the Fish links was at a high level and gave information about events to come over the next few weeks – one decrypt gave details of Kesselring's preparations for a defensive position which showed that it would take two months before it would be ready. Interestingly, Bletchley Park concluded that the Bream link had only been opened because of the threatened Allied invasion of Sicily. Decodes of Codfish traffic showed that, despite pleas from the operating staff at Salonika for a lightening of their load, the German army signals corps intended to carry on using the Codfish link as the connection between the Axis Mediterranean forces and Berlin. 'It should be noted that, in spite of the effect of all this increased and projected [wireless telegraphy] activity [by the German armed forces in the Mediterranean], there is no real evidence that it is the result of a long-premeditated plan... It is hardly too much to suggest that the move from Athens [to Salonika] and [the opening of Bream and other changes] may have been caused by the successful invasion of Sicily.'[6]

On 6 June 1943, Kesselring advised his commanders that the expected 'sea and air landings on the Italian mainland [demand] the active employment of every German of all three services. Every defended locality, airfield, etc., must defend itself to the last man with its own forces.'[7] A decode of 27 June 1943 from Kesselring to all the forces in the Mediterranean under his command revealed him telling them that 'the hour of decision was at hand and they must be prepared to protect the homeland "on Italian soil".'[8] When the invasion of Sicily was launched, the Allies got ashore successfully, the Italian forces putting up little real resistance to the landings. Counter-attacks from the German divisions were duly beaten off and the Allies threatened to divide the German forces on the island into two.

Both the Bream link and Enigma traffic gave the Allies good intelligence on German reactions. A decode on 14 July made it clear that the German command was ready to abandon the west and concentrate on holding the east of Sicily. But even this rapidly became unsustainable with the forces Kesselring could afford to station there. The possibility of another invasion elsewhere in the Mediterranean meant that Hitler could not take troops away from other potential targets to help defend Sicily and Italy. And, as the Allies had hoped, a political crisis was developing in Rome, which led to the toppling of Mussolini. Italy's leaders had never shared Hitler's war aims, having sought an empire in Africa, not a conflict with more powerful western economies. The country's economic mobilization was a 'risible' effort, according to one historian, and underlined the total failure of the Fascist regime which had ruled Italy for twenty years: 'Here, it seemed, was a dictatorship so weak that, under the first test of war, nobody seems to control it.'[9] The political crisis was resolved only in the autumn with a German military takeover. Elsewhere, the situation on the eastern front was becoming very serious for the German army. Indeed, decodes showed that, despite the Allied landings in Sicily and later on mainland Italy, Kesselring was ordered to send troops to the eastern front to shore up the battered front line there. As a result, on 26 July 1943, an order, which was intercepted and decrypted, was sent from the German general staff of the armed forces, the OKW, to Kesselring instructing him to prepare to evacuate Sicily.

The German withdrawal from Sicily in August was followed by Allied landings on the foot of Italy and at Salerno, near Naples, in September. The landings at Salerno came close to disaster as the German army counter-attacked, but the Allies did secure a foothold. Kesselring successfully managed to stop the Allied advance some hundred miles south of Rome, taking refuge behind the hastily prepared Gustav Line. His success encouraged Hitler to decide, between October and November 1943, to hold the Allied forces as far south as possible, rather than to withdraw to a strong defensive line in the northern Apennines.[10] As it was, it took eight months of bloody battle before the Gustav Line was eventually broken. During this entire time, Bream decodes 'threw a light on the enemy's determination to carry out this battle, the state of his divisions, his supply situation and the development of his defensive preparations'.[11] According to the official history of British Intelligence, Bream provided the single most important piece of strategic intelligence during the war. It concluded, 'a fair appraisal shows not only how intelligence helped to overcome [the] handicaps, but also how it made possible the integration of the Italian campaign with converged attacks on Nazi Europe from east and west'. Hitler's determination to hold on to Italy after the fall of Mussolini in 1943, and the hard battles that followed, drained the supply of troops that could have been deployed against Russia in the east or made ready to ward off the Allied invasion in the west. 'No German division left Italy for the western front in 1944 and only one for the eastern… Too much cannot be claimed for a single piece of intelligence, but it is clear that the discovery in October 1943 that, contrary to expectation, Hitler would not give up Italy without a fight was pivotal to [overall] Allied strategy.'[12] Since the war Allied tactics in Italy have attracted much criticism for the slow, costly advance that followed the initial landings. But, however valid those complaints may be, the tardy progress of the Allies did succeed in holding substantial numbers of German troops away from north-western and eastern Europe. A Bream intercept in 1944 showed a ration strength of around over million men for the German armed forces in Italy. Slow progress may not have been the plan, but it served the strategic purpose fairly well.

The network of radio links carrying Geheimschreiber-encrypted messages was expanding rapidly. In August 1943 a memo from Bletchley Park to US codebreakers recorded that 'The amount of information which we are now obtaining from our sources in Western Europe is very small and inclined to diminish, whereas the demand for it is increasing. As you know, we have been successful in our attacks on the German Scrambled Teleprinter [i.e. the Geheimschreiber], and I think that there is no doubt that, if we had traffic from the teleprinter lines, we should be able to read [i.e. decode] it, especially if we could get it in some quantity.'[13] On 10 August 1943, the Bream transmitter in Italy was switched off and moved north to a new location, before coming back into service two days later. Just before the link closed, the office at the Berlin end asked the operators at Rome for information about all the messages sent on the link between 1 June and 31 July. When the reply to that request was successfully intercepted and decrypted, it gave the Bletchley Park traffic analysts a much fuller picture of the link at work than they had seen so far from the successfully intercepted and decoded messages.[14] The codebreakers knew that they were regularly breaking the wheel-pin positions for a month, and that they managed to decode about 25 per cent of messages that were intercepted within each period, but what this represented as a proportion of total traffic was unknown. The statistics sent by the German operators in response to the request for details about traffic in June and July 1943 on Bream gave the codebreakers an answer to that question. In June, they decoded 114 out of 575 messages sent from Rome to Berlin, and 108 messages out of a total of 876 sent from Berlin to Rome (each message, of course, contained several individual messages to be forwarded to different recipients). That represents an overall percentage of 15.2 per cent. But this bald statistic masks the difference in the percentage of each end – for Rome to Berlin it is 20 per cent, but for Berlin to Rome it is only 12 per cent. Similarly, in July, 184 messages from Rome to Berlin were decoded out of a total of 1,205 (15 per cent) and 142 out of 2,438 sent from Berlin to Rome (6 per cent). The report was written in mid-August and the author expected that several more messages for July would be decoded, so the average figure for messages decoded in July, of 9 per cent, slightly understates the true success rate.

The intelligence gleaned from the decrypted messages was seldom of immediate tactical importance for Allied armed forces in the field. Out of the total of 222 messages decrypted in June, only forty-two contained information that was sent out to intelligence officers in the Allied armies; similarly, the 326 decodes in July generated only forty-three teleprinted messages to Allied intelligence officers. The other information, however, was carefully studied at Bletchley Park and at intelligence offices in the general staffs and armed forces headquarters, resulting in considerable numbers of reports about a vast variety of subjects relating to the Axis command of the war. Some were everyday matters, but others were highly significant. According to the Bletchley Park report on the intercepted German Bream statistics, 'Bream, like all Fish traffic, on the one hand carried a fair burden of routine administrative signals... [and that,] on the other hand, many of the [Ultra] tele-prints from Bream belong to the category of "war-winners".' Of course, if the 10 to 15 per cent of the total produced forty-odd items of intelligence of considerable tactical and strategic value – even if the label 'war winners' is somewhat of an exaggeration – it was clear that the other 85 to 90 per cent should also contain intelligence of a similar quality. The figures in the Bletchley Park file now in the National Archives suggest that on some days more messages were decoded than were sent, but this is due to different timings used by the various organizations. In general, Bletchley Park's figures were about twenty-four hours behind those of the German operators. What the figures show is that Bletchley Park was only managing to decode a small proportion of messages that were being sent. But better interception and more successful decryption would increase the amount of information the codebreakers could obtain.

In October 1943, the dedicated non-Morse interception station at Knockholt was aware of nineteen different German army Fish links. The Bletchley Park codebreakers had already succeeded in break-ing the cipher systems used on thirteen of these links, but they did not have complete mastery of the situation. One new, apparently experimental link between Berlin and Bordeaux and codenamed Swordfish defied analysis by the interception engineers at Knock-holt. They were able to work out that it was teleprinter traffic, but could not work out the transmission techniques properly, or whether it was Tunny enciphered traffic or some other type of Geheimschreiber. 'All that can be said... is that two slightly different systems of teleprinter modulation are being compared, still without a conclusive result.'[15] It later turned out to be a test link connected with Siemens, as were several other links that opened later. Furthermore, the traffic analysts were aware that there were growing numbers of German air force, navy and SS links. These links mainly used the Siemens and Halske T52 version of the Geheimschreiber (codenamed Sturgeon) which Bletchley Park had diagnosed but did not exploit. One link used yet another Siemens machine, the T42, with yet another design, codenamed Thrasher. Details of these machines and some of the links are given in Appendix K – Sturgeon and Thrasher. The traffic on all these links had to be forgone.

There were only enough interception sets and operators at Knockholt to cover seven of the links all the time. Full-time cover resulted in increasing the effective interception to about 70 per cent of the traffic on the Bream link. The seven links that were covered full time provided intercepts almost every day of the month. Other links, such as the now well-established Codfish link to the Balkans, could only be covered for about half the days in the month of October 1943, so little traffic was taken on them. By December 1943, the number of Fish links in use had risen to twenty-four, of which only seven were covered.[16] In the summer of 1943, consideration had been given to using French resistance supporters in the French Post Office to tap landlines for tele-printer traffic,[17] but the risks were too great and, besides, resources were too scarce. Eventually, in December 1943, eight new non-Morse interception sets were brought into operation. 'We have made good steps towards getting on top of the German Non-Morse circuits,'[18] reported Harold Kenworthy, who was in charge of the interception station at Knockholt. 'Supply of [interception] apparatus is getting a little easier now that our Workshops are going.[19]

An illustration of the frustrations of interceptions comes from a report in November 1943. Traffic on Bream on 1 October had been particularly troublesome (QRM and QRN are forms of interference, human-induced and natural, respectively; QMP38 is a message serial number). 'Very heavy QRM and fade, end of QMP38 unreadable. Continues bad until 2045 hours, then improves. Located again at

0045 on 2 October, but very weak and sometimes completely un-recordable through QRM, QRN. Traffic lost through QRM at 0610.' The following day it was just as bad: 'Tone completely swamped by Morse QRM and QRN. Traffic [so bad, that] not submitted [to Bletchley Park]. Barely audible from 0001 to 0130 hours. Conditions very bad from 0416 to 0515.' Interception of traffic on Codfish and the other links also suffered badly from interference and fading.[20]

The waiting for Colossus was indeed hard, as the amount of Fish traffic that could be decrypted was limited not just by interception capacities. There were limits on codebreaking, too. In August 1943, Newman wrote to Travis, reporting that 'progress in the last two weeks has been slow'.[21] The German signals corps had introduced a measure known as a limitation that required new methods of breaking. This technique had first appeared in North Africa on the Herring link, but was soon abandoned as the Allies closed in on Axis forces in the first half of 1943. But in May 1943 limitations, though not the same version, started to appear on other links, beginning with Codfish, spreading to Tarpon, Trout and Bream. There were different types of limitation, which affected the turning of the motor wheels and thus of the Psi wheels and the extended-Psi stream. They generally required extra processing to decrypt.

The Chi-2 and the Psi-1 limitation, respectively, used the second unit of the previous Chi character and the first unit of the previous Psi character to influence the movement of the motor wheels. But the most troublesome was the P5 limitation, which used the value of a unit in the plain language two characters previously to control the movement of the motor wheels. This reliance on the plain (which other limitations did not share) meant that errors in transmission made the message indecipherable – for the Germans as well as the British. But as Newman said, 'These... features are not enough to keep us out, but they do remove any margin for faults.' They also put more pressure on the Robinsons. These new measures could be countered only by developing new means of

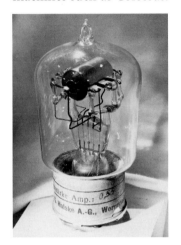

2. Schottky Tube invented by Walter Schottky in 1916. The first use of electronics was as analogue amplifiers in wireless equipment. Only later did electronic valves become used as switches in machines such as Colossus.

1. German teleprinter, Siemens Fernschreiber 37, 1936/1937. The teleprinter, invented in the 1920s, brought telegraphic machines into offices and could be used by anyone who could use a typewriter. The coding systems used for teleprinter communications are the same as those that underlie modern computer communications.

3. The first German teleprinter exchange, linking Berlin and Hamburg, 1933. The teleprinter network eventually formed a massive web of communications links across Occupied Europe.

4. Lorenz SZ 42 Geheimschreiber on-line cipher machine. The twelve wheels used to generate the cipher key can be seen in the centre. The machine would also be attached to a teleprinter.

5. Marconi UG6A undulator. The needle (seen in horizontal position on the cylinder on the right) is deflected by magnets depending on the nature of received wireless signals. The needle leaves a record of the signal on the paper tape or 'slip'.

6. British Post Office international wireless telegraphy operators in the 1940s. The operator types the message via a key punch onto paper tape. The tape is fed into the transmitter at a steady pace by the reader to the left of the key punch.

7. General Erich Fellgiebel was head of the Germany army signal corps and led the introduction of the Geheimschreiber and wireless teleprinter transmission into Occupied Europe. He was tortured and executed for his part in the attempt to assassinate Hitler in July 1944.

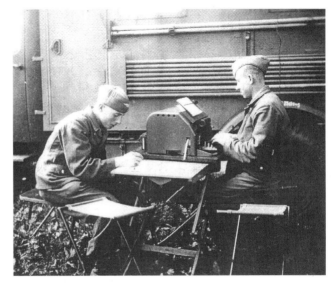

8. German signal troops using a teleprinter outside a wireless unit wagon.

9. Overhead cables arriving at a well dug-in German field communications exchange on the eastern front.

10. Post Office wireless station near St Albans.

11. 'Wireless War' poster. One of a series of propaganda posters issued by the Post Office during the war.

12. Max Newman in 1940. Newman conceived of using a machine to perform a statistical method of identifying the correct wheel settings for German enciphered Geheimschreiber messages intercepted by British wireless operators. The first machine designed was called Robinson, but was mainly electro-mechanical and was too slow. Colossus was designed with electronics to speed up the process.

13. Tom Flowers started his career as a lowly telephone engineer, but rapidly worked his way up to a senior position in the Post Office Research Establishment, where he pioneered the use of electronics in transmission and switching systems. He proposed the construction of an electronic machine, eventually known as Colossus, to overcome the limitations of the electro-mechanical Robinsons.

14. Sir Gordon Radley. Head of Post Office Research Establishment at Dollis Hill, North London.

15 & 16. Unidentified Fish decryption machines, 1945.

17. Part of the Fish Sections. The machines on the desks are possibly Garbos.

18. Dragon 2. An electronic machine used to 'drag' a 'crib' or likely word through an encrypted message looking for a match. The knobs at the top of each rack allow the crib and other information to be 'entered' into the machine to control the run.

19. A Robinson Fish decryption machine which was a forerunner of Colossus. Note the two taped 'bedsteads'. The semi-electronic counting sub-system is in the middle of the right hand rack and can be seen projecting backwards.

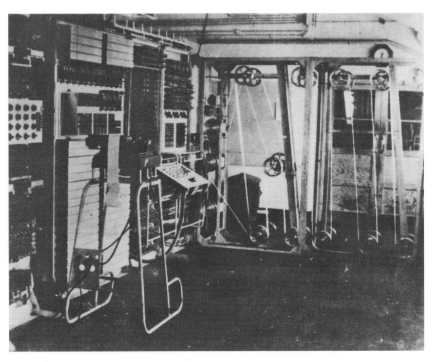

20. Colossus.

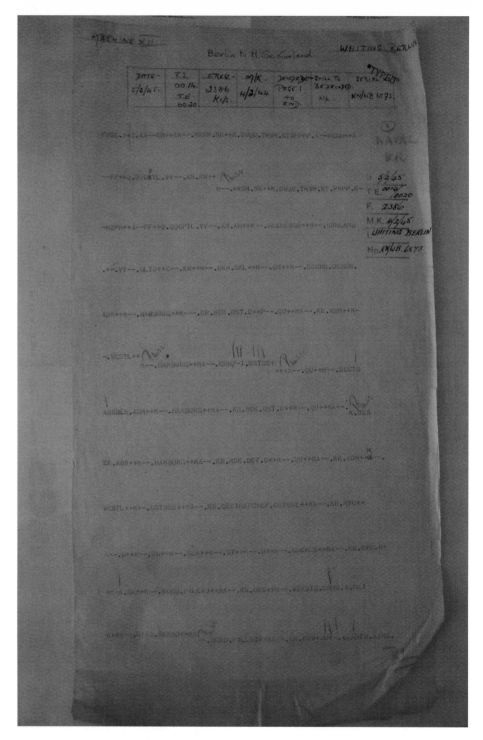

21. Whiting Decode. This is an example of the finished product of the Newmanry and Testery, a plain-language print including teleprinter commands, produced by a Tunny machine after a Colossus machine had worked out the cipher settings. Dating from early 1945, this is one of very few originals to survive the destruction of Fish material at the end of the war. See Appendix O for a further explanation.

de-Chi'ing which relied on machine-based techniques rather than hand methods (see Chapter eighteen). The net result, however, was that from mid-1943 to the end of the year, while the number of links in use by the German army and intercepted by Knockholt was increasing (from 6–7,000 per month in the middle of the year to 11–13,000 at the end), the number of messages that could be successfully decoded remained static at about 220 to 280 per month.[22]

In mid-December 1943 the troublesome P5 limitation was introduced on Bream and Codfish. 'The wheel patterns for the month had been recovered [i.e. the wheels had been broken] before the change took place, so the immediate problem was that of attempting to set the Chis of all messages in the Newmanry, depths no longer being available. [The introduction of the P5 limitation meant] the adoption by us of new techniques and a consequent re-organisation of staff to deal with the various processes. The re-organisation was necessarily a slow process, but as most links continued without using [the P5 limitation] for some time, the change-over kept pace with requirements.'[23] A further change on Bream in February 1944, described in a Bletchley Park document as a change of 'wheel characteristics', combined with the extra processing needed to cope with the P5 limitation 'hit the section hard', and output of decoded messages fell to half of what it had been in January.

Before the problems hit the section, in August 1943, Newman reported that 'The [Robinson] machines are now settling down; [the] faults are mainly concerned with the tapes.' The machines were kept busy with setting the Chi wheels for intercepted Bream messages. Bream took priority because of the importance of the Italian campaign and because operator habits at the Rome end of Bream made it one of the easier links to break (see Chapter seventeen). Despite these successes, there was also trouble with the quality of interception at Knockholt, which undermined the hard-won success with the Robinsons. Slides, where messages were recorded with dubious interspersed characters, became a problem. 'In the first two weeks [during an inspection] a number of messages were attacked which had slides but had such rich language properties that the Chi wheels could be set nevertheless.'[24] But increasingly that was becoming impossible as hand methods were displaced by the need for statistical, machine techniques. A report from September 1943 concluded, 'Tester with his [hand] method can tolerate four or five slides in a message and still be able to break it. His whole success, however, hangs from the slender thread of German signals carelessness, for they have been repeatedly ordered not to use the same indicator more than once during a day. In static moments, these instructions are fairly implicitly carried out and it is clear that future success of non-Morse cryptography must depend largely on Newman's machine methods.'[25]

Planning and preparation for using the super-fast machine were put in hand well before its arrival. Nor was it the only machine on the horizon. The Robinson and Colossus were primarily conceived of as performing the wheel-setting task, the wheel-breaking already having been done in the Testery using hand methods, such as a newly developed technique known as 'rectangling' as well as more established methods. But the Testery had conceived of its own machine, one that could help test out potential cribs automatically by looking for the crib in the cipher text. Newman observed,

> After a preliminary discussion with members of this and Tester's section I feel that the question whether the machine methods would compete with the hand methods already in use depends, first, on the setting-up and finishing-off time (finding the motor settings), secondly on the number of different cribs, and versions of the same crib, that have to be tried to give a good chance of success. Counts on material to answer the second of these questions are now going forward in Tester's section. If Colossus is a success, it will be far quicker than any possible cribbing machine, besides having a

better chance of success in most cases. This would not entirely rule out their machine, if they are prepared to develop it as an auxiliary, since we shall probably want to use Colossus in the first place mainly on difficult traffic, for runs too long to be done on the Robinsons.[26]

This Testery machine was developed and became known as Dragon (see Chapter twenty) as it dragged a crib thought the cipher text looking for a match – this was, of course, the same task that the room of Intelligence Corps NCOs had been assigned the early days of the Testery (see Chapter ten).

Following Colossus's dismantling and transport to Bletchley Park, on 18 January 1944, the computer age was born. Max Newman expressed his barely contained excitement in a terse final point to an otherwise dry, detailed technical memo: 'Colossus arrives today.'[27] It finally came into operational use in February 1944 and almost immediately proved its worth.

The first Colossus machine performed brilliantly, better than anyone had expected, and the fears about the unreliability of the machine proved to be unfounded. The failure rate for the valves was 'negligible'. Indeed, most problems occurred with the electro-mechanical components, such as the typewriters and uniselectors (which stepped the starting point of a valve ring used for internal generation of key streams). The photocells, which read the paper tape, and did so by being sensitive to light shining through holes in the paper tape, had to be given rest periods in the dark every so often to recover their sensitivity. But otherwise the machine worked as required. One maintenance engineer, Bill Chandler, ascribed the ease of maintenance and reliability of Colossus to three factors. First, 'most of the machines, having been installed and handed over, had their valve heaters on literally until the end of the war', proving that valves left running continuously did perform as Flowers had promised. Second, Colossus used a fairly low frequency in its the electronic cycle – there being no need to speed up the

cycle because of the limit at which the paper tape could be read –
and thus there was no need to push the components. And, third, the
valves were physically well spaced, so preventing the development
of hot spots.

According to an assessment made at the end of the war, 'The
flexibility of Heath Robinson for experimental purposes made it
easy to discover the essential requirements of a Tunny-breaking
machine. As a result, Colossus 1, the original experimental model,
really lacked surprisingly little for a first model.'[28] And the flexibility
built into the basic Colossus architecture meant that it could undertake new tasks.

'The Bream Chis for January 1944 were broken within the first
fortnight with the comparatively primitive equipment of the time –
Colossus 1 was not yet in action. [But]… the breaking of the
February Chis was greatly assisted by the use of Colossus 1. No
pairs of messages on the same QEP [indicators] were available, and
attempts by the Testery to break the Psis from the de-Chis sent over
were at first fruitless. Finally, however, the Psis were broken with
great difficulty and effort from one de-Chi.'[29] The problems created
by the introduction of limitations, and the consequent need for
extra processing, meant that the arrival of Colossus was extremely
well timed. Originally conceived as a machine for wheel-setting, it
increasingly became employed as well in wheel-breaking. By the
end of the war, six of the ten Colossi in operation were being used
to perform wheel-breaking, while the other four were devoted to
the original task of wheel-setting.

When Flowers first delivered Colossus, he and his team fully
expected to receive orders for more machines, yet initially they
heard nothing. So, once again, the Post Office engineers carried on,
relying on their own initiative, assuming that more models would
be needed. Flowers and Coombs started to design and improve the
machine: Colossus 2, which was to be equipped with 2,500 valves,
would be much faster and more versatile in the routines it could
perform. A method of parallel processing allowed the tape speed to

be increased to an effective rate of 25,000 characters per second, but it did so by performing five parallel sets of electronic processes for each character read, so the actual tape speed remained at 5,000 characters per second. As Flowers later pointed out, it would have been 'difficult to construct a reader to read five tapes simul-taneously... [so,] shift registers were invented for the purpose. Data read from the tape were read into six-bit shift registers, which meant that six consecutive characters from the message tape were available for processing', so that five processes were going on in parallel, all operating the same program but with different input data from the message tape.[30] The term shift or shifting refers in this situation to remembering one character back. Also, a switch-panel replaced some of the plugboard connections to make it easier to set up the machine. Captain Walter J Fried, an American liaison officer, reported back to Washington, 'The new machines have an extensive switchboard in addition to a plugboard. They carry a great many more patterns than the old and these can be switched in or out with triggers. Furthermore, it is unnecessary to plug up Delta patterns because the machine itself can difference if required.'

Then, suddenly, Flowers and his team received an order for more machines – more than they had expected, and to be delivered in a far shorter timescale than seemed practicable. The invasion of mainland Europe from across the Channel – the second front long demanded by Stalin to relieve the pressure on Russia – was clearly going to happen sometime in 1944. Many of the new machines were needed to help improve the odds for the Allies in the battles that would ensue after a successful invasion. But Flowers and his colleagues were being asked to perform the impossible. As many machines as could be produced would be taken into service. The electronic machine was to become a family of electronic machines. All Flowers could offer was that the Post Office engineers would do their best. If he could get the resources, and get permission to reorganize the Post Office factory in Birmingham into working on the production of special parts, then it might just be possible to produce about one Colossus per month, but it would be a challenge. This time there was no problem in getting Travis to write to Radley and Angwin asking them to dedicate the necessary Post Office resources to building a 'special' programme of machine manufacture as an absolute priority. Flowers and his team worked long hard hours and in March Radley was able to write to Nigel de Grey, assistant director at Bletchley Park: 'You will be pleased to hear that our Colossus programme appears likely to work out satisfactorily.'[31] Even the extremely tight security was relaxed slightly. Welchman, now assistant director, Mechanisation, wrote to Travis in May 1944, 'Until now the periods of the wheels have been concealed from all but a select few [Post Office staff], but it looks as if it will be necessary to allow parts which give this away to be made at the factory.'[32] But on a more optimistic note, Welchman was also able to report that, though 'It was thought that factory made Colossi could not begin to operate until early October', three Colossi being made at Dollis Hill would be ready for delivery in June, July and August.

chapter seventeen

Fish Dialects

Bletchley Park was a particularly unmilitary institution. In many ways, it was more like a university or a commercial research laboratory than a unit of the armed forces and the secret services. Max Newman's Machine Section, when it came to suggesting new ideas, was run in an informal fashion, although not in day-to-day work. Anyone could suggest new techniques or improvements, and meetings were held to discuss issues where all were encouraged to contribute. The cryptographers and machine-designers worked 'sabbaticals' in other parts of the Fish section for a week each month so that they could learn about the methods, techniques and problems of other departments – although this required some creative administrative measures to overcome organizational obstacles to staff exchanges between the Testery and the Newmanry (see Chapter twenty).

It was the policy of the section that all its members should be encouraged to interest themselves in all its activities and to improve their theoretical knowledge. In practice, it became increasingly hard for Wrens to get a complete picture of an organization in which they might have only done one job. Moreover, the mathematical style of the Research Logs made them unreadable for Wrens, and before they (or new men) undertook Chi-breaking and Colossus-setting on their own, some other introduction to the theoretical side was needed. Screeds and lectures on aspects of the work were issued or given from time to time in 1944, but nothing was done systematically till the Education Committee was founded in January 1945. This committee of four men and 14 Wrens chosen democratically and was [it] arranged general lectures or seminars for small parties of Colossus operators or other specialized groups. All lectures and seminars were given outside working hours and were voluntary. The seminars for Colossus operators were a complete success. The less mathematical general lectures were also appreciated. The Education Committee co-ordinated the production of screeds and started a General Fish Series of papers which were duplicated and available in every room.[1]

One lecture given by Wing Commander Oeser of Hut 3, which translated and distributed decoded Fish and Enigma messages, was entitled 'The intelligence value of Fish'. It was given in the run-up to D-Day when the use of Colossus machines was due to expand rapidly and it was considered that making staff aware of what their job was all about merited a temporary halt to the urgent day-to-day work of decrypting current traffic. The lecture was open to all members of the Machine Section ('including machine-maintenance staff') and the Testery, though they were warned not to discuss it with anyone outside the blocks housing the Fish sections. As the lecture was at 4.05 p.m., just after the start of the evening shift, attendance was voluntary for the day shift, but compulsory for the evening shift. Staff were advised that 'permission has been given to stop the machines for half an hour in view of the importance of the lecture'.[2]

When the statistical methods were being developed, at one stage 'A controversy broke out in the Research Section over the problem of the best method of continuing the analysis from [the] point' where the first set of wheels, the Chi wheels, had been worked out.[3] Some wanted to carry on with statistical work on the next set of wheels, the Psi wheels, while others thought that 'attempts should be made to guess the clear [i.e. the plain] at some point... and thus to obtain a short stretch of extended Psi key, on which the wheels could easily be set.' Initially, the second method was used, but the first method was adopted later when there were enough machines. The encouragement given to staff to develop new ideas and methods was to prove crucial, for example, in the way in which new counting methods were developed to supplement Tutte's double-delta method. These new statistical techniques will be the subject of this chapter.

Only three months after Colossus was delivered, when the statistical machine methods were at last fulfilling their potential, Newman commented in a memo, 'The future is brighter in that Flowers now promises a Colossus 2 which is far speedier than Colossus 1, and should therefore more than treble the output; and that Colossus 3 is not quite as remote as it seemed. On the other side is our absolute ignorance of the proportion of time that Colossus will be out for maintenance and repair; and the very serious difficulties that may be encountered in breaking the wheel patterns every month.'[4] There were also limits to the effectiveness of the crude double-delta test. The arrival of effective high-speed machinery thus prompted the Newmanry in particular to formalize processes and techniques.

Jack Good was a mathematician who, when he first joined Bletchley Park, had been assigned to help with the work on Enigma. He made some important contributions by reviewing statistics relating to Enigma messages, applying and building on some original insights made by Turing into the application of probability theory to statistical analysis. As statistical issues were of growing importance to Fish, Good was moved to the Newmanry in the spring of 1943 and immediately conducted a review of the Fish statistics, setting up a comprehensive system of statistical logging and analysis. This was to pay off handsomely in providing the tools that supplemented the cruder statistical searching technique of the double-delta method. Good recalled that, when he arrived, 'the future of the Newmanry was in jeopardy' because of the problems with the Robinson, but, thanks to his collection of statistics and the imposition of stricter checking, 'progress improved to the point where a big investment' in machines was justified.[5] According to Shaun Wylie, his colleague and fellow mathematician, Good 'once told me that he wanted to win the war by himself, and, from the way he set about Tunny, you could tell that he meant it'.[6]

Good's work led to the use of specific statistics for each individual link, even for individual types of message. For example, the messages sent from the two different ends of the Bream link between Berlin and Rome had quite different statistical profiles – the Rome end using a 'dialect' of German military teleprinter language that was more easily subjected to the statistical processes of working out the Chi settings than the language used on the Berlin end. (The messages sent by the Rome end were also longer, on average 3,600 characters, compared with the Berlin end, with an average of 2,000 characters, and, of course, the longer the intercepted messages, the easier it was to break them.)[7]

Colossus was used to identify a statistical bulge in the delta-de-Chi, which should occur when the correct delta-Chi settings were combined with the delta-cipher (see Chapter thirteen), as it would expose statistical traces of the delta-plain wherever the delta-extended-Psi had a / (00000), which would happen whenever there was a repeat in the extended-Psi. This was the wheel-setting operation (i.e. determining the wheel starting positions for individual messages, once the wheel-pin pattern of raised and flush pins was known for all messages in a fixed period). Colossus would count the number of times a condition occurred in the cipher text after the delta-Chi setting had been stripped out (the / characters produced by the delta process in the Psi stream within the cipher text would be transparent and allow the plain-language delta statistics to be counted). This was a general statistical test and gave a fairly weak signal in the form of a barely identifiable divergence from the statistical average. The higher the number of dots (0s) in the two motor wheels, the higher the number of repeats or stutters in the extended-Psi stream. Thus, the statistical evidence was easier to spot when there was a high level of motor wheel dots. The success of the method thus depended quite closely on what Bletchley Park called the 'dottage' of the motor wheel with thirty-seven pins.[8] For example, the length of cipher text needed to work out the correct Chi settings was directly related to the dottage. A dottage of 15 demanded a cipher text 6,200 characters long before it could be used for wheel-setting. A dottage of 18 reduced it to 4,800 characters; a dottage of 21 to 2,400 characters, a dottage of 24 to 1,700 characters, and the high dottage of 27 needed only 1,200 characters.

Tutte's double-delta test was a general one. As more and more messages were intercepted and decoded, the codebreakers began to look more closely at each link. Different types of message and operator habits produced statistics that were specific to a link. They began to categorize messages into 'language' and 'punctuation' types. Then they developed methods of searching for statistical clues specific to the link. It was seen earlier that all languages have their own characteristics, including teleprinter language, and that character count for a delta stream depends on the count of pairs of characters in the plain text. At Bletchley Park, an enormous amount of time and effort was devoted to identifying the letter frequencies of the language I have called German military teleprinter language and, in particular, the delta patterns produced by common combinations. It was a combination of standard written German, military German, and teleprinter punctuation and commands. Teleprinter commands created very common combinations, and indeed sequences of common combinations. In particular, combinations of SPACE and commands, such as 'shift to letters' and 'shift to numerals'. So, for example, 5M89 (5 – shift to numerals, M – full stop, 8 – shift to letters, 9 – SPACE) was a very frequent sequence, thus creating three common pairs (5+M, M+8, and 8+9) which produced a characteristic sequence in the delta-plain (UA5).

It was also quite common for operators to repeat teleprinter commands, especially figures-shift and letters-shift, so that many links used 55M889 (delta – /UA/5) or 55M8899 (delta – /UA/5/). Habits such as these had quite a noticeable effect on the statistics for each link. The double-shift practice was common at the Rome end of Bream, and at the Koenigsberg exchange, Amtes Anna. After Anna was closed down and moved back to Berlin, the double-shift habit 'made a general appearance in the west'.[9] Appendix E lists some common sequences and their delta equivalents.

As well as these teleprinter command sequences and operator habits, the actual words and characters used in the original message would also affect the delta statistics. EI, SC and CH are particularly common combinations of letters in German, both standard and military. On the other hand, there are plenty of letter combinations that do not occur at all. As an anonymous codebreaker observed at the end of the war, 'The plain and delta-plain counts for these components [of German military teleprinter language] are strikingly different and, even within each type, the form of the count depended on the operators' spacing and punctuation habits. The tank returns and other standard military reports which appeared on several links could also often be in highly formatted form, with lots of abbreviations, shift commands, and punctuation marks. Some messages consist entirely of German, or abbreviations and punctuation, or even of numerals, but in most messages there is a heterogeneous mixture of hand patches (German language with irregular spacing), addresses (abbreviations and punctuation), message content (language usually with some abbreviations) and occasional places where the tape sticks and the same letter of P is transmitted until the tape is adjusted.'[10]

Naturally, these different characteristics produced different statistics for each link. These specific statistics meant that Colossus could be used to search for the correct wheel settings for that particular link rather than, or in addition to, the standard double-delta search. Increasingly, rather than searching for a statistical correlation with the average, Colossus was used to search for a statistical correlation with known or likely characteristics of a link. This also enabled Colossus to be used to perform different tests on a message if one test failed to produce a statistically significant result. Of course, this was only possible once enough messages had already been enciphered on a link to amass the plain and delta-plain statistics needed to decide what to search for. But it provided a much surer tool. A run on Colossus would thus be tailored to search for statistical bulges that occurred only on specific links.

A report at the beginning of May 1944 recorded that the Bream link was one of the easier ones to break because the operators tended to use a lot of repetitive words and phrases. Indeed, Max Newman reported, 'Some lines use favourable language in a much more marked degree than others and consequently require much less time to break. For instance, the Rome end of Bream probably takes about half as long to break as the Berlin end.'[11] 'Favourable language' here means using words/punctuation etc. that was highly amenable to statistical analysis.

> The capacity of [the machinery in Newman's section] for breaking messages depends on the degree of favourable language used. It should be able to produce 20 messages of Rome–Berlin Bream per day but would probably only be capable of 10 Berlin–Rome Bream messages. It is probably true to say that its present capacity is just sufficient to absorb both ends of Bream. While the number of Bedsteads [Robinsons] will show continual increase, no great gain in capacity will be achieved until the arrival and setting up of Colossus No 2, which according to present plans should take place in about two months' time. This should immediately double the figures.[12]

The general statistical test, the double-delta, was performed initially only on units 1 and 2, and then, once a setting had been found on those two wheels, the other units could be counted. To perform a count on all five units in one run would take too many calculations to be practicable. Similarly, the tailored statistical tests would also be confined to a pair of units at most – 1 and 2 were usually the easiest to start with. But some messages responded better to counts on units 4 and 5. Unit 3 was the hardest of all to test and so was usually the last. Once the setting of the other four wheels had been found, it would only be necessary to test twenty-nine possible start settings (the number of pins on wheel 3).

Good's statistical analysis was really focused much more on the statistics of the individual units in the delta-plain rather than characters. The assignments of the Baudot code had been real-located when the teleprinter was developed to minimize and equalize machine wear and tear. This meant that the common language character frequencies left traces in the statistics of the individual units, which in turn affected the probabilities of statistical profiles of the units in the delta-plain. These probabilities were the consequence of those code assignments to characters. The probability that unit 1 of a standard German language delta-plain character will be a '1' is 0.5599, for unit 2 it is 0.5118 and for unit 4, 0.5316; on the other hand the probability that unit 3 will be a '0' is 0.5316 and 0.5796 for unit 4.

The statistics were analysed using a technique which Turing had introduced for work on the Enigma ciphers. This was adapted to work out a probability of one or more units being equal to a cross or a dot and to identify the statistical bulges that pointed to a non-random occurrence. This was called the Sigmage, from the Greek letter Sigma, frequently used as a symbol in equations by statisticians. Statistical techniques were employed to define the ratio of a bulge to the standard deviation for random scores. 'It is a measure of the improbability that the sum will occur at random in a single trial, i.e. a particular setting.'[13] The statistical theory was vitally important and allowed a method of defining significant count results as 'good' or 'certain'.[14]

Colossus would be used to identify settings that produced counts on one or more units that exceeded the expected random level, the Sigmage or the set level. A count above the set level was statistically significant, and thus a possible candidate for the correct setting. 'No simple formula for weighing the evidence of a run can be exact. Evidence is derivable not only from the sheer magnitude of the bulges but also from having bulges on the right letters, or on a consistent group of letters (e.g. on all language letters); in other words, it is unjust to take a message as a fair sample of itself, and [it is] necessary to include other messages.'[15] From this close statistical analysis, a 'processing tree' was established which specified the most productive tests – i.e. on which units a count should be performed, with follow-on stages for counting subsequent units to complete the setting process. The processing tree, and the statistical analysis which underlay it, was the core of the Colossus technique. Without the ability to perform counts looking for statistical correlation with specific message types, Colossus would only have been able to perform the standard double-delta process. This could produce a result, but the tailored techniques allowed many more positive results to be obtained from messages that failed on the standard technique. The processing tree shows different sets of tests for different types of message (depending on whether they were language- or punctuation-oriented). In addition, different runs had to be devised to cope with limitations (see Chapters sixteen and eighteen).[16]

Furthermore, the statistical tests could use the logical flexibility built into Colossus. The basic double-delta test used the Vernam cipher combining rules to check if units 1 and 2 were both the same. Other logical rules could be used to check whether a pair or units were different, and so on – as shown in the processing tree. Usually, there was a limit to the number of runs that would be performed on a message. If it did not show any good or certain results, it would be abandoned – processing time was limited and had to be devoted to messages that were likely to yield results. Occasionally, however, a message demanded extra attention, in which case it would be subjected to 'flogging'. 'Flogging is trying all methods which may possibly help to set a message. This may be done because of intelligence or cryptographic priority, lack of work, or for ostentatious display (towards D.O. [Duty Officer] or Wrens).'[17] The use of the processing tree may be compared with any diagnostic routine. The obvious things are tried first and if these fail to give a clear answer, more refined, specific tests are applied, based on intuition and experience. If none of the tests shows a significant result, they are abandoned.

With the development of the statistical techniques, Bletchley Park's ability to decrypt Fish messages was considerably refined. And, as the codebreakers gained more experience, they developed new techniques. This applied to both the Testery and the New-manry. Initially, the Robinson and Colossus were intended to perform the job of working out the Chi-wheel settings to produce the de-Chi stream. The wheel-breaking process and the separation of the Psi stream and the motor stream were to remain manual tasks for some time. But, as the codebreakers looked into what they were doing, they discovered all sorts of new ways of developing techniques, especially machine techniques, for both wheel-breaking and wheel-setting. Indeed, they evolved indeed a coherent set of methods that was called the 'modern strategy':

> The theoretical base of wheel-breaking and setting is very similar, and for every method of setting there is a corresponding method of wheel-breaking which uses more traffic and more information. Normal practice is therefore to select the most promising material enciphered on a given set of wheel patterns and to use this for wheel-breaking. When the wheel patterns are known, they can be used for setting other

enciphered messages on them... The fact that Tunny can be broken at all depends on the fact that plain, Psi, Chi, cipher and de-Chi have marked statistical, periodic or linguistic character-istics which distinguish them from random sequences of letters... There are three main methods of Tunny analysis, each of which can (in suitable circumstances) be used for wheel-breaking or setting.[18]

The first method was the general technique in use when the motor-wheel patterns were unknown. It depended on a string of text consisting of about 4,000 characters for wheel-breaking, or 1,000 characters for wheel-setting. The first step was the process of identifying the Chi stream by testing every possible Chi setting (of units 1 and 2) and counting the double-delta or other statistical test using a machine. The other units would then be set by machine in subsequent runs. In the second stage, the extended-Psi stream was then removed by hand by cryptographers skilled enough to recognize the patterns created by the common character combina-tions even in the delta stream. Finally, the motor wheels were also identified by hand analysis.

The second method was entirely mechanical, 'and as soon as there were sufficient machines available, became the general method of setting as soon as the motor patterns were found'.[19] The first stage was the same as in the first method. The second stage involved the mechanical/statistical identification of the motor wheels by the statistical properties of the delta-de-Chi stream. Then, in the third stage, the extended-Psi stream was identified by testing all possible Psi streams and looking for the one with the statistical correlation with plain-language text. The disadvantage of this method was that it depended on a stream of characters longer even than that required by the first method.

The third method, which pre-dated Colossus, but was revived when security measures prevented the other methods for a while in 1944, made use of either depths or cribs and could be applied to streams of as few a hundred characters. In the first stage, either a depth or a crib could be identified mechanically/statistically through the properties of delta-key. In the second stage, the two component key streams were stripped apart by mechanical/ statistical analysis of the delta-extended-Psi stream. The motor wheels were then identified by hand methods.

This short summary really does not do justice to the full complexity of the methods and the statistical theories underlying them. The processes described above give an outline of the fundamental technique used for cracking the Geheimschreiber – the stripping apart of the key by identifying its component parts, by the statistical means of testing every possible combination to look for the right one. And it was the statistical approach that triumphed – thanks to both the theory and the machine.

chapter eighteen

Fish – Landing the Catch

Colossus's arrival was certainly fortuitous. Britain and the United States had postponed the opening of the second front in western Europe from 1942 to 1943, and once again until 1944. In 1943, they had decided that it would be more productive (given the lack of preparations for an invasion to be launched against Hitler's Atlantic Wall defences) to invade Sicily and then Italy. It was hoped that this would hold in Italy German troops that Hitler could otherwise have placed in defence of the Atlantic coast. Hitler's decision to occupy Italy in October and November 1943, and to hold the Allies as far south as possible, validated that strategy.[1] But, despite Churchill's fears of a bloodbath, continued pressure from Roosevelt and Stalin made an invasion of north-west Europe, and the opening of the second front, a political necessity in mid-1944. And Colossus was to prove instrumental in helping to fill a large gap in Allied knowledge about the state of the German armed forces that would be ranged against them and of the defensive works they would have to overcome to get troops ashore.

The German army had been in occupation of the entire Atlantic and Channel coasts of France, Belgium and the Netherlands since mid-1940. Not only had there been time to prepare the Atlantic Wall defences, but also to develop landline communications links that minimized the need for wireless traffic. A senior naval officer attached to the headquarters of Rommel, the German commander-in-chief in north-west Europe, later recalled how his days in early 1944 had been spent with Rommel visiting various units on the Atlantic coasts and dealing with an endless number of telephone and teleprinter messages. However, for long-distance backhaul links between the commanders on the spot and the high command at Berlin or Hitler at Koenigsberg, wireless communications became essential. And those who used such links became convinced that they were safe. The same naval officer wrote 'For those who came from the navy, the immense number of telephone calls between the higher and the supreme army command staffs concerning the most important matters seemed rather odd. After the First World War, the navy had found out that the enemy had read most of its wireless messages, which seriously affected Germany's conduct of the war. Because it had learned its lesson, and also because of the inherent dangers of direction finding, it limited its wireless traffic to a minimum. It had introduced a totally secure code system with coding machines and had applied this experience to the use of the telephone and transmitted urgent and secret information only through a teleprinter with a built-in code [i.e. cipher] key. One could never be sure if a telephone call was monitored, illegally through wiretapping or legally through a second listener, as was often the custom in higher staffs… [but the Geheimschreiber was] now a completely secure way to communicate which made wire tapping impossible. In addition, there was an immediate typed copy at one's fingertips. No doubts would arise later about what actually had been discussed.'[2]

In any event, as has been seen, Bletchley Park had had relatively little success with German army Enigma keys, but the introduction of a Fish link between Berlin and north-west Europe made British 'wire-tapping' a possibility. The invasion of north-west Europe would be the largest combined arms operation in history, far bigger than Sicily or Salerno, and it would be launched against a much bigger and far better-prepared defensive force. In retrospect the

D-day landings appear to have been foreordained to succeed. But, at the time, this did not seem so clear-cut. At Sicily, Salerno and Anzio (in January 1944), landings had all succeeded, but they also showed how easily the scales could have been tipped to create a disaster, as at Dieppe in 1942. The Allies had significant – in fact, vital – advantages with their dominance of the air and sea. But, with the notoriously hazardous nature of sea crossings and landings, it could so easily have gone wrong.

Colossus contributed in two ways to the success of the D-day landings. First, it helped provide the information about the German army's order of battle, and about the state of the units and their supplies. Second, it helped the Allies confirm that a massive deception campaign had largely succeeded in holding German army reserves away from Normandy – where the landings were planned to take place. This combined intelligence was vital to planning the landings and to ensuring that the armed forces were not driven back into the sea on day one or two. As Montgomery, who was to command the landings, put it, 'We must blast our way ashore and get a good lodgement before the enemy can bring sufficient reserves up to turn us out.'[3]

The deception campaign, Operation Fortitude, needed to allow for flexibility, adjusting intentions as and when necessary, depending on what decodes revealed about German reactions. A Bletchley Park report from March 1944 on the role of intelligence from decrypts noted, 'At all stages we should be practising deception, and [seeking] information about the enemy's reactions to our actual movements, therefore, in all that follows we are dealing with any reactions to our deception as well as to our actual movements.'[4] The main conduit of misleading information was the ring of double agents who passed false reports to Berlin. This stream of misinformation was supplemented by dummy wireless traffic, generated to give the impression of a build-up of forces in southeast England ready for an invasion directly across the Channel to the Pas de Calais.[5] The wireless traffic for a non-existent army of

150,000 men even included plain-language snippets which the German interception service could pick up, and which apparently gave away information. The dummy network's wireless call-signs were printed in Allied call-sign listing books in case any were captured in due course by the German army.[6] An entire fictional army was eventually 'based' in the south-east, keeping the German high command's eye off the real target by convincing them that an attack would happen in the Pas de Calais, and that any landings in Normandy were a diversion, designed to attract reserves away from the main point of attack.

By trying to convince Hitler that the main attack would take place on the Pas de Calais, the deception planners were building on his preconceptions – in their position, he would have decided to invade via the Pas de Calais, and so he assumed that the Allies would. In December 1943, Hitler had discussed the expected Allied invasion of western Europe with his generals. The main problem they faced was deciding where a landing might be attempted so that they could position their forces to meet the threat. The Pas de Calais was the obvious choice, but it was far from being the only one available. Hitler surmised that 'We must also expect [a landing in] Norway, as well as probably a diversionary attack in the Bay of Biscay and maybe in the Balkans.' What was not at issue was the importance of any invasion. 'If they attack in the west, then it will decide the war... If the attack is driven back, the whole affair will be over', although, to an inner circle, he added, 'If the invasion is not driven back, the war will be lost.'[7] The deception campaign succeeded in building on this weakness.

However, the Allies also badly needed information about the dispositions of German forces in north-west Europe. The official history of the British intelligence during the Second World War observes:

> The [German] army all together was a huge and complex structure and the task of acquiring comprehensive information

about it, and of keeping that information up to date, was always going to be more difficult than that of keeping abreast of the strength and order of battle of the Air Force or the Navy... Its armies, corps, divisions and non-divisional units were frequently redistributed between the various theatres. New formations were always being created... Before the spring of 1943 it was not easy to achieve accuracy in these studies and still less easy to do without considerable delay. Enigma and Army Y[8] threw a steady light on operations and orders of battle in North Africa and on some sectors of the Russian front, but about the Army as a whole and about its order of battle in theatres where is was not engaged in active operations – and especially in Europe, where it used landlines for its communications – Sigint still only provided fitful intelligence.[9]

Then, during January 1944, a new Fish link, Jellyfish, was opened, connecting the general staff of the armed forces, OKW, near Berlin with the Oberbefehlshaber West, ObW, Commander-in-Chief West, Field Marshal Karl von Rundstedt. During March 1944, Wing Commander Oeser of Hut 3 at Bletchley Park reported that Bream 'is the only Fish being broken at present. Some Octopus and Squid (South Russian front to the OKH at Koenigsberg) and Jellyfish (Paris to Berlin) could probably be broken, but only at the expense of Bream, since not enough manpower or machinery is available at GC&CS.'[10] The fact that Bream was relatively easy to break made it highly attractive in terms of overall intelligence output and the tendency was to break as much of it as was possible. However, with the paucity of information about the state of German forces in north-west Europe, it was essential to exploit the new link, even at the cost of reducing the amount of information derived from Bream.

Jellyfish was first intercepted in January and was still unbroken in March when Bream, thanks to the processing power added by Colossus, produced a bumper harvest of 1.5 million decoded plain-language characters.

But in many respects the next month, April 1944, was a particularly difficult one in the Fish sections. Difficulties in breaking the pin patterns introduced at the beginning of the month on Bream, Jellyfish and Stickleback meant that the task was not completed until the second half of the month. This left those deciding on work priorities to determine how much of the backlog of unset messages to tackle, or whether to ignore it all and shift focus to putting all efforts into an early break of the wheels on these links in May. In the end only about one-third of potentially decodable Bream messages were read. However, there was also one major achievement in the same month. Captain Walter J Fried, an American liaison officer at Bletchley Park, reported back to Washington on 3 April 1944, 'Strenuous efforts have been and are made to determine the Jellyfish Chi patterns statistically. The circuit Paris–Berlin is believed to be very important. Messages with the same QEP [indicator] numbers [cannot] be read in depth [i.e. when two messages sent with the same initial wheel-settings] so presumably Jellyfish has some [special] element. Very likely it is the P-5 limitation but this is not certain. The circuit started in early 1944 and the [special] feature has always existed. Since the traffic has never been read [i.e. decoded] nothing is known about its plain-text characteristics.' However, a fortnight later, on 17 April, Fried was able to report, 'The March Jellyfish wheels have finally been broken and a few messages have been read. They have fulfilled all expectations with respect to intelligence value. The circuit uses Chi-2 and P-5 limitations precisely as does Bream. The Motor-37 patterns contained 22 dots. This is quite favourable so that it is probable that a substantial amount of March traffic can be read if time permits. Work on the April Jellyfish wheels is in progress and they look hopeful.'[11]

The break was achieved by the use of another new statistical technique designed for use on Colossus. It would search for statistical evidence of an entire message that had already been sent on Bream being retransmitted on Jellyfish. This wheel-breaking technique depended on the retransmission being exactly the same as the original – any differences would prevent it from working. These retransmissions often occurred at regular times, perhaps even daily, and involved standard reports from one army command that were copied on to others. Once the wheels had been broken, about 20 per cent of Jellyfish messages sent during March could be set individually using the Robinsons or Colossus as they would all use the same pin positions. These decodes then provided plain-language information about the traffic on the new link which could be used for preparing the statistics that would allow further breaks when the pin positions were changed. Success would breed success – and provide a mass of valuable intelligence. Bream not only contributed so much intelligence directly; it also gave entry to an equally important source of material, Jellyfish.

This break into Jellyfish was to provide details of the Germans' strategic appreciations, their order of battle, the strength of individual divisions in the ObW's command, and much more. One of the first Jellyfish decodes – dated 21 March 1944 and decoded on 6 April – was an appreciation from ObW giving a detailed assessment of Allied intentions and included the view that an invasion was not imminent. Another appreciation of 20 March, which was decrypted on 12 April, expressed the view that any Allied invasion would take place in Normandy.[12] But this view was only one of many pouring into the army high command. There was also the information which was fed through the double agents and successfully diverted attention to the Pas de Calais and to Norway, the Balkans and elsewhere. As D-Day neared, and the build-up of forces in the south and south-west of England became unavoidably obvious, decodes showed that, although the German high command was increasingly concerned about Normandy, it still believed that the Pas de Calais was the main target and that any attack on Normandy would be secondary. This was precisely the message being passed back to Berlin by double agents working to the orders of the deception organizers in British Intelligence. A decode of an

ObW appreciation sent on 8 May revealed that von Rundstedt believed that an assault in Normandy would 'be the enemy's prerequisite condition for a subsequent descent on the Channel coast' in the Pas de Calais.[13]

As for the German order of battle, an appreciation from ObW during April 1944 – decrypted on 2 May – gave the details of a planned tour of inspection of the German panzer troops in western Europe by the panzer commander, Heinz Guderian. The itinerary revealed the date, time and place of each of Guderian's intended visits – and the location where each unit was based. This confirmed, at least for the panzer formations, the German order of battle that Allied intelligence had surmised a few days earlier. The decode also gave useful information about the extent of damage to a central tank-repair site at Mailly following an Allied bombing raid.[14] More Fish decodes, issued from Bletchley Park on 24, 25 and 27 May, of messages which dated back to the middle of April reported a considerable reinforcement of the Contentin peninsula in Normandy, 'and gave exceptionally full details of the locations, boundaries and subordinations of the formations involved'.[15] By the eve of D-Day the Allies had some reasonable idea of the forces ranged against them.

There were also hints that the flow of decode intelligence might not be so easy to maintain at the same high level.

The whole position regarding the breaking of [Fish] messages has been altered by the introduction of the P5 attachment [limitation] on practically all lines (the only three exceptions at present are Octopus, Squid and Stickleback). Before the introduction of this attachment over half-a-million letters of decodes a month were produced by the application of hand-methods to messages sent on the same wheel-setting. Also wheel patterns which change every month could be obtained relatively easily by the same means. Under these conditions, the number of decodes obtained by machine methods were only a small proportion of the monthly output. [With the P5 limitation, so that] the key is dependent on the clear text, messages that are sent on the same wheel settings can no longer be broken... nor can the monthly wheel patterns be obtained by hand methods... the five Chi wheel patterns and settings have to be obtained on Newman's machine. The Psi wheel patterns and settings can then still be obtained quicker and more economically by hand.[16]

In other words, depths were no longer breakable, and Colossus would have to be used for both Chi-wheel-breaking and Chi-wheel-setting.

Meanwhile, in Italy, the Allies had reached Rome by early June 1944, following eight months of hard battle against the defensive Gustav Line, which encompassed the monastery at Monte Cassino. Allied landings in the rear of the German line, at Anzio in January 1944, had come close to being driven back off the beaches, but they held and, eventually, led to the break out towards Rome just as the Allies were finally driving through the Gustav Line itself. Bream provided information about planned German offensives against the Anzio beachhead and later continued to provide a useful flow of intelligence about German plans as they retreated to new defensive positions. The last and most northerly of these was known as the Gothic Line – so called in an attempt to derive some psychological boost from this association with the Visigoths, the Germanic tribes who had overwhelmed the Roman Empire in its homeland.

A report of 13 April 1944 at Bletchley Park gave details of some of the 'outstanding intelligence' that the Bream link between Berlin and Italy had gleaned in the previous few weeks. On 28 February, it had revealed the German plans for an assault on the Allied beachhead at Anzio.[17] On 1 March, a message gave details of Kesselring's appreciation of the beachhead in which he said that all his divisions were badly in need of rest and refit and that two new divisions were needed if the beachhead was to be cleaned up. The messages also revealed that Kesselring desperately needed an early attack: any delay would work to the Allies' advantage as they could build up the number of troops and guns landed.[18] It was information such as this that enabled Allied policy-makers to press ahead with their strategy of fighting for Italy. The failure to reach Rome in 1943 had turned the situation in Italy into one of stalemate, but knowledge that the German army had to divert resources to Italy to keep the army there in a functional state made it seem worthwhile.[19]

Bream also informed the Allies about other fronts. On 5 March 1944, another message contained a German naval assessment of the situation in the North Sea. The same day a message reported on the state of the partisan war in Italy. On 10 March, the link opened to the Allies an appreciation of the situation on the entire Russian front. On 16 March, the link was used to report on the ration status of the German armed forces in Italy. Three days later, a report gave details of the state of the German Tenth Army. There are several other similar messages outlined in the report, and they give a good flavour of the immensely detailed view this Fish link could offer of the strategic and operational situation. The information mostly related to the link's own area, but it was also capable of offering valuable insights into the condition and plans of the German armed forces in any theatre of the war.[20] Although Bream was an army link, the messages it carried even gave information about the navy and air force. The appreciations to and from the ObSW (Commander-in-Chief South-West), Kesselring, included reports on 'ground, sea and air'. In all, about 5 per cent of the Bream traffic that was decrypted concerned naval matters.[21]

While Bream continued to produce its copious intelligence, Jellyfish provided the information that the Allies needed to launch the D-Day invasion on the night of 5–6 June 1944 with a degree of confidence that they might succeed. The landings on four beaches were successful, but on the fifth, Omaha, there was a bloodbath. 'Troops landing on the [one] exposed beach were simply worn down... Omaha gave a terrifying taste of what the landings could have faced elsewhere had the German defence been properly prepared and waiting.'[22] Just prior to the launch of the landings, the German command believed, because of the very bad weather, that an invasion was not imminent. A decode of a message sent by ObW on 1 June concluded that 'as yet there is no immediate prospect of the invasion'. Rommel even thought he had time to return to Germany and visit his wife – which indeed is where he was when the invasion started. Other senior officers were at a conference. So, with Rommel absent and von Rundstedt having decided that nothing at all would happen over the next few days, it took some time for the German army command to react when it learned that the invasion was indeed under way. More time was taken to inform Hitler, who was asleep, and no one dared wake him up. The request for his approval to move up the reserves was thus delayed beyond a critical point, and this gave the Allies vital early time to secure the beachhead and to ensure that it remained beyond the reach of German artillery. These delays, along with the continued deception measures which convinced Hitler that the landings in Normandy were a ploy that would precede a bigger assault on the Pas de Calais, created the basis for a successful invasion. Over 150,000 Allied troops were on French soil at the end of the first day.

A few days later, once Stalin had satisfied himself that the D-Day landings had succeeded, the Russian army unleashed a new and powerful offensive, smashing German lines and advancing westwards in overwhelmingly massive and mechanized force. The fear of the main invasion in the Pas de Calais, the Russian offensive and the fighting in Italy, combined with Hitler's determination to keep troops in Norway, the Channel Islands, Denmark and elsewhere, meant that, in the critical period of D-Day itself and immediately afterwards, Allied troops found the German defences severely stretched. In land war, an attacking army is at its strongest at the moment of launching an attack, and thereafter its power is weakened. In marine assaults, however, the moment of attack is the attackers' time of greatest weakness and vulnerability. Once successfully ashore, the attackers' strength increases, as supplies and reinforcements are landed.[23] In failing to deny the Allies the ability to land, the German army could not make its most effective, and perhaps only, response.

Even after the invasion, the conviction of Hitler and the German high command that Normandy was a diversion remained very strong. Hitler held reserves away from the sagging German front in Normandy for several weeks as he awaited the main attack near Calais from the phantom forces. Indeed, it took a good eight weeks before the Allied forces had been built up in the beachhead in Normandy to launch a breakout – eight weeks of desperate fighting where Allied manpower was drained away daily in a terrain that was ideal for defensive fighting.[24] The battle developed so that Montgomery's British, Polish and Canadian troops held down the German panzer divisions around the eastern end of the beachhead at Caen, launching hard-fought attacks and soaking up the German counter-attacks, while allowing Bradley's American troops to amass forces for a break out further west. All the while, any sufficient German reserves that might have been able to swing the battle in Hitler's favour were held back east of the Seine awaiting the main invasion in the Pas de Calais. A senior German naval officer later recalled, 'The spectre of an added landing… still haunted the OKW. Concern about these yet-to-be-attacked coastal sectors prevented energetic measures to strengthen the heavily struggling front. OKW still did not release any of the divisions standing in double rows along the narrows of the English Channel.'[25] On the eve of the Allied breakout from Normandy, in late July 1944, the deception was still working. As one British staff officer commented at the time, 'It is quite incredible that today, seven weeks after the campaign was started, twenty German divs including two Panzer divs are stationed… north of the Seine, awaiting the arrival of a notional Army Group.'[26] The most successful strategic deception in history was an essential part of the success of D-Day.

*   *   *

In a report written shortly after D-Day, it was recorded that 'Fish comprises the communications network of the [German] supreme command. Traffic passing over this network has the highest strategic value of all sources of Signal Intelligence.'[27] But it also recorded that serious problems had hit the supply of decodes. The widespread adoption of the P5 limitation and, more important, daily change of the pin patterns meant that wheel-breaking now had to be performed for each link every day, not once a month as had been the case. The combined effect of these two developments was to hinder the flow, but not to staunch it. Machine methods of wheel-breaking (see Chapter seventeen) had become essential, as had the arrival of more Colossi.

A report to the USA in July 1944 gave details:

I mentioned... that the Jellyfish patterns changed on 14 June. The wheels were broken on 18 June (through a crib from Bream) but only messages of that day could be set. This led to the suspicion that wheel patterns were changing daily... However, 24 June has now been solved (also though a Bream crib) and the patterns are different... No other day can be set on these patterns so it is reasonably certain that they are now changing daily. As a result, principal reliance is now being placed on an attempted solution through cribs although rectangle analysis[28] on this link has not been abandoned. Grilse, a new link between Berlin and somewhere in Northern France was solved for the first time a few days ago. The solution was statistical on a single message of 10,000 letters. It is the only long message of that day (21 June) and no other messages can be set. Attempts to set five long messages of other days have been unsuccessful so it looks as though patterns change here daily as well... Bream wheels changed on 22 June and have been solved... Messages of subsequent days are being set on these patterns... Gurnard patterns continued in force without change to the end of June.[29]

These changes meant that the workload for Colossus 1 and its soon to arrive successor machines increased enormously. Because the P5 limitation depended on the clear or plain text, it was vital for both the legitimate German users and the illegitimate British interceptors to ensure precise accuracy in reception of messages. But, assuming that this was a practicable proposition, the P5 limitation did not prevent codebreaking – although it certainly demanded more processing, as did the daily pin changes. The limitation did affect which messages could be decrypted – namely those with distinct, language characteristics that made them susceptible to statistical analysis, what were known at Bletchley Park as 'favourable' messages. The basic methods remained applicable once they had been adjusted. Bletchley Park had acquired massive processing power, but these two developments demanded even more of it. In the meantime, however, the changes reduced sharply the number of messages that could be decrypted. The new Colossi were now absolutely vital just to restore previous levels of decryption. 'It will be seen that our resources for breaking Fish messages are at present extremely limited and will not be capable of dealing with the whole traffic available in any foreseeable future. This means that there will be a constant problem facing us as to how the available resources should be employed,' concluded Lieutenant-Colonel Pritchard, a senior officer in GC&CS's military section.[30]

Planning for D-Day had involved a massive increase in the strength of GC&CS. By the spring of 1944, staff numbers had reached 5,600 – up from 3,800 a year earlier – alongside a substantial increase in the number of operators deployed in the 'Y' Service, especially mobile units that would be needed in the days following the invasion. The official history later noted, 'By the beginning of 1944, for the first time in the war, the resources available for Sigint were temporarily in excess of what was necessary for current purposes.'[31] However, there were always bottlenecks affecting Fish output – if it was not lack of machines or extra processing requirements, it was Knockholt (in part because machine methods of wheel-breaking demanded the interception of more long messages). Several new non-Morse interception centres were opened in different locations which were better placed than Knockholt to pick up signals from western Europe. The siting of the new stations was vital. Knockholt, for example, was not well positioned to pick up signals from the non-Morse links based in France – Jellyfish (Paris–Berlin), Anchovy (Paris–Koenigsberg) and Swordfish (Bordeaux–Berlin). A report from Lieutenant-Colonel Pritchard pointed out that this was because 'Knockholt was not in the extended line of transmission. Generally speaking, North and South transmissions will be well intercepted, East and West badly.'[32] One of the new stations, Hawklaw in Scotland, was much better at receiving such signals. 'Interception of the Paris Jellyfish was particularly good while I was there,' reported one of Harold Kenworthy's engineers in May 1944. 'No doubt when the aerials have been erected... and full diversity [reception] is available, it will become solid throughout.'[33] Some non-Morse interception had been undertaken since 1943 at Wincombe, but in 1944 the need for a wider range of locations was urgent and interception was tested at sites at Keddlestone, Forest Moor, Hawklaw and Brora – which last station proved to be the best site for picking up the Jellyfish signals. A new type of aerial, a 'sloping-V', was tested and proved to be quite effective, and later a long Beveridge aerial was also installed, both of which gave very good interception right up to the end of the war. In the meantime, mobile interception units, 'Army Y', and decryption teams had to be set up to accompany the armies that would be heading for the mainland of Europe. But most spectacular of all was the massive expansion of Fish decryption at Bletchley Park.

In March 1944, there was still one Colossus at Bletchley Park used purely for de-Chi'ing processes for eighteen hours every day. It could handle about fifteen messages a day, while three single Robinsons handled one message a day each, and one coupled Robinson handled two messages a day, making a total of twenty decrypted Fish messages a day. By early April, an additional five messages a day were handled on Colossus 1, by then fully operational, and two extra messages each a day from three new coupled Robinsons, giving a total capacity of thirty-one messages a day. By mid-June, it was expected that Colossus 2 would be in operation – shortly after D-Day – and it would include the new parallel processing technique that increased the speed of the machine fivefold. Yet, the increased difficulty caused by limitations and daily pin-pattern changes would offset the greater capabilities of the new machine. It was thought, therefore, that Colossus 2 would be able to cope with another fifteen messages a day. Then, by mid-July, Colossus 3 and 4 – 'These are promised rapidly after C2' – would tackle still harder messages and between them handle another twenty-four, bringing the overall total output up to an expected seventy messages a day – from the handful per day of a couple of months previously. [34]

With the introduction of limitations and the daily change of pin positions (introduced on the 17 June on Jellyfish) it meant that these calculations were potentially overoptimistic. But the threat to continued decoding was eased by the gradual introduction of both limitations and daily pin position changes to other links. This stepped approach gave the codebreakers the time to adjust, whether it was new techniques or added processing power from new machines as more and more Colossi, Robinsons and other machines came on stream. One link could be decoded to supply continuing information while techniques to deal with the changes were developed. But the main relief came from the programme of Colossi construction being undertaken by the Post Office. As a Bletchley Park report put it, 'This daily change [i.e. of pin positions] spread gradually to other links, so giving the necessary time to re-organise… Colossus II arrived on 1 June, so removing in part the bottleneck experienced at the beginning of May, and further Colossi arrived gradually.' The number of decodes hit 476 in May, then dropped to 339 in July when Colossus 3 arrived, but hit 404 in August and went on rising steadily as Colossi 4, 5, 6 and so on arrived, so that in September there were 391 decodes produced from a total of eighteen daily pin positions broken for various links. Serious improvements soon followed with 533 decodes in October and 831 in November.[35] Without the Colossi, the introduction of limitations and daily pin-position changes would undoubtedly have overwhelmed the Robinsons, and Fish decodes would have all but dried up during that summer of 1944. But the timely arrival of Colossus 1 and its offspring meant that the Newmanry was able to ride the wave of processing demanded by these German security measures rather than being drowned by it. However, the two measures did have one effect – they increased the time it took between interception and decoding – and it often took as much as ten days until the decoding operation was completed.

However, in September the awkward P5 limitation started to disappear (having caused the Germans as many problems as the British) and the average time for decoding during September was one week, falling even further so that during October several messages were decoded within twenty-four hours. By November 1944 the P5 limitation had disappeared from all but Bream, Codfish and Gurnard. November also saw a record month for interception at Knockholt and new stations – during one week over 7,000 army messages were intercepted. The interception teams at that time were aware of twenty-seven army links, twelve belonging to the Luftwaffe and three used by the Navy.[36]

According to a Bletchley Park report, written in March 1945 and looking back at D-Day, entitled 'The Value of Ultra – accurately handled',

> Our role in Intelligence is strategic rather than tactical, and our value is therefore far higher in a pre-offensive planning period than during a battle... ours is outstandingly the best strategic source – it is, indeed, worth far more than all the others put

together – it is only one of many tactical sources, and at that probably not the best of them… In a pre-offensive planning period, Ultra is normally supplemented by such sources as ground reconnaissance patrols and, in consequence, by captured documents and prisoner interrogation. But these supplementary sources have rarely been thinner than they will be with Allied forces [in western Europe]… All this goes to show that we have reached a planning period… in which Ultra will be at least as valuable as it has ever been, and perhaps more valuable than it can ever be again.[37]

While Fish intercepts and Colossus decodes had played a role in allowing the Allies to measure the success of their deception measures and in turn to make D-Day a success, the war was far from over. It would, in fact, become more violent than ever, with twice as many bombs, for example, being dropped in the last eight months of the war than in the whole of the previous five years.[38]

The German wireless teleprinter network started to become more fluid as both Russian and Allied armies pushed back the German armies. The location of the Jellyfish transmitter retreated from Paris eastwards, ending up in Koblenz. On 20 July 1944, a bomb planted by an army officer at Hitler's war headquarters, the Wolfschanze, failed to kill him. One of the key conspirators was General Erich Fellgiebel, head of the German army signals corps. Indeed, the signals corps and the staff of Army Group Centre on the eastern front were hotbeds of the conspiracy. Fellgiebel's 'fellow officers and his subordinates had an extraordinarily high opinion of him; he was regarded by as a highly educated, sensitive soldier, upright and human, well-versed in the natural sciences with a bent for philosophy and an outstanding expert in everything to do with communications… He also knew, however, how indispensable he was; he remained fearless and straightforward. He loathed Hitler as an unintelligent, inhuman tyrant; in wartime he loathed him even more as a military incompetent, [and] culpable instigator of destruction.'[39] The conspirators were able to organize and communicate precisely because they had access to the army communications network so their messages were relatively safe. Furthermore, Fellgiebel possessed secret codes, which were impenetrable to the secret services.

On the day of the bomb attack, Fellgiebel's task was to 'secure' communications between the Wolfschanze and Berlin for the conspirators, thus allowing them to stage an army coup, displacing the Nazis.[40] Unfortunately, Fellgiebel found it impossible to sever all communications – it was something that an engineer might have been able to do, but a general could hardly go to the exchange with a pair of wire cutters, or pull out the connections. Nor was there any reason why he should turn up at the amplifier station at Rastenberg and instruct the engineers working there to close circuits. Also, given the redundant circuit design with double rings, it would be impossible to cut all communications even if one station was closed down. In any event, there were 'secret' lines beyond Fellgiebel's control, some belonging to Martin Bormann, head of the Nazi Party, as well as links to the special trains of Hitler, Goering and others which, when stationary, were plugged into the local network near the Wolfschanze. 'Technically it would have been easier for two or three junior post office officials to isolate Wolfschanze than it was for Fellgiebel or [fellow conspirator and signals officer] Hahn. For them it was almost impossible to find the assistance for their project', as the conspirators were all army officers.[41] They did consider whether to recruit some non-commissioned officers, but decided the risks were too great.

So, although Fellgiebel never managed to sever communication completely, following the bomb attack, he did make it extremely difficult for several hours. Nevertheless, news of Hitler's survival was telephoned to Berlin in time to undermine the momentum of the coup. In Paris, there was confusion until 8 p.m. over whether Hitler was dead or not – and, in the meantime, a number of army officers effectively signed their own death warrants by arresting the SS/SD establishment in Paris.[42] Another factor in the failure of the plan was the timing of the message ordering the coup. The conspirators intended sending an order to the army commands to arrest Nazis loyal to Hitler on fabricated accusations of an attempted takeover, and this order was to be dispatched by a conspirator in Berlin on hearing news of the bomb blast. He duly took the order to the teleprinter exchange at Zossen and gave it to an operator who asked if it should be sent over enciphered links. When the conspirator said that it should, it was placed in the pile of other messages awaiting enciphered transmission. But there were so many secret messages that it took three hours before the cipher machine operator had worked though to the conspirators' message and it was sent out too late. The Nazi party, the SS and much of the army instead rallied around the singed, dazed and furiously vengeful Fuehrer. Fellgiebel, like several other conspirators, suffered torture and an agonizing death. He had never made a serious attempt to hide his dislike for the Nazis, but his technical and organizational competence had forced Hitler to tolerate him. His replacement, Albert Praun – 'a good Nazi' according to Guderian – had to press Hitler not to purge the signals corps too deeply, despite the number of sympathizers it clearly contained, since it risked undermining the ability of the organization to carry out its duties. As a result, many signals corps conspirators survived the war, ensuring that the story of Fellgiebel's death was not forgotten. Other army units were not so fortunate.

Admiral Canaris, the head of the German armed forces intelligence department, the Abwehr, was another victim of Hitler's vengeance. He, too, was involved in the resistance to Hitler within conservative and military circles in Germany. There have been persistent suggestions that either Fellgiebel or Canaris, or both, supplied intelligence to the British (or via other nations to the British) including information that helped the breaking of the Enigma and/or the Geheimschreiber machines. There is no documentary evidence to support these theories, however, and, unless such evidence is eventually released or uncovered, it is safest to dismiss them.

According to official accounts, no prior hint of the conspiracy reached Allied intelligence via Enigma or Fish decodes. Yet, one message was picked up on the day of the bomb attack, detailing the attempted anti-Nazi coup and its short-lived existence. 'Source has found parts of one such telegram: General von Witzleben... styling himself Commander-in-Chief Armed Forces, announced the death of Hitler, and warned that an unscrupulous clique of front-shy [Nazi] party-leaders was attempting to seize power, and declared a state of emergency... [but] this copy at least broke off in the middle.'[43]

Hard on the assassination attempt, Hitler suffered another devastating blow. On 27 July 1944, the Russian army reached the Baltic Sea on the Bay of Riga, isolating Army Group North in the Kurland, or Courland, pocket. 'Instead of withdrawing the thirty battle-ready divisions (accounting for nearly one-third of the total strength of the German army in the East) to defend the East Prussian frontier, Hitler ordered them to stand firm.'[44] Later that month, the Amtes Anna exchange, at Mauerwald, was closed down as the Russians moved closer to occupying Eastern Prussia and Hitler's Wolfschanze. Hitler withdrew to his bunker in Berlin, where he was to end his days less than a year later, and the OKH, the army command for the eastern front, retreated to Zossen, just outside the capital. The OKH teleprinter exchange was located seven floors below ground level to avoid damage from the now daily Allied bombing raids. Jellyfish and Bream, two of the most productive of the Fish links, also had to move their field bases, as Allied armies pushed them into retreat, with the Bream station in Italy pulling back to near Florence.

Historians have pointed to a major difference between the way in which the two powerful dictators, Stalin and Hitler, conducted the war. 'As the war progressed Stalin came to rely more on the advice of the professional soldiers' especially after 1942. 'Stalin accepted the new balance of power, since he had little choice, and focused his efforts on mobilising the domestic economy and workforce... [While] Hitler refused to accept his limitations, perhaps because he saw his calling as Germany's warlord as the central purpose of a dictatorship based on the ideal of violent self-assertion of the race, where for Stalin supreme command was above all a political necessity.'[45]

The number of fronts on which the German army now had to fight did not result in Hitler ceding his detailed control. The attempt on his life also increased his distrust of the army and strengthened his belief in their treason. He did not blame the defeats on his own increasingly unrealistic orders but on the generals' unwillingness to carry them out. So he restricted the reaction time of army units even further by insisting that all commanders, down to divisional level, had to report their plan to him personally in sufficient time for him to be able to countermand them if he so desired. And as the commands became more mobile, and as bombing raids made cable communications more difficult, so more of the commanders found they had to put details of their plans into radio transmissions for Hitler's approval (see Appendix P – 'Hitler as seen by Source').

> The attitude of Hitler, in [Ultra] documents, shows a violent stiffening from Normandy on. One has the impression of a growing despair (whether or not he owned it to himself), a growing distrust of his generals, as either knaves or fools who would let him down whenever he gave them a chance... But the more numerous and minute his orders, the less possible they become to carry out; the more they were disobeyed, the more ubiquitous become his interferences, his threats, his flying-court-martials. There could be no more flagrant contrast than between Hitler's behaviour through these last battles in the West and Fieldmarshal Montgomery's principles of an HQ well forward, personal contacts with subordinate

commanders, and an absolute refusal to get muddled up with details... [During the autumn], though the spate of Fuehrer orders persists, they are of a longer-term nature, and concerned with administration, man-power, defence-lines, morale, punishments of waverers, scatterings of oak-leaves [i.e. military decorations], swords and crosses, and designation of more and more 'fortresses' to be held to the last round.[46]

An analysis at Bletchley Park of the wireless teleprinter links of German Army Group B, based in north-west Europe, showed that there were two different wireless teleprinter links maintained with the general staff of the armed forces, OKW, in Berlin by different signals corps sections. One was the main link, while the other served as a back-up and provided uninterrupted communications when the main Army Group headquarters had to close down to shift its location. Communications between Oberbefehlshaber West, ObW, Commander-in-Chief West, and the OKW went via the Army Group signals section, with a forwarding link between the signals section and ObW's personal headquarters. This set-up also enabled the OKW to have direct communications with individual armies within the Group nominally under the command of ObW.[47] The topology, or layout, of the communications network betrayed the fault line that undermined the efficiency of the command structure of the German army.

General der Infanterie [Infantry General] Günther Blumentritt was von Rundstedt's chief of staff during the Normandy invasion. After the war, Blumentritt recalled at a critical point in mid-June, when the Americans were cutting off the northern part of the Cherbourg peninsula: 'OKW, bypassing ObW and Army Group B, gave a direct order to Seventh Army to... maintain sufficient forces in the north for the defence of Cherbourg and still have enough forces to withdraw south... this was an impossible order... The Fuehrer wanted to throw the strongest force possible into the defence of Fortress Cherbourg. We, on the contrary, wanted the strongest possible force to be in the south. To us, Cherbourg was not so important as the need for a southern front to prevent the enemy from breaking through into France.'[48] But Hitler ordered otherwise. Hitler's communications network increasingly turned into a noose around the neck of his army, slowly strangling it. Two different forces pulled the noose ever tighter: Hitler's own compulsive need to interfere and the constant leakage of information to the Allies.

Yet the flow of this intelligence to the Allies was not entirely smooth. The daily change of the pin positions was causing a substantial amount of work and would reduce the output of decodes until improved methods and machines became available. A report written in August 1944 assessed the great success of Fish decryption – and the continuing challenges: 'Fish... has the highest strategic value of all sources of Signal Intelligence. The problem of solution has always been most complex and, owing to the introduction of new precautions by the enemy, has recently become tougher. Hence, the diminution in intelligence suffered lately. The solution has always had to be carried out by mathematicians of the first rank. The number of these men available is small and the problem from its new complexity demands an increase in their numbers unless the position is to be allowed to deteriorate.' As it was, the situation did not deteriorate, and, in fact, the teams working in the Testery and the Newmanry ensured a renewed supply of that vital intelligence.[49]

chapter nineteen

A Day in the Life of Fish I

On 4 February 1945, a message was sent from Berlin on the Whiting link to the German army command teleprinter office in the Courland, where some thirty German divisions had been cut off. Some troops were being evacuated, but it seems that Hitler was prepared to keep almost a third of his armies on the eastern front in the west Latvian peninsula, either as a bargaining chip for negotiations or to launch a counter-attack on the exposed Russian left flank as it moved further into East Prussia, north Poland and the Reich itself. The message, serial number KN/WB6573, has multiple addressees, mainly in the German navy, and appears to give shipping instructions for the evacuation. The message is one of very few of which the original Fish decode has been preserved. All the original intercept slip and perforated tape, as well as all the perforated tape used in the decryption processes, was burned after it was no longer needed, partly for security reasons and partly to avoid creating an impossibly onerous amount of filing. The small amount of original codebreaking material that has survived has done so by chance – perhaps because it was kept for an investigation after an incident, or for training purposes, or because it was filed in the wrong place. Effectively, our knowledge of the Fish decodes comes entirely from those decodes that, after translation, were considered worth sending immediately by teleprinter to army intelligence units (though only after being redrafted to more or less conceal details of the origin of the information) and from reports written in GC&CS based on these and other decoded messages. One further problem is that it is seldom made clear whether information sent to the army intelligence units or revealed in a report comes from Enigma or Fish decode(s).

The KN/WB6573 decode is reproduced in the photographic plates and is transcribed and annotated in Appendix O – Whiting decode, 5 February 1945. It is an example of the end product of the main Fish process, following interception at Knockholt or one of the new stations, and decryption by the combined efforts of the Testery and the Newmanry. Bletchley Park would still have to translate, assess and annotate the decode and send out any important information to the intelligence units with the armed forces, but these tasks were handled by the unit which performed the same function for Enigma messages. Because hardly any original intercept or decode material survives, it is impossible to reconstruct the passage of a real Fish message through the processes at Knockholt and Bletchley Park. It is nonetheless clear that, from its vantage point on the North Downs, a few miles south-east of London, the non-Morse interception station at Knockholt picked up the message sent on Whiting on 4 February 1945 (as indicated by the KN in the message serial number). But nothing survives to show details of its interception or decryption. One clue, however, does exist which may well indicate the intense pressure under which the work was done. The photograph of the decode shows information written in boxes across the top and in the right-hand margin (repeating the same data). The date entry under 'MK' across the top shows the date of origin of the message as '4/2/44'. A check on the other dates in the boxes will show that this is an error, and should be '4/2/45'. This small, insignificant mistake reminds us that this is a real document, not a carefully amended one that has been translated, interpreted, reordered and published (if only to a tiny audience), but an actual working document used by someone rushing to get the job done, one job among many on the Fish decode assembly line. In this chapter and the next, the various stages of the process will be studied in some detail to give an idea of how a message was intercepted, its key worked out and then decoded. Different messages will be used to illustrate the various processes when the role of Colossus is examined in the next chapter.

What can be seen is a veritable information-processing factory in operation, with people and machines working in an unusual synthesis. Incoming electronic wireless signals were processed into outgoing intelligence, which in turn contributed to strategic decision-making by the Allies and which thus affected the course of the war. The large electronic machines naturally sit at the centre of the picture, but they were dependent on meshing successfully with a considerable number of other technological processes. To observe Bletchley Park at work is to witness not just the birth of the electronic computer, but also the birth of the age of electronic information-processing.

Colossus was not quite what is meant by the term computer nowadays, yet it was the first prototype, *the* stepping stone to the modern computer, so completely different was it from all that went before it (see Chapter twenty-three). One important difference in later computing machines was the way in which the operator-cum-user and the machine were unusually closely linked. Colossus's interaction with the user was rather more like that of a complex piece of scientific apparatus than that of a modern personal computer; the results it produced needed to be interpreted and they were not presented in an especially user-friendly fashion. Similarly, the hive of activity at Bletchley Park (and Knockholt, of course) does not reflect the activities of any modern computer centre, although it does perhaps have modern counterparts in large computer-using organizations which include manual processes (for example, the printing and enveloping of tens of thousands of computer-generated bills). Rather, Bletchley Park was like a cross between a noisy factory, with its machines working at full tilt, and a research laboratory/non-teaching university, with rooms full of people working quietly away, obviously applying their full attention to the detail of some complex subject.

This meeting of two worlds was marked as well by the sharp gender division between the cryptographers, who were almost exclusively male, and the machine operators, who were exclusively female. There were, of course, other groups at Bletchley Park, security troops, maintenance engineers, general workmen, cleaners, caterers and so on – all the sort of peripheral but essential support staff one meets in any organization. The engineers who built and maintained the machines were also very important, but the core workers were divided into these two largely gender-based grades, codebreakers and Wrens – members of the Women's Royal Naval Service (or, in the case of Knockholt, women from the Auxiliary Territorial Service, ATS). In fact, as time progressed, the hierarchical divide was not so much between the tasks performed as simply between male codebreakers and the female Wrens. Naturally, the capabilities of individual Wrens varied enormously and some became quite adept at running Colossus and interpreting its results – a task that was initially the duty of the codebreakers. But, whatever tasks some Wrens performed, they generally retained the status of less capable assistants to the real stars, the codebreakers.

The majority of both the codebreakers and the Wrens were young people, in their twenties and single. So, naturally, there was much social intermingling and many a romance, to use the term of the times. For many there was an easy relationship between the genders, but for others, unprepared to suddenly find themselves in this weird, artificial world, it was unsettling. The presence of so many young women leading independent adult lives upset some of the older and more staid military types at Bletchley Park, as well as setting the tongues of locals wagging. One security officer tacked an illuminating observation on to the end of an assessment of security at the Park. He was concerned about potential implications in the high staff turnover of the catering department, which recruited locally. 'I feel sure they have no suspicion of the work being carried on, but they certainly have a lot to say as to the way some of our young ladies dress for business.' And to underline the point he added a personal observation: 'I have seen a young married woman leaving the Park, coming off night duty, dressed as if she had just left a Turkish Harem.'[1]

In addition, most of Bletchley Park's core workers had to be brought in from outside and lodged as nearby as possible. The early arrivals got the best accommodation – in local hotels and inns – but increasingly staff had to be put up in institutions and lodgings further and further away. As the numbers employed at the Park increased, so it spread its influence. It was rather like the very first factories some two centuries earlier, which turned smithies into machine-makers and agricultural workers into machine-minders, drawing them away from the land and the rural life into the industrial revolution, ineluctably effecting deep social change. Bletchley Park was the first electronic information factory. It drew in academics from ploughing the furrows of their particular field of research and Wrens from their permitted status as teacher, maid or housewife. The employment of women for the Fish work was first mooted in early 1942, when the overall shortage of men meant an acute lack of wireless operators. Harold Kenworthy, who was in charge of the wireless interception station, reported, 'The possibility of women [wireless telegraphy] operators must not be overlooked. Women could easily be trained and be expert in dealing with the large amount of slip that will have to be read up.'[2] He gained approval, and a few months later, in July 1942, he reported, 'Women slip-readers are being recruited and specially trained.'[3] Later, women were also employed to act as machine-operators at Bletchley Park, running the Robinsons, Colossi and other machines, as well as the Enigma Bombes and a massive punched-card operation.

Paul Gannon

The employment of women to fill the labour vacancies at GC&CS was part of a wider wartime movement – one that would have far-reaching effects on the patterns of women's work. Between May 1939 and May 1944, the number of women in work in Britain increased by over two million. And the patterns of work also changed radically – the number of women employed as domestic servants or maids fell from 1.2 million in 1939 to under half a million in 1944.[4] One historian has concluded that 'Within the overall picture of the British war-economy, the most striking success was the mobilization of women... the largest single source of extra manpower was womanpower.'[5] The numbers at GC&CS were a fraction of the total of women employed in war work, but it is important to record that women came to make up the greater part of the workforce at both Bletchley Park and Knockholt.

The first women at Bletchley Park had been employed on the Bombes in 1941. A job specification stated, 'Wrens are required for interesting and extremely important work in the county, 50 miles out of London, necessitating the operating of light electrical machinery. Girls should be of good physique and education, quick, accurate and keen, with good powers of concentration.'[6] A later history recalled, 'Their progress was watched with great interest, and doubt was felt as to whether women could undertake the work', but the doubters were soon proved wrong and numbers began to increase.[7] By the end of the war, there were nearly 3,000 Wrens at Bletchley Park and outlying sites, over half of them working on Bombes. Apart from the cryptographers and engineers, the Newmanry was entirely staffed by Wrens who worked under the control of the male civilians. The Newmanry started in May 1943 with sixteen Wrens (all ratings) and grew steadily until, in May 1945, it employed 270 officers and ratings.

Bill Bundy, an American codebreaker, who worked on Fish decryption at Bletchley Park and was used to overheated offices recalled, 'We were told the entire available output from the Scottish universities came to Bletchley Park. These were fine stalwart ladies for the most part, wearing tweeds and flat shoes that we in Boston call butter-spreaders. They were vigorous and very, very good at their jobs. They also had a great sensitivity to temperature in huts. This was not kept exactly torrid at the time. But when the Scottish ladies got there, if the temperature crawled above sixty [degrees Fahrenheit], you would hear this anguished cry: "Stuffy in here" and the windows would be flung open to let some fresh air in.'[8]

Most non-Morse messages were intercepted at Knockholt. This too was a task mainly carried out by women, members of the Auxiliary Territorial Service – and pronounced 'Ats'– a name which, unlike that of the Wrens, has not survived in popular use. At its height, Knockholt employed 600 staff working round the clock in three shifts – allowing for weekend coverage, some 150 staff were due on duty at any one time, to run the intercept sets and associated equipment. 'Nevertheless there were times when traffic ordered by us [i.e. the Bletchley Park cryptographers] was more than they could handle.'[9]

During the period immediately before D-Day, the commanding officers of other 'Y' stations had been asked to sacrifice some of their operators to help boost numbers at Knockholt. Colonel Balmain, chairman of the 'Y' Committee, reminded a meeting of station commanders in March 1944 of 'the extreme seriousness of the woman power situation. For the non-Morse commitment alone, 144 operators had to be produced.' So far, just thirty-nine had been offered up by other stations and forty-eight new operators were under training. However, commanders were warned not to send 'unsuitable operators', such as those who 'could not stand up to night shift'.[10] They were being asked to offer up their best staff, not to grasp an opportunity to get rid of their also-rans.

The daily output from Knockholt in August 1944 was 250,000 characters of intercepted Fish messages. Newman reckoned that, with the arrival of Colossus 2 and the expectation of more Colossi, his machine department could cope with 320,000 characters a day immediately and 500,000 by September. Overtime working increased production at Knockholt to 300,000 characters later in the month, but the existing organization was stretched to its limit. 'There seems little hope, therefore, of giving Newman all the perforated tape he can use unless an immediate increase in the Knockholt staff can be obtained.' Colonel Wallace, who had nominal charge of Knockholt, declared that the lack of suitable staff was the only cause he could identify for the problem, and he concluded, 'I am satisfied that the best possible use is being made of the available personnel at Knockholt. We simply have not enough girls to keep the machinery working... Mr Janes has made great efforts to increase the efficiency of the Station, but the poor quality of the staff and the lack of good supervisors have been a handicap.'[11]

However, this was not good enough for the senior GC&CS managers. During 1944 all the 'Y' stations were inspected to see what improvements could be made. For unknown reasons, the planned visit to Knockholt was postponed.[12] But in January 1945 the long-delayed inspection took place, over three and a half weeks, and the report, marked as being for the 'Director only', made uncomfortable reading for the supervisors at Knockholt who, under Harold Kenworthy's wing, had been kept from external scrutiny for so long.[13] It was perhaps a coincidence – or perhaps it was not – that Kenworthy was, in January 1945, on a rather trying trip to Brussels and the Rhine to check on the quality of non-Morse interception there (see Chapter twenty-two) – just at the time that an outsider was penetrating his sanctum and exposing his management shortcomings, whatever his technical brilliance.[14]

Colonel Jacob, who conducted the inspection, noted,

First impressions in the Slip-Reading and Reperforating Sections were not favourable. Slip-reading calls for quiet application, yet at all hours the Slip-Reading Section gave an impression of movement and bustle. There were whole days when the Reperforating Section had little work, whereas on others the section was fairly fully employed – yet the quantity of material being transmitted to Station X [Bletchley Park] was always well below requirements. The causes of this unsatisfactory state of affairs were investigated... What particularly impressed me there was that, apart from the essential information... extracted daily for Station X purposes, no precise data on the performance of Slip and Reperforating Sections, and, indeed, some other aspects of the organization, were available. Such data cannot be sacrificed if the [officer in charge] is to manage his station satisfactorily, and be in a position to report accurately to those interested.[15]

Another set of problems was the inadequate supervision of the work, badly organized staff rostering and poorly managed shift patterns. 'My impression was that, with some notable exceptions, insufficient attention was being given to supervision by the Supervisors and their assistants... undoubtedly there is a feeling among both Supervisors and Staff that the girls are not being paid enough for what we expect of them.' Part of the problem was that the intercept operators were kept in the dark about much of the effects of their work. It was work that required intense concentration over long hours and for poor pay. Some hints were given to them about the importance of their work, but not much was conveyed for fear of a leak, a fear proved entirely unjustified by the remarkable secrecy which was maintained for several decades after the war by all who worked at Knockholt.

The dissatisfaction over pay and lax supervision affected output. One Sunday during the inspection, just ninety-eight people were on duty, with sixty-five on leave and thirty-nine 'absent', while on another weekday, 'the respective figures were 168, 5 and 29'. Not surprisingly, output went up during the week and down at weekends. In one week, on the Sunday 217,000 characters were output, while on one weekday it was a massive 403,000 – a record achievement at the time. A new shift system and, in modern jargon, a management-reporting system were introduced. Jacob also reorganized the tea breaks. 'The members of slip and reperforating sections are allowed two ten-minute tea intervals per shift – in addition to the regular meal-break of one hour.' But, to get the tea, the staff had to go to the canteen and the time taken was stretching to twenty or even thirty minutes. 'With an average of 240 people on duty daily in the two sections the loss in output from this cause is obviously considerable.' Delivering the tea to the section improved output and added twenty extra minutes' work per person per shift. Jacob concluded, 'Given adequate traffic and with certain improvements already under way and others in prospect, I feel that an average daily transmission from the Reperforating Section to Station X of 400,000 letters (about two-thirds of our total requirements) is well within the capacity of the present staff.' The success of Jacob's reorganization of operations demonstrated that Wallace's confidence that the staff were being employed as best they could had been misplaced. Thus, the immediate crisis at Knockholt was ended by the application of a fairly new discipline, then known as 'operational research', later becoming called 'systems analysis'.

The main challenge for the interception team was to ensure absolute accuracy of all the characters in an intercepted message, and then to give the cryptographers at Bletchley Park any extra information they needed, who transmitted the message and to whom, when, from where to where, what time, and so on. But accuracy remained paramount. As an internal Bletchley Park account observed, 'A tape with a single letter inserted or omitted in the middle would almost certainly fail to set'.[16] That Bletchley Park could expect this quality of interception of distant directional radio signals is a tribute to the work of Knockholt staff and the remarkable performance of the wireless equipment, much of it developed in-house. A priorities meeting held every morning at Bletchley Park determined which links were to be covered in any one day at Knockholt. Until mid-1944, the priorities tended to be set by the officer in charge of Knockholt, Harold Kenworthy, but, with the opening of the second front in June 1944 following the landings in Normandy and the need for specific intelligence, Bletchley Park asserted its primacy.[17]

The receiving room at Knockholt was fitted out with thirty interception sets in what was known as the Set Room.[18] Messages were generally recorded in three different ways to ensure a good copy. The most accurate record was produced by the undulator which recorded the individual mark/space units on a slip. A skilled slip-reader could observe the pattern recorded on the slip and recognize the shape of signals representing different characters (long runs of the same signal – i.e. all spaces or all marks – and slides, repeated signals, had to be measured with a ruler). The slip-reader would write the characters on a form known as the Red Form, which included other information such as the link, trans-mission frequency and tones used, transmission starting time and date.[19] Also the intercepted signal could be printed out – in the basic teleprinter code – on a strip of paper tape which was then cut into suitable lengths and stuck on to paper. And the intercepted signalling units were punched or reperforated directly on to paper tape in the Baudot code. This was the most useful form as, once it had been checked and copied, it could be sent simultaneously on two teleprinter links to Bletchley Park, where it could be used as input to Colossus and several of the other machines. The Red Form and less urgent material went by motorcycle courier.

The operators in the teleprinter room at Bletchley Park would take the two punched tapes on receipt and slide one on top of the other to check that all the holes coincided on the two tapes. If they did, it had passed the first check; if they did not, Knockholt was asked to retransmit. Accuracy improved after Knockholt was issued with a relatively low-tech piece of equipment, a hand counter which could be used to count perforations in tapes. Looking back at the Fish decryption operations immediately after the war it was noted, under the heading of the 'Relative importance of machines', that while 'The pre-eminence of Colossus and Robinson is manifest... The need for efficiency in other [less sophisticated] copying machines is apt to be overlooked; one of them, Miles [see later in this chapter], was in fact unduly neglected. The supply of spare parts for readers and re-perforators generally has been inadequate. The hand counter is very simple and quite indispensable; a long time elapsed before a reliable one was produced. The amount of Colossus time wasted because tapes were delayed or incorrect [because of the lack of a hand counter] is difficult to estimate but it *is certainly very considerable*' [italics added].[20] This is a common phenomenon, even if it is one that is seldom acknowledged – underestimating simple technology because too much attention is paid to high technology, even when that high technology needs the low technology to function at its best.

The work on the Fish intercepts at Bletchley Park began with Colonel John Tiltman, in a room on his own, standing at his high desk. By early 1945, it had grown to a unique electronic information-processing factory, with one new Colossus machine arriving every month and a couple of dozen other electronic and electro-mechanical devices working steadily. The Testery and the Newmanry were spread around several buildings in the north-west corner of the Park – the Testery in Block F, the Newmanry in Hut 11 and Block H. The buildings housing the machines were certainly not humble huts but were, in fact, extremely strong, steel-framed, brick-walled buildings. There was a fire-brigade team maintained at the Park and it was called to put out a fire in one of the workshops used by the engineers who maintained Colossus. Arthur Chamberlain was Duty Officer the night that the fire broke out and later recorded that, though there was a lot of smoke, there was little damage. 'Newman arrived about 4am, very angry because several hours had elapsed before he had been notified. He instituted a rigorous enquiry, but he was unable to find out the cause.' Chamberlain later learned that it had in fact been started by an engineer showing off to a Wren. 'He had spilt some lighter fuel on the floor of the workshop and tossed a lighted match on to it. Though all the Wrens knew this, none of them let on to Newman's enquiry.[21] This was the only serious external disruption to the service provided by the Colossi and other machines.

Even the most advanced computing tasks involve tedious, manual work, often with the help of simple machines or ones of intermediate complexity – work that has to be done if the complex machines are to do their job properly. It was with such tedious, but vital, tasks that the decryption process began. Paper tape was the means of passing data from one process or room to another and of storing it when not in use. An important part of Bletchley Park's practical achievement was managing all that paper tape, keeping it under control while ensuring the value of the data it contained was not inaccessible. In January 1944 a Joint Registry was set up to monitor all material entering or leaving and kept note of where any particular piece of information could be found in the system. The Registry also created a master card for each message, which recorded its essential details, and procedure cards, which accompanied any tapes sent to the appropriate codebreaking department. The system was tightly enforced, so that, 'few messages strayed and those that did were quickly recovered'.[22]

When tapes arrived at Bletchley Park from Knockholt, they first underwent extensive checking. One of the lessons learned early on – albeit not as early as it could have been – was the vital importance of testing everything at every stage. 'The number of operations performed on a message from the time it was received at Knockholt to the time it is decoded is very large and therefore it is essential to have systematic checks at every stage. These checks are equally important for processes which are done by hand and by machine. Checking has become a mental habit with all the cryptographers who have been in the section for any length of time.'[23] However, while the lesson was being learned, much intelligence was lost. 'The importance of checking was not realized at first and it is generally believed that *the comparative lack of success in the earliest days was largely due to the use of incorrect tapes'* [italics added].[24] This was, of course, a lesson which had to be relearned by post-war computer engineers and systems analysts and which they characterized as 'garbage in, garbage out'. What came to be called, rather confusingly, the British Tunny machines started out as simple 'analogues' of the Geheimschreiber which could be used to perform decoding once the wheels had been broken and set (i.e. the key used for an individual message had been identified). But they were also developed into much more flexible devices, capable of performing tasks such as calculating the delta streams for input to Colossus and Robinson. The Tunny machines also came to serve a very useful function in performing checks and tests.[25]

One testing technique exploited the consequences of using the Vernam cipher addition rules which mean that combining two identical characters results in all spaces. Two tapes could thus be compared by checking that all the characters were identical by adding them all together – which should produce a third paper tape with nothing but 'all spaces' for every character. Any hole punched into the output tape would indicate that the two input tapes were not identical. A family of machines, one of them electronic, was designed to perform this task. These machines were known as the Miles – although it was sometimes also called Mrs Miles, after a woman of that name who had attracted newspaper publicity when she had given birth to quadruplets in 1935. But, before looking at the Miles, it is worth discussing the Fish machinery in general, to see how the various machines developed for Fish codebreaking fitted into Bletchley Park. The hand counter, the Tunny machine and the Miles have already been mentioned, but there were also Angel, Insert, Garbo, Aquarius, Proteus and Dragon.

The Robinsons and the Colossi were the most conspicuous of the devices invented at Bletchley Park to handle the digital Baudot code and perform arithmetic/logical processes based on the rules governing the Vernam cipher and other similar logical processes. One point should be clarified. The five units representing each character are transmitted, whether by cable or radio, in sequence, one after the other – in serial. If five wires (or five radio frequencies) were available, all five could be transmitted simultaneously – in parallel – though for practical and economic reasons this was not done.

In the Baudot code and Vernam cipher, each group of five units represents a single character, and it is possible to conceive of many of the enciphering and deciphering, as well as decryption, processes as happening to the five units of one character at one time – and this is implied in some of the explanatory diagrams. Several of the machines designed at Bletchley Park did operate on all five units simultaneously. 'Both types are used for Tunny cryptography, though for this purpose [serial] apparatus has no advantage except availability; it is clearly much easier to add and permute' in parallel 'though requiring more complex machinery.'[26] The hand perforator, the Insert machine, Junior, Garbo and the punch of Colossus 6 all used parallel processes. Angel, Tunny and the decoding machine used successive units, i.e. serial processing. To complicate matters, some Miles machines, including Miles A, read the five units in parallel but perforated them in serial.

Bletchley Park divided its ranks of machinery into three general categories: counting machines, copying machines and general machines. Colossus and the Robinson were the top-of-the-range counting machines – if the label seems rather prosaic for the first electronic computing machine, it is important to recall that the basic function was to count the number of times that, for example, units 1 and 2 of the delta of two streams equalled a dot (0). The Tunny, Miles, Garbo, Junior, Insert and the Angel were all copying machines although some versions of them were fairly complex with, as mentioned, the capability to perform logical binary calculations to produce differenced or delta streams. The output of all the copying machines was another paper tape – or tapes in the case of some of the more sophisticated versions. Angel was the simplest of the copying machines, making straightforward copies, and consisted of just a tape-reader linked to a reperforator. However, it was awkward for making corrections. Insert was a development of the Angel, and had a keyboard attachment for easier correction and insertion of characters. Junior was somewhat more complex and consisted of a tape-reader, a steckerboard and an electric typewriter. The steckers – short cables (also known as plug cords) – could be used to connect an output socket on the steckerboard to any input socket. This allowed any one character to be made to print out as any other one character.

Garbo was a more advanced version of the Junior and could also perform differencing or delta processing on the input-tape characters and could output to a typewriter or a reperforator. Here the logical processing – the combination of two characters or a number of units according to the Vernam cipher rules – of the Geheimschreiber, Robinson and Colossus is seen performed in ever more complex and flexible copying machines. Garbo was primarily used for setting up rectangles for rectangling, a means of wheel-breaking. The later version of Garbo had its own memory made up from electro-magnetic relays arranged in four small banks on a rack, with switches used to set up the machine for a particular run. One important point to note is the increasing reliance on equipment sourced from the USA. In March 1944, Max Newman was looking forward to the manufacture of more 'Garbo outfits from long overdue IBM typewriters'.[27]

The Miles machines formed another family of complex copying machines and they came in various generations (following the order of versions used at Bletchley Park): the early Miles, Miles B, Miles C, Miles D and Miles A. The early Miles machine could only perform a straightforward combining operation (this was needed to check whether two tapes were identical), but the later versions, Miles B, Miles C and Miles D, were more flexible. Processing and combining of the individual units could be handled, as well as whole characters. The Miles machines were used to check the two copies of the incoming teleprinted messages, and to check copied tapes to ensure that they were indeed perfect copies. It could also spot slides or spurious characters.

All the machines described so far, with the exception of the Tunny machines which employed a few electronic valves, were electro-magnetic devices which operated at fairly slow speeds. However, Miles A was almost entirely electronic – which is why, though the name implies it stands in between the early Miles and Miles B, C and D, it, in fact, stands alone. It contained only seventy valves – not many compared with the vast number deployed in Colossus, but it is an indication of the gradual expansion of the use of electronic machinery at Bletchley Park beyond Colossus. The valves proved to cause fewer problems in operation than relays and at the end of the war a new version of the Miles was under construction that also had an electronic ring counter. The use of electronics was, indeed, far more extensive than the impression given by most accounts of Bletchley Park.

Miles A could difference up to eight times using its own memory circuits to remember previous characters – a feature that was of great use in tackling limitations. However, even though the trouble was not with the valves, Miles A was 'rarely in proper working order, the existing model being the experimental one, not really intended for regular use: this rather than the extra plugging, explains the operators' preference for B, C, D'.[28] Again, the glamour of the big machines meant that less sophisticated ones, such as the Miles family, were undervalued. Their performance was 'not entirely satisfactory… The design is believed to be sound, but there has been no adequate supply of spare parts.'[29] In March 1944, Max Newman reported to Travis that the two 'Mrs. Miles' machines were 'very unreliable' and in the future two updated Miles machines would replace 'the present Mrs. Miles condemned by Flowers as unsound'.[30] At the end of the war, only two Miles machines were still in use and two more were nearly completed.

chapter twenty

A Day in the Life of Fish II

An anonymous account, written at the end of the war but held secret until recently, gives a feel of Colossus in action:

> It is regretted that it is not possible to give an adequate idea of the fascination of a Colossus at work: its sheer bulk and apparent complexity; the fantastic speed of thin paper tape round the glittering pulleys; the childish pleasure of not-not, span, print main heading and other gadgets; the wizardry of purely mechanical decoding letter by letter (one novice thought she was being hoaxed); the uncanny action of the typewriter in printing correct scores without and beyond human aid; the stepping of display; periods of eager expectation culminating in the sudden appearance of the longed-for score; and the strange rhythms characterizing every type of run: the stately break-in, the erratic short run, the regularity of wheel-breaking, the stolid rectangle interrupted by the wild leaps of the carriage-return; the frantic chatter of a motor run, even the ludicrous frenzy of hosts of bogus scores.[1]

By November 1944, there were six Colossi at Bletchley Park and by mid-1945 there were ten such machines at work, five in F Block and five in H Block, with an eleventh under construction. And there was that host of other machines that aided the codebreakers in their work. While Fish decryption was an intensely intellectual feat, it was also a mindless machine task. It required from everyone, Wrens and codebreakers alike, an attention to detail, consistent concentration and an ability to cope with the unexpected – the barely visible pattern in a stream of characters on a paper tape or the unusual sound that signalled a relay slightly out of synchronization. Indeed, the physical working environment at Bletchley Park was a strange, hybrid one. On the one hand, the electronic machines had paper tape-readers running as fast as was practicable and their operation, as well as that of the clattering relays, was as noisy as any factory floor. On the other, their electronics operated in complete silence and were comprehensible on a theoretical level, like the environment of a modern computer room. The intercepted messages arrived in the Newmanry or the Testery once they had been through the various checking and tape-making processes. The Colossus runs that will be followed in this chapter, however, will all be wheel-setting runs. This was the original reason that Colossus was built, and was its bread and butter work.

With the completion of the copying and testing operations, it was time for the decryption work to begin. The cipher text message tapes were sent, via the Registry, to the Tunny Room for preparation of the delta tapes, then to the Colossus Room for the Chi wheel-setting runs. For the purposes of following three messages processed on Colossus, it will be assumed that the wheel-breaking had already been carried out by hand methods in the Testery. The task for Colossus was to find the Chi-wheel settings.

There were, usually, more messages intercepted than there were machine and human resources to decrypt them. Which messages were to be dealt with first depended on a mix of factors, the most important being military need on the various fronts. But workaday cryptographic measures also played a role – after all, it also made sense to tackle first the messages from links which were easier to break. The priority given to different links in the allocation of machine time was determined by a small group consisting of Wing Commander Oeser (of Hut 3), Major Tester (as he had become) and Max Newman. Edward Travis, director of GC&CS, informed those involved, 'Wing Commander Oeser will represent the Intelligence priorities and it will be the business of Mr Newman and Major Tester to interpret that priority to the best of their ability, taking into account the cryptographic position. In the event of any one of the three feeling that the situation requires further discussion the matter shall be referred to AD(3) [Assistant Director 3], AD (Mech) [Gordon Welchman] and Lt Colonel Pritchard [Military Section].'[2]

Once the daily priorities had been set, the Newmanry code-breakers and operators knew which messages to tackle. The usual first step was to run a statistical count based on the double-delta counting method devised by Tutte (see Chapter thirteen) or one of the punctuation- or language-oriented statistical tests (see Chapter seventeen). The double-delta would run repeatedly through a message tape, each time stepping one place to start the Chi wheels in a different initial position, and perform the double-delta count on units 1 and 2 for each character, scoring the number of times the result equalled a dot (0). The Chi settings with the highest count would probably be the right ones.

The process started with the duty codebreaker looking at the incoming message tape, using his knowledge of the link's characteristics to decide what initial test to perform. He would then specify the instructions for the set-up of Colossus for the run. The Wrens operating the machine would set up switches with the delta pin positions on each wheel derived from the earlier wheel-breaking, and connect up the logic switches so that they performed the processing run specified by the duty codebreaker. In effect, they were programming the machine, defining the variables and the processes that the machine would go through once it was started. A key step in the post-war development of the computer was to bring this process inside the computer as the program – an extension of Flowers's insight that it was the data that mattered, not the tape. For the time being, however, the set-up process defined the precise processes the machine would follow.

There were far more Wrens working in the Newmanry than any other group (Appendix Q). One male codebreaker at least was happy that there were people who could be allocated the fiddly tasks.'They controlled the flow of tapes and ordered the runs to be made, with occasional advice from the analyst who was the duty officer. They operated the machines, including the Colossi, with aplomb. Some of them would be in charge of Colossi on their own, moving expertly from run to run. For wheel-breaking, there was always an analyst in charge, but he would be helpless without a Wren to wind the tapes on to the Bedstead and plug up the runs.'[3] But, in fact, many Wren operators became far more skilled than this implies, eventually taking over some of the tasks performed by the duty codebreaker, for example, determining which tests to run.

There were sharp distinctions between the cryptographers and the Wrens in terms of the division of labour.'The method of division of labour is a principle which applies to all grades.' But, in fact, it applied quite differently to the grades:

Cryptographers are given a definite job for at least a week at a time. Wrens have a definite job more or less permanently. An experiment was tried once of changing the jobs of the Wrens around, but it was unsuccessful. The cryptographers, on the other hand, need to have a complete and detailed knowledge of the entire section if they are ever to act as duty officer. The principle of moving from one job to another after a week or two is particularly important as regards research. No important theoretical advance was made by anyone who did not have a good knowledge of the practical side... The possibility of cribbing by long retransmission would probably have been discovered much earlier if a definite individual had been made responsible for looking into the question (as a part-time job).[4]

Training of the Wrens was mainly given on the job and only became formalized over time. 'When [Colossus] routines were first spread round the section in the form of notices there was an immediate decline in the number of mistakes. Previously the Wrens had been taught mainly by word of mouth. Later instruction books were introduced and each entry was signed by all who read it. This is the best method.'[5]

Wrens were chosen by interview from those in HMS Pembroke V (Category – Special Duties X). No fixed qualifications were required, though a pass in mathematics in School Certificate or 'good social recommendations' was normally considered essential. Though a few of the earlier Wrens were rather older and more experienced, 96 per cent of those who came were between the ages of seventeen-and-a-half and twenty. Twenty-one per cent had higher Certificate, 9 per cent had been to a University, 22 per cent had some other after school training and 28 per cent had previous paid employment. None had studied mathematics at the university. On arrival, all Wrens were given up to a fortnight's training in the teleprinter alphabet, the workings of the Tunny machine and (in some cases) computing [of rectangles]. This was followed by a conducted tour of the section and a written test. Wrens (unlike men) were organized in fixed watches and given fixed jobs in which they could become technically proficient. While the section remained small, it was possible to try new Wrens at various jobs soon after arrival, but later, allocation was made on the basis of the test held at the end of the their initial training period, and on the bases of the jobs available. The cheerful common sense of the Wrens was a great asset. Several of them showed ability in cryptographic work and several others were trained by the engineers to undertake routine testing of machines.[6]

The third work group in the Newmanry was made up of the forty-five Post Office engineers who maintained the machinery, 'made up almost entirely from men in these grades aged 20 to 22 years'.[7] The presence of so many, often so young, men and women led to the occasional problem. Some of the few surviving papers in the files of Max Newman relating to the war describe an incident late one evening in December 1944. A couple of passing engineers stopped to chat noisily in a corridor of the Newmanry, when a Wren appeared. One of the engineers produced a sprig of mistletoe, causing, the engineers later claimed, the Wren to let out a shriek. At that, again according to one of the engineers, 'Mr Newman came out of his office shouting. As he did not appear to be shouting at me I proceeded to the workshop.'[8] All those involved scattered and Newman wrote angrily to the head of the engineers demanding an investigation and disciplinary action. There is no indication that any such action was taken, but the incident illustrates the stresses and strains of the variety of work in the Newmanry. Newman needed quiet so that he could concentrate on solving complex mathematical issues. But the young, hard-working engineers and Wrens needed to let off steam now and then so that they could cope with concentrating on their often tedious, repetitive tasks or, in the case of the engineers, very long hours.

There were fifteen Post Office maintenance engineers looking after the Fish machinery – chosen from among the 'very bright' ones who had worked on the building, with some also contributing to the design, of Colossus at Dollis Hill.[9] Most of the maintenance work they carried out was with the electro-mechanical components of Colossus and the other machines rather than the electronics, which performed almost flawlessly. 'We depended totally on our engineers, who installed the incoming machines and maintained the battery already installed. It was only because of them that we could keep on increasing our output,' said Shaun Wylie, a codebreaker in the Newmanry.[10] Great efforts were made to recruit the Post Office's best available men from the automatic telephone construction and maintenance staff throughout the country, to employ them at Dollis Hill and the Post Office Factory at Birmingham to build the equipment so that they should be thoroughly familiar with it, and to give them, before taking up maintenance duties, any supplementary instruction that was necessary. As the work developed, the complexity and novelty of the equipment increased and further maintenance training was needed, but technical staff were often hard pressed to produce the equipment and instruction was neglected. A number of maintenance men made up for this deficiency by their own initiative and exertions, and passed their knowledge on to others... The total manpower available at the beginning of 1944 had been so depleted by the demands of the Armed Forces on the Post Office staff that no further suitable men were available, and the men already engaged – including all the manufacturing force at Dollis Hill and the Post Office Factory – worked over 70 hours a week for many months.[11]

The only maintenance problems arose over the machines built at the TRE whose transfer to Post Office care 'was never officially authorized', leading to a 'most unsatisfactory state of affairs, in consequence of which, despite their relatively simple character, they are less reliable than Colossus'.[12]

By early 1945, there were about fifteen mathematicians working in the Newmanry – Donald Michie, Jack Good, Shaun Wylie and Henry Whitehead among them. There were new buildings too, with the Newmanry occupying a solid-brick two-floor building, called Block F, and later another single-storey brick building, Block H, as the Colossi accumulated and demanded more space.[13] Howard Campagnie, an American codebreaker who joined the Newmanry in December 1943, recalled that,

Colossus was the epitome of an adult toy. For the

mathematicians it was marvellous. It would tabulate five thousand frames of teleprinter tape a second so if you did a ten-minute run you were probably getting close to three million tallies. It was fascinating really. You didn't see the plain text, the Testery was the one that recovered the plain text. You were dealing entirely in a statistical world. You would toss out the random scores and look for anything that looked like it was [significant]. The operator had to make a decision right there, in your head, sitting on a stool in front of Colossus. You depended entirely on the probability of being right as far as the random scores were concerned. If you got a [significant] score you would try to confirm it one way or the other on some of the other wheels, or by another run.[14]

This is the other aspect of stored program control – conditional branching – that was brought inside the computer after the war. With Colossus, the operator or cryptographer would assess the results of one run, decide what run to perform next, set up the machine, run it and assess the results once again, perhaps leading to yet another set-up and run process until a good result was obtained, or the message abandoned. Conditional programming simply means putting the assessment of the results into the computer program, so that the decision on how to proceed is determined by the machine, rather than by an operator.

There were so many messages which needed to be set and such a limited amount of processing time available that a maximum of about an hour of machine time could be devoted to attempting to set the wheels for a message of known wheel-pin positions. If no significant results could be found in that time, then the tapes would be returned to the Registry for storage. More time might be allocated if it seemed there were indications of a successful run, but the need for successful decryption and the demand for machine time enforced tough limits on how much effort would be expended on a recalcitrant message. To illustrate how Colossus was used, three runs on different messages will be followed in more detail, with different results. One illustrates a straightforward run and the other two illustrate rather more complex ones. Whatever the nature of the run, Colossus first had to be programmed, by setting up the processes it was to follow in the plug- and switchboards, and inserting the U-links to specify whether the generated delta-Chi settings would be dot or cross. Nineteen-year-old Wren Jean Thompson was a Colossus operator in 1944.

> If the pattern of the wheels was already known you put that up at the back of the machine on a pinboard. The pins [or U-links] were bronze, brass or copper with two feet and there were double holes the whole way down the board for a cross or dot [unit] to put up the wheel pattern. Then you put the tape on round the wheels with a join in it so it formed a complete circle. You put it behind the gate of the photo-electric cell which you shut on it and, according to the length of the tape, you used so many [Bedstead] wheels and there was one moveable [wheel] so that you could get it taut. At the front there were switches and plugs. After you'd set the thing [i.e. after completing the counting run to set the wheels] you could do a letter count with the switches. You would make the runs for the different wheels [or units] to get the scores out which would print out on the electromatic typewriter. We were looking for a score above the random and one that was sufficiently good, you'd hope was the correct setting. When it got tricky, the duty officer would suggest different runs to do.[15]

Once the machine had been set up, the run could start. Appendix I contains an annotated copy of the printout produced by Colossus for the first message to be followed. The printout has been annotated to explain what the information means – the step numbers in the text below refer to the notes in that appendix. Reference is also made in the account that follows to the processing trees and statistical counts of groups of units, outlined in Chapter seventeen – for example, the double-delta is labelled on the Colossus printout as '1p2/' and means 'adding units 1 and 2 results in a dot', and a count is made of each hit or time that this condition is met.

The first message is from a link that had poor security measures and its message was usually quite easy to set, so the duty cryptographer for Colossus 3 decided to give it priority. The whole setting process took about twenty minutes – probably about as long as it takes to read this account thoroughly in conjunction with the annotated printout in Appendix I. The message was sent on 23 October 1944 on the link codenamed Stickleback (between OKH, then in Berlin, and Army Group South on the retracting eastern front). The message had 9,567 characters – a good long stretch of text which means it was likely to set fairly easily – Step 1. The message will be put through the double-delta count on units 1 and 2. This is indicated in the printout by 1p2/ – Step 2. The number of times the double-delta condition should be satisfied by a random stream of characters is half the total, 4,788. The duty codebreaker would tell the operator that the machine should be set to record details only of those counts which exceed 4,912 – the set level (this figure is determined by the probability calculations and the Sigmage – see Chapter seventeen). The set level was well in excess of the random average, and thus would print out details of only the most significant settings when the process is run. This data is all entered into Colossus by the setting-up processes described above (there was no interactive communication with the electric typewriter which was used purely for output). The printout of this data gave the operator a means of checking that it had been set up correctly before the run.

The double-delta was then run and printed out its results – Step 3. These showed the starting positions of Chi wheel 1 (K1) and Chi wheel 2 (K2) whenever a count exceeds the set level of 4,912. Out of 1,271 possible starting positions, eighteen settings show a potentially significant count, of which four stand out with counts of 5,005, 5,015, 5,038 and a whacking great 5,384. This highest count was produced when Chi wheel 1 had a starting position of 36 and Chi wheel 2 a starting position of 21. This was such a clear statistical bulge that it is almost certainly correct and the message was deemed to be set for Chi 1 and 2.

The operator now had to repeat the runs, but this time choosing one of the processing conditions from the processing tree to work out the settings for the other wheels. In many cases, this would have started with a run on wheels 4 and 5 and these were easier to set once wheels 1 and 2 were known. Wheel 3 would then be worked out last of all. Runs could be made looking at just one unit (known as a short run), two units together (a long run), three, four or even five units. Of course, the more units involved in the count, the longer the run. Thus, the processing tree indicated the best conditions to search for depending on what was already known. In the case of this message, the operator chose a multiple test which looked at all three remaining units, albeit independently, as three separate short runs. This gave a score for each unit, rather than for a combination, thus necessitating fewer possible positions to test. The text length was again 5,384 characters, the random average was 2,692, and the level at which counts were to be printed was anything in excess of 2,728 – Step 4. As can be seen, there was one significant count for each wheel – with Chi wheel 3 in a starting position of 1 (Step 5), Chi wheel 4 in a starting position of 19 (Step 6), and with Chi wheel 5 in a starting position of 4 (Step 7).

The operator had now worked out the settings for all five Chi wheels, but still needed to instruct Colossus to do a count of the letter frequencies in the delta-de-Chi stream at those settings to provide a final statistical confirmation. This is shown in Step 8 and Step 9, and reveals a very high count for the characters 5 and /, and a reasonably high count for 8. This sort of count was very unlikely indeed to be produced by random, so it was taken as confirmation that the counts had thrown up the right solution. The right settings could now be passed to the Testery who would then strip out the Psi and motor stream settings by hand for the message to be decoded on a Tunny analogue. Colossus had done its job in an incredibly short time, pointing to the statistical sore thumb sticking out in the delta-de-Chi stream of the message.

But, of course, not all runs went so smoothly. The basic double-delta was used as the initial way in, but sometimes messages refused to be set on units 1 and 2, and then the initial run had to be replaced with a count on another statistically useful condition – that units 3 and 4 added together produced a cross (1). Albert Small, an American cryptographer, reported back to the USA on the operation of Colossus: 'There is no rigid rule or procedure in wheel-setting; each operator has his pet methods... The important consideration is "how high is the score itself as against all the other ones?".'[16] Another frequent problem was slides where characters were missed out in the intercept. A slide fed corrupt characters into the count and so reduced the effect of the statistical anomalies that were being searched for.

The second message to be followed proved to be more difficult owing to a slide in the intercepted text. The message, which was 6,020 characters long, was sent on 24 February 1945 and an attempt to set the Chi wheels was made on Colossus 7 (the Colossus printout for this message is reproduced in the *General Report on Tunny*, see Further Reading). The initial run was the same as the previous two examples, 1p2/, the double-delta count on wheels 1 and 2. The duty codebreaker wanted the machine to print out those Chi settings which produce a count in excess of 1,624. The Colossus run produced details of nine settings with counts in excess of 1,624, of which the highest was 1,655. This was not even a good result, and certainly not statistically significant enough to be considered as giving the right settings. 'The solution... is not considered complete unless the results match the expected delta-de-Chi characteristics,' observed Albert Small, and this one did not measure up to that standard. The operators and cryptographers knew exactly what the figures typed out by Colossus on its IBM electric typewriter implied and knew what was an acceptable result and what wasn't. 'It might almost be said that the whole of the Newmanry is told in the [delta-de-Chi characteristics] table... [it is] so important to the successful prosecution of the Fish problem, that practically every man, every Wren, in the Newmanry and in the Testery, knows them by heart, together with the variations to be expected on the different [links... which] have not been computed for all cases where they are needed, [though] they exist in the minds and experience of the Colossus operators.'

Returning to the specific message – although the result was not good enough to be considered definitive, it was significant enough to be worth probing further. If the message did indeed have a slide, then that could undermine the results, throwing out of kilter the statistical patterns being searched for. So the operator instructed Colossus to do a span count, also known as spanning, which simply meant performing the double-delta count in spans or groups of 1,000 characters and printing out the results for each span separately. The operator then looked at the results and saw that one span, between characters 4,000 and 5,000, had quite a different count than all the other spans. So the operator ordered a further span count, this time from 4,000 to the end of the message in spans of 500 characters. This showed that the slide occurred somewhere in between character 4,500 and 5,000. So the operator could re-run the basic double-delta count on the message from character 1 to character 4,500, which should have been enough to give a result and indeed, once completed, it strengthened the probability of the result sufficiently to convince the operator that she had found the right settings for Chi wheels 1 and 2. Spanning could also be used to isolate parts of a transmission to check for specific types of message within the overall transmission. Each intercepted trans-mission contained several individual messages for different organizations attached to either end of a link, so one transmission might contain formatted reports, such as tank returns, that were amenable to statistical identification in spans, but not in the overall message.[17]

The operator then decided to follow up with a count on the condition that both unit 4 and unit 5 equalled a dot (0). She could have chosen other conditions, but, when run, the count threw up one marginally significant result. This was taken as providing the settings for Chi wheels 4 and 5, even though it was a bit weak. The operator knew that the most likely characters to be searched for in setting the third and final wheel are /, 5 and U. To decide which to look for, she instructed Colossus to count the occurrences of the combinations which produce these characters and discovers that the best results are likely to be produced by 5. A further run based on counting the number of 5s then gave one setting for unit 3 that was statistically significant and thus all five wheels had now been identified. However, given that one weak count, the operator decided a letter-frequency count was needed. Colossus performed this, printing out a block of numbers in two columns of thirty-two numbers. There was no labelling explaining what character each number represented, but an operator would know perfectly well which number related to which character. In this case, she spotted that the counts for 5, U and F were all highly significant and thus she was able to confirm that Colossus had indeed managed to set the Chi wheels for that message – but only on the evidence of the first 4,500 characters. The full message may have given a different statistical result. Indeed, methods were developed for stepping back and isolating a slide so that a run could use the entire message in a count. Another electronic machine, Aquarius, was designed specifically to handle that task so that the Colossi could be concentrated on their main processing task.

The third message to be followed was run on Colossus 3 and had been sent on 22 October 1944 (the printout for this message is reproduced in a report by US cryptographer Albert Small's report which is now available on the internet – see Further Reading). The message was 2,683 characters long, and on the 1p2/ test would have an average of 1,341, so to filter out non-significant results Colossus was instructed to print out the count for settings over 1,404. One setting stood out at 1,605, which was calculated to be 150 to 1 against being a chance occurrence, so the multiple test was performed on units 3, 4 and 5. However, the results were mixed – there were no significant counts for unit 4, and only a single poor count for unit 5, but it did produce a reasonable count for unit 3. This was assumed to be correct, and another run was made with units 1, 2 and 3 considered as set and a statistical test on units 4 and 5. But this run produced no significant scores, so another run was done to check unit 3 and it indicated yet another setting for unit 3. So, once again, the machine was set to run a check on units 4 and 5. And once again it produced nothing worthwhile. Several more counts were performed in case a statistical bulge could be found by one or other of the processing-tree counts. Eventually, a reasonable count was found for all wheels, though it took nearly two hours, double the maximum time normally allowed. The Chi-wheel settings and a de-Chi print were sent to the Testery for the Psi and motor wheels to be set, but they eventually abandoned work on the message. For some reason, it was one of the messages that refused to be set. The higher the number of dots (0s) in the first motor wheel, the easier it was to decipher the messages and, indeed, success was highly proportional to the dottage. The lower the dottage, the more resistant it was to statistical decomposition, so that the real delta-de-Chi stream was within the random range of counts and so could not be identified. Perhaps one or two of the units within the message above were correctly set, but clearly not all were and this prevented the Testery from finding valid ways of identifying the rest of the key settings.

So, of the three messages followed, two were set successfully and one was not. Each had required a different degree of machine analysis before it yielded its secrets or was jettisoned as being unbreakable in a reasonable time. (Some figures for output of the Newmanry are given in Appendix Q.) Once the

Newmanry had worked out the Chi-wheel settings, the results would be handed over to the Testery, where the Psi and motor wheels would also be set so that the message could be decoded.[18]

The Testery used hand methods to pull apart the de-Chi'ed message, identifying the Psi and motor settings. Mathematical, linguistic and military expertise would be deployed in the task. Albert Small, the American cryptographer, reported back to his colleagues in the USA, 'Setting Psis… is done by hand just as [in Washington]; but they do it much smoother here. Experience, and I believe experience alone, has made these capable lads artists at their work. The time usually required to set all five Psis varies: given known patterns, and high motor dottage, they can set in twenty minutes. Adverse conditions can require eight hours or more. Day in day out, the average time is four hours counting the unbroken ones in that average; one hour is the most usual time.' He also observed, 'Last spring [1944] when Chi and Psi patterns remained permanent throughout each calendar month, the setting of Psis might possibly have become a bottleneck. At that time the Newmanry used to make motor or Psi runs to help the Testery. But this is done only about twice a week today [December 1944], because the pressure to get out the daily Chi's is too great.' Informally, the process of Psi-setting, or de-Psi'ing, was known as deep-sighing, an expression the frustration at the many dead-ends that had to be followed before the right answer was found.

But this sharp division of the Newmanry and Testery into machine and hand work became blurred as the war progressed. In general, the Newmanry used Colossus to work out the Chi settings and the Testery used hand methods to identify the message and strip out the Psi and motor settings. The Testery also did the wheel-breaking from depths and using other techniques. But wheel-breaking methods were also developed that could be run on Colossus. For example, rectangling, which was originally a hand method of wheel-breaking, was later performed on Colossus using a special rectangling gadget or attachment and became a vital technique following the introduction of new security measures from mid-1944 which made it impractical to do wheel-breaking by hand methods alone. Rectangling gadgets were fitted to Colossi 2, 4, 6, 7 and 9. Colossi 5, 6, 7, 8 and 10 all had a large Bedstead capable of handling tapes up to 30,000 characters long. In fact, Colossus 6 was used almost continuously for rectangling. Colossus was also used to break wheels by statistical analysis of long re-transmissions of identical messages on different Fish links (as happened with messages sent on both Bream and Jellyfish allowing the later to be broken for the first time in the run-up to D-Day).

The Testery also invented its own electronic cribbing machinery, Dragon and Proteus (see below), so, even though hand methods remained in use until the end of the war, wheel-breaking and wheel-setting could both effectively be handled entirely by machines. 'In general, Testery methods were hand methods based on language properties, and Newmanry methods were statistical and needed machines. But there were many contradictions. The computing of rectangles is a statistical hand job undertaken by the Newmanry, and on the other hand Dragon is a machine designed to do a language job in the Testery. Hand analysis of key (by methods elaborated from that devised by Turing in 1942) is a statistical hand job involving probability techniques which was done by the Testery before (and after) the Newmanry was founded.'[19] In other words, there had to be great flexibility and co-operation between the two Fish departments, deploying their combined human and mechanical resources to the best effect as new techniques and new needs evolved.

Donald Michie, a young classics student who had been one of the first members of the Newmanry, learned his mathematics in situ. He did such a good job that one day he proposed a method of using Colossus to perform wheel-breaking as well as wheel-setting. He worked with his colleague Jack Good to devise a way to program or set up Colossus to perform wheel-breaking. Jack Good recalled, 'Once again then, a simple idea that we had been overlooking led to a major saving of time. Since the mid-1960s, if there is a laborious calculation to be done, everybody thinks of programming it for a computer; but the mid-1940s were not the mid-1960s.'[20]

Dragon was a series of electronic cribbing machines which was invented by the Testery.

Dragon 1 was built in the USA using advanced electro-mechanical techniques, while Dragons 2 and 3 were built in Britain using electronic valves. Dragon 1 and 2 each had a ten-character memory, while Dragon 3 could store sixteen characters. The machine was used on a message that had already been de-Chi'ed, in search of an underlying stretch of plain language containing the crib. This meant looking 'behind' the Psi stream for a match with the crib, thus giving the correct settings, which was the object of the search. The crib could be up to ten characters long, or sixteen characters with Dragon 3 – typical cribs and the links they appeared on are given in Appendix N. As can be seen, punctuation and other aspects of the teleprinter shift function played an important role in these cribs – most of them included at least one or two characters of basic teleprinter code and some consist of nothing but the teleprinter-oriented characters.

The crib would be set up on the machine on an array of fifty jack plugs (ten by five, for ten characters each of five units) using plug cords. Above the jacks there was a display which showed, in dots and crosses, the crib that had been set up on the array. A second array was built into the machine so that, while one crib was being searched on the machine, the operators could be setting up the next. The de-Chi'ed message was read from a paper tape fed into a tape-reader. The machine remembered its ten crib characters and would then search for that crib in every possible position for each set of ten message characters at a time. It did this by combining the crib with a stretch of de-Chi in all possible positions. If a stretch contained the crib, combining it would wipe it out of de-Chi stream, leaving the extended-Psi stream. A compatibility gadget called Salamander was built for the Dragon but its purpose is not clear.[21]

According to Gil Hayward, a Post Office engineer, the American version of Dragon was shipped to Bletchley Park in a strong wooden case and guarded by an armed US signals corps sergeant who refused to allow anyone to unpack it. Eventually, however, he was persuaded to relent. As the wooden case was made of good solid planks the British engineers, after years of shortages, were at first more interested in what would happen to the wood than in the machine it encased. 'A quiet word with the sergeant revealed that he had no instructions as to the disposal of the crates, which he clearly regarded as rubbish, and he readily agreed that we undertake the onerous task of disposal for him. We did. I have never seen such a rapid vanishing trick.'[22] When Dragon was assembled, the British engineers were disappointed as they had expected a slick and sleek machine. It used advanced new crosspoint relays, but it was very noisy and soaked up so much power that at times it caused the lights to dim. Indeed, Dragon was an appropriate name for the machine that one engineer described as sounding like a monster munching its way through tin-plate. After a few weeks, Dragon 1 expired, having chewed its own electrical contacts. A newer British version, Dragon 2, which used electronic valves, was set up in one room at Bletchley Park and, when one American engineer saw it, he asked when it would be switched on. Gil Hayward recalled, 'I replied that it was already running. I am afraid that for once Sam [the US operator] was speechless. Our Dragon, except for a very faint background pitter-patter, was practically silent. Soon after this, Sam dismantled his Dragon, and it was removed.'

However, a history of the Fish section written at the end of the war gives a slightly different assessment. 'Dragon arrived from America [in October 1944] and Rooms 22, 23 and 24, Block F, were made into one room to house it. Considerable success was achieved, 31 de-Chis on low motor dottage being broken by the end of October. Improvements, such as counters, were added to it and plans started for an improved model.'[23] Unfortunately, these two short and discordant accounts are about all that we know of the Dragons and their role in the success of the Fish decryption operation.

With the development of Dragon, there was a greater need for precise information about likely cribs. The Testery was concerned that Hut 3, which translated the decrypted messages, was concentrating on those which revealed information of intelligence value to the armed forces rather than information of use for decrypting more Fish traffic. 'There is a danger of not only messages not being broken on the Dragon (which depends on cribs), but also that wheels that would have been broken by means of a crib will remain unbroken. There is a further danger that messages of technical interest will... not be reported at all and that vital information will be lost.'[24] However, the demand for skilled German linguists and the need for immediate intelligence meant that the Testery itself would have to do more to look for cribs and technical information.

Another electronic Testery machine was Proteus, which was used to 'anagram' depths, as the codebreakers described the process. Two messages sent in depth would be combined to wipe out the common key and leave the combination of the two plain-language messages. This would then be tested simultaneously against six common cribs, plus another crib from a dictionary of several hundred frequently used cribs. If a pair of cribs was correct (i.e. that each crib was present in one or other or the combined messages) then the result would be a /, all dots. The six cribs were set up using jacks on a plugboard, but the depth text (the combination of two plain-language texts with the key stripped out) and the dictionary were held on paper tape. All six cribs were then tried simultaneously, but independently, with the depth text, a character at a time (in groups of seven characters) and for each character scanning the entire dictionary of its hundreds of words looking for a hit. (This was thus the equivalent of a program that ran loop within a loop, with a six-part parallel process.)

Another machine, Aquarius, was a go-back device, which could recover the flow of a text distorted by slides or spurious characters. It had a 400-character memory, built up of over 2,000 capacitors (400 characters times 5 units per character), making it a significant development in terms of memory technology. It could remember up to 218 de-Chi characters before a pause and 87 after a pause, which could be used to recover from a slide and allow a mechanical wheel-setting or wheel-breaking run to be resumed.[25] These machines, and those discussed in the previous chapter, were built by engineers at Dollis Hill and by the small team based at Bletchley Park under Godfrey Wynn Williams, who had been a major figure in the development of the first Robinson. Unfortunately, most information on the construction and use of these machines has been lost – and therefore so has an opportunity for fully under-standing the role in the development of digital technology of the rich array of digital machines that appeared at Bletchley Park in the last two years of the war.

Once the Testery had identified the Chi, Psi and motor settings, details were passed to the Decoding Room, where a Tunny ana-logue would be set up with the appropriate settings and the tapes were loaded and run though the machine – and out of the printer would come the plain-language message. Post Office engineer Gil Hayward recalled how he was serving overseas as an intelligence officer when he was summoned back to Dollis Hill in January 1944 to join the Tunny design team under Sid Broadhurst. According to Hayward, the Tunny was much easier to change (for example, when altering the pin positions) than the Lorenz original, and it could perform many more functions. An example of a decode produced by a Tunny machine is reproduced with the photographs in this book and transcribed and annotated in Appendix O – Whiting decode, 5 February 1945). As can be seen from the photograph of the decrypt, it was printed in the basic teleprinter code format, so that the statistical work on teleprinter punctuation could be advanced. This printout used a somewhat different set of characters from those used in the text and examples in this book

(+ instead of 5 for figures-shift; – instead of 8 for letters-shift; and . instead of 9 for SPACE).

Once the decode had been printed, the tapes were returned to the registry for storing and the plain-language copy went to Hut 3 which received the decrypts from both Enigma and Geheim-schreiber traffic and it was responsible for translating, annotating and writing up the intelligence gathered from decrypts for onward transmission to the handful of senior intelligence officers and general staff officers permitted to receive Ultra intelligence. Hut 3 did not generally make assessments or point to the value of intelligence. This was left to the recipients, who would have received intelligence from other sources (such as photo-reconnaissance and prisoner-of-war interrogations) and were best placed to decide what weight to place on Ultra material. However, Hut 3 maintained a massive index, so that, when a unit, person or technical subject was mentioned, any previous mentions and connections could be added to the annotated report sent out to intelligence officers. Hut 3 also performed important traffic analysis of Fish traffic and wrote innumerable reports on a variety of different subjects. Reports on German wireless telegraphy and interception operations are particularly frequent, but others cover subjects as diverse as German codewords and 'Hitler as seen by Source'.

Two other aspects of the role of machinery at Bletchley Park are worth noting here. First, the Bombe operation had become a substantial undertaking, dwarfing the Newmanry. Nearly 1,700 Wrens were employed in operating the Bombes at Bletchley Park and other sites (not counting Bombes in the United States). A family of 211 machines of different versions was in use at the highest point. The table in Diagram 20.5 shows some sample Bombe processing figures for the autumn of 1944. For example, in the week ending 14 October, nearly 200 different Enigma keys were broken. During that week, an average of 4,608 Enigma message parts (Enigma messages were restricted to 500 characters so longer messages had to be sent in a number of parts) were intercepted each day of which an average of 2,040 parts were decoded, with the help of 36,361 Bombe hours.[26]

The other massive machine-processing operation at Bletchley Park involved punched-card machinery. Punched cards (which had 80 columns with which up to data 80 items of basic numeric or alphabetic data could be stored by punching a combination of holes in each columns) and the machines that handled them (which could sort and 'tabulate' – or help analyse – the data stored on the cards) served two fundamental functions in the pre-computer age: commercial and administrative data storage and processing; and scientific calculations. The cards could be counted and sorted on different criteria, and the data they held subjected to limited processing. By the start of the Second World War, the punched-card installation was ubiquitous in industry and in many academic institutions, and was dominated by a company called Hollerith, which was renamed IBM in the inter-war years and came to dominate the post-war commercial computer industry up until the 1980s. Naturally, punched cards also played an important role in the administration of the war. Two examples will illustrate their multiplicity of roles before their use at Bletchley Park is examined briefly.

Tom Watson Junior, son of the chairman of IBM, served in the Second World War before going on to take over the company and steer it to its pre-eminent position in the post-war computer industry. He recalled in his autobiography,

> I steered clear of IBM for most of the war… yet IBM was hard to avoid. The entire military was beginning to move by IBM cards, because warfare had become so big and complicated that book-keeping had to be done right on the battlefield. Toward the end of the war, I'd land on some Pacific atoll just taken from the Japanese and find a mobile punch-card unit there, tabulating the payroll… IBM cards kept track of bombing results, casualties, prisoners, displaced persons, and supplies.

There was a punch-card record of every man drafted, and it followed him through induction, classification, training, and service, right up to his discharge. There were also IBM machines involved in a lot of top-secret applications. Our equipment was used to break the Japanese code before the Battle of Midway.[27]

Indeed, IBM's sales tripled over the war, turning it into a major corporation.

Punched cards were also used by the Nazis. In 2001, Edwin Black, the American writer, who was the son of Polish survivors of the war, caused a sensation when he published an account of how IBM punched cards were used to organize the Holocaust and keep track of the millions of slave workers in Germany. Part of IBM's success with selling business processing machines had been the way it would help users identify the most efficient way of using punched cards for their own particular application – and, according to Black, via its German Hollerith subsidiary, the company offered the same service to the organizers of the slave and extinction camps.

Nearly every Nazi concentration camp operated a Hollerith Department known as the *Hollerith Abteilung.* In some camps, such as Dachau and Storkow, as many as two dozen IBM sorters, tabulators and printers were installed. Other facilities operated punches only and submitted their cards to central locations such as Mauthausen or Berlin. IBM's equipment was almost always located within the camp itself, consigned to a special bureau called the Labor Assignment Office, known in German as the *Arbeitseinsatz*. The *Arbeitseinsatz* issued the all-important daily work assignments, and processed all inmate cards and labour transfer rosters. This necessitated a constant traffic of lists, punch cards and encodeable documents as every step of the prisoner's existence was regimented and tracked.[28]

The Germans, the Americans and the British all made significant use of punched-card machines in codebreaking. Indeed, the American and British codebreaking punched-card installations were the biggest single punched-card-processing sites in each country. It has been estimated that as many as 300 different punch-card machines – counters, sorters and tabulators – were used at Bletchley Park, and there was a much bigger operation in the United States.[29] Such machines had been in use in cryptographic work before the war – the first recorded use was in 1932 – and there have even been suggestions that they were employed by Room 40 during the First World War. As war drew near, arrangements were made for expansion of punched-card installations and a special secret unit was set up at BTM, Letchworth, to build and develop special code-breaking equipment. BTM was the main punched-card supplier (of IBM-licensed machines) in Britain and became the main supplier of Bombes once the war started. It received a similar, if significantly smaller, boost as IBM from the vastly increased use of punched cards during the war and later entered the post-war computer industry, becoming one of the companies that formed ICL, which in turn competed unsuccessfully with IBM for the British computer market.[30]

The punched-card installation at Bletchley Park was run with a firm hand by Frederick Freeborn, who ruled over some 300 people, mainly Wrens, in his section and anyone who was not up to scratch was quickly shipped out. He reported in mid-1942 to Commander Edward Travis, director of GC&CS,

> As you are probably aware, we are having exceedingly great difficulty in keeping our machines maintained on account of the unskilled staff which are handling them at present. The small number of unskilled messenger jobs in this section are already filled and I am therefore unable to make use of these people in any alternative manner [i.e. two young women who had left school at 14 and been dressmaking machinists]. Neither of

these people is in any way suited for the work of this section as they have not sufficient education to understand our problems at all, nor are they in any way suited to handle our delicate machinery. Neither of these people was interested in coming to Bletchley when first called up… I must confess that I find it incredible at this late stage that every reference, verbal or written, which is made to the staff here still speaks of 'Punch Operators'. Until this can be changed, as I have so repeatedly asked, so we shall be sent unsuitable, uneducated workers who would be much better serving the country in the munition plants. I made it quite clear at the meeting with Miss Sharp and Miss Moore and various Ministry of Labour Officials that I must have intelligent young women and that the work can best be described as 'clerical', pure and simple. Can steps be taken finally to ensure that the requirement of this section are recorded as approximately ninety Clerical Staff, and not Punch Operators?[31]

Despite the problems Freeborn faced in finding staff who lived up to his expectations, his department processed on average some two million punched cards every week – with about 40 million 'passes' though machines. Indeed, there were so many cards used at Bletchley Park that special arrangements had to be made for their secure disposal. GC&CS's security requirements were so tight that the HM Stationery Office refused to help and told the codebreakers to organize their own recycling contracts.[32] One routine used to assist in decrypting Enigma intercepts was known as a Tetra search. Turing had worked out that about 80 per cent of Enigma messages contained the characters EINS and developed a technique to exploit that observation. The technique could be performed on the punched-card machines rather than the Bombes. A search took 102 hours of machine time and involved 439,400 cards.

Other punched-card-machine uses included jobs such as group

report searches, production of difference tables, cataloguing and Playfair deciphering, and the machines could also be used for the production of pseudo-random setting tables for keys to be used in one-time pad ciphers.

As the complexity of the work increased, it became vital to find more and more skilled operators. 'It has been found that it is necessary to employ higher-grade staff with the greater ability to meet the more difficult problems now arising from the deeper penetration of mechanization necessary to overcome more complex subject matter.' Friedman pointed out that in recent months his department had already achieved 80 per cent expansion, and still he was faced with a further 25 per cent increase in the number of machines in the immediate future, and 20 per cent more on order. However, it should be pointed out that the USA made considerably more use of punched cards and their machinery than did Bletchley Park and had done so from the early days of the war. This no doubt reflected the greater use of the same machinery in US businesses.[33] Indeed, it is perhaps part of the reason why Bletchley Park was so productive in terms of new machines that its academic and military denizens were culturally less firmly wedded to punched-card machinery and systems than their American counterparts. Even so, it was the American punched-card industry that came largely to dominate the post-war commercial computer market.

Machine-decryption was the great triumph of GC&CS in the Second World War, with Colossus and all the other Fish machines, the Bombes and the great variety of uses of punched cards. Yet the punched-card operation was almost closed down in 1938. Not everyone thought that codebreaking and machinery should be mixed, and the purists believed that machinery would undermine the skills needed for hand solution of codes and ciphers. One senior codebreaker wrote, 'Quite early on tabulating machines had been brought into use and while in certain circumstances they were of great use, they did, in my opinion, a good deal of harm as many idle people thought they relieved them of personal indexing; this, I think, led to the failure to solve many of the hand codes, as contrasted with machine types.' Freeborn reported on the consequence of this attitude to be found in some parts of GC&CS: 'This section had a narrow escape from extinction, as Quex [head of the secret service], impatient of the little information we had been able to get at that time sent a minute to Denniston [director of GC&CS until late 1941], asking if he thought our work was going to be of any use in view of the increasing difficulty of foreign codes. Denniston, always a pessimist, said, "No", but I wrote a very strong minute, taking the opposite view: in it I said that machines were in use and this type of cipher would spread and that in war there was a good chance of their capture.'[34]

One obvious characteristic is shared by perforated paper tape carrying Baudot code units and the intermediate processed binary streams produced by the Testery and Newmanry machines, and lightweight cardboard punched cards holding various information: they both use punched holes to identify data. Those who worked with five-hole paper tape or punched cards frequently would often develop the ability to 'read' the data by recognizing the meaning of the five Baudot code units or the strings of holes in the 80-columns of the punched card. Both tape and card survived well into the age of the electronic computer, most especially punched cards. But, step by step, all sorts of data have been digitalized (or digitized) and held almost exclusively on less visually informative media (magnetic disks, electronic memory of various sorts, optical disks and so on), so that now perforated paper tape and even the punched card seem but part of some distant archaeological find. Yet those paper-bound technologies, based on the regular positioning of 'holes and not-holes', formed a key stepping stone from the pre-electronic data and communications era to the modern computer age. Flowers's great step was to recognize that the data could be held internally within a machine – but it was a recognition that was essentially drawn from a practical realization that the data had to be held internally if the machine was going to work steadily at electronic speeds.

The traditional theory has it that writing developed from symbols of the things represented. But this view is now challenged by some archaeologists. In ancient Mesopotamia (modern Iraq), small clay tokens were used to represent goods for recording and accounting purposes – different-shaped tokens represented wheat and other produce. The farmer who delivered the produce to a depot, it seems, received tokens representing what he had delivered as a record, perhaps for later exchange for other goods or services. The tokens were placed in a clay envelope that was then sealed for storage. At some stage the practice developed whereby the tokens were impressed on to the still damp clay envelope before they were placed inside and the envelope sealed so that its contents could be established without breaking it open. The fundamental step came with the realization that the impression on the clay was sufficient, and the tokens could be done without. The impression represented the 'data' in the tokens just as well as the tokens themselves, and the envelope became the flat mud tablet. The impression thus became the written symbol for the produce and, over time, the system was expanded to allow impressions of other symbols to represent the words, through their constituent sounds, of the language. Flowers's insight was of a similar order, seeing that it was the data that mattered, not its form.[35] The clay cuneiform tablet was soon augmented by the development of papyrus as a writing material, and to a lesser extent by parchment. From the late Middle Ages, paper began to provide the writing material that underlay the rapid development of early modern Europe, aided by the introduction of printing (both techniques of paper-making and printing having made their way to Europe from China via medieval Islam). The rise of Europe is tracked by the rise in its use of paper. European overseas dominions were truly, in this sense at least, 'paper empires'. And the Second World War was a paper war. One writer has commented that the Second World War was 'a conflict in which the tonnage of paper probably ran a close second to that of bullets'.[36] It was also a conflict that gave birth to the gradual substitution of paper by new electronic and optical media, which are progressively displacing mashed wood pulp as the key means of storing information essential to humanity's daily undertakings.

chapter twenty-one

The Technology and Organization of Fish

Economic historian Alan Millward has written that

The experience of recent history has been that the substitution of labour by capital is greatly speeded up in periods of warfare. War may be a potent inspiration to technological innovation because the bounds of economic practicability set for inventions are usually set much wider by the removal of constraints imposed in peacetime by the high relative cost of innovation... [On the other hand] while speeding up technological innovation, at the same time [the technological trajectory of particular wars may] divert its main thrust away from those objectives which economists usually consider desirable... It is in fact not at all established that the so-called 'spin-off' from armaments development into more peaceful lines of scientific and industrial development was superior to or even equivalent to what would have occurred without the pressure of war... [indeed,] only in certain precise circumstances does the experience of war stimulate technological innovation.[1]

What can be said about Colossus in this regard? Did the war accelerate the development of the electronic computer? Or did it divert the path of commercial technological progress? Colossus was not invented in a vacuum. Telecommunications engineers in Britain, the United States, Germany and elsewhere had been building electro-mechanical analogue and digital computing devices; some even experimented on a small scale with electronic machines. Scientists, too, were interested in calculating machines and electronic counters. The theorist of technological change R Heilbroner has written that the frequency of the simultaneity of invention 'argues that the process of discovery takes place along a well-defined frontier of knowledge... [and technological 'clustering' or similarity of invention] again suggests that technological evolution follows a sequential and determinate rather than random course'.[2] In this sense, Colossus was part of a technological trend. Heilbroner later softened his views somewhat, suggesting that, while technology moves forward in a general trajectory, 'soft', or social, factors also influence precise development and thus there are often many ways of developing an item of technology.[3] So, in this sense, the particular choices made for developing Fish machines were determined by different individuals and organizations, but within a general trajectory determined by the particular historical circumstances in which Colossus was born.

Colossus was an intensely specific machine designed to perform Fish cipher analysis and closely related tasks. In that sense, it was a diversion. But, in two other important senses, the opposite is also true. First, in the widespread use of electronics, there is no doubt that Colossus sped up development. Second, despite its specificity, Colossus was also a precursor of later technology in its approach to data and process. The deliberate design choice to incorporate an element of flexibility into the structure of Colossus ensured its wider role in the development of post-war computing devices. Colossus took the work that was being done to a new level, scaling up dramatically the practicability of high-speed computing devices. The use of a mass of electronics, the complex control and timing sub-systems, and Flowers's core insight of the importance of the data rather than the tape, were all new, groundbreaking advances.

But they were developments in a direction towards which scientists and engineers were already heading, though probably with less focus and more variety of technological possibilities. Colossus was clearly the result of urgent practical decisions about how to tackle the Geheimschreiber cipher. That urgent application led to a technologically advanced machine. Without the war, it is hard to see what urgent application could have had the same effect of reducing the time taken to conceive of and construct such a machine. No doubt the electronic computer would have been invented, but probably some years later. The Second World War did speed up the development of the integrated, self-managing machine we now call the computer. And there is no great doubt that it would have been invented at some time or other if the war had not happened. In the case of the electronic computer, war hastened the development of a product that was to have incalculable consequences for society generally and specifically for the global economy.

What Millward says suggests that, even if the computer would have come about without the war, the course of its development may have been altered by its military genesis. It has been emphasized that, from the very start, machines were designed to be as flexible as possible – a policy that was to pay great dividends especially with Colossus. But there was also the urgent pressure of the war to ensure that machines were kept as simple as possible and to rein in the tendency of engineers to want to make their machines ever more complex. The machines, their technologies and the concepts behind them were often utterly new, forging ahead at the boundaries of mathematical, scientific and techno-logical endeavour. Even before a new machine was completed, someone would suggest an improvement, a new function or a better wiring solution. Naturally, the engineers and mathematicians wanted to incorporate these new insights, but, equally naturally, the management had to be pragmatic and resist this or machines would take too long to be designed and built.

This was a common wartime problem. In 1940 and 1941, Winston Churchill had insisted on reducing the time allowed for developing a new British tank, the Churchill, as it was called. Unfortunately, this resulted in a tank which was less powerful and more vulnerable than those it later had to meet in battle.[4] Getting the balance right between research and production was probably the most difficult task facing those running wartime operations, whether it involved armaments or electronic machines. The evidence of later performance suggests that Bletchley Park found that balance easier to maintain than did the British armaments sector. It was shown in Chapter fourteen how Newman tied Flowers and Radley into accepting a 'freeze' on design if the different parts of the Robinson, built by different workshops, worked once they were connected. New features were to be built into later models of machines if they were needed – and, of course, they were indeed needed. Bill Chandler, who worked on the design and maintenance of the Colossus machines, recalled, 'Although all the ten machines that were completed before the end of the war were of the same basic design, almost every one differed in some respect from all the others. Some of the modifications were extensive, involving extra panels, while others were trivial, and needed only a few extra components and wiring changes.'[5] (The German armed forces were particularly bad at this aspect of technology management, leading to their demanding lots of short runs of new armaments from manufacturers, each run producing different and incompatible weapons and the other equipment, thus cancelling out the advantages of high quality of manufacture which often gave the German better weapons than those of the Allies.)

There was also a balance to be struck between complexity and practicality. The complexity of designs could all too easily get out of control and take over if not carefully managed. The desirability of a new function had to be weighed against the complexity it would generate. For example, 'Many features recognized as desirable in Tunny-breaking equipment were not incorporated because they required equipment which was either non-standard or not readily available.' Six-unit paper tape, for example, would have been a real advantage (such tape was produced in the USA towards the end of the war).[6] But the policy was that standard parts were to be used wherever possible so that machines could be built and put into operation as quickly as possible – a policy that also had benefits for maintenance. 'Indeed, it is a recognized principle that a machine which can be assembled from standard parts, even though more complex, is preferable to a machine requiring special parts. This is due in part to availability, in part to the probability that the special parts will not work properly. This is one advantage of electronic equipment: the amazingly reliable counters of Colossus are of novel design but do not need special parts, being made from standard valves and other standard equipment.'[7]

This account of the development and achievements of the Fish sections at Bletchley Park has concentrated on what happened and who did it. Organizational issues have not been considered in any great detail (apart from the odd case of friction, usually involving either Harold Kenworthy, who led the interception operations, or some branch of the Post Office, or both). However, those issues are relevant ones. GC&CS and Dollis Hill, with some assistance from the TRE, managed to harness some of Britain's best mathematicians and other academics, as well as excellent telecommunications engineers, to develop a wholly new technological paradigm – all while fighting a war and having to deliver results, and doing so daily in difficult circumstances. Obviously, resources were made available in adequate measure, but it is clear that those resources were at least fairly well managed. People with ideas and ability, often difficult and sensitive people, had to be found, motivated, enthused and provided for in order to bring out their best performance. Not only did the Testery and the Newmanry manage to provide vital intelligence, but also, with Knockholt and Dollis Hill, they managed

a revolutionary technological research and development programme of an outstanding nature. It was pointed out in Chapter
four that British success in the Battle of Britain was not due to
pragmatic amateurism, but to a well-managed blend of technology
and people. The same is true of GC&CS in general and Fish in
particular. The technological challenges of overseeing a moving
programme of machine development demand first-class management skills. T P Hughes, a historian of technological systems, has
written that 'Some broadly experienced and gifted system builders
can invent hardware as well as organizations, but usually different
persons take these responsibilities as a system evolves. One of
the primary characteristics of a system builder is the ability to
construct or to force unity from diversity, centralization in the face
of pluralism, and coherence from chaos.'[8]

The success of Fish was perhaps all the more surprising given
that there was no single person in charge of the Fish operations at
Bletchley Park. Indeed, the organizational structure was diverse,
with no clear lines of control and direction. The sections set up to
handle the various activities developed as a reaction to immediate
need, not as part of a well-rehearsed plan, despite the realization
that Fish decrypts were at least as important as the Enigma
decrypts, if not more so. The original work on the Geheimschreiber
was handled by Colonel Tiltman's Research Section headed by
Gerry Morgan. Fish rapidly took over the Research Section's entire
resources. Once the machine had been diagnosed, the Fish Section,
or the Testery, was set up in mid-1942 to handle daily codebreaking
tasks, and the Research Section could look at a number of other
ciphers. As the information derived from the Fish intercepts was
mainly, but not exclusively, about the German army, the Testery was
formed as part of the Military Section, later the Military Wing,
at GC&CS – which handled German army and Luftwaffe intelligence (while a separate Naval Section handled German navy
intelligence).

During the next few months, a substantial quantity of messages was successfully decoded by the Testery using hand methods, but the fear that these techniques would be excluded by German army security measures led to the development of the theory of the statistical method towards the end of 1942. Between then and early 1943, the idea for a mechanical approach was born. According to an internal history written at the end of the war, when Newman's idea for mechanization was given approval in early 1943, the Machine Section, the Newmanry, was set up outside the Military Section, first as part of the civilian Research Section and later coming under an Assistant Director, Mechanization. GC&CS was under overall Foreign Office control, but, as it served the armed forces as well as government, the Military Wing was under military control, whereas the Research Section was a civilian unit, so the Newmanry started life in the same mode. The Newmanry was

> conceived as part of the Research Section specializing in high-speed methods of tackling all problems beyond the practical reach of hand methods, but that the intricacy, instability and increasing ramifications of the non-Morse problems in the event devoured the whole of the Section's available resources. Hence its interest tended to be limited to the solution of the problems presented to it, and most of the business of co-ordinating interception, traffic analysis and exploitation generally was left to the Military Section... Some [Fish] links became soluble by machine methods only, others could be dealt with by hand, and others again by a partnership of both. But, though there was the closest liaison and constant interplay between the two Sections, they were never amalgamated.[9]

The success of the overall Fish project suggests that the two departments, despite reporting through different wings, co-operated effectively under the stewardship of Newman and Tester. This must have been particularly true when machine methods took over much of the wheel-breaking previously done by hand from mid-1944.

Donald Michie thought that the organizational divide between the two departments was failing to exploit the full potential for decryption of Fish traffic at Bletchley Park. Although the two departments performed separate parts of the overall task, there was a need for more exchange of ideas and understanding. The various rules applying to the military and civilian units meant, for example, that it was bureaucratically all but impossible to arrange a continuous programme of exchange between the Testery and the Newmanry to ensure an effective exchange of information and experience. However, when Michie started agitating for a merger, he found himself in some trouble. Major Tester

> had to summon me (presumably at Newman's request) to reprove my conduct. Why had I been canvassing the crypto-graphic staff of both Newmanry and Testery for signatures to a petition for the administrative merging of the two sections? With the naivety of a nineteen-year-old, I was oblivious of such facts as that, even if a Foreign Office section and a War Office section *could* have been merged, one or other of Tester and Newman would have had to be dumped, and that it would not have been Newman. An ingenious administrative compromise resulted. A fictional 'Mr. X' appeared on Newman's books whose fake identity four selected Testery staff assumed for periods in rotation, acting as a species of internal consultant [so that they could spend some time in the Newmanry bypassing the bureaucratic problems of organising official transfers between civil and military sections].[10]

No doubt it was not the perfect organizational arrangement, but it worked effectively under intense time constraints.

One negative consequence of the lack of a directing influence was that traffic analysis was not organized properly for some time.

As the Testery members lacked experience of traffic analysis, it was left to a group at Knockholt, the wireless interception station, who naturally knew most about the German wireless technology and which units used what technology, but little or nothing about whom the units served. And, anyway, a significant part of the traffic information – including the teleprinter call-signs and addressing/copying information – was held in the enciphered part of the transmissions and this was not available to the staff at Knockholt, who were not informed of whether any messages were decrypted, let alone of their contents. 'Without knowledge of these call-signs it was impossible to tell the origin and distinction of many messages which passed only one stage of their journey by radio link and were sent the rest of the way by landline teleprinter.' Once several Fish messages had been successfully decrypted, Hut 3, which translated and annotated decrypts for distribution to intelligence officers in operational commands, noticed the significance of these teleprinter call-signs and started its own basic form of traffic analysis. However, it was only in early 1944 that two members of the section known as the Sixta, which handled Enigma-traffic analysis, were put to work to study the Fish-traffic data. And, indeed, it was only in October of 1944 that the Sixta Fish team was moved to Block F to be closer to other teams working on the cryptographic aspects of the same messages. Eventually, nineteen people worked on what turned out to be an important source of information, especially about the German army order of battle, so that yet another blurred organizational line of reporting was established – Hut 3 and the Sixta were part of the Military Wing – and it was only in mid-1944 that Bletchley Park was managing to produce all the information that could be extracted from the analysis of Fish traffic. An internal history concluded, 'The early successes [with decrypting Fish] obscured the need for the highest quality of interception, together with rigorous control, and the methodical study of traffic analysis, which later became vital. Again, earlier development of machine methods would probably have led to a better balanced whole, for possibilities for their extension were continually being revealed as the work progressed.'[11]

One area of GC&CS that did not work well was the organization of its own communications links, which never really managed to provide a satisfactory service. An internal review at the end of the war concluded, 'In sum, largely through failure to recognize the magnitude of the problem in time, GC&CS communications remained inadequate for the task throughout the war' and this was due to the 'appalling difficulties that arise from running communications largely on an emergency basis without direct control of either the engineering or operating departments'.[12] Yet, despite similar organizational ambiguity, the Fish operation managed to provide an effective service at the forefront of mathematics and technology. The same internal analysis concluded, 'In general, the non-Morse, like the army-air Enigma, complex seems to have suffered from the lack of someone in charge of the whole enterprise. Nevertheless, it produced first-class intelligence when most needed, notably from D-Day onward.'[13]

However, there remain significant gaps in our knowledge about the thoughts and plans of senior management at Bletchley Park. It is hard to imagine that decisions could have been taken on developing machines such as the Robinson and Colossus, not to mention Dragon and other lesser machines, without written proposals and assessments. If there were such papers, they have either not survived or have not been released. Some documents are still retained on the grounds that they may reveal something about cipher techniques that are still in use today. If such papers are still withheld, it is perhaps because they reveal something about the reasoning behind the adoption of codebreaking techniques as much as about the techniques themselves. In the absence of these papers, it is difficult to make a full assessment of this aspect of the Colossus story. Our knowledge of what happened – proposals, opinions, personnel, and so on – is minimal. And, unless GCHQ is sitting on the documents, that will probably remain the case. The planning and administration of Colossus remains a secret success story, which is a pity, as the papers would surely make up a superb and informative case study for effective administration and computer-system development – something at which the post-war British civil service has, with some exceptions, proved to be repeatedly inept.

A report in *Computing*, the weekly computer industry newspaper, of 4 December 2003 is worth noting. It reports, under the headline 'Naivety Led to GCHQ Crisis',

> Moving the headquarters of the GCHQ government communications centre cost more than seven times the original estimates because no one had understood the complexity of IT operations, MPs [Members of Parliament] were told this week. But the Commons Public Accounts Committee was also told that the cock-up had actually delivered 'lasting value' – by forcing a major network upgrade. GCHQ director Dr. Pepper admitted that when plans were drawn up in the 1990s to move to a £1.2 billion headquarters in Cheltenham, it was not understood how much networking there would be between computer systems. The National Audit Office said the miscalculation meant the cost of the move had risen from an original estimate of £41 million to £308 million. Dr. Pepper said the plans to transfer the computers had been based on systems used during the Cold War when GCHQ had to deal with a relatively static threat from the Soviet Union involving little interaction between different systems. However, the growing complexity of the threats facing the UK in the 1990s meant there had been an increase in networking between computer systems. The engineers simply didn't understand the complexity of the IT transition, he said. Sir David Omand, the Cabinet Office intelligence and security co-ordinator who was GCHQ director from 1996 to 1997, said, 'I cannot excuse the failure to recognize these issues earlier. I take

responsibility.' However, he said that the result had been a much improved computer system with a new information technology architecture. If the system had not been upgraded as a result of the move, they would have been left with a 'decaying' system that would now be in urgent need of an emergency update. 'The large expenditure which was authorized on the technical transition has produced lasting value in terms of the new architecture, the ability to manage it and considerably more resilience,' said Omand. 'It is a very large sum of money but it does represent real value.' An Office of Government Commerce spokesman said the 'Gateway Review' process should prevent a repeat of the disaster.[14]

Reading this report, it is difficult to determine whether the management skills shown during the Second World War at GC&CS have been lost by GCHQ – or whether GC&CS's success was, in fact, due to having to respond to wartime demands and upgrade decryption technology from hand to machine methods, and so just happened to produce a machine of value. In both cases it is possible that senior management took a back seat and let the technologists do their thing. In the absence of documentary evidence, we simply cannot judge.

chapter twenty-two

Transatlantic Fisheries

The codebreaking effort of GC&CS, especially the cracking of the Enigma and even more so the Geheimschreiber, was undoubtedly one of Britain's wartime successes. It has been said that 'Russia defeated Germany, America defeated Japan, and Britain defeated Italy'. Yet Britain was pitched against Germany in a number of ways – in the air, at sea and in the ether. Measured against the performance of the German Intelligence and code-breaking services, the British achievement was significantly better. But it is unlikely that German engineers were any worse than their British counterparts, or their intelligence officers less able. The reasons for the differing performance must be sought elsewhere. Britain staved off defeat in 1940, but had no means of defeating Germany until either the United States or Russia joined it as an ally. Russia was forced reluctantly into the role by Germany's invasion in June 1941; the United States, somewhat less reluctantly, by Japan's attack on Pearl Harbor. Russia, it is true, performed the essential defeat of the German army by the intense application of its resources to enable it to wage mechanized warfare on a gigantic scale. In contrast, Montgomery, like a careful storekeeper with a limited stock, tried to minimize casualties and to avoid depleting the comparatively small number of British troops. So, the British effort was crafted, while Russia employed traditional sledgehammer methods and the United States brought mass production to the war.

The American strategy was to harness the productive power of the economy to out-produce the enemy, and then to use those resources in concert with its allies to defeat, first, Germany and, then, Japan. The US economy could continue to maintain a high standard of living even while devoting 40 per cent of output to war production. By 1944, the Allies had a three-to-one superiority over the Axis in terms of munitions. 'Eisenhower was once accused of having a mass-production mentality, which was true but beside the point. He came from a mass-production society, and like any good general, he wanted to use his nation's strengths on the battlefield,' wrote Stephen E Ambrose, a biographer of the Supreme Allied Commander in Europe.[1] This was to manifest itself in a strategic divergence between Montgomery and Eisenhower. After the defeat of the German army in France and Belgium, Montgomery wanted to concentrate efforts and resources on a narrow, armoured thrust to the heart of Germany, delivering a deadly blow using minimum resources. Eisenhower, however, wanted to attack all along the line, exploiting the power of American factories, and fresh supplies of troops, until the entire front crumbled under the weight of overwhelming pressure. Germany's army was only partially mechanized (for example, it had employed over 600,000 horses in Operation Barbarossa), but America's was fully motorized, the fruits of an economy which had thrived on oil production and car use.

During the nineteenth and twentieth centuries, the industrialization of war-fighting capabilities meant that, if war between major powers came about, it would inevitably be an overwhelming experience for the whole of society. War was no longer something that could exist almost outside society, impinging only through taxation or the devastation caused if a population was unfortunate enough to find itself in the path of an advancing army. It would no longer involve just a small proportion of the population – the nobility to direct it, some stout fellows to do the hard work, and a few merchants and financiers to make it all happen. The industrialization of war – total war – demanded the participation of the whole of society and the muddying of the distinction between peace and war. Scientists and technologists were put to the permanent service of the military – primarily in inventing and improving weapons – but also in the organization and supply of armies. The 'military-industrial complex', identified after the war by the then President Eisenhower, had, in fact, long been in development. The scientific development of weapons and related systems and their production on an industrial scale – and the resulting destructive power – began to transform war most dramatically from the mid-nineteenth century.[2]

The command and communications possibilities of the telegraph and, later, the wireless meant that telecommunications engineers were as essential as any other part of the war effort. Britain had long exploited its domination of the seas and far-reaching empire to control the world's international submarine telegraph cables and managed to ensure early domination of the wireless industry too, developing successful strategic and tactical use of telecommunications as a weapon of diplomacy and war.[3] By the time of the Second World War, telecommunications had become a central tool of the organization of all aspects of modern warfare from tanks, submarines and aircraft to administration. The industrialization of war meant that the ability to mobilize and use technical resources was vital and that bigger and better weapons alone could not guarantee victory. Hitler had started rearmament and the diversion of resources from civil to military production as soon as he gained power, but he was planning for a general war in the mid-1940s. He had not expected Britain and France to honour their obligation to Poland and as a result found himself at war somewhat earlier than expected. Both Britain and Germany started serious mobilization of the economy from September 1939 and in crude figures Hitler achieved more, devoting by 1944 a larger share of the German economy to war production than Britain had. But there were constraints inherent in the Nazi system which meant that Britain's mobilization – and those of its major allies, the USA and Russia – was more effective.[4]

By 1942, the conquests of the German armed forces meant that Hitler could theoretically muster as much economic potential and output as his combined enemies. And, indeed, it was Hitler's clear strategy to achieve economic growth through military conquest. But, in fact, wherever the Nazis took control, economic output fell. Historian Richard Overy concluded that Germany's problem was not a lack of mobilization, but a failure of organization, a failure to ensure sufficient productivity. It was ironic that 'the one country, whose political and military leadership had thoroughly grasped the importance of Wehrwirtschaft [war economy] and prepared for economic mobilization on a large scale, failed to produce weapons in the quantities expected and called for'.[5] The reason is quite clear – enforced exploitation was less productive than trade and co-operation. 'The German authorities made little effort to pretend that that areas they had conquered were not German colonies, outposts of a new German racial power... the unremitting violence [in the east especially] of the occupier against the civilian population alienated much of the potential for political collaboration.'[6]

Dutch historian Pieter Geyl, who spent time in a German concentration camp, was active in the resistance and survived the war, observed how the Germans squandered any opportunities there may have been from the beginning: 'As it was, no planning, no large-scale political or social reconstruction was possible, nothing that might be termed a policy for the occupied territories. Nothing but subjugation, oppression, exploitation.'[7]

Economic historian Alan Millward has concluded,

From the outset Britain gave priority to the production of the most technologically sophisticated and the most costly of available modern armaments... it was a decision taken with an awareness that the economic resources of Britain could not match those of possible aggressors and that an adequate defensive strategy could only be sustained by capitalizing on the major advantages of a highly developed economy, research and innovation and modern production methods. In contrast, these were the very things that [Hitler's]... strategy discouraged in Germany... At the end of the war Allied interrogators were amazed to discover how slight, inadequate and inefficient had been the administrative apparatus in Germany for fostering research and development... The fruits of these early [British] decisions did in fact turn into the prolonged struggle which had been anticipated.[8]

This divergence of strategy lies behind the relative success of Britain, Russia and the United States in mobilizing their economic resources. Germany's economic policy was essentially based on autarky, acquiring the economic resources it needed by conquest rather than by international trade. One historian has concluded that, despite significant losses of industrial areas and manpower and resources during 'Barbarossa', 'over the course of the war the Soviet Union succeeded in producing more tanks, guns and aircraft than Germany by a wide margin, even within a year of the catastrophic defeats of 1941.'[9] Russian production of weapons was supplemented by supplies of vehicles, communications equipment and food from the Allies, but its recovery and outperformance of Germany illustrates the poor achievements of the Nazi regime in overall economic mobilization for the war effort.

The mobilization of telecommunications resources was a part of the overall effort. Radar was an offshoot of wireless technology and drew on similar academic research and industrial experience. And efficient modern networks, with secure ciphers, were essential to the smooth running of the war effort. The different relative weight given to codebreaking as well as cipher development became evident in the First World War, in particular with the success of Britain's Room 40 which broke tens of thousands of German naval wireless messages.[10] It was the later awareness of this which led to the inter-war emphasis in the German armed forces on machine ciphers. The solution the German armed forces identified was to create bigger, better ciphers, rather than to pay greater attention to codebreaking and the lessons it could offer. British codebreaking efforts in the First World War, during the inter-war years and with the success with both Enigma and the Geheimschreiber (as well as the Italian Hagelin and Japanese Purple machine ciphers) influenced how the British used their own machine ciphers. The Second World War British TypeX teleprinter cipher machine, for example, was secure, in part at least, because the British knew that Enigma-type ciphers could be broken, whereas the Nazi dictatorship was predisposed to believing that blame for all problems could be attributed to human failing and traitors within. And the organizational needs of the leaders, with their disregard for the unpleasant detail of logistics and organizational coherence, effectively suppressed any idea that ciphers were vulnerable. Accepting that would have meant allowing technical cipher experts to demand too many changes that would have crossed the boundaries of the Reich's powerful fiefdoms.

Certainly, there were several occasions when different parts of the armed forces came to suspect that ciphers were possibly being broken. The changes in the Geheimschreiber system, widespread use of limitations and the daily change of wheel-pin patterns were introduced in part because of German fears that cipher material had been captured by the Allies in North Africa and Sicily. Previous measures followed German awareness of the Swedish break of the Siemens T52. But, despite such scares, there was no individual or organization at a high enough level capable of insisting on a thorough reappraisal of cipher security among all the organizations, military, police, paramilitary and civilian, using high-level ciphers and wireless transmission.

Since the war, it has become commonplace among British and American writers to attribute the failure to appreciate the extent of

Allied codebreaking to German arrogance and certainty in the perfection of their codes and systems.[11] But the evidence presented by a Swedish writer suggests a more plausible explanation. Before the war Dr Eric Huettenhain, the chief of decryption at the general staff of the armed forces, OKW, cipher branch, reported that he had worked out how to crack the Siemens T52 with around 100 characters of cipher text. And the German Foreign Office rejected the same machine as too insecure to risk using for enciphering diplomatic traffic. However, these warnings were ignored by the armed forces at higher levels. Further evidence of the potential vulnerability of the Geheimschreiber came later. The Swedish secret service intercepted a telephone call where a middle-ranking German officer advised a counterpart not to use the T52 as it was not 100 per cent safe. And in mid-1942, the German armed forces had become fully aware of the Swedish break of the T52, introducing new security measures on both the Siemens T52 and the Lorenz SZ with the launch of the SZ42 which handled limitations. Thus the leak of the Swedish break led to the introduction of limitations and daily pin position changes which would have overwhelmed Bletchley Park were it not for the production line of Colossi and other machines coming into operation.

'The documentary evidence suggests that a more powerful factor was also at work, namely a desire, quite natural in the circumstances, for fast and [relatively less irksome] communications. In a situation where the amount of information to be processed is expanding rapidly and the pressure from central offices is great, the risk that breaches – indeed, serious breaches – of security rules and regulations will occur, also increases.'[12] This effect, which is applicable to all organizations, is particularly marked in dictatorships and totalitarian systems where the top leadership will not listen to 'bad news'. Despite numerous worries about leaks at operational levels, the German high command insisted on progress as usual. It was because it found such issues a nuisance, and in any event the natural Nazi response to a setback was to seek traitors.

The leaders recognized the need for ciphers, but were not interested in how they themselves could give sufficient authority to those who would ensure the security of the ciphers in use. Churchill's intimate understanding of the importance of signals intelligence stands in stark contrast to the views Hitler derived from his narrow horizons. The transcripts of Hitler's daily military briefings offer a glimpse of him and his peers discussing ciphers but clearly lacking any real understanding of them or any informed and active advisers to whom they could refer.

At the midday briefing on 26 July 1943, when addressing the problem of keeping secret orders for preparations for the military takeover of Italy, General Alfred Jodl, chief of the OKW operational staff, told Hitler and Goering, 'I've just transmitted an order to Kesselring [in Italy].' Goering, concerned about the security of the messages, asked, 'Are we really giving these orders?' Hitler responded, 'They all come by enciphered teleprinter.' Jodl backed up the Fuehrer: 'It's perfect.' Hitler asked Goering, 'What do you want? Otherwise we can't give anything – no orders at all any more.' Goering explained that he thought 'in this case it could be done with special secret couriers'. But Hitler was adamant. 'Couriers are even more dangerous, if they have anything on them. It must be enciphered again.' Himmler chipped in that 'I can also radio to my division in Rome.' Hitler enquired whether it was enciphered or not, and then asked, 'Is it completely secure?' Himmler replied, 'Completely secure. We've agreed on a brand new key. Yesterday we made the latest key.'[13] It is extraordinary to see three of the highest-ranking figures in the Reich discussing whether a cipher is secure or not. It is equally astonishing that no informed military contribution is put forward and an apparent absence of any alternative view-points. The attitude to cipher security was driven by wishful thinking and the need to get things done, rather than arrogance.

The British codebreakers had ample evidence that operator practice and the interaction of cipher and machine characteristics (such as teleprinter punctuation) could offer ways of reducing the odds from the astronomical to the almost feasible – and some brilliant mathematicians and engineers found ways of making the almost feasible almost possible. In essence, the breaks into both Enigma and the Geheimschreiber were dependent on repeated error – operators who reused keys, or users who were attached to formulaic openings and contents – as well as underlying weaknesses in the cipher technique. These operator and user errors opened up the weaknesses inherent in machine ciphers to exploitation. The same operator and user errors taught the British how not to employ their own cipher machines, and to attend to the detail of protecting their own ciphers. The only major breaches in British cipher use during the Second World War were in the Royal Navy and in North Africa. The German navy read British wireless messages to convoys that were designed to help them evade the U-boats, but actually helped direct them into ambushes. Poor cipher security was the cause of the problem, and an unwillingness to believe that the code could be being cracked allowed it to persist. But, overall, Britain's codebreakers decisively outperformed their German counterparts.

Why should this have been the case? Was it really due to the work of a gaggle of geniuses at Bletchley Park? A certain degree of scepticism must temper this suggestion. Certainly, Alan Turing was a genius and applied his original mind to different problems both inside and outside GC&CS before and, for a short time, after the war, until his untimely death. But Turing was probably the only such creature at Bletchley Park. More likely, Bletchley Park was the home for a gathering of brilliant mathematicians and engineers. And, crucially, it operated in an atmosphere and for a cause that brought out and encouraged their creativity. Yet it is clear from the accounts of veterans that it was not just the cream that gave of its best, for the operation of Bletchley Park depended on the thousands of intelligent and highly capable women who managed the decryption machines and processes.

And, in any event, it would be quite wrong to think that Germany did not have its share of brilliant academics and engineers. Indeed, the career of a man such as Konrad Zuse, who built a range of electro-mechanical computers, shows that brilliant technicians did exist in the Reich, but they were isolated and ignored. Resources went to the interests of those with power and influence to the extent that those wanting to build bigger bombs or create ever more efficient means of exterminating people inevitably found a much more receptive hearing. An apparently complex machine that appeared to have no direct use on the battlefield itself could not attract the same interest or support. The failure to exploit the potential of men such as Zuse or Helmut Schreyer, who built a small-scale electronic machine during the war, illustrates the relative German inability to mobilize academics, engineers and scientists. Schreyer originally proposed a machine with 1500 valves, but, refused resources, had to content himself with a mere 150 valves. Zuse was fair-weather Nazi and Schreyer a keen one, but that did not improve the prospects of their respective machines. These weaknesses seem to have been inherent in Nazism and Hitler's style of absolute leadership. Hitler's management philosophy was based on his interpretation of a Darwinian struggle for domination, and he maintained his own power in part by preventing the development of any rivals by ensuring that his underlings were kept at one another's throats. The unified command of the armed forces, the OKW, was undermined by the independent fiefdoms of the Luftwaffe and the navy, and by the elevation of the army general staff, the OKH, to direct control under Hitler of the army on the eastern front (leaving OKW with the other fronts – in particular, the Mediterranean and north-west Europe). The army and the air force each built their own networks of landlines and wireless links, with the landlines often running next to one another alongside roads or railways. In addition, there were competing organizations – in particular the SS – within the military structure. And other institutions, such as the Nazi Party, Ribbentrop's Foreign Office, and Goering's economic empire, all intervened in policy.

And Hitler, of course, was always willing to order individual army units, as well as to direct the army overall. Over time, the economic, administrative and military command structures of the Reich became increasingly dysfunctional. On the other hand, Britain and America, who had the apparently severe disadvantage of being two independent sovereign nations, managed to develop the means of agreeing aims, strategy and operations, despite their different outlooks and national interests.

Similarly, one of the great strengths of GC&CS was that it was a single organization which undertook all aspects of governmental and military interception and codebreaking. It pooled all talents and benefited from doing so, whereas, in Nazi Germany, there were nine different organizations which had their own interception and codebreaking operations.[14] Far from combining their capabilities, they often expended considerable resources in fighting one another rather than the external enemy. So, the very organizational nature of the Nazi state bred a weakness, one that was fatal in a collegiate activity such as codebreaking, which demands a wide range of talents and experience. The differences between sides in a war are often minimal, and they often depend upon who can make fewer mistakes, and who can exploit technology slightly better. One military historian has concluded that 'the virtue of a technologically superior device is not in its technical novelty, but in its mode of employment… In weapon technology as in other areas, the Nazis lost a major advantage simply as a result of their style in tackling organizational problems.'[15]

The pre-war process of Nazification also weakened Germany's resource base. It promoted the fawning in academia and demoted the questioning, and it killed many or possibly even most of the country's Jewish, left-wing and homosexual intellectuals. The 'victim-turned-bully' appeal of the Nazi Party demanded social discord and social enemies. Tens of thousands of Germans disappeared into the Gestapo torture chambers or the extermination camps never to reappear. While most Germans welcomed Hitler's rise to power – and the self-confidence he gave the nation after the shock of defeat in the First World War and the humiliation of the Versailles Treaty – large sections of society passively resisted the Nazi ideology. The management of Siemens and other electrical and communications companies, which thrived on international markets, opposed both the First and the Second World Wars, for example, and thoroughly disliked Hitler. And while many, indeed, most, German soldiers fought hard for their country, many did not want to and had to be compelled to do so. The German army is known to have executed 15,000 of its own men, sentenced 23,000 to long terms of imprisonment and 404,000 to shorter prison sentences. The bald figures do not reflect the extent to which the need, or urge, for punishment stretched even to the highest levels. Both General Erich Fellgiebel, the head of the German army signals corps, and Admiral Canaris, the head of the Abwehr, the Military Intelligence organization, were among those executed by their own side. Many more were shot or hanged during the terror of the last months of the war as commanders and the SS desperately tried to force men to stay at the front. The Russian army, too, punished thousands of men savagely – but it is estimated that its overall punishment rate was 1.25 per cent, contrasted to the 3.3 per cent of the German army.[16]

Hitler's response to the bomb plot of July 1944 is indicative of the preference to seek people to blame for setbacks:

> But this act which happened here is, I would like to say, just a symptom of an inner circulatory problem, of an inner blood poisoning, that we are suffering from. What do you expect when... as we can see now [i.e. since the bomb plot], the most important positions are occupied by absolutely destructive people – not defeatists, but destructive people and traitors? Because it is like that. If the Signals Corps and the Quarter-master's office are occupied by people who are absolute traitors – and you don't really know how long they have been in

contact with the enemy or the people over there – you can't expect that the necessary initiative to stop such a thing will come from there… But our morale doubtlessly became worse – became worse because we had this place over there, which constantly spread poison over the path of these General Staff organizations… So we only have to ask ourselves today – or rather we don't have to ask ourselves anymore: how does the enemy learn about our thinking? Why are so many things neutralized? Why does he react to everything so quickly?[17]

The Nazis were conditioned by their prejudices. Machines could be controlled and were trustworthy. But their political philosophy drew its sustenance from identifying and annihilating human enemies (and 'sub-human' ones too).

This, too, contrasts strongly with the evidence from Bletchley Park, and elsewhere, that there was a common purpose in Britain in achieving the defeat of Hitler and then getting back to 'normal life'. Hitler, like other dictators, believed that the corrupt and decaying democracies would not be able to stomach war against a deter-mined, disciplined army. The evidence of the late 1930s shows that the people of France, Britain, the United States and other countries did not want war. The evidence of the early 1940s shows that, once war was inevitable, the democracies were far more effective at mobilizing the full array of talents and capabilities of the modern industrial nation – and this proved to be a more powerful weapon in the long run than Hitler's disciplined army and the force of his will.[18] One writer has observed that, in Britain, 'The most effective individuals viewed themselves as taking part in a collective effort and had a realistic view of the value of their own effort's contribu-tion to it.'[19] In Britain's case, a numerically small, but strategically significant, aspect of that effort was the chance that brought together a team that at various times drew on, from among others, an awkward, socially ill-at-ease, homosexual genius (Turing), the son of a German migrant (Newman), a quiet academic chemist-turned-mathematician (Tutte), a clever working-class lad from the East End of London (Flowers), and one military man, albeit a delightfully eccentric one (Tiltman). It was the fact that Bletchley Park could exist, could draw together such disparate people and exploit their creativity, that made its success possible and, to some extent, enabled it to affect the progress of the war. While similar people were no doubt to be found within its boundaries, it is difficult to envisage how such a group could have been nurtured in Hitler's Reich.

The recruitment criteria for work at GC&CS permitted those of unorthodox political views, such as communists. The test was whether someone was in favour of prosecuting the war to victory. So members of the Peace Pledge Union, who wanted to end the fighting, were not eligible. The question to ask about a communist was whether he or she was the sort of communist who would betray their country or not. Such a policy could never have been applied in Hitler's Germany, where people could be executed for their thoughts and beliefs as well as their deeds. In December 1944, as Germany's enemies were preparing to cross its borders, Hitler told Albert Speer, then his armaments and industrial chief, 'It is those who are ruthless, not the cowards, who win! Remember this – it isn't technical superiority that is decisive. We lost that long ago.'[20] An observation of military historian Martin van Creveld is worth noting: 'The greatest victories that have been won in war do not depend on a simple superiority of technology, but rather on a careful meshing of one side's advantages with the other's weaknesses so as to produce the greatest possible gap between the two.'[21] One key advantage which Britain was able to mesh with Nazi Germany's weaknesses was the achievement of decisive technological and organizational superiority in the vital areas of telecommunications and codebreaking, from which it gained an unparalleled oversight of Germany's military and strategic communications. But, clearly, the Second World War was not a matter of Britain versus Germany. Other powers were involved, and none more intimately connected with Britain than the United States.

As the Allied beachhead in Normandy was built up, and even more so after the breakout and the liberation of France, the preponderance of the troops and supplies came from the United States. Britain had reached the limit in the number of troops it could provide, but the US army was receiving one new division roughly every week. The influence on strategy and command shifted correspondingly. Britain's role as junior partner to the new world power became more apparent every day. At this point, therefore, it is worth examining US involvement in the Fish project. The post-war partnership between Britain and the United States was particularly strong in the realm of intelligence and Sigint, signals intelligence, in particular. Wartime co-operation and transfer of technology and knowhow laid the basis for an enduring post-war Sigint alliance.

Co-operation between British and US Intelligence services started tentatively, with the support of both Roosevelt and Churchill, shortly after Marshal Pétain signed an armistice with Hitler in June 1940. By the autumn, the two leaders were prepared to consider 'a free exchange of intelligence'.[22] It took several months to get agreement – codebreakers on both sides of the Atlantic were reluctant to share the secrets of their successes – but in 1941 a team from the United States visited Britain. The links were strengthened following the entry of the United States into the war in December 1941 after the attack on Pearl Harbor by the Japanese. Bletchley Park was concerned about security and feared simply handing away its hard-won achievements, and so only slowly gave up details of what it had managed with Enigma, and even more grudgingly information about the Geheimschreiber. But by mid-1942, US codebreakers were fully informed of the material Bletchley Park had gathered on Fish.[23]

William Friedman led the US Army codebreaking team (unlike GC&CS, which was a single unit, the US navy maintained a separate codebreaking operation) and was determined to build up American experience in teleprinter cipher decryption, although Britain remained the operational centre for both interception and decryption. Colonel Tiltman, who made the first break into the Geheimschreiber, wrote to Friedman in May 1942 about the problem: 'The Geheimschreiber is in production and it is a great worry to us as we have had difficulty in finding the staff to service it. As it is, the whole of my Research Section has had to be turned to it, to the consequent detriment of the Japanese military investigation.'[24] Friedman, commenting on the information that had been sent back to him in Washington, said in a memo to Tiltman, 'This looks like a most interesting problem and has quite stymied us at the moment. I am beginning to suspect certain things and will communicate with you as soon as we reach what appear to be valid conclusions.'[25] There is no hint as to what Friedman suspected, or whether it paid any dividends. In any event, a few weeks later, an American codebreaker based at Bletchley Park informed a colleague in Washington: 'Almost all messages begin with the letters ++ZZZ in the clear text, on the basis of which, with some depth, the machine had been reconstructed in May... Will bring back complete details and expect two lunches from Friedman.'[26] So, from at least May 1942, full details were made available to US codebreakers.

Historian David Stafford has written that, in late 1942, Travis went to Washington 'to sign a deal on a joint Anglo-American codebreaking effort in the Atlantic, the first of two remarkable wartime agreements that broke the taboo on keeping one's closest secrets hidden even from one's allies. The second accord, this time between the Allied armies, followed in March 1943. No such intimate an intelligence alliance between two sovereign powers had been seen in history before.' The BRUSA (BRitain/USA) agreement provided for the complete exchange of all information about the detection, identification and interception of wireless and cable communications. 'This historic BRUSA agreement, which later formed the foundation for all Cold War Sigint cooperation, was only one of several advances in Anglo-American intelligence cooperation that spring.'[27]

But, initially at least, there was clearly going to be a big gap between the levels of experience available in Bletchley Park and Washington: the British at GC&CS were under urgent daily pressure to achieve results. A British report on the Geheimschreiber, written in November 1942, betrays the writer's antipathy towards the Americans: 'All practical work on this cipher has been and is being done in this country. The Americans ask for and receive copies of our registers and carbon copies of hand-read messages on which presumably they are training their personnel... So far as is known, they do not intercept any traffic in the States, nor would it be possible to do so... It cannot be emphasized too strongly that the Americans are at present contributing nothing to the common effort on the types of cipher under consideration.'[28]

An American report, written by Albert Small in December 1944, was penned in a more generous tone, but made a similar point: 'Daily solution of Fish messages at GC&CS reflects a background of British mathematical genius, superb engineering ability, and solid common sense. Each of these has been a necessary factor. Each could have been overemphasized or underemphasized to the detriment of solutions; a remarkable fact is that the fusion of the elements has been apparently in perfect proportions. The result is an outstanding contribution to cryptanalytic science.'[29]

Small also reported on the extent of what would later be called 'technology transfer'.'The original mathematics of the Fish problem was brought to us from England by Captain Seaman and Mr. Ferner, and kept scrupulously up to date by Captain Friedman. There is little difference therefore between the mathematics at [Washington] and that now existing at GC&CS. We have all the elements of the story – in fact, many more elements than are used in the story – and we lack only the operational perspective to piece them together. It is a perspective that we can hardly attain unless we ourselves do operations on an "assembly-line" basis.' The US codebreakers tried to set up their own Fish-decryption plant, but not using Colossus. Instead, they attempted to develop an alternative technological approach – one they believed would lead to a general-purpose technique for codebreaking.

According to an account by an American historian of US codebreaking,

> During the cryptanalysts' Golden Age, World War II, the codebreakers and their technological allies built many impressive machines. The Americans created proto-computers as advanced as those of the British, whose Colossus has gained a reputation as one of the world's first modern electronic computers. But America's devices fell short of the country's technological and scientific potential. For example, America's versions of the devices used to attack Germany's World War II encryption machines were technological compromises rushed to completion. Those Bombes, and even America's 'Colossus', the 5202, arrived a bit too late because during a critical decade army and navy codebreakers had been unable to establish a development program or to convince the leading universities and corporations to bend their research to the special needs of code- and cipher-breaking. The unprecedented millions of dollars and the hundreds of skilled engineers and scientists assigned to crypto-technology during World War II could not make up for the lost opportunities of the 1930s.[30]

The 5202 was only completed in April 1945 – just in time for the end of the war in Europe. Its late arrival and technological compromises may have been caused by US policy in the 1930s, but one can only note that a similar lack of a development programme in Britain did not prevent a few score of engineers and mathematicians from making up sufficient time to ensure the worthwhile exploitation of German cipher machines, including the

Geheimschreiber. The latter was diagnosed in January 1942 and Colossus had been created by the end of 1943.

In mid-1944, the US army's codebreaking organization had decided to build its own machine to do the same work as Colossus, but using a quite different technology – photographic film. 'Although designed for the Fish problem, it was hoped that the 5202 would become the foundation for the long-sought universal microfilm cryptanalytical machine.'[31] The idea of using microfilm technology for a general-purpose cipher-breaking machine had been developed in the mid-1930s by Vannevar Bush of the Massachusetts Institute of Technology, MIT. Bush had constructed the world's largest analogue computer in the 1930s. It used variable electric currents driving rotating wheels with interconnecting rods and gears to solve differential equations. As Bush was America's leading expert on machine computation, it was to him that the navy turned in 1935 when it was considering decryption machines that would be faster than the IBM punched-card machines then being used. Bush developed an idea for a Rapid Analytical Machine, RAM, using microfilm techniques (and a limited amount of electronics for essential high-speed counting purposes). Although Bush's RAM project was never progressed beyond an unsuccessful, small-scale trial device, his idea for using film merely lay dormant until America's involvement in the war revived it. After Pearl Harbor, Bush persuaded Eastman-Kodak to start making parts for a new film-based machine, and work on a limited-function device was started in 1942 to tackle Japanese or German ciphers, and several other film-based devices were developed. Eventually, the line of film-based machines led to the 5202.

The US codebreakers had often considered using electronics, but had repeatedly rejected the idea because electronic valves were considered unreliable. In 1942, NCR, the cash-register and office-machine company, was given a contract to build an electronic four-wheel Bombe, but 'within a few weeks the company had to notify [the codebreakers] that the experienced [NCR engineers] found electronics impractical'. And around the same time, AT&T, the US telephone company, agreed to make one electronic Bombe and one using advanced, high-speed relays. 'Quite soon, electronics was declared possible but impractical and Bell's engineers concentrated on what became the largest electromechanical relay computer in the world, the $1,000,000 "Madame X".' But this monster performed no better than an ordinary Bombe costing less than $50,000, so Bush's film technique apparently remained the only high-speed option.[32]

In essence, the 5202 worked by superimposing two lengths of standard 35mm photographic film on top of one another and measuring the amount of light that flowed through them. One film held images of the delta-cipher stream of an intercepted message. The other held images of the delta streams of the Chi settings. When the two films were superimposed, more light came through where dots were in the same places on both films. The amount of light detected at each Chi setting was measured and the one with the highest level of light indicated the right Chi settings. According to a Bletchley Park report, 'The light shining through the two films is proportional to the number of coincidences of transparent spots.'[33] This is a considerable simplification but describes the basic technique, which was performed by the 5202's Comparator. The 5202 had various components – including circuits and wiring to perform the delta or differencing processing on the cipher and Chi streams, a film generator to produce the Chi setting and cipher films from the delta-streams, counters and a display system. There were a number of advantages to the 5202. The actual process of comparing the films was a much faster process than the technique employed by Colossus with its repetitive counting of the double-delta test, as the Comparator could measure the light over an area of film in one go. So it took the same time for the Comparator to measure the light for five units at a time as for just one or two, whereas Colossus could not really be expected to count related settings for more than two units in a single run.

A version of the 5202 was shipped from America to Bletchley Park and arrived just as the war in Europe ended. However, it was tested for two months to see how it compared with Colossus. Several messages were tried out – for example, messages from the Squid and Dace links, which had given clear settings on initial Colossus runs for units 1 and 2, but had refused to be set on the remaining units. The 5202 gave mixed results.[34] It was especially effective at setting normal messages, but, as was noted at the time, 'unfortunately a large proportion of messages are not normal'. And the 5202, despite its origins in Bush's vision of a general-purpose decryption machine, was inflexible. If the standard test did not show up a statistically significant result, it could not simply be re-run using more specific tests, as would happen with Colossus. 'Thus the standard procedure which we adopted could set messages [on the 5202] which conformed to the usual long supply reports with a considerable amount of punctuation, but would fail on a message which was, say, an appreciation of the chances of an expected opera-tion, in which case strong language differences would predominate and different types of run would be successful. On Colossus it would be easy to try both hypotheses, but at the moment to try both hypotheses on the 5202 requires the making of two films.'[35]

Furthermore, when the time taken for generating the film data, exposing it to the film, and then developing it was calculated, the actual time taken for a run was in fact comparable with Colossus. Bletchley Park concluded that Colossus was more flexible, had shorter preparation times, a much longer maximum character length (30,000 instead of the 5202's limit of 5,000 characters) and could also perform character counts and spanning. Overall, the 5202 had limited use: 'Chi setting is only one of the Tunny-breaking operations performed on Colossus. The following are impossible or impracticable on 5202: Chi-breaking; rectangling; [and] Psi-setting. The lack of these facilities is due in some cases to inherent characteristics of the 5202 principle; in others their provision would require a very precise technique.'[36]

The US codebreakers lobbied for a big funding increase to build three more, even larger specific-purpose film-based machines and also tried to develop a general-purpose technique based on film. But that only represented technological inertia, a determination to push a previously favoured technology rather than adopt a better alternative, especially one that had been invented elsewhere. The influence of Bush and others who were doubtful about electronics took US codebreakers down a technological byway.[37] Only when their preference for film-based techniques was dropped did US codebreakers begin to construct general-purpose machines using electronics – 'one much more like later electronic computers', the completely electronic Superschritcher – and to absorb the lessons of Colossus, copies of which were constructed in the United States towards the end of the war.[38] The digital, electronic approach pioneered by Newman and Flowers clearly triumphed over the optical approach promoted by Bush. The two key technologies of the post-war interception world were to be non-Morse wireless interception and electronic, binary decryption technology. Both were developed in Britain for use by the emerging transatlantic Sigint operation, which was dominated by the enormous budget that the USA could devote to interception and codebreaking operations.

Continued British dominance of international cable networks, however, did not sit easily with the increasingly important global role of the USA. Once US troops were active in North Africa and Europe, 'The Americans… were not happy to see their most secret military messages pass through British cable stations in Britain and Gibraltar. They wanted their own cables.' In 1943, the US military communications services proposed to patch circuits by linking US cables with sections of German and French cables that had been cut earlier in the war. The British Wireless Telegraphy Board was most upset: 'These proposals are an attempt on the part of US commercial interests to encroach on British interests on this side of the Atlantic, with a view to reaping post-war advantage.' A compromise was reached, allowing the US signals service to operate part of the capacity on a British-owned cable between Gibraltar and the Azores, where traffic could be forwarded to New York on a US-owned cable. This arrangement was intended to respond to US concerns about British eavesdropping on US communications, but not to alter the economic status quo. However, this did not satisfy those who did seek to upset the British, pre-war, imperial network, for commercial, political or military reasons. As the dominions and colonies also wanted to have independent communications links, the US case received support from within the Empire. Such pressure eventually became too great and the British government had to accede. 'Since the Americans held the purse strings, the British, however reluctantly, had to give in. In late 1943 US-controlled transatlantic channels – to Algiers, to Italy, to England – proliferated.' It should be emphasized that British policy was intended to ensure continuation of the Empire after the war. Edward Wilshire, managing director of Cable & Wireless, the British cable company, argued that the British government had breached an agreement made in 1928 that it would defend the existing communications system of the Empire, against any 'attempt on the part of foreign governments to secure an increased share in the control and operation of world communications... It is therefore with profound misgivings that the Company is now forced to look upon a future where foreign interests have been permitted to make inroads on the communications of the British Empire, with possible disastrous results upon Empire communications as a whole and this company in particular... It might have been thought undesirable, from a security point of view, that messages which up to date have transmitted to London should no longer continue to do so, but should go direct between the countries concerned without the same facilities for the interception and scrutiny of such messages by those charged with the preservation of security.' As historian Daniel Headrick has written, 'Britain's century-old monopoly of Empire communications began to crumble. In its place there appeared a new policy of "partnership", with the United States as a benevolent patron.'[39] Wilshire's concern for 'national security' and the loss of access to intercepted intelligence proved to be unfounded as long as Britain was prepared to play the role of loyal junior partner. Traffic was in fact not diverted away from Britain – indeed, London retained its position as the international node, the large number of cables terminating there attracting other cables aiming to benefit from the network effect of extra connections. No doubt the convergence of international teleprinter cables in London was extremely useful for the joint UK-US post-war interception operations, bringing the greater bulk of international communications within easy reach of the eavesdroppers. While residential and business users were formally forbidden from using ciphers on international teleprinter circuits, a considerable mount of diplomatic traffic in cipher was carried on the same links, no doubt at least some of it using Vernam type on-line teleprinter ciphers. Even after telecommunications liberalization in the 1980s and 1990s, US companies building global fibre-optic and satellite networks still often chose to put their network control centres in London. And intelligence agreements continued to ensure a comprehensive exchange of information between USA, Britain, Australia and New Zealand.

chapter twenty-three

Siginstitutionalization

On 16 November 1944, Field Marshal Bernard Law Mont-gomery, commanding British and Canadian forces on the northern flank of the Allied advance to Germany, issued an appreciation: 'The enemy is at present fighting a defensive campaign on all fronts; his situation is such that he cannot stage major offensive operations. Furthermore, at all costs he has to prevent the war from entering on a mobile phase; he has not the transport or the petrol that would be necessary for mobile operations.'[1] At three o'clock the following morning, Hitler launched his last great gamble, an attack on the weakest spot in the Allied line, in the Ardennes, starting what became known as the Battle of the Bulge.

Montgomery's misreading of the German army's capability to resist was only the latest example in a long line of overoptimistic assessments by Allied commanders following the Allied success in the Battle of the Normandy (although not in Italy, where any optimism had long since been eroded by the hard fighting required to make even slow progress). Shortly after the liberation of France in July and August 1944 and Russian successes in the east, British Intelligence had issued the opinion that 'it is difficult to see how Germany... can prolong the struggle beyond December'.[2] In Normandy, the German army had lost 400,000 men, killed, seriously wounded or captured; 1,300 tanks had been destroyed, twenty-five divisions eliminated and another twenty 'severely mauled'. The Supreme Headquarters of the Allied Command (SHAEF) on 2 September 1944 concluded, 'the enemy had no coherent order of battle and no strategy outside [retiring to a defensive position on Germany's border, the] West Wall, his armies having been reduced to a number of fugitive battle groups'.[3]

A belief took hold that it would all be 'over by Christmas'. The disorganized German retreat after the fall of Paris was so rapid that it appeared that the Battle for Normandy had truly ended the German army's capacity to fight. The US army headed directly eastwards, threatening the German border. German troops in the Pas de Calais had to escape being surrounded by British troops aiming for Belgium. Brussels was liberated and the port of Antwerp, the second largest in Europe (after Rotterdam), was captured in an undamaged state. A rumour swept through the Netherlands that Allied troops had crossed the border and that liberation was at hand. The Dutch railway managers called for a strike and thousands flocked on to the streets to celebrate. But the Allies were stuck at the border and the Dutch were forced to endure their worst period of the war, the Hunger Winter, when 18,000 died of starvation, bringing a taste of the war in the east to the western shores of Europe. A retired doctor living in Rotterdam wrote in his diary, 'We have cheered too soon... They [the Allies] seem unable to progress farther, as they have in fact only one good port (Cherbourg) where they have to bring in all their men and military supplies.'[4] The doctor, despite not sharing the information flowing to the Allied commands, was able to diagnose the latter's weakness.

The Allies, in the flush of victory, had allowed strategy to be subordinated to wishful thinking. Their forces had indeed moved ahead on all fronts towards Germany, but they overlooked the urgent need to secure access from the sea to Antwerp – which lies some sixty miles inland at the head of a deep channel – and had enabled German forces on the seaward approaches to the port to dig in for a long and bloody defence. The Allies thus created a logistics bottleneck for themselves. They had fallen prey to their belief in their own invincibility. In this situation, the value of intelligence supplied by decrypted messages was effectively worthless, as the best intelligence could not change established preconceptions. Indeed, the exceptional string of good intelligence provided by Ultra may have contributed to a belief among Allied commanders that the enemy was beaten with collapse of the German army in France and Belgium, when in fact the Allies were about to be held once more at bay.

Perhaps the highest accolade that could be awarded to the value of Fish intelligence was just this – that at times it became an excuse for lack of progress. A telex from the US army codebreaking unit in Washington to GC&CS, dated 5 January 1945, reported that it had heard from US officers with SHAEF in Europe 'that some of intelligence troubles connection reverses on western front due to difficulties with Fish… before we attempt to assist we must have necessary ammunition. Please confirm above statement. Would also appreciate your views on any other assistance we may give on Fish project.'[5] It is not clear exactly what these difficulties were, as December 1944 saw 86 per cent of de-Chis from the Newmanry fully decoded by the Testery, and 60 wheels were broken from 9 links, producing in total 4,313,000 decoded characters in one month.[6] There was a sharp decline in the performance of the interception stations at the end of 1944. Harold Kenworthy wrote to Edward Travis, the director of GC&CS, explaining the latest problems: 'Conditions are very poor at present on non-Morse links. Owing to seasonal conditions, frequencies have all come down below 7 M/cs. Other countries have come down as well at night time nearly all the frequencies are between 3 M/cs and 1 M/cs. A lot of interference is experienced during this period. It is [also] surmised that a reduction in power has been found possible [by the German army operators] owing to the shorter distances to be covered. The whole subject is being examined from the technical angle and additional amplifiers are rapidly being made up to extend the range of our aerials.' Kenworthy also proposed a trial at intercepting non-Morse in Belgium.[7] Nonetheless, five new links in north-west Europe were broken between June and December 1944: Grilse (Army Group B to Berlin) was broken in June; Bleak (Army Group H to Berlin) in August; Lampsucker (Army Group H to Berlin) in November; and Toadfish (Army Group B to Berlin) and Triggerfish (Army Group B to Berlin) both in December. On the eastern front, there were new links to be broken, too: Whiting (Army Group North cut off in the Courland); Crooner (Army Group Vistula) and Gurnard (Army Group East). The task facing the Fish section and the Newmanry in particular was to harness the expanding range of Colossi to handle this growing number of links that required machine time for breaking and setting, and much more frequently than ever before.

Even as late as 31 August 1944, Hitler had not taken any steps to fortify the half-built, pre-war line of defensive positions, the West Wall (known in Britain, though not in Germany, as the Siegfried Line). The wall had originally been built before Hitler reoccupied the Rhineland in 1936, as a defensive measure against any French reaction, but work ceased on it when Hitler saw that his first military adventure attracted no military consequences. On 7 September 1944, Hitler ordered von Rundstedt to hold the Allies on the Albert Canal, the Meuse and the upper Moselle to gain time for the West Wall to be brought up to a defensible state – something von Rundstedt estimated would take up to six weeks. But the Allies had already crossed the canal and Meuse the day before the order had been issued. With the German army in disarray and the West Wall derelict, the way to Germany beckoned. Then, however, the Allied advance stalled as the logistical needs outran supplies because of the failure to capture the sea routes to Antwerp so that everything had to be driven from distant Cherbourg. At Arnhem, Aachen and Antwerp, the German armies won important defensive, delaying battles and kept the war going into 1945, aided by confused Allied strategy and tactics.[8] Some have blamed Eisenhower's broad front strategy, which meant that no one Allied army could have enough supplies to break through effectively, while others have pointed to the vulnerability of a single advancing army to an enemy counter-attack aimed at cutting that army's lines of communication. Politics probably played the most important role in determining Allied strategy. It became unacceptable for Montgomery to be allowed to lead an attack while US generals, including the impetuous George C Patton, were held back. In any event, Hitler gained time to strengthen the West Wall, so that, far from the war being over by Christmas, the Allies would have to fight yet another horrific battle to break into Germany. And, while the Allies prepared for that battle, Hitler was planning his own counter-offensive – hitting the Allied line at the very spot in the Ardennes he had chosen for his attack on Belgium and France in May 1940 – and hoping that his panzers could cause the Allies sufficient casualties to weaken the political will cementing their effort.

If Allied overconfidence and logistical problems gave Hitler time to prepare defences on the West Wall and the Rhine – the so-called Fortress Area West – and plan for his winter offensive, the Allies also gained time to discover the details of those defences and the internal problems faced by the German armed forces. The first information came as early as September 1944, when a British Intelligence appreciation noted, 'Source has reported considerable constructional manning and other defensive activities in the general area of the West Wall.'[9] Decodes gave details of where constructional work was ordered, and which troops were to be sent where. They revealed the orders stating where anti-tank defences were to be built and, later, further reports on which ones had been completed and which were unfinished when the time came to launch the Allied offensive. Cologne and Bonn were declared 'keypoints'.

The decodes also revealed that, so desperate were the shortages of soldiers, young boys and very old male civilians were organized as a Home Guard – Volksturm – to be used in some areas, for example, the upper Rhine, where natural defences were thought likely to deter an Allied assault.[10] Use of the Volksturm released some troops for the danger spots, but never enough, and all sorts of desperate measures were demanded of units that had not expected to be sent to the front to face the Allied assault. Decodes showed that the Luftwaffe objected when its air-defence troops were told to become infantry subject to army orders. The army objected when the non-commissioned officer training school staff were told to stop teaching and join the troops at the front. 'The forces available for defending the Rhine crossings against airborne landings or surprise breakthroughs... were a scratch lot' – engineer bridge builders, training units and their instructors, Erstatz (substitute) units, and so on.

Meanwhile, Hitler's strategic position steadily deteriorated. His insistence on maintaining troops in Norway, Denmark and elsewhere – even an experienced division marooned on the Channel Islands – meant that he wasted troops who could have eased the shortages elsewhere. And the Allied strategy in Italy of drawing troops away from the front in north-west Europe only exacerbated the situation. A Bream decrypt issued on 20 December 1944 by ObSW, Commander-in-Chief South-West, revealed that the ration strength of the German armed forces under his control in Italy and the Balkans was one million men and 125,000 horses.[11] There were shortages of equipment, too. Some examples from the signals corps illustrate the situation. In December 1944, on the western front, 'various [German army] signals stations were told that precautionary building of heavy field cable and trunk field cable in defence installations was forbidden owing to shortage. Such cable was to be dismantled, stored and reported.'[12] And another order was issued to German army units because of the chaos caused by telephone enquiries following air raids. The volume of such calls and the shortage of cables meant that lines were congested. The practice 'must stop [and] violations are to be punished'.[13]

411

While the Allies suffered thousands of casualties in attacks on the West Wall, Hitler was weakening his defences in order to build up the forces he needed for his planned offensive in the Ardennes. There were indications of the attack in Ultra, but they could just as easily have been interpreted as preparations to parry the next major Allied attack with a counter-attack, rather than the pre-emptive counter-offensive that was actually planned by Hitler. As the Allied commanders saw it, a counter-offensive by Hitler would be reckless, for it would reduce the number of aircraft and tanks available for the defence of the West Wall and the Rhine. But, once again, Allied commanders made the mistake of imagining that Hitler would think like them. The Nazi leader hoped that a defeat inflicted on the Allies would sap their will for the hard struggle and destroy co-operation between them; he did not anticipate the military destruction of the Allied armies, only severe disruption of their will to advance. As it was, his unexpected move merely caught the Allies off guard. In fact, the Battle of the Bulge was probably doomed to failure given the growing preponderance of Allied forces and their almost complete domination of the air. Germany's air defences, indeed, had to be denuded to provide fighter aircraft for the Ardennes offensive. And, far from being shaken by Hitler's attack, the American troops were angered by it, and their own deter-mination to defeat the German army and their commanders' eagerness to resume the offensive was bolstered.

When the Ardennes offensive did fail, it was the Russian army which benefited most immediately from the destruction of Germany's mobile reserves. Since October, the Russian army had been rebuilding its forces in preparation for the launch of a massive offensive in January 1945. On this occasion, German Intelligence was fully aware of Russian intentions – a decrypted Fish message reported a German army intelligence appreciation which con-cluded, 'Continual advance of [Russian] attack preparations in the Schwerpunkt [keypoint] areas are clearly distinguishable today. The time of the attack seems close at hand.'[14] The Russian offensive opened in relays, eventually encompassing the whole front, with six million troops undertaking the biggest military offensive in history. Several army groups – the First, Second and Third Belorussian Fronts, and the First and Fourth Ukranian Fronts – under the command of Marshals Zhukov, Rokossovsky and Konev, moved forward from their positions west of the Vistula, with German army groups putting up a fierce but now wholly underarmed and undermanned defence. The Russian army was now at its zenith, stronger, better armed and more confident than ever.

As one historian has concluded,

> The Soviet war effort focused above all else on the prosecution of war at the expense of everything else... Soviet factories produced artillery pieces in hundreds of thousands, German factories in tens of thousands. The balance of tank production was also heavily in the Soviet favour [as early as] 1942 and 1943. Red Army mobility was higher than German... The increased modernisation and mechanisation of Soviet forces took place against a declining level of supply on the other side... It was not the Soviet 'masses' that defeated Axis forces, but ever larger numbers of the weapons of modern warfare... The key component in the [Soviet] reforms [of the armed forces] was radio communications, which had been primitive or, in some cases, non-existent before 1942. Neither tanks nor aircraft had been routinely fitted with radios, or kept in contact with battlefield commanders. Under lend-lease, the Soviet Union was supplied with 35,089 radios stations, 380,000 field telephones, 5,900 radio receivers and almost a million miles of telephone wire. These supplies revolutionised Soviet battlefield performance.[15]

The decisive battles of 1945 were those fought on the borders of Germany and Poland as the Red Army pushed directly into the territory of the Reich, smashing the core resistance and morale of the German army, heirs to the traditions of Frederick the Great, Moltke and Hindenburg. The latter, along with Ludendorf, was celebrated for his victory against the Russian army at Tannenberg, East Prussia, in 1914, but on 21 January 1944, the Red Army occupied this precious site of Prusso-German military heritage. In Italy, the bloody struggle continued, drawing German troops away from north-west Europe and the eastern front. On several occasions, Allied commanders used deception measures to divert the German commanders into expecting an attack in one place, and then, when Fish and Enigma decodes showed that German troops were being sent to that place, launched an attack elsewhere. The benefits of Ultra decodes were by now integrated into the planning of military operations.

Soon the rate of advance of the Russian troops meant that they would threaten Berlin, capital of Prussia and now of the Nazi Reich. Hitler had no choice but to shift troops from the west to face the immediate threat to his adopted city. As one of his biographers, Ian Kershaw, has observed, 'As the war that Hitler had unleashed 'came home to the Reich', the dictator, now rapidly ageing, becoming increasingly a physical wreck, and showing pronounced signs of intense nervous strain, distanced himself from his people.'[16] Losing touch with reality, Hitler placed his faith in super-weapons that would terrorize his enemies into surrender and in ever greater doses of Nazi fanaticism stiffening the 'will to win'. His chaotic command structure also showed signs of diminishing. Fish decrypts revealed constant confusion within the German armed forces over the chain of command. Initially, for example, the defences of the vital Rhine crossings were under control of the local Wehrkreis (military districts) commanders, but ObW, Commander-in-Chief West, and Army Group commands also had some responsibilities, as did the Luftwaffe's Air Defence Zone West (itself officially under command of ObW, but with a considerable degree of independence). In December 1944, when preparing for a withdrawal from the West Wall to the Rhine, ObW complained to the general staff,

OKW, in Berlin about the state of defensive measures on the Rhine crossings. He was anxious about the lack of heavy weapons and the stationing of tactical reserves at too great a distance from the Rhine. He pointed out that the Wehrkreis command could not provide infantry protection for flak gun positions outside the inner bridgeheads as its own forces were barely sufficient to occupy the most important positions. He 'stated that the Rhine bridge situation required at once unified designation of responsible officers with dictatorial powers for all military measures'. A further measure of confusion was caused by the creation of a special command, Oberbefehlshaber Upper Rhine. 'This is a different category [of command] and appears to be an operational command created by Himmler for himself.'[17] Again, all this information was revealed to Allied Intelligence primarily by Fish decodes.

Decodes also revealed that the disastrous Allied parachute landings at Arnhem in late September had one advantageous consequence: they elevated the fear of further airborne assaults to a prime concern of Hitler and the German army – and led them to withdraw defensive forces from the front to cover against such possible attacks in the rear.[18] After breaching the West Wall, the Allies undertook preparations for a broad attack aimed at gaining crossings of the Rhine. Early in February, decrypts of Fish messages showed that the German high command expected a major Allied attack but could not predict precisely where it would fall.[19] The Allies learned that German Military Intelligence had concluded, 'Eisenhower's aim was to surround and annihilate the German formations West of the lower Rhine.'[20]

The number of decodes produced by the Fish operation rose throughout the first half of 1945 up until the end of the war in Europe. February saw over 5 million characters decoded from 696 intercepted transmissions on 13 links. The joint efforts of the Newmanry and the Testery saw 97 successful wheel-breaking operations. Using rectangling it took an average of 3.8 days to achieve a wheel-break, 2 days using a depth, and 7.1 days by use of cribs. March was the all-time record as the retreating German armies took to the airwaves in ever greater numbers, interceptions soared and more machines were available to decode them. In all 6,037,000 characters of decode were produced from 1,063 broken de-Chis (356 in the Newmanry and 707 in the Testery) and over 100 wheel pin patterns broken. And, to cap it all, there was a marked improvement in the time taken to produce a decode – an average of just 3.24 days.[21] All in all, decodes gave the Allies invaluable intelligence about the preparations and difficulties of the defences they had to overcome to gain entry to German territory and to finish the war. The battles of early 1945 must rate as some of the most intense of the war. On the eastern, western and Italian fronts, the Allies were involved in hard struggles against an increasingly desperate German army emboldened both by the fact that it was now defending the homeland, as well as by Allied demands for 'unconditional surrender' (which was the only objective capable of holding the Russia and the USA in continued alliance) and ill-judged proposals, for example, to reduce Germany to a pre-industrial, rural state.

In early January 1945, Harold Kenworthy, the leading wireless engineer in the interception of the German non-Morse trans-missions, visited Brussels with three other GC&CS wireless experts to find a suitable site for an interception station closer to the German army. Despite the thousands dying not far away on the front, Kenworthy – ever concerned to record his personal sacrifices – ensured his report included note of the difficulties he had had to endure. The party set out on 8 January, but did not get to Brussels until 3 a.m. on Sunday, 14 January. Kenworthy noted that 'weather conditions were extremely bad throughout, and a lack of fuel did not add to personal comforts. In spite of these adverse conditions, the team worked very well throughout the period, putting in long hours to get results quickly.' They had tried a site near Verdun but found Brussels gave better reception and they started setting up a station at Bel-Air in the Belgian capital where, 'In general, signal strength was up and recordability very good.' Some captured high-quality German aerials were also put to good use. However, while reception of transmissions from western Germany was good, signals from occupied Copenhagen were difficult to intercept.[22]

Care was taken to ensure that the flow of intelligence was not disrupted unnecessarily. Plans to bomb major telecommunications centres in Germany were not considered to be likely to disrupt interception of Fish messages. 'Little is known of the exact whereabouts of the Fish transmitters, but [they are] likely to be fairly near the headquarters served and not in large towns [where main telecommunications nodes are usually located, so] the chances of their suffering under this programme is slight.'[23] With the growing number of Colossi at work at Bletchley Park, the number of messages being decrypted grew towards the end of the war. Through March 1945, Knockholt was successfully recording an average of 729 messages a day, and slip-reading some 400,000 characters. At Bletchley Park, the codebreakers were also doing well, cracking on average 3.5 keys (wheel-breaking) a day. Indeed, March 1945 saw some record-breaking days, with 455,847 characters being perforated on 30 March (the previous record being 426,380 characters on 28 February 1945) and a record of eight keys being broken in one day on 10 March (the previous record being seven keys broken on 18 February 1945).[24]

As Allied attacks on the Rhine intensified, it became apparent from decrypts that preparations were in hand for the retreat of German armed forces staff and administrative units to a mountainous part of inner Germany. Analysis of teleprinter traffic showed that several OKW, OKH, SS, Abwehr (Military Intelligence) and cipher and cryptography units were on the move away from Berlin. The first indication of any shift of location usually came from messages between signals corps units, and requests for teleprinter links and wireless telegraphy stations. 'Important inter-service telegraphic exchanges which about three months ago moved from Berlin and a site east of Berlin to locations in the Zossen... area, are now believed to be setting up in the area of Muelhausen [which] is about as central a spot as can be found in Germany.'[25]

The Dace link had first appeared in 1943 and provided for communications between the OKH, the high command on the eastern front, near Koenigsberg (teleprinter call-sign HOSF), and the OKW, the high command for other fronts, near Berlin (HZPH/FF1). The link opened and closed at various times until early 1944, when the OKH headquarters and its signals section evacuated East Prussia, to move near Berlin. The move had long been fore-shadowed, with the opening of a second signals centre near Berlin in October 1944, stationed in an army headquarters building at Zossen – eight floors underground to protect it from the heavy Allied bombing of German cities. This new station, HZPH/FF2, gradually took control of the links previously managed from near Koenigsberg until the station there was closed in January 1945. In February, a new station, ODO, was opened in the Erfurt area as the Russian army closed in on Berlin, and it took over communications with Bream, Sailfish, Weaver, Mullet, Bullhead, Gurnard and Squid. 'Very shortly, however, the advance on the Western Allies rendered the ODO exchange untenable and on 14 March a link was set up between HZPH/FF1 at Zossen and a station in the Munich area.'[26] Several more moves were also logged until the war ended, giving the Allies advance notice of where Hitler and his generals intended to carry on their duties commanding the German armies. In fact, the planned resistance proved to be fantasy, but that is the benefit of hindsight.

The German army 'Chi' branch[27] – which handled cipher and cryptanalytical operations – was also searching for a safer spot. On 22 February 1945, a request was issued to the local Wehrkreis for sufficient motor transport to take about fifty tons of cipher-related material (probably including printing presses) to the railway station for relocation to a safe hiding place. 'It is clearly of the utmost importance to the Germans that these documents should never fall into Allied hands.'[28] The anonymous author of a British Intelligence summary of Allied knowledge about these plans for the redoubt and other panic measures to evacuate secret documents and personnel from Berlin, asked a number of questions: 'Who are the "cipher personnel" (Schluesselkraefte) and what are the "documents" (Akten) for whose sake certain old ladies are to be denied asylum in the paper-mill at Rudolfstadt-Jena?' Some of the answers may well only have come somewhat later. In October 1945, it was reported that 'European TICOM materials [i.e. captured cipher documents] were pretty well exhausted with the exception of materials being recovered from a lake in Germany known as Schliersee. The most recent report concerning this material is that some additional 2,000 lbs of documents [have been] found. It has been indicated that this material is the most interesting to have been uncovered so far.'[29] The reports about the redoubt offer an example of how signals intelligence can mislead, rather than enlighten. The move of the signals corps and other headquarters units, and decrypts which referred to an 'Inner Redoubt', led Eisenhower to fear that a hard core intended to fight on taking refuge in the mountainous parts of south-east Germany.

With the Allied crossing of the Rhine and the Russian approach to Berlin, the war in Europe was clearly drawing to a close. In fact, Hitler decided not to flee to his mountain eyrie. He chose to stay in Berlin to the bitter end, hoping that, like his hero Frederick the Great who had founded Prussia's military reputation, he would inflict some crushing defeat on his enemies at the last moment. And failing that, feeling that the German race had let him down, he intended to bring about their annihilation along with his own. Indeed, one biographer of Hitler concluded that 'he would blame the German people themselves, whom he would see as too weak to survive and unworthy of him in the great struggle'.[30]

The relentless pressure on the Reich can be illustrated by a few examples from the contracting German communications network and its increasing difficulties. In February 1945, the Luftwaffe had to station supervising officers at wireless stations to enforce rules that forbade private traffic being sent on congested wireless links. In mid-March 1945 the Luftwaffe in Berlin reported that all telephone lines from the Reich to Italy had been put permanently out of order by enemy action. The non-Morse link from Treuenbrietzen to Italy had also experienced difficulty in receiving transmissions during the previous few days and there were just four hours a day when traffic could be passed. On the eastern front twenty-six balloons had to be floated aloft with directional wireless relay receivers/transmitters to carry telephone and teleprinter communications to the surrounded Army Group North in the Courland on the Baltic coast. Command and communications began to break down as Allied troops poured across the Rhone and, at last, the German army started to crumble. At the end of March, Army Group B in the west asked the OKH to provide a wireless teleprinter link between them, but was told that it would take between six and eight days as there was no equipment at OKH.[31] Because of all these communications difficulties, more and more reliance had to be placed on non-Morse wireless links. As Allied forces moved ever closer to the transmitters, the easier it became to intercept the transmissions. And, as has been seen, as more and more Colossi were delivered to Bletchley Park, the more decrypts there were. Between November 1943 and the end of the war, 63,431,000 characters were decrypted in total.

Hitler's armies, which had some years earlier spread out across so much of Europe, had now retracted fully. So too had Hitler's communications networks with which he directed his troops. In his Berlin bunker, Hitler and his entourage lost all contact except for two telephone links to the nearby telephone exchange. They resorted to dialling telephone numbers at random, hoping someone would answer the phone and tell them what was going on in their locality. 'Have you seen any Russians?' they would ask if they got a connection.[32] Hitler, full of frustration and rage, exploded, telling his generals, 'The only thing crippling us is that fact that we don't know exactly what's happening and we don't have precise data and are dependent on chance news.'[33] But, of course, Hitler was entirely wrong. Even if he had had good communications, he would still have refused to believe that his forces were defeated, and he would still have wanted to fight on, to see yet more lives lost. SS Brigadefuehrer Wilhelm Mohnke said to Hitler, 'We haven't quite brought about what we wanted in 1933, my Fuehrer.' Hitler, in reply, laid the blame on his having come to power too soon. 'You regret it afterwards that you are so good' was his final judgement on himself.[34] A day later, he committed suicide and the war effectively ground to a halt.

For the Fish team, it had already become clear that the end of the war was close. In the preceding few weeks, the amount of traffic dropped off as the German army ceased to exist. Work on assembling Colossus 11, which had started on 8 May, was stopped and this last machine was left unfinished. Essentially, the task for which Colossus had been invented was over. Attempts were made to decrypt messages that had not succumbed to earlier efforts. On 5 May 1945, the Fish interception unit attached to Montgomery's 21st Army Group, reported, 'We are getting [plain language] on a Fish link here one end of which says he is at Pfunds about 45 miles south-south-west of Innsbruck and is about to be overrun by American... [We are asking the US HQ] to try and contact the troops concerned and instruct them to put a guard on any [wireless telegraphy] equipment.' Two days later, a special unit with the 6th US Army Group issued an order stating, 'To insure no Fish escaping the net and to capitalize on drama of surrender, I have today presented Winterbotham's [memo] of 21 April to all concerned and had all customers sign off' in preparation for closing the service.[35]

One month later Edward Travis, the director of GC&CS, issued a notice stating, 'Mr. M. H. A. Newman left on 6 June 1945 to take up another appointment.'[36] Others left in slightly less haste. Turing, Flowers, Tutte and many others left Bletchley Park and Knockholt, and made the return to civilian life. There, some of them, Newman in particular, developed one of the world's first electronic, stored-program-control computers, building on the work they had done at Bletchley Park. Others returned to old occupations, with Flowers, for example, resuming his work at the Post Office. But some stayed on, and the Government Code and Cipher School, GC&CS, became the Government Communications Headquarters, GCHQ. Fish had given birth not just to the age of the electronic computer but also to its sibling, the age of electronic surveillance.

While the Second World War in Europe was drawing to a close, the interception and codebreaking organizations of the Allies were being prepared for a new world order. As early as August 1943, a new section had been set up in GC&CS to look for weaknesses in the communications of other countries in preparation for a refocusing of the interception effort for the post-war era.[37] The approach was to 'assume all countries have a weak spot'.[38] Early on, it was imagined the number of interception stations and sets after the war 'gradually diminishing as the political situation returns to normal'.[39] But there would be no return to the pre-war world. The war had changed society – economically, politically, socially, militarily – far too much. Besides, interception and decryption had obviously played such an important role in the war that there could be no question of reducing its role once the fighting had stopped. It would grow, become central to governmental and military activity, and develop into a permanent, secretive but pervasive feature of post-war life. The basis for that process was laid in the last months of the Second World War as hundreds of Bombes and ten Colossi churned out their vast outpourings of decrypted enemy intelligence. In the last year of the war, the post-war organization of interception and codebreaking was established. It was to be absolutely secret and wholly independent. The institutionalization of Sigint was one of the enduring changes brought about by the Second World War.

The issue, as the title of one report put it, of the 'Re-orientation of Cover' rose up the agenda.[40] It was claimed in one report, in August 1944, that no Russian traffic had been intercepted since 1941 and to start now would require thirty receiving sets (eighteen in Britain and twelve in the Mediterranean) – although this is almost certainly an exaggeration as several existing documents refer to earlier interception and analysis of Russian wireless traffic.[41] To cover Italy, Sweden, Czechoslovakia, Poland, Norway, Finland, Belgium, the Netherlands, Yugoslavia, Hungary, Bulgaria, Rumania and Turkey would require another ninety-eight sets (thirty-five in Britain and sixty-three in the Mediterranean).[42] 'Our cover of neutral countries is inadequate at a time when they call for increasing watch. As recently liberated countries resume wireless telegraphy activity, we shall have no resources for covering them.'[43] Despite the broad range of targets which quickly widened to cover every independent country, Russia was the main target. One section at Bletchley Park was allocated the daunting task of going back through all the tens of thousands of pages of Ultra source material that had been gathered during the war for any and all information about the Russian armed forces.[44] Robert J Aldrich, a historian of the secret services, has observed, 'The British official history of intelligence has declared that Britain stopped breaking Soviet communications traffic on 22 June 1941. But this is no more plausible than the contention that the British ceased work on American communications traffic after Pearl Harbor on 8 December 1941.' He contends that 'At some point during late 1943 or early 1944 Western signals intelligence priorities shifted dramatically, giving the Soviets much greater emphasis.' Before that turning point, the British had warned the Russians of weaknesses in their ciphers – weaknesses the British had learned about from decodes of German messages (see Chapter twelve). After the change in course, the British kept quiet and drew a lot of information about the Russian armed forces from decodes of German intelligence reports on the Russians. The Russians, of course, were aware of the change of sentiment and, by the end of 1944, 'almost all exchanges [between Russia and the Western Allies] on the German order of battle, the main areas of intelligence cooperation, had ceased'.[45]

And, while Enigma traffic was set to decline substantially, all forms of non-Morse and auto-Morse were expected to increase significantly. The role of the teleprinter as a form of electric mail had been firmly established by its widespread wartime use by both sides. The wartime teleprinter networks were redirected to support commercial use. Teleprinter traffic would grow very rapidly in the post-war decades, only being superseded as a vital means of printed business communication by 'e-mail' in the 1990s. The number of interception sets forecast to be needed for non-Morse coverage grew as the end of the war drew near. In April 1945, one estimate thought that one hundred more sets for non-Morse interception would be needed. But, by May, Knockholt had already logged some 200 stations transmitting non-Morse signals.[46] Some of the non-Morse traffic that was taken was commercial traffic.[47] Other non-Morse techniques were also coming into use – especially transmission of pictures or images, now known as facsimile or fax.[48]

A report noted, 'The present trend of Commercial activities points very strongly to the expansion of printing systems, e.g. Teleprinter, multiplex (multi-channel circuits), of all kinds… These various types call for special apparatus such as "crystal controlled" receivers for stability etc…. Teleprinter technique, which includes both American and British machines, is now well developed and a first-class team of teleprinter personnel have been part of the FORDE Staff for some time.'[49]

With non-Morse transmissions, it was essential to 'continue our research and so keep ahead and be able to intercept any of these forms of transmission… Coupled with [non-Morse] is the problem of high-speeds of Morse, particularly favoured by Russia. Very good apparatus must be used in this connection.'[50] Russia had achieved transmission speeds of up to 500 words per minute by the end of the war and was pressing for faster speeds, leading Knockholt to develop its own reception techniques for high-speed Morse. This meant strengthening GC&CS's technical and scientific resources so that it could cover whatever wireless traffic there was to be intercepted. Travis wrote to his deputy telling him, 'I would like plans... for scientific search of [the] ether from end to end.'[51] The research department at Knockholt was charged with developing the equipment that would be capable of performing such comprehensive searching of the airwaves.[52] The wireless research department would have to become the equivalent of a research and development section of a major manufacturer or a leading university. It would need to attract its research engineers from among the best graduates each year and compete with commercial companies for the brightest talents – to work in secret.[53] The war had changed Britain's – and the United States' – interception and codebreaking units from a last-minute effort to a sophisticated operation. In July 1945, it was decided that Knockholt would, in fact, need over 300 hundred non-Morse receiving sets.[54]

A report entitled 'Development of a Modern Interception Service', written in April 1945, expressed the outlines of an integrated interception service as the basis of a codebreaking operation.

The art of interception under modern conditions is therefore one of considerable and increasing difficulty. To be successful, it must be developed as a special art; the use of personnel, methods and equipment of normal [wireless telegraphy] will not lead to success. Operators must be trained ab initio in intercept work, with particular emphasis from an early stage upon weak signals, interference, fading, poor Morse and all the phenomena and atmosphere of interception. Aerials, receivers and associated equipment, which together form the intercept station, all require independent study and continual development as the interception problem changes... It will therefore be evident that, under modern conditions, 'Y' work has become an extremely complex and 'specialist' matter. It is certain that size alone (measured by the number of receivers available) is no measure of success; a small, highly skilled and homogeneous team will undoubtedly produce better results than a large unwieldy organization of low ability.[55]

In truth, the organization was to become both highly skilled and large in size.

The codebreaking and traffic analysis sides were also institutionalized and their operations refocused. There are fewer hints in the surviving files about codebreaking and traffic analysis than about interception, but some glimpses are provided of the conscious expansion of cryptanalysis into the most challenging areas. Colossus had been designed for a specific purpose, but always with as much flexibility as practical in mind. Several small jobs had already been found for the Colossi as soon as the Fish traffic started dropping off. But, as the war drew to an end, Gerry Morgan reported to Travis, 'more ambitious ones are under discussion and another problem of a somewhat similar kind is coming to the fore in the Research Section – namely of solving a transposition. Several of the projects, or more vaguely "requirements", need a high-speed or instantaneous memory of code groups.'[56] In other words, Colossus-like machines were essential to modern post-war codebreaking. It should be pointed out, though, that this conflicts with the official view put forward nowadays by GCHQ – that after the war one or two Colossi were kept, but used purely for supporting tasks, such as letter frequency counts, and not for key-breaking purposes (and also that GCHQ had to wait several years for one of the first post-war computers and, even when it arrived, it did not work anything like as reliably as the Colossi, it is claimed).

One interesting insight comes from a short memo, in the Bletchley Park files which have been opened to the public, regarding what are known as one-time pads. Mathematicians can prove that truly random keys are completely undecipherable.[57] A truly random key is known generally as a one-time key or a one-time pad. If a key really is random, then it becomes impossible for patterns to be detected (unless the key is reused, i.e. creating a depth of two or messages enciphered with the same key). However, the problem – just as it was for Vernam – was creating truly random keys in sufficient quantity. Hand methods were simply impractical, and machine methods could not (and still cannot) be developed that generate truly random numbers. So the term one-time pad represented an objective which was virtually unachievable, and which could only be approximated.

The memo reads (in full): 'The following is a note of suggested procedure for detecting possible cribs from Fish into Diplomatic One-Time pads. Research Section will provide Major Tester and Major Crawford (3L) with clues to detect cribs, i.e. places and some guide to addresses and signatures. Major Tester's Section will inform Major Morgan when they find a likely message, 3L will act as a long stop.'[58] Again, this documented use of Colossus, for non-Fish diplomatic codebreaking tasks, conflicts with GCHQ's official position on the use of the Colossi after the war. The memo also suggests that British and American codebreakers had learnt the lesson better than the post-war theorists. James Bamford, the American author of two of the very few books on post-war interception and decryption activities in the United States, *The Puzzle Palace* and *Body of Secrets*, cites one codebreaker as saying that 'no cipher is unbreakable'.[59]

A memo written by Newman to Travis on 3 June (three days before Newman left Bletchley Park) notes that 'When the back work on Fish comes to an end in 2 months' time, there will be no further use for Colossi, but some specimens will be wanted for future investigations.' Newman also recommended that a useful combination of machines for other (unidentified) immediate cryptographic needs would be: 4 Robinsons; 2 Miles; 1 Insert machine; 1 Garbo; 4 hand-counters; and 2 hot stickers. Other memos from after Newman's departure show that Robinson, Miles, Dragon and, especially, Proteus were all thought to be of use in dealing with Japanese ciphers – though some argued that

427

Freeborn's punched card section was more efficient than Robinson at character frequency counting. A memo from Tester's section in August asked for 4 Tunny machines to be retained, while 9 would be dismantled. Dragon 2, Dragon 3, Proteus and Aquarius 'are being retained for research work as their capabilities have not been fully decided'. Dragon 1 was to be dismantled.[60]

Newman also pointed out that Colossi 4 and 5 had self-contained counter racks that could be saved. 'It would be a great service to research in this country if these institutions [engaged in computer research after the war] could have the chance to acquire some of these racks... [it] would be most valuable to the computing machine research units which are being projected.'[61] He recommended that the counters and Bedsteads should be packed and stored for possible reuse in this fashion. The available documents show that they were indeed dismantled and packed away in storage, but there they stayed and no word, let alone any physical manifestation, of the existence of these electronic counters was made public until 2004. The post-war computer teams had to redevelop any counters they needed for themselves.

The question of what role, if any, there was for the Post Office in post-war interception activities also had to addressed. From before the Second World War, it had played a key part in aiding diplomatic interception for the Foreign Office. But the attitude of Post Office staff was not helpful in day-to-day operations.[62] Even as early as mid-1943 GC&CS was thinking about the post-war interception organization. 'The obvious way to avoid the anomalies and difficulties inseparable from joint control by FO [Foreign Office] and GPO [General Post Office] is to delete GPO. To do this during the war is however definitely undesirable [because of dependence on Post Office staff and technical expertise]... At the end of the war the situation will be radically different... it is desirable to take the long view.'[63]

According to one report, when GC&CS tried to control the Post Office operations, 'most stations showed unveiled hostility'. One of the worst offenders was the Post Office station at Sandridge and 'it is still necessary for us to keep a very tight control and to check the frequent transgressions in their early stages'.[64] A plea also came from Knockholt to sever the links with the Post Office and strengthen internal capabilities. According to Kenworthy, 'The advantages would all be on our side. Endless discussions as to why we want things done a certain way and the attitude of procrastination... would be obviated... Knockholt are now actively engaged in investigating Russia and other Baudot circuits', and would be better off handling the work themselves.[65] They could react quickly to new types of transmission without the delays involved in asking Post Office engineers and managers for help.[66]

The deputy director wrote to the director, Edward Travis, 'I do not consider the standard of the Post Office intercept stations to be good enough, but I have suggested nothing beyond a general policy of doing away with them as soon as possible... We need to get some promising "young blood" introduced into the interception organization... Put a bright young man in each interception station as an outpost of tight central control... young men [who will] develop into key figures in future... My only essential qualification would be that they should be of second-class honours degree mentality.'[67] While the very brightest were needed as cryptographers, the engineers needed to be slightly less brainy – it was assumed that such people were more likely to be unquestioningly loyal.

In this manner, the new interception and codebreaking organization GCHQ was set up. The technical and mathematical tasks facing it were numerous given the spread of its ambitions to keep abreast of as much wireless and landline traffic as possible as it worked in conjunction with equivalent organizations in the USA, Australia and New Zealand. The end of the war brought not a period of relief for GCHQ, but a massive expansion of the tasks it had to cope with. Travis himself commented in October 1945, 'One thing after another has been happening, so that... war seems to have [had] less problems than peace.'[68]

Fish had proved to be one of the most spectacular coups of the Second World War. Ultra, and Fish in particular, almost certainly did not win the war for the Allies, but probably hastened the end of the war by a year or two, and in doing so probably saved several million lives. Two of the last reports in the existing files on Fish are a memo of 22 June 1945 noting that two Sturgeon machines and a power unit were being shipped to Washington, and another memo of 10 July 1945 reporting that mobile communications wagons and teleprinters from von Rundstedt's headquarters had been captured.[69] The final memo is dated 9 July 1945 and simply records that Fish operations were to cease: 'The work on old material which has been proceeding since VE Day can now be discontinued... Those concerned should take the necessary steps to wind up those parts of their sections which have been engaged in this task. Those responsible for the machines used for this purpose should report to me, before taking action, their plans for dismantling etc.'[70] Most of the Colossi were dismantled and much of the documentation about them was burned. Some machines and documents were retained for the use and instruction of post-war codebreakers in Britain and the United States. And enough documentation survived, and has now to come light, for the Colossus story to be told at last.

chapter twenty-four

Colossus – The Legacy

In the valleys towards the western edge of the South Wales coalfields, the intrepid rambler can stumble across a massive masonry wall running down a steep valley side for a hundred metres or so. Originally the construction went all the way down to the valley floor, but it was too obvious from the air and offered a good navigational beacon to German bombers heading for the industrial centres and docks of South Wales. So, early in the war it was blown up, and now only an isolated part stands, apparently purposeless, high on the valley side. In fact, it is not a wall, but a forgotten relic of the early railway age. Before the arrival of the railway, coal was too heavy to move far, and, at the most, it could be lowered by gravity down the valley side in wagons on an inclined plane to a close-by navigable river or canal. The rich coal seams of the upper Glyncorrwg valley were too remote from navigable waterways to make them worth exploiting until growing demand made new sources essential. The first attempt to get coal out of the Glyncorrwg valley took the existing technologies of horse-drawn tramways and inclined planes to a wholly new landscape. A fine surveying and engineering feat, the tramway twisted and contoured for twelve kilometres across the heads of several small valleys, losing just enough height to ease the horse's task with a full load. So far, so good. But the coal-carrying wagons then had to cross one valley on a high, slender viaduct, drop down, on an inclined plane, into the next much wider valley, and then be hauled up the other side on another inclined plane, by a stationary steam engine, before finally being lowered into another valley, there to meet the Neath canal. In all, there were one powered incline and six gravity inclines. In the words of one industrial archaeologist, 'This took the principles of the powered-incline and intermediate level sections of... [the] tramroad and included them in a final heroic engineering work of the pre-locomotive age.'[1]

It was all a heroic engineering effort, but a financial flop. Parson's Folly, as it soon became known, took a number of existing technologies and, in combining them, tried to extend considerably the distance and the terrain over which heavy goods could be carried – it was, in the term of the time, a long-distance railway and one that traversed unfavourable terrain. But it was effectively impractical, too slow, with too many stages where the wagons had to be manhandled from one means of haulage to another. And, in the scale of its civil engineering works, it was recognizably a narrow lightweight tramway, each horse drawing just one small coal-bearing wagon. Even as it was being built, other engineers were developing a new technology – the steam-powered loco-motive. Civil engineer Kingdom Isambard Brunel was engaged to build a branch of his Great Western Railway, which had already reached the docks at Briton Ferry, up to Glyncorrwg. The civil engineering required for the railway proper was on a much greater scale than that of horse-drawn trams. A railway demanded gentle inclines, which meant the coming earthworks of cuttings and embankments that characterize railway engineering, slicing through hillsides and moving them out of the way rather than contouring round them, and, if necessary, using tunnels to drive straight through hills. Steam locomotives hauled trains with scores of large wagons, so that Brunel's Glyncorrwg Mineral Railway was recognizably a modern railway. Except, that is, for one final section. Brunel drove his railway to the top of the valley side above Briton

Ferry, and there the coal wagons were unhitched from the train and lowered down the valley side using old technology of an inclined plane. Not surprisingly, this particular piece of Brunel's engineering oeuvre is usually omitted from the heroic accounts of his life.[2] The delays caused by working the incline were to make it a short-term solution, and some time later another railway was built by competing interests at the dock in Port Talbot, so that, finally, Glyncorrwg coal could travel in one journey all the way from the minehead to the dock. The transition to what we now recognize as standard railway technology took time and a number of inter-mediate steps to achieve. Parson's Folly and Brunel's incline were hybrids that led to the fully integrated railway system.

It would not be wise to stretch the analogy too far, but we might usefully compare these stages in the development of the railway in the Glyncorrwg valley with the birth of the computer. The Heath Robinson took some existing technologies, assembled them in a novel way and tried to scale up the amount of processing and counting that could be done. Like Parson's Folly, it was not quite up to the job – but it did show that the concept of mechanizing statistical methods could solve the basic problem, just as Parson's Folly had shown that coal could indeed be hauled out of the remotest valleys. Colossus can in some ways be compared with Brunel's hybrid. It was a step change in technology, almost a completely modern railway, but it was dedicated too much to a specific purpose – coal trains – and lacked the integrated end-to-end railway concept. Colossus, too, was a step change in tech-nology, and it was almost a completely modern computer, while it too was dedicated to one purpose – Fish decryption (although, as has been seen, flexibility of design allowed Colossus to perform a variety of processes in pursuit of that one purpose). Colossus lacked some vital features of the modern computer – in particular, what came to be called stored-program-control. Colossus had an extremely close relationship with its operators, who had to set up the processes and conditions for a machine run and then make the sort of decisions about subsequent processing steps that were later embedded within computer programs. We might, therefore, usefully compare the unhitching of the wagons at the incline with the operators' tasks on Colossus.

The computer can also be compared with the true end-to-end railway. The railways may have started as a coal-carrying technology, but soon transported all sorts of other freight and passengers too – and became a multi-purpose technology in the way that neither Parson's Folly nor Brunel's incline could ever be. Similarly, the computer is defined, from one point of view, as a general-purpose machine. The railway demanded an integral technological approach and engineering to match. The first post-war computers were conceived as machines that would have an integral store and program control system.

According to a recent book, *Turing and the Computer*, 'Turing's decoding machine was known as Colossus' and it 'cracked German Enigma codes'. Turing did, indeed, design a decryption machine used for Enigma messages, the Bombe, but it was an electro-mechanical device and not a forerunner of the modern computer. Also, Turing was not part of the teams whose work led them to devise and build Colossus. Colossus certainly was not 'his' machine, although he did contribute his pre-war ideas about universal machines. And, of course, Colossus was used to crack the quite different teleprinter codes, not the Enigma Morse messages.[3] Yet these confusions are understandable. It was the aim of post-war guardians of Britain's wartime codebreaking effort that the Colossus story should be inextricably linked with that of Enigma when, in the mid-1970s, the Ultra secret finally surfaced. However, these are matters of fact, and are easily cleared up now that more documents have been released, allowing us to see that the Enigma story is, in fact, the lesser and quite separate part of the overall account of what happened at Bletchley Park.

On matters of interpretation, it is somewhat harder to clear up the fog that surrounds the birth of the computer. Corelli Barnett, the eminent historian of British wartime and post-war military and technological performance, says in *The Verdict of Peace*, 'Popular British myth has it that the wartime Colossus used to break the German Enigma ciphers was the world's first computer in the modern sense. It was not; it was a giant electronic calculator designed for the special purpose of breaking the German Enigma ciphers.'[4] Leaving aside the references to Enigma, rather than the Geheimschreiber, there is indeed room for debate about whether Colossus was a calculator, a computer or a binary/logic processing machine. It is perhaps to be expected that Barnett's choice of appellation should be the one that minimizes Colossus's role as that fits most neatly with his thesis on British muddle and decline. But it has the effect of undervaluing what Colossus represented in the development of the computer. This can be illustrated by comparing Colossus and the US electronic machine, Eniac. Eniac was intended to help with ordnance calculations, and the project to build it was started in 1944. It employed an incredible 20,000 electronic valves, but was not finished by the end of the war and later served to perform calculations for the future development of the atom bomb. It had many similarities to Colossus – it was programmed in similar external ways via plugboards, for example – but it was a decimal and arithmetic machine, rather than a binary/logic processing machine.

The modern computer can be defined as an electronic, binary/logic-processing, conditional-programming, stored-program-control, general-purpose machine. Eniac can be defined as an 'electronic, decimal-processing, programmable, limited purpose machine'. And Colossus can be defined as an, electronic, binary/logic-processing, programmable, specific-purpose machine.[5] Thus, it can be seen that Colossus was closer to the modern concept of the computer than Eniac was in some significant ways. So, if Barnett's definition of Colossus, in relation to the computer, as a giant electronic calculator is valid, it becomes difficult to define Eniac satisfactorily, for it is indeed best described as a gigantic electronic calculator. It may be fair to call Colossus a programmable, binary calculator, but that label diminishes Colossus's technological closeness to the computer.

However, in terms of immediate post-war influence, Eniac was indeed significantly more important – because it was not kept so utterly secret in the way that Colossus was. Open almost any book on the history of the computer, even quite recent ones, and Eniac is invariably introduced as the first modern electronic computer, or as its most immediate ancestor.[6] This is not surprising. The best-known outline of the essentials of the modern computer is a paper written by mathematician John von Neumann when he joined Presper Eckert and John Mauchly, inventors of Eniac, in developing the post-war Edvac computer. This gave us the unfortunate formal name for the basic architecture of almost all subsequent digital computers, the 'von Neumann machine'. The link with Eniac was clear and direct, while no one knew of the existence of Colossus, yet alone any connection between it and subsequent ideas about computing machines. Yet, equally clearly, with our present knowledge of Colossus, now the veil of secrecy has at least been partially lifted, it can be seen that there was knowledge of Colossus in the post-war computing milieu of both the United States and Britain.

It has been established that there is no surviving evidence to show that von Neumann was let into the codebreaking secrets of the Allies, although it was 'During a visit to England in the first half of 1943 that von Neumann became seriously interested in computational mathematics.'[7] His interest was generated by his involvement in computing for ordnance work (which was also Eniac's original purpose). However, '[Max] Newman reports that he met [von Neumann] during his visit, but that he did not visit Bletchley Park.' It is safest to assume that von Neumann remained unaware directly of Colossus. On the other hand, there is sufficient evidence to show that information about Colossus was available in the United States within codebreaking organizations, and reasonable evidence to suggest that that information was subsumed into generally available technical knowledge. Documentary evidence of how complete information was sent to Washington on Colossus and the Fish project was given in Chapter twenty-two, and an alternative machine using techniques based on photographic film was also described. This machine was based on an original conception of Vannevar Bush. Bush was centrally involved in US cryptanalytic automation, and there is documentary evidence that he was fully briefed about developments in Britain prior to a visit in late 1944.[8] After the war, Bush was not directly involved in any of the US computer-development projects, but he was a key policy adviser and highly influential in directing funding and support for computing technology.

And, of course, there were all the Americans who worked full time on the Fish project both on attachment in Britain and in Washington. One reflection of this is the significant amount of technical documentation on Fish which is available in the United States archives, but which has not survived or was never kept in Britain. Some of these documents are reports written by Americans who were based at Bletchley Park for the very purpose of learning about Fish and Colossus. Some of the reports may well not have been given to the British codebreakers – they quite likely did not have time to read about what they already had learned by hard work in getting the project going in the first place.

Components of Colossus were shipped to and reconstructed in America at the end of the war based on the copies of documentation and machines then being destroyed in Britain. After the war ended, a group of those who had been involved in the US navy codebreaking operation in America started a commercial company, Engineering Research Associates, to develop computer technology, for both cryptanalytical and commercial/scientific customers. The company was contracted by the US navy to compile the existing knowledge on computing technology. 'Information for the survey was collected and assembled in 1947 and 1948. ERA technical people visited laboratories where work was being done under government, particularly Navy, sponsorship. Other survey material was based on work in progress on other ERA projects, and on unpublished reports by government agencies and by organizations doing work for the government.'[9] The report digested all the material into an account of the state of the art that had considerable influence in spreading knowledge of electronic digital techniques.

The published result of this comprehensive research, *High Speed Computing Devices*, did not mention any projects by name, but its chapter headings clearly reflect matters that were of importance at the time. After two introductory chapters, the first main topic is 'Counters as Elementary Components', followed by 'Switches and Gates', then 'A Functional Approach to Machine Design' and 'Arithmetic Systems'. The concept of the stored program control only comes in this fifth chapter, and it is hard to imagine that any work on computing devices would have opened with a discussion of electronic counters even shortly after this report was published. It would, of course, be rash to ascribe too much of this to Colossus, as many other machines of the day employed electronic counters and this was indeed a key pre-war use of electronics. But, on the other hand, it seems clear that Colossus and its techniques were known to some or all of the authors, as well as to a crucial small number of policy-makers, such as Bush, and leading engineers. Although it is not possible to pinpoint technology transfer directly derived from the key developments made with Colossus – the use of binary, the use of electronics, control and timing systems, the centrality of data – in this work, it is clear that these lessons were absorbed and resurfaced in de-sourced form to become part of the given background of post-war American technical understanding of computing machines. The legacy may be impossible to measure, but it is not insignificant.

The key step following Colossus and other machines of its generation – electronic ones such as Eniac and a bevy of electro-mechanical monsters, as well as programmable punched-card machines – was the internalization of the program. But another key feature is that the computer is a general-purpose machine. Turing's pre-war theoretical concept was of a universal machine which could undertake any mathematical/logical routine that could be expressed as an algorithm – a set of processes. Von Neumanns's account of the computer is generally taken as the first description of these concepts of the general-purpose, stored-program-control machine.

But there is an earlier hint, in respect of the idea of the general-purpose machine at least. As has been seen, Colossus was designed with flexibility in mind. Flowers gave his machine, not just the logic circuits for the Vernam cipher rules (exclusive-or), but other logical operations too. Within the fairly strict limits of its overall architecture, Colossus was general-purpose. It could count the number of specified outcomes in an input tape and the internally generated bit stream. According to Professor Brian Randell, who interviewed several of the main actors in the Colossus story in the mid-1970s:

> During all this time [i.e. from mid-1944] Newman and his mathematicians were having frequent discussions to explore the possibilities that had been opened up by the Colossi, and their requirements for further facilities... Although a special-purpose device, it turned out to have considerable generality within its own subject area, more, in fact, than Newman and his team had asked for, although Newman was a strong believer in the importance of having flexibility in the design of the machine. The flexibility was exploited fully, once it had been appreciated, and the Colossus ended up being used for several types of jobs which had not been anticipated when the machine was first designed... Colossus could be plugged up so as to do multiplication: 'It took a great deal of plugging and it wasn't worth while... but the flexibility was such as to let it be used for something for which it was not designed'... 'the

use of Colossus to do other things unconnected with the purpose for which it was built, although possible, would have been strained and artificial... we could fake up some of the properties of branching on a condition, essentially through manipulations of the data tape, but that sort of thing stopped a long way short of a Turing Machine'.[10]

However, in terms of its legacy, what is important is whether those who developed and used Colossus understood the implications of universality and of the stored program. A sentence in the 500-page-long, dense and essentially mathematical account of the Fish codebreaking techniques, *General Report on Tunny*, written at the end of the war, suggests that some did: 'The method of making a machine adaptable is first to think of a number of things required of it and then design the machine to cope with a general class of problem which includes all the special ones as particular cases.' Certainly, Max Newman, who had conceived of a machine solution to the Fish decryption problem, was aware that what he, with the help of Flowers and others, had achieved was revolutionary in its implications, and for the last year of the war he was itching 'to get out' of his wartime duties and get on with taking automated computing machinery to the next stage in its development. Certainly the almost indecent haste of his departure at the end of the war was much more than lesser mortals in the GC&CS hierarchy, let alone the general run of service personnel, could expect to achieve, and betrays his desperation to end his time working in secret codebreaking activities and get on with implanting similar technologies in machines for scientific and mathematical uses.

However, there is little other evidence about the issue. Colossus was kept secret until the mid-1970s, its processes till 2000 and beyond. The thoughts and memories of those involved were thus either guarded or lost. Where the legacy of Colossus would definitely have been important was in the many post-war computer-development projects in Britain. As in the United States, that legacy is hard to measure and can only be estimated by guesswork. What is not in doubt is that it was necessary to import back from the other side of the Atlantic the distilled technical knowledge of wartime computing projects produced by ERA and the inventors of Eniac and by von Neumann. There was no equivalent of the ERA's *High Speed Computing Devices* published in Britain. No means was sought of spreading technical advances without compromising the source, except to allow those who worked at Bletchley Park to carry on with their own computer projects.

Max Newman went to Manchester University, where he became Professor of Pure Mathematics in October 1945, accompanied by two of the Fish team, Jack Good and David Rees. Newman was highly relieved to put aside the interruption to his mathematical work. Mathematics, he thought, would be of more importance in the long run than the war and even Colossus. Another Manchester academic, P N S Blackett, had been director of naval operational research during the war and had recruited Newman to Bletchley Park. He encouraged Newman to apply for a grant to open a 'calculating-machine laboratory' at Manchester. Professor Hartree of the Royal Society was allowed into the Ultra secret and was invited to Bletchley Park to see Colossus and to get his support for the project. Two radar engineers, Fred Williams and Tom Kilburn, from the misleadingly named the Telecommunications Research Establishment, also joined the team – but were not told about Colossus. However, by this time, the lessons of Second World War computing were being circulated in recycled form in the United States and the lessons of Colossus could be quietly subsumed into that flow of ideas. Within eighteen months, the Manchester team had designed and built one of the first modern computers, the Manchester Mark 1. The other contender for this title was a small-scale project at Cambridge University led by Maurice Wilkes who knew nothing about Colossus, but who had travelled to the United

States and had managed to pick up some of the information that was circulating there. Wilkes, however, had been at the TRE and had learned much about electronics and digital circuits while he was there, and went on to build the world's first full electronic, stored-program-control computer, Edsac.

The British projects were the first to develop computers because they were much smaller, and thus less constrained by the need for intra-project management, co-ordination and communication, than the much more lavishly funded projects in the United States. American companies, however, proved to be more willing to take risks and to convert the research machines into commercial products. And, in the background, a large potential market existed of commercial and military organizations willing to risk using these new machines. In Britain, government support was more constrained, suppliers were more cautious and users were more conservative in the technology they were prepared to buy. Thus, despite secrecy over Colossus, while Britain did make the world's first computers, it was in the United States that the computer was established as a widely used technology. Indeed, the computer became as emblematic of the post-war evolution of the United States as the automobile had been of the pre-war decades – and the electronics and computer industry became part of the leading edge of America's multinational corporations, taking its place alongside the oil industry.

Many of those at Bletchley Park went on to work in various computing projects, including Donald Michie, who became a professor of machine intelligence. He later wrote to Max Newman, 'My years in the Newmanry were the most thrilling experience of my life, and also formative – for good or ill.'[11] The influence of Colossus thus spread quietly in this way into the various scientific, industrial and commercial computers that were developed in Britain in the 1950s.

It is unlikely, however, that wider public knowledge of Colossus would have made any difference to the long-term prospects of the

British computer industry. Repeated strategic mistakes were made in the technological and commercial strategies of the companies that were eventually forced to merge into a single British national champion, ICL. (ICL was eventually taken over by Fujitsu of Japan in 1990.) ICL's fundamental mistake was to persist too long in trying to match the US giant IBM with British-designed technology, rather than either selling IBM-compatible computers or trying to identify technological alternatives to IBM's stranglehold on mainframe technology with smaller computers.[12] The knowledge that Britain had designed the world's first electronic computer with Colossus might well only have strengthened that insistence on home-designed solutions. The computers at Cambridge and Manchester were the first two true computers in the world, but that did not save the British industry in the long term, let alone propel it to leadership. Being the first to invent something does not guarantee leadership of, or even necessarily participation in, its industrial production. The effect of the restriction of knowledge about Colossus was more particular. It was psychological, as it denied those involved both recognition and what we would now describe as closure on their wartime effort – especially those who found it difficult to adjust to normal life after the intense intellectual excitement of Bletchley Park.

Alan Turing was awarded an OBE for his wartime work, and he initially joined the National Physical Laboratory, NPL, at Teddington, West London, where he worked on another computer project, ACE (Automatic Computing Engine), but he found the atmosphere bureaucratic and uncomfortable, so he left to join Newman at Manchester. There he had difficulty integrating with the team and his interests moved away from computing to other areas, such as plant morphology where he made important advances – illustrating yet again the potential for his incredibly original mind to make contributions in all sorts of fields. When his homosexuality (illegal in Britain until 1967 when Bletchley Park and Testery veteran Roy Jenkins was appointed Home Secretary and changed the law) brought Turing to the attention of the police and the courts, he underwent chemical treatment rather than imprisonment. He later, illegally, removed the chemical hormone implants that caused him to grow breasts.

Surprisingly, given the extent of his knowledge about Bletchley Park, not to mention the value of his wartime contribution, no one at high level intervened in Turing's prosecution. No one, it seems, considered Turing a security risk during the war, even though he was one of the very few people who knew about every project at Bletchley Park. Yet, during the emerging Cold War, Turing was deemed a potential threat to security, precisely because of the extent of his knowledge, particularly if he was to be sent to prison. Nor is it at all likely that Turing would have got into trouble if he had returned to Cambridge University where homosexuality was quietly accepted. But in Manchester, isolated and lonely, Turing faced a second prosecution. And the fear of a second court case, it seems, led Turing to his tragic suicide.

Max Newman had the unpleasant task of visiting Turing's home (Holymeade) to collect his academic papers (once Turing's brother had sorted out personal papers) and of attending the inquest into Turing's death:

> I went out to Holymeade before the inquest. Everything was lying about just as it had been. There were two unopened letters, one accepting an invitation for a day or two later, also a parcel just opened containing three new pair of socks, evidently bought the same day. The cyanide was made by some electrical process, which the pathologist, a man presumably with a respectable knowledge of chemistry, said he did not fully understand. He first thought the fumes might have been inhaled, but later formed [the opinion] that the liquid must have been drunk. There was also an apple which had been bitten to suppress the taste, which is so bad that it is difficult to keep down otherwise. The most natural explanation

is, I think, that he made the stuff perhaps just as a difficult experiment (it has plenty of other uses) and then suddenly thought, well there it is, why not take the stuff... There was no one to dissuade him. Apart from the press there was nobody [at the inquest] except for J Turny and the daily help.[13]

A local newspaper reported, 'The Coroner Mr J A K Ferris remarked that he was forced to the conclusion that it was a deliberate act for, with a man of that type, one would never know what his mental processes were going to do next. He might easily become unstable and unbalanced when he decided to end his days.'

Tom Flowers, too, had some problems in adjusting to peacetime conditions. His boss, Gordon Radley, was knighted, but Flowers was only given an Award to Inventors of £1,000 (a sum which recouped some of the cash he had paid out of his own pocket for hard-to-find items of equipment for Colossus). And his disappointment at such lack of recognition was equalled by his frustration of not being able to explain to sceptical colleagues the potential of electronics. Many of the codebreakers in the United States and Britain went on to join computing projects where they could consult information circulating in the US on wartime lessons from electronic computing. There was no such opening in the telecommunications world. In the Post Office, efforts were devoted to restructuring operations for resuming commercial and residential services which had been neglected for six years. Flowers was to have worked with the TRE on developing a secret computer, MOSAIC, but the demands of peacetime recovery at the Post Office forced Dollis Hill to back out of the arrangement. There was a strongly conservative streak in the industry, too. 'To work in the [Post Office Telephone Division] just after the Second World War was considered a great privilege and achievement by those in the service,' one senior Post Office engineer later recalled. 'Life was very solid and ordered, and seemed as if it would go on forever without change.'[14] In such an atmosphere, Flowers had an uphill struggle to promote electronics (and, in any event, the government controlled and limited Post Office investment). He was involved in the design of an electronic exchange but the Post Office did not take up the idea seriously till later on. Flowers remained head of the switching division of the Post Office until 1964, when he moved to join a telecommunications equipment supply company, STC – and again the electronic exchange he worked on was not developed commercially. He retired in 1970.

Listening to Flowers on taped interviews, one cannot avoid the feeling that Flowers was not a man who suffered fools gladly and who was saddened, not to say somewhat embittered, by the lack of recognition or influence that followed on from his momentous invention. Unlike one of his senior colleagues, Allan Coombs, Flowers faithfully followed his instructions and burned all his documents at the end of the war, recalling how he took them down to the boiler room himself to oversee and ensure their destruction. Later, when the secret was partially let out in the late 1970s, Flowers maintained that Britain had lost a post-war lead in electronic telephone exchange technology because of the secrecy over Colossus. In a lecture to the National Physical Laboratory in 1977, he said that he had failed to convince the Post Office that it was feasible to build an all-electronic exchange, thus surrendering the chance of Britain leading the telecommunications industry worldwide. This was actually as unlikely a prospect as British leadership of the computer industry – having the advanced technology in itself is not sufficient without the resources and culture to develop and deploy it. It was the culture of the industry, of both the Post Office and its equipment suppliers, which determined that Britain would be a follower, not a leader, in the application of modern telecommunications technology in the post-war decades. Flowers's real frustration was that, having seen the future, he could not get on with building it, but instead had to fight against the bureaucratic conservatism of the British post-war telecommunications industry.

Even when Colossus was first made public, Flowers could say little about it, as tight security restrictions on the processes performed by Colossus remained in place until after his death, although he did recall his wartime experiences and colleagues with great warmth. He also recalled Max Newman telling all the people who had worked on Colossus at the end of the war, 'One of the prices of peace must be the losing of the most interesting job we've ever had.'[15] In that sense, while Newman and others carried on their interesting work, Flowers – like Turing – did not. Everything else was an anti-climax to that incredible thing they did in their youth and about which they could only hold their silence.

Epilogue

The wide-ranging effects of the Colossus story permeate society today. The advent of the electronic computing machine has led to inestimable consequences. Similarly, digital communications, not least the internet and the mobile phone, have transformed work and home life. The institutionalization of Sigint and the devotion of considerable resources to interception and decryption has been an important, if largely veiled, aspect of the world since the end of the Second World War. An indication of how common eavesdropping has become came from Clare Short, former British minister for overseas development, who resigned her post in 2003 over the war in Iraq. She related how transcripts of conversations held by Kofi Annan, the UN secretary-general, were regularly included among the ministerial papers she received. Alongside the largely accepted official world of interception and decryption is the insidious growth of illegal hacking and on-line fraud. Indeed, in some respects, the Colossus episode can even be viewed as the first great computer hack with the electronic computer first being devised for the specific purpose of breaking into a digital communications and cipher system. So, while it is natural to focus on the role of Colossus in the development of the computer, we should not lose sight of the fact that the computer was preceded, in total secrecy, by the anti-computer.

With the widespread development of corporate and public computer networks, and the digitization of the telecomms networks, computer network security is no longer the concern of a few closed segments of the secret services. Today, the internet, a network of computers, and the electronic commerce and private communications it carries depend on secure communications. Any on-line purchase or transaction entails disclosing one's credit or debit card details, which means that secure, enciphered transmission is vital. Digital communications security and encryption is no longer only the concern of the military and the state's approved eavesdroppers, but of all citizens, who need to understand the extent and limitations of digital security in the age of the internet. Mathematicians and computer scientists proclaim that modern cryptographic systems are unbreakable, but so did their counterparts of the 1920s, 1930s and 1940s.

The Geheimschreiber was not broken because of a single user error – the 'long depth' of August 1941 which allowed the machine to be diagnosed – but because of a series of mistakes in its design and, more importantly, in its day-to-day use. Computer security is often as much at risk from such mundane security breaches as the password written on a piece of paper and taped to the side of the monitor, or the somewhat unimaginative use of 'password' as an ostensibly secret password, as it is from the sophisticated hacker. Similarly, the breaking of the Geheimschreiber was not a single event, but a process of cipher breaking that had to be repeated relentlessly and continued to depend on security errors as well as on unprecedented levels of machine processing using Colossus and the other machines. Evidently, the Colossus story has much to tell us about computer security today.

There are also important lessons for today in the wider story of Colossus's contribution to the strategy of the Allies in the Second World War. Although militarist dictators are no longer a direct threat to democratic societies, there are other equally serious security considerations. Intelligence gathering and analysis has

449

come to play an ever more important role, not just in secret circles, but also in the public debate over defining, assessing the extent of and deciding how to respond to terrorist threats. The example of the misuse of intelligence before the second Gulf War in 2003 underlines the challenge facing policy-makers in the inevitable process of the politicization of intelligence. It also illustrates how the instinctive secrecy and manipulation of information – a trait common to most governments but one developed with special force by the British and US security services in response to leaks at the end of the First World War – is increasingly at variance with the need for the integration of intelligence with policy debate within democratic societies.

I would like to conclude with a more recent episode. In the USA, five different computer scientists recognized and took up the challenge of how to automate the distribution of keys for enciphered transmissions. Key distribution of course was one problem that faced the German signals units with both the Enigma and Geheimschreiber machines. In both cases, initially some of the key information was included in the preamble to messages, then it was distributed in codebooks to both ends of a link (details of the pin positions for a month or a day were distributed to operators of Fish links in printed booklets). Neither solution was really satisfactory, although the latter was more secure. Some decades after the Second World War, the information-technology industry grew increasingly aware that, if electronic commerce over the internet was to become viable, it would require a structure that was not reliant on key distribution. Thus, keys would have to become fully automated. This required a system, which later became known as 'public key cryptography', whereby two users pass sufficient information for each to be able to generate a commonly usable set of keys for a single transaction, but which an interceptor could not calculate. An excellent account of how this works can be found in Steven Levy's book, *Crypto*, which includes an accessible technical explanation, but, for brevity, there are two essential components to a workable solution – an overall concept for secure key exchange, and a mathematical process to implement it. Some readers may recognize the names of the two Americans who first thought up a solution – Whitfield Diffie and Marty Hellman – from the well-known Diffie–Hellman algorithm. The names of three others who converted their ideas into a practical method – Ronald Rivest, Adi Shamir and Leonard Adleman – are present albeit with less prominence in the name of the 'RSA Public Key Cryptogram' system. All these researchers and engineers encountered considerable disapproval and discouragement for their work from the USA codebreaking authority, the National Security Agency (NSA). But, convinced of the need for public cryptographic systems, they persisted with developing their concepts into practical systems. The solutions they developed have now become the international standard, and the 'secure' on-line channel used to pass card details is made safe by the Diffie–Hellman concept implemented by an RSA algorithm.

This story is not just another example of how the US computer industry and its offshoots have pushed to the fore, establishing the computer and now the internet as quintessentially American technologies, even in the areas where Britain was once in the forefront, such as cryptography. In fact, the story is almost a re-run of the Colossus story in one significant aspect. For, in fact, an automated key system, identical in all essential points to the Diffie–Hellman and RSA solution, had already been developed in secret in Britain at GCHQ some years before it was reinvented in the public sector in the USA. In the late 1960s and early 1970s James Ellis, Clifford Cocks and Malcolm Williamson, between them, had become the real inventors of public key cryptography. But they had not applied for a patent, not even when the software engineers in the USA started making their own patent applications, and the concept irretrievably entered the public domain. Indeed, it was only in the late 1990s that GCHQ announced that it had indeed beaten Diffie–Hellman and RSA to the mark. Williamson later reported that he 'tried to get [GCHQ] to block the US patent. We could have done that, but in fact people higher up didn't want us to. Patents are complicated... The advice we received was "Don't bother".' Cocks recalled that 'you accept that [when you work for GCHQ]. Internal recognition is all you get.'[1]

The now public stories of Colossus and of public key crypto-graphy serve to remind us of the immense hidden effort being put into eavesdropping in modern societies. Although we can now read much of the detail of Colossus and the overall Fish inter-ception and codebreaking operation, we can only guess at the extent of its modern-day equivalent and whether the statistical approach that underlay the need for the Robinson and Colossi was used in post-war codebreaking, or whether cribbing techniques came to predominate. What is certain is that general-purpose electronic computers provided the processing power for the techniques that are used. A general-purpose computer could be programmed to perform Colossus-style logical counts, letter-frequency counts or the complex cribbing techniques used in the special-purpose machines, Dragon and Proteus. The enduring significance of Colossus, therefore, is as the first electronic computer, being a multi-purpose machine applicable to different uses, rather than as a new type of cryptographic machine.

part three – appendices

Appendix A: The Baudot Code with Shift Function

1	2	3	4	5	Basic teleprinter code	Letters shift level	Figures shift level
0	0	0	0	0	/	not used(in plain)	
0	0	1	0	0	9 or .	'SPACE'	
0	0	1	0	1	H	H	£
0	0	0	0	1	T	T	5
0	0	0	1	1	O	O	9
0	0	1	1	1	M	M	.
0	0	1	1	0	N	N	,
0	0	0	1	0	3	carriage return	
0	1	0	1	0	R	R	4
0	1	1	1	0	C	C	:
0	1	1	1	1	V	V	=
0	1	0	1	1	G	G	&
0	1	0	0	1	L	L	)
0	1	1	0	1	P	P	0
0	1	1	0	0	I	I	8
0	1	0	0	0	4	line feed	
1	1	0	0	0	A	A	-
1	1	1	0	0	U	U	7
1	1	1	0	1	Q	Q	1
1	1	0	0	1	W	W	2
1	1	0	1	1	5 or +	shift to figures	
1	1	1	1	1	8 or -	shift to letters	
1	1	1	1	0	K	K	(
1	1	0	1	0	J	J	ring bell
1	0	0	1	0	D	D	who R U?
1	0	1	1	0	F	F	%
1	0	1	1	1	X	X	/
1	0	0	1	1	B	B	?
1	0	0	0	1	Z	Z	+
1	0	1	0	1	Y	Y	6
1	0	1	0	0	S	S	'
1	0	0	0	0	E	E	3

Note: The 'basic teleprinter code' provides a single character for mid-transmission analysis. The actual meaning is determined by the last prior shift command. It will be noticed that the basic teleprinter code identifier is the same as the letters-shift level for alphabetic characters. It may also be noticed that in the figures-shift level, the identifier for numerals is the same as the top row of the keyboard (Q=1, W=2, E=3, R=4 and so on).

Appendix B: The Vernam Cipher

Note the '+' sign is used to indicate 'combine according to the Vernam cipher rules':

	0	0	1	1
+	0	1	0	1
	0	1	1	0

1. Enciphering a message using Baudot code
1a. – with 'basic teleprinter code' identifier:

Input text	P	L	A	I	N
(plain)	01101	01001	11000	01100	00110
+ Key	H	9	M	T	O
	00101	00100	00111	00001	00011
= Cipher text	4	P	8	P	H
	01000	01101	11111	01101	00101

1.b – without 'basic teleprint code' identifier:

P	01101	01001	11000	01100	00110
+ K	00101	00100	00111	00001	00011
= C	01000	01101	11111	01101	00101

2. Deciphering a message
2.a – with 'basic teleprinter code identifier (note the key is the same):

Input text	4	P	8	P	H
(cipher)	01000	01101	11111	01101	00101
+ Key	H	9	M	T	O
	00101	00100	00111	00001	00011
= Plain text	P	L	A	I	N
	01101	01001	11000	01100	00110

2.b – without 'basic teleprinter code' identifier:

C	01001	01101	11111	01101	00101
+ K	00101	00100	00111	00001	00011
= P	01100	01001	11000	01100	00110

3. Expressed as formulae

To encipher:		To decipher:	
Plain text	P	Cipher text	C
+ key	+ K	+ key	+ K
= cipher text	= C	= plain text	= P

or,

To encipher:
Plain text + key = cipher text   P + K = C

To decipher:
Cipher text + key = plain text   C + K = P

Appendix C: Extended Example of 'The First Break'

Message One (P1):
Plain language '55ZZ88SPRUCHNUMMER55ZZ88AN9OBERKOMMANDO9DER9...'

Message Two (P2):
Plain language '55ZZ88SPRNMR955ZZ88OBERKMD9DER9...'

The two messages are identical except for short cuts in the second message due to the sending operator having to type out the same message twice. The message was sent twice with the same key and with these small variations; this is known as a 'depth'. The first message has been sent with the German for 'serial number' (Spruchnummer) and 'high command' (Oberkommando) spelt out in full within the encrypted part of the message. The receiving end operator has asked for the message to be sent again, and the second time the sending operator has taken a few short cuts, for example, abbreviating it to SPRNMR to save having to retype the whole word. The extract of the messages above shows only the first few characters of the messages. The example below is based on characters 7 to 14 only (i.e. SPRUCHNU from M1, and SPRNMR95 from M2).

Key (K)

JKRWUAQBXDFYZSE/9THN3GP4M.......

This is a pseudo-random sequence (normally generated by the Geheimschreiber machine wheels).

P1 = 'SPRUCHNU' = 10100 01101 01010 11100 01110 00101 00110 11100 (1)
                   S   P   R   U   C   H   N   U

P2 = 'SPRNMR95' = 10100 01101 01010 00110 00111 01010 00100 11011 (2)
                   S   P   R   N   M   R   9   5

K = 'BXDFYZSE' = 10011 10111 10010 10110 10101 10001 10100 10000 (3)
                   B   X   D   F   Y   Z   S   E

Step 1 – encipher message one (by German operator):

```
  P1  S P R U C H N U   10100 01101 01010 11100 01110 00101 00110 11100  (1)
+ K   B X D F Y Z S E   10011 10111 10010 10110 10101 10001 10100 10000  (3)
= C1 = M J A R 5 S D I (4) 00111 11010 11000 01010 11011 10100 10010 01100
                       M     J     A     R     5     S     D     I        (4)
```

Step 2 – encipher message two (by German operator):

```
  P2 = S P R N M R 9 5 =  10100 01101 01010 00110 00111 01010 00100 11011  (2)
+ K    B X D F Y Z S E =  10011 10111 10010 10110 10101 10001 10100 10000  (3)
= C2 = M J A E D 5 E G =  00111 11010 11000 10000 10010 11011 10000 01011
                        M     J     A     E     D     5     E     G        (5)
```

Step 3 – add the two ciphered messages together (by Bletchley Park):

```
 C1   MJAR5SDI    00111 11010 11000 01010 11011 10100 10010 01100 (4)
+ C2   MJAED5EG    00111 11010 11000 10000 10010 11011 10000 01011 (5)
= Q = ///JLV3M    00000 00000 00000 11010 01001 01111 00010 00111 (6)
                    /     /     /    J     L     V     3     M
```

Step 4 – check the result by adding the messages one and two in plain language to verify that the assumption does work (added just to show this gives the same result as step 3):

```
 P1   SPRUCHNU    10100 01101 01010 11100 01110 00101 00110 11100 (1)
+ P2   SPRNMR95    10100 01101 01010 00110 00111 01010 00100 11011 (2)
= Q   ///JLV3M    00000 00000 00000 11010 01001 01111 00010 00111
                    /     /     /    J     L     V     3     M    (6)
```

Step 5 – combine the content of message two from the combined stream (Q) from step 3 to reveal the content of message one (this was done at Bletchley Park by trial and error using the serial number as an expected piece of information within the message near the beginning):

```
 Q    ///JLV3M    00000 00000 00000 11010 01001 01111 00010 00111 (6)
+ P2   SPRNMR95    10100 01101 01010 00110 00111 01010 00100 11011 (2)
= P1 = SPRUCHNU =  10100 01101 01010 11100 01110 00101 00110 11100 (1)
                    S     P     R     U     C     H     N     U
```

Appendix D: Structure of the Lorenz
Schluesselzusatzgeraet SZ40/42

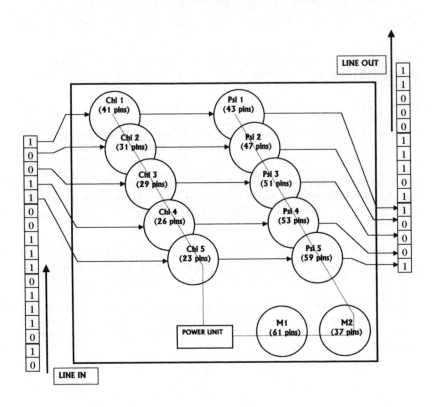

Appendix E: The Delta Technique

1. The 'delta' or 'difference' – glimpsing the delta-plain in the delta-de-Chi

A) Plain: 9 I M 9 K A M P F 9 G E G E N 9

B) Delta-plain: 4 **G̲** O J **N̲** **8̲** R 5 D **V̲** 5 **5̲** **5̲** P 3

C) Delta-extended-Psi: 8 / 5 3 / / P Q K / 5 / / V /

D) Delta-de-Chi: X **G̲** A A **N̲** **8̲** M N I **V̲** / **5̲** **5̲** W 3

In the above example, the plain language (A) message reads "im Kampf gegen" ('in struggle against'). The delta-plain (B) is achieved by adding each character in the plain to the next character in the text stream (see example below). The delta of the 'extended-Psi' stream (C) contains a '/' (all '00000') wherever there is a repeat in the Psi stream (about one-third of the Psi stream usually repeats). Wherever there is a '/' in the delta-extended–Psi stream, then the same character will occur in both the delta-plain (A) and the delta-de-Chi (D) – where this occurs the characters have been set in bold type and underlined to show the result.

As about one-third of the Psi-stream consists of repeats, there can be enough '/'s in the delta-extended-Psi to allow the statistical character frequency of the delta-plain to be glimpsed in watered down form in the delta-de-Chi if a message is long enough.

To create the delta-plain for the above example a copy of the text stream is placed under itself, but displaced by one character. Note that there is one less character in the delta stream than in the original as there is no 'subsequent' character to add to the last one in the original stream:

9	I	M	9	K	A	M	P	F	9	G	E	G	E	N	9
I	M	9	K	A	M	P	F	9	G	E	G	E	N	9	
4	G	O	J	N	8	R	5	D	V	5	5	5	P	3	

2. The delta process in formulae
(note: the '+' sign is used to signify 'combine according to the Vernam cipher rules'.)

A – The SZ40/42 cipher system in formulae
Key = Chi + extended-Psi

The basic cipher action is: Plain + Key = Cipher
this is the same as: Plain + Chi + extended-Psi = Cipher

Decipherment is: Cipher + Key = Plain
this is the same as: Cipher + Chi + extended-Psi = Plain

B – de-Chi

    de-Chi = extended-Psi + Plain

But also: De-Chi = Chi + Cipher (i.e. combining Chi with the cipher
                       text strips out the Chi within the cipher)
                       Cipher + Chi = de-Chi = extended-Psi + Plain

C – The delta process
ΔPlain = Plain 1 + <u>Plain 2</u> (where the <u>Plain 2</u> indicates the next or succeeding Plain
character in the stream),
ΔChi = Chi 1 + <u>Chi 2</u>
ΔCipher = Cipher 1 + <u>Cipher 2</u>.

D – Combining the above
To recap:
1) Cipher = Plain + Chi + ex-Psi
2) de-Chi = Cipher + Chi
3) de-Chi = Plain + ex-Psi

The same equations also apply to delta streams:
1) ΔCipher = ΔPlain + ΔChi + Δ-ex-Psi
2) Δde-Chi = ΔCipher + ΔChi
3) Δde-Chi = ΔPlain + Δex-Psi

E – Delta and '/' ('all dots')
As has been seen: Δde-Chi = Δex-Psi + ΔPlain
Therefore, where Δex-Psi = '/' then Δde-Chi = ΔPlain

*(because '/' = 00000 ('all dots') and when this character is combined with any other
character, that character remains unchanged).*

F – The 'double-delta' method
(Δ-Cipher-Unit-1 + Δ-Cipher-Unit-2)+(Δ-Delta-Chi-Unit-1 + Δ-Delta-Chi-Unit-2)=0

3. The delta – common characters

Each Fish wireless teleprinter link, each end of each link, and indeed each type of
message, had its own set of statistics for the frequency of characters in the plain and
the delta-plain streams. The frequency of each character in the delta-plain depended
on the frequency of the thirty-two 'bigrams' in the plain which add up to each delta-plain
character. For example, the character 'U' in a delta stream can be the result of adding
any of the following combinations: '/U', '9A', 'HW', 'TQ', '08', 'M5', 'NJ', '3K', 'RF', 'OD',
'VB', 'GX', 'LY', 'PZ', 'IK', '4S', 'A9', 'U/', 'QT', 'WH', ''5M', '80', 'K3', 'JN', 'DO', 'FR', 'XG',
'BV', 'ZP', 'YL', 'S4', 'KI'.

The delta-plain frequency of each character can be illustrated using statistics derived
from a series of decrypted Jellyfish messages from June 1944, totalling 25,600
characters (this information is derived from the *'General Report on Tunny'*). The
character 'U' appears in the delta-plain 1,472 times – indeed it is the most common
character in the delta-plain. Of the bigrams, or letter pairings, in the message's original
plain text that produced the character 'U' in the delta-plain, fourteen of the possible
bigrams score zero, showing that they did not appear at all in the plain language (for
example, '/U', 'TQ' and 'S4'). On the other hand, some bigrams appear frequently, '9A'

appears 218 times, 'IK' appears 107 times, 'A9' appears 185 times, '5M' appears 617 times and 'NY' appears 214 times. Thus these five bigrams account for 1341 appearances of 'U' in the delta-plain out of 1,472 times that it occurs, that is, for 91 percent of occurrences. '5M' alone accounts for over half the occurrences of 'U'.

The most common delta characters are: '/', '9', 'O', '5' and '8' (on the other hand 'H', which has only 542 occurrences, is typical of an infrequent character in the delta). As was the case with 'U', there are specific plain language bigrams which produce the bulk of these common delta-plain characters, while many bigrams do not appear at all in the plain language. Which delta-plain characters were most common on a link depended on whether, for example, it used double-punctuation or single, formatted reports or free language and so on. The frequency counts of the plain and delta-plain varied from link to link, each having its own characteristics (Type 'A' uses double punctuation, Type 'B' uses single punctuation, and Type 'C' is language oriented). The most common character in the delta-plain on the 'double punctuation' link is '/', while for the 'single punctuation' link it is '5', and on the 'language oriented' link '3' and 'F' are just about equally predominant.

4. Common delta-plain sequences

Plain:	5M89	Delta-plain:	UA5	Plain:	5M98	Delta-plain:	U05
	55M889		/UA/5		5M989		U055
	55M8899		/UA/5/		5MMA89		U/8M5
	5N89		QW5		55KK889		/H/T/
	55N8899		/QW/5/		55LL889		/D/P/5
	EI		U				

Note
1. '55KK889' & '55LL889' – 'open brackets' and 'close brackets'
2. Operators on several links repeated commands such as 'shift'

Appendix E

5. Statistics

Table 1: Plain and cipher text character frequencies

	Plain	Cipher
/	4	110
9	544	81
H	67	94
T	123	124
O	89	108
M	180	89
N	212	95
3	1	114
R	159	110
C	44	105
V	21	98
G	94	93
L	87	104
P	51	123
I	137	87
4	3	93
A	161	82
U	81	99
Q	23	88
W	38	104
5	200	106
8	197	112
K	60	95
J	6	77
D	71	85
F	42	104
X	1	106
B	57	101
Z	26	108
Y	7	106
S	110	110
E	304	98

Source: 'General Report on Tunny'

Notes:
/ should not occur in plain, so it can be assumed that these represent corrupt signals, the same is true '3' and '4'.

Table 2: Delta plain, delta-de-Chi, delta-extended-Psi

b	Delta plain	Delta-de-Chi	Delta-ex-Psi
/	91	128	1159
9	78	127	4
H	82	128	17
T	56	98	4
O	121	128	18
M	69	105	47
N	66	78	7
3	157	118	2
R	77	87	11
C	73	84	53
V	64	80	153
G	127	125	32
L	76	98	17
P	90	99	47
I	50	94	10
4	52	71	5
A	136	96	13
U	224	148	52
Q	79	92	186
W	67	70	52
5	326	170	160
8	144	170	572
K	45	66	154
J	194	115	46
D	83	7	14
F	156	107	56
X	83	87	168
B	32	55	47
Z	65	81	13
Y	84	88	62
S	90	109	14
E	63	96	5

Appendix F: Robinson – Block Diagram of Major Function Units

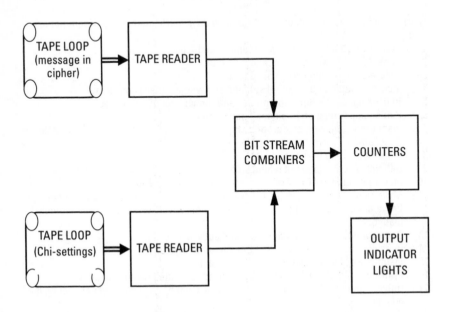

Appendix G: Non-machine Problems Identified During the Heath Robinson Period

A list of "difficulties that occurred in the early days, particularly in the Heath Robinson period":

1 – Sprockets on paper tape tearing and stretching
2 – Paper tapes breaking and coming unstuck
3 – Failure of experiments with oiled tape
4 – Incorrect setting up of wheel settings and wheel patterns on Tunny
5 – Blurred figures on Robinson printer and running out of printer ink
6 – Putting paper tape on Robinson back to front
7 – Inaccurate punching of start and stop signals – high standards required by Heath Robinson
8 – Incorrect setting of repeat dials
9 – Difficulty in calculation of wheel settings from readings, especially motor settings
10 – Incorrect setting of Chi-2 when contracting a tape on Tunny
11 – Mysteriously long time taken for production of de-Chi tapes and contractions
12 – Prevalence of transient faults on machines which were therefore difficult to diagnose
13 – Badly written figures and figures incorrectly written down
14 – Runs not checking with de-Chi tape and other mysteries
15 – Insufficient handing over from one shift to the next
16 – Print-outs with letters erroneously inserted or omitted by the machine
17 – Habit of guessing the average from readings in the run, instead of calculating it in advance
18 – Using even length of paper tape for runs involving Chi-4
19 – Inaccurate counting by Heath Robinson
20 – Damaging paper tapes by maltreatment
21 – Numerous slides in paper tapes provided at that time by Knockholt
22 – Presumed certainty of 4 on a long run
23 – Running out of bensens, squared paper, and method of obtaining bensens, paint brushes and rubbers from legal sources
24 – Difficulty of getting supplied with the small machines like hand counters and stickers
25 – Setting tape in wrong place (on any machine). Forgetting Chi-2 limitation for Tunny contraction. Forgetting to read a tape when restarting a job
26 – Sickness due to intolerable working conditions
27 – Knockholt perforating the wrong tapes
28 – Mechanical relays developing 'pips'
29 – Over emphasis on (temporarily meager) operational results at the expense of research work

"Suffice it to say that most of these difficulties and troubles were eventually almost entirely eliminated."

Source: 'General Report on Tunny' (National Archives, London), pp 110–111

Appendix H: Basic Functional Sub-systems of Colossus 1

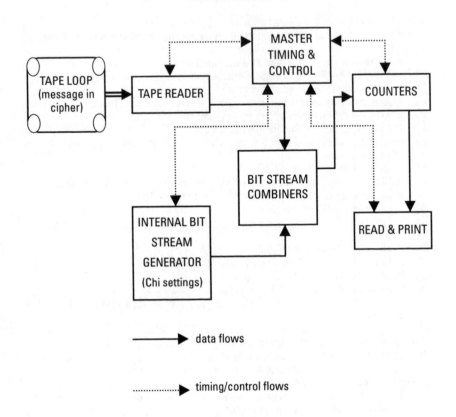

Appendix I: Annotated Printout of Colossus 3 Run 23/10/44 (Stickleback)

```
SB3115      0100/23/10
COL 3

T 9567

1P2/    R 4788   S 49    ST
4912
```

STEP 1: SB3115 – Serial number
0100/23/10 – Time (01.00 or 1am) and date (23/10) of message origination (year not included)
Col 3 – Colussus 3
T 9567 – Text length 9567 characters

```
K1      K2
06      11      A 4921
06      13      A 4948
06      15      A 4920
02      16      E 4977
02      18      E 4988
02      20      E 4954
06      21      A 5005
03      25      D 4925
02      26      E 5015
25      19      B 4930
25      21      B 5038
29      18      C 4946
36      13      A 5055
36      15      A 4995
36      19      A 5047
36      21      A 5384
36      23      A 4975
38      08      D 4933
```

STEP 2: 1P2/ – 'Double-delta' test (on bits 1 and 2)
R 4788 – Random number of 'hits' expected (half of 9567)
S 49 – 'Sigmage 49' measure of statistical probability of non-random score
ST 4912 – 'set total' 4912 – i.e. only print details of settings if count exceeds 4912

STEP 3: Colossus runs and prints out the results.
K1 K2 – Chi wheel 1 and Chi wheel 2 settings
Eighteen settings produce results in excess of 'set total' of 4912. Four produce count over 5000 – highest one at 5384 far in excess of all others. Represents 'sigmage' of 12.2 – a very good score, almost certainly the right setting of Chi 1 and Chi 2 wheels.
SET K1 36 K2 21 – Starting positions 36 and 21 'set'

```
SET K1 36  K2 21

C 1, 2 & 4

A 5384

R 2692   S 36.5   ST 2728

K3  K4  K5

01              A 2938
    01          B 2763
        01      C 2803
    02          B 2733
    04          B 2782
        04      C 3003
05              A 2829
    05          B 2783
06              A 2740
    08          B 2774
    09          C 2811
10              A 2769
11              A 2751
    11          B 2742
        12      C 2759
    13          B 2823
        14      C 2733
15              A 2750
16              A 2743
    16          B 2826
    19          B 3093
```

STEP 4: The operator decides to run three simultaneous 'short runs' – single bit analysis on bits 3, 4, 5.
A 5384 – Only this number of characters is analyzed rather than the whole message.
R 2692 – The expected random scores are 2692 (half of 5384).
Sigmage is 36.5 and 'Set Total' is set at 2728.

STEP 5: Colossus runs and prints out results.
The very first result for Chi wheel 3, is a good score and identifies the starting position for Chi wheel 3 as position 01.

STEP 6: The score for Chi wheel 5 is also a good one at 3003, so it is set at position 04.

STEP 7: The third very good result is a score of 3093 for Chi wheel 4 at starting position 19.

STEP 8: All five wheels are now set, but the operator must check by instructing Colossus to perform a character frequency count (see continuation).

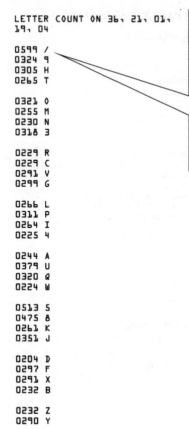

LETTER COUNT ON 36, 21, 01,
19, 04

```
0599  /
0324  9
0305  H
0265  T

0321  O
0255  M
0230  N
0318  3

0229  R
0229  C
0291  V
0299  G

0266  L
0311  P
0264  I
0225  4

0244  A
0379  U
0320  Q
0224  W

0513  5
0475  8
0261  K
0351  J

0204  D
0297  F
0291  X
0232  B

0232  Z
0290  Y
```

STEP 9: The operator instructs Colossus to perform a character frequency count with the identified settings (36, 21, 01, 19, and 04). The count gives high scores for 'basic teleprinter code' characters such as '/' (599), '5' (513) and '8' (475), giving confirmation of the right settings.

The Colossus run is completed successfully. Details of Chi settings are passed to the Testery (via Registry) for Psi and motor setting and decoding.

Appendix J: Colossus 'Processing Tree'

Type A ('stroky') messages, '/' is very common

Type B (language) messages, '3, J, F, G' are common

Type A

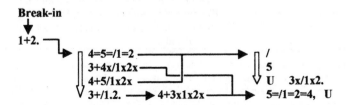

Type B

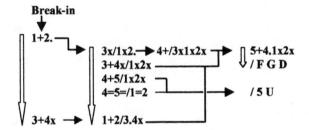

Notes:

1. Runs are tried in descending order, following the white arrows, until one of them gives a 'certain' or 'good' rating. If such a rating is achieved, the following run is then determined by the horizontal black arrows. The runs for the last wheel should be 'certain'. If all runs fail the messages are abandoned. The table was described by cryptographers as "crude". Once a few messages had been broken on a link and some statistics on it were gathered, the codebreakers and operators would develop specific sets of runs best suited to that link. The table shows a handful of the full range of runs that were developed for different processes such as de-Chi setting and breaking, Psi breaking, key breaking, and so on.

2. The '/' character is used to indicate that the bits to its right have already been set.

3. The 'break in' is the initial run (thus there are no bits to its right following a '/', so nothing has so far been set). In both instances this is the 'double-delta' run. Type B messages offer an alternative 'break in', checking that bits 3 and 4 are different (i.e. combining the two together results in a 'cross'). 1+2. stands for the double delta test which counts the number of characters where bits 1 and 2 are both the same (i.e. both 'crosses' or both 'dots'). Statistics for one message showed that bits 1 and 2 were both

'dots' in 26.7 per cent of characters, and both crosses in 26.8 per cent. Thus bits 1 and 2 were both the same in 53.5 per cent of characters. This is 113 more characters than would be expected at random (1,600 in this message, i.e. half of the total of 3,200). The chances of this happening by random are 25:1.

4. After the initial 'break in', the first test to be applied would usually be 4=5=/1=2 which means that, having set bits 1 and 2, the number of characters where bits 4 and 5 were both the same were counted. This occurred in 28.7 per cent of characters in the message, making it the second most sensitive average test after the 'double delta'. If the 4=5=/1=2 test succeeded, then the next test would be letter-frequency counts on /, 5 and U, then the 3x/1x2. test to try to set bit 3.

5. But if the 4=5=/1=2 test failed to give a good result on any setting, another test would be applied. Having set bits 1 and 2, the test 3+4x/1x2x prompted a count of the number of characters where bits 3 and 4 were both different (i.e. bit 3 is a 'cross' and bit 4 a 'dot', or vice versa, so combining them results in a 'cross'). This condition occurred in 14.5 per cent of characters, so was a far less sensitive test, but if the previous test failed, this one could show a particular type of message, so was worth a try. If it succeeded, the follow-on run would be 5=/1=2=4, followed by a letter-frequency count on U. If this 3+4x1x2x test failed, then the next test 4+5/1x2x would be tried (which shared a follow-on stage with 4=5=/1=2 run if it was successful).

6. Finally, if none of the three tests — 4=5=/1=2, 3+4x/1x2x, and 4+5/1+2x — were sucessful, the last test would be run. The test 3+/1.2. would be followed by 4+3x1x2x and 5=/1=2=4, with a check on the character frequency count for U. A similar route can be traced through the second part of the tree for Type B messages.

Source: 'General Report on Tunny' (National Archives, London)

Appendix K: Sturgeon and Thrasher

The Lorenz SZ40/42 was not the only version of the Geheimschreiber used by the German armed forces. According to a post-war GC&CS internal assessment, 'Success, both then [mid-1942 when the Lorenz SZ40 Tunny machine was first broken] and later, was limited almost entirely to German military [i.e. army] traffic, for, though analogous methods were used by the German Navy and Air Force, Allied resources did not permit of their regular solution, and it was only possible to conduct a very limited watch on them.'[1] These so-called analogous methods were two different versions of the Geheimschreiber produced by the Siemens and Halske concern, the T52 and the T42, codenamed respectively Sturgeon and Thrasher at Bletchley Park. In fact, both machines were diagnosed and some messages enciphered on a T52 were broken, while the T42 was considered to be unbreakable. Some accounts state that no means were developed to exploit the diagnosis of Sturgeon, the T52, but others indicate that a method was developed, but resources were devoted instead to ensuring the continued flow of decodes from the Lorenz cipher machines used by the Germany army.

In mid-1944, the codebreakers at Bletchley Park worked out the logical structure of the T52, Sturgeon, used by the Luftwaffe and other organizations. The break was made using traffic from a link known as Halibut. Captain Walter J Fried, an American liaison officer at Bletchley Park, reported to Washington in May 1944, 'A substantial amount of research is being done on this problem at the moment. Solution through depths cannot be relied on for the future because of the apparent introduction of the [P5 limitation] element. One problem being considered is a statistical means of differentiating between this traffic and ordinary Fish traffic... The possibilities of statistical and cribbing methods are being studied. Without a machine to assist in enciphering and deciphering [i.e. an analogue of the Sturgeon], all necessary operations are exceptionally laborious... No plans have yet been made to construct such a machine... [Also] cryptanalysis of traffic enciphered with this machine seems to present extraordinary difficulties.'[2] Sturgeon had ten wheels which could be linked in any combination. Five would be used to perform a vernan cipher operation and five to perform a mutation of the order of the five output units.

Sturgeon was used by several different organizations including the Wehrkreis (internal military district commands), the SS and the German Air Force. The Wehrkreis, for example, had a wireless teleprinter link between Berlin and Vienna which first appeared on 5 June 1943 and carried traffic until 3 April 1945. The link was codenamed Sole at Bletchley Park. Several other links – Devilfish, Sild, Tilefish, and Basker – were also heard transmitting at various times between 1944 and May 1945. Most of these links were thought to use the Sturgeon cipher machine. Several other unclassified transmissions were also picked up and were thought to be Wehrkreis. No doubt, other links existed but were not heard due to low power needed for transmission within the core territory of the Reich, and most of the links named above were indeed only intercepted because the invasion of mainland Europe by the Allies in mid-1944 meant that aerials could be stationed close to the legitimate users.[3]

A link that was first picked up under such conditions in February 1945, codenamed Moonfish, was initially thought to be an army or Wehrkreis circuit, but close analysis of

Appendix K

'indicators' and a small amount of plain-language chat showed that it was in fact an SS link, between Berlin and South-West Stettin. A total of 110 messages were sent over the link in April, then it moved to Salzburg, before becoming less active and ceasing transmission in May 1945. No messages from any of the above links is recorded as having been deciphered, and it appears that the transmissions were recorded for traffic analysis only. It has always been claimed, both in public and previously classified documents, that only German army links were broken and that only the army used the Lorenz machine. However, one recently released document shows that up until October 1943 the Luftwaffe links transmitting to the air force headquarters near Koenigsberg, Robinson 2, used the Lorenz SZ40 Geheimschreiber.[4] It is not known whether any of these links were broken or not. Whether they were broken or not, from late 1943 the Luftwaffe replaced the Lorenz SZ40 with the Siemens T52. 'The absence of [Siemens] T52 machine breaks, and the consequent lack of cover on [German Air Force] links, makes it difficult to give the German picture at all completely', for Luftwaffe use of wireless teleprinter networks. German air force links using the Sturgeon machine multiplied in late 1943 and early 1944. Links codenamed Sprat, Dab, Vendace, Groper, Loach, Monsun, Salmon, Sardine, Halibut and Conger were all first intercepted in 1943 and identified as air force locations from direction-finding, chat and intelligence derived from associated Enigma links. Various fixed air force wireless transmitter exchanges were also identified, at Treuenbritzen, south-west of Berlin, at 'Robinson 2', 'whose transmitter was placed by [direction-finding] some 20 miles West of Goldap', and at Biesenthal, north of Berlin. In 1944 several new links appeared, including Char, Bass, Sandeel, Rocksalmon, Tinker, Loach, Elver, Carp, Blenny, Goldfish, Gudgeon, Anchovy, Pilchard, Gilthead and Needlefish. These lists are not comprehensive. As existing links closed or moved, and new links and exchanges opened regularly from 1943 to 1945, the moves were closely watched by the British interception engineers, but without success in breaking the many links.

The German navy used wireless teleprinter links far less frequently than the German Air Force. Its bases tended to be more stable than that of the air force which had to respond to developments in the land war more closely than the navy with its bases near serviceable ports. With memories of the British codebreaking success in the First World War, there was also more emphasis by the navy on security. Landlines were commonly used to connect ports to command and supply centres, rather than wireless links. Its wireless teleprinter network was known as the 'Barbel' network, first heard working between Athens and Belgrade in January 1944, and from August between Athens and Berlin. Over the next few months several new links were identified linking Oslo, Libau, Sofia, Kiel, Trieste and other places. 'One of the distinguishing features of working on the Barbel set-up was the large amount of plain language in chat and traffic references.'[5]

Finally, there was Thrasher, the Siemens and Halske T42 machine, which had yet a different architecture to the T52. It was diagnosed but considered as unbreakable.[6] It appeared only on one Wehrkreis link and caused the codebreakers a lot of trouble. 'Thrasher was a Fish link whose only manifest abnormality was its QEP system. Between consecutive transmissions the QEP number increased not by one, but by an amount roughly proportional to the length of the earlier transmission, approx. 1 per 120 letters. After some 30,000–40,000 letters there was a change of "Rolle" [roll]. The obvious interpretation was that the Rolle was an expendable key tape of which each terminal had a copy, containing 30,000–40,000 letters'.[7] Having established this, the codebreakers went on to analyse the machine's structure, but decided that it could not be broken at all.

A number of other links were also detected between 1943 and 1944, some of which were clearly used 'for testing purposes only'.[8] Other test links took more patience. One, Swordfish, between Bordeaux and Berlin had caused much confusion for many months. The operators on this link had learned not to discuss technical details in plain language test transmissions and chat, but to exchange useless pleasantries, so little information was forthcoming. The Berlin operator mentioned swimming in the Wann and Fahrlander lakes, leading Bletchley Park to conclude that the station was near Potsdam, and his counterpart in Bordeaux related how he had been swimming in the sea, which confused them given the distance of Bordeaux from the sea. Both operators revealed that they were in wooded areas when they chatted about the trees interfering with reception. It was learnt that the Berlin end often experienced interference from three nearby transmitters for other links. And they exchanged information about bombing damage, but 'Although there were many items of chat during the periods under review [in November 1943] conclusive evidence of actual working details, intentions, etc., can not safely be assessed.' No one at Knockholt was even sure if Swordfish was transmitting messages using Tunny or Sturgeon versions of the Geheimschreiber because no one could diagnose the transmission tone signals system that was being used.

The only useful information picked up in the chat showed that the now familiar 'Wapruef7' (which had developed the directional radio transmitters used for the Fish links) was experimenting with new cipher devices and two suppliers, Siemens and Telefunken, were involved in the experiments – though, clearly, as rivals. A report on interception at Knockholt during the autumn of 1943 recorded that the only definite information was the transmission times and the frequencies. 'Nothing useful was given about the teleprinter apparatus… [making it difficult to determine the transmission technique]. Such details can only be provided by Mr Kenworthy and a Technical Report from him would amplify or disprove' the assumptions made. But, Kenworthy 'gave the impression that he was losing interest in the investigation.'[9] When the Sixta section, which had been set up for traffic analysis of Enigma wireless networks, took on analysis of Fish traffic in 1944 additional expertise could be applied. 'The outstanding characteristic of this group was its frequent use of code names, Tiger, Tigerleute, Panther and Pantherleute at the Berlin end, and Edelweiss, Falke and Wolf at Bordeaux.' In the end traffic analysts concluded that, 'This was neither an army nor a [German air force] link, but probably used by the Siemens firm.'[10] Stingray, between Berlin and Nuernberg, 'was also probably used by the Siemens firm. It was heard on Jan 18 1944, and continued regularly till the end of June 1944, and at intervals after that date till Nov 7. It used the codenames Wilhelm, Ferdinand and Richard. This link experimented with Speech as well as Tone transmission.' A link between Nuernberg and Vienna/Budapest, codenamed Uncl. 13 (presumably its wireless call-sign), appeared in 1944 and was suspected to be a test link but the traffic analysts could not be certain. Another link known by its call-sign, D2iW, also appeared but could not be categorized.[11]

These experiences with Sturgeon, Thrasher and a growing number of experimental links confirmed the management at Bletchley Park in their decision to concentrate on

Appendix K

Tunny, the Lorenz 40/42 machine. It was producing intelligence of enormous value and required all the resources that could be given just to keep up with the size of the task. Sturgeon and Thrasher would be a demanding catch and so were off limits for Bletchley Park's anglers.

Appendix L: Bream Message Types and Examples – Early 1944

There were roughly five types of Bream message:

1 – Situation reports ('sitreps'): from ObS (Commander in Chief, South), Kesselring, covering the whole Italian area, and daily reports from the fighting fronts – Kesselring's intentions and appreciations, casualties, reinforcements.

2 – Supply returns: tank returns (which gave a lot of information on the German 'Order of Battle') and ammunition and fuel returns.

3 – 'Y-appreciations': Axis appreciation of Allied 'Order of Battle' in Italy (derived mainly from Axis wireless interception, traffic analysis and direction-finding) also information on Allied 'Order of Battle' in the Mediterranean and in Britain.

4 – Secret service: information about airfields, harbours and shipping movements.

5 – Miscellaneous: administration and supply, etc.

Examples from January and February 1944

Type 1

Kesselring's review and appreciation of the German bridgehead situation. All divisions badly in need of rest and refit. Two new full divisions needed if bridgehead to be cleared up. In emergency retreat to new position, unifying all fronts and still holding onto Rome.

Appreciation of Allied forces at Nettuno; their strength, fighting value, reinforcements. Allied conduct of the whole operation and its weaknesses. Front opposite 10th Army being weakened.

Intentions of Kesselring: to attack at Bridgehead on 29/2, because delay works against the German army.

Casualties: losses of German 14th Army 20 to 31 January 1944. Third degree frostbite troops from Russia to be exchanged for fit troops in Italy.

Coordinated attack on Aprilia prevented by destruction of wireless telegraphy network.

Lower state of training of German troops being sent to reinforce bridgehead and excessive demands on the troops causing anxiety.

Type 2

Detailed tank returns of Armies in Italy.

87th Corps (North Italy) has no reserves, therefore weakness at the junction of the 19th and 14th Armies cannot easily be remedied. Complete strengths of 10th and 14th Armies and Army Group von Zangen.

Some new identifications: First mention of PanzerGruppe West in France; Panzer Division Hermann Goering to go to sphere of ObW (Commander in Chief, West in France); II Parachute Corps in Ghent; 333 and 92 Infantry divisions in Mediterranean area; SS Division Hitler Jugend (Hitler Youth) at Leopoldsburg; Panzer Regiment 69 in the Rome area; elements of I Parachute Division and I Parachute Corps moving to Brest area.

Type 3

Review of Allied forces in Great Britain and Mediterranean area. Summary of RAF and USAAF new tactical and strategic commands. Emphasis on success of British wireless telegraphy silence in preventing German army from gaining an insight into Allied 'Order of Battle'.

Type 4

Instruction to all Army and divisional commanders to attend a conference in Posen on 24 to 27 January 1944 under aegis of the Nazi Party.

Source: HW13/217, 13/3/44

Appendix M: Some Jellyfish Messages from May and June 1944

Sent 0200 on 20 May 1944
1 SS division: 39 panzer tanks; 2 SS division, had 37 panzer tanks (deficiency 62) and 55 panzer IV (deficiency 46). 1 SS division: fully serviceable, one Panzer Battle Gruppe, one Artillery Battle Gr, one Battle Gr reconnaissance 'Abteilung' (section) of three companies; one Battle Gr with three rifle and one headquarters company.

Sent end of May 1944
Commander-in-Chief, Netherlands to Commander-in-Chief, West. The armament of 19 Panzer division is entirely inadequate even for defence against air landing.

Application for weapons arranged by 48th Panzer Corps.

Sent in 25 May 1944
Tank return from Commander-in-Chief, West, mentioning names of many units.

Sent at 2250 on 6 June 1944
Officer requirements listed by 85 division, Lille area, amounts to 36 officers needed.

Sent at 2250 on 6 June 1944
To OKW (Army High Command, Berlin) from Commander-in-Chief, West. In consideration of developments here (Cherbourg Peninsular) we request that Obstlt Perau be left as commander of Grenadier Regiment 936 (in 245 infantry division).

Sent at 1000 on 10 June 1944
Move of 1st Panzer division into previous area of 19 Luftwaffe field division (mouth of Scheldt) also to same location temporary transfer of 2 Flak abteilungen of 65th Air Korps.

Subordination of 1st SS Panzer division to 99th Corps at Antwerp. 116 Panzer division subordinated to 81st Corps at Rouen.

Sent at 1000 on 10 June 1944
Details of locations of battle headquarters:
1 – Panzergruppe West: La Caine (10km north-west of Thury-Harcourt)
2 – 364 infantry division: Brucourt (4km south of Dives)
3 – 21 Panzer division: Andre-sur-Orne (2.5km north-west of Caen)
4 – Panzer Lehr division: Hotlot
5 – 352 infantry division: Littry
6 – 716 infantry division: Caen ("not employed at the present moment")

Source: HW13/153

Appendix N: Cribs Used on Dragon

Crib	Frequency per month	Length	
Gurnard (Berlin end)			
89ROEM95	65	8	
M89ARMEE	64	8	Armee – army
ANGRIFFE9	37	9	Angriff – attack
9DER9FEIND	34	10	Der Feind – the enemy
5M89GR5M89	29	10	
M89PZ5M89	28	9	
TAETIGKEIT	23	10	Taetigkeit – activity
9ANGRIFF9	28	9	
5M89DIV5M	20	9	
DG9HOSF95	16	9	
Jellyfish (Berlin end)			
89ROEM95	61	8	
5M89KDO5M8	38	10	
9DG9HOSF95	29	10	
5M89ROEM95	27	10	
ABSCHNITT	23	9	Abschnitt – section/sector
9ANGRIFF	31	8	
5M89D5M89	20	9	
5M89A5M89	20	9	
5M89GR5M89	16	10	
5M89WEST	34	8	
TAETIGKEIT	15	10	
AUFKLAERUN	14	10	Aufklaerun(g) – intelligence
9NACHR5M89	15	10	Nachr(ichten) – message
Stickleback (Berlin end)			
889ROEM955	53	10	
55M889SUED	24	10	
9ROEM955	83	8	
955LL8899	51	8	
88ARMEE55	26	9	
9LM9AUM9	27	9	Raum – space
SUEDUKRAIN	21	10	Sued Ukrain – South Ukraine
GRUPPE9SUD	20	10	Gruppe Sud – Group South
999PZ55M88	20	10	
ANGRIFF9	32	8	
HEERESGRUP	17	10	Heeresgrup – Army group
TAETIGKEIT	16	10	
Whiting (Riga end)			
95L5L595M5	19	10	
95K5K58	21	7	
89A5M89K5M	16	10	

HEERESGRUP	13	10	
95AA95M5A8	11	10	
95M5A899	27	8	
89ROEM95	15	8	
M5QP5M5R5R	9	10	
WIRTSCHAFT	8	10	Wirtschaft – economy

Source: NARA 4628, Special Fish Report, Box 1417

Appendix O: Whiting Decode, 5 February 1945

Whiting/Berlin, 5/2/45, KN/W6573.

This is one of only a very small number of decodes that has survived. The surviving decodes all come from traffic on two days in February 1945 on the Whiting link between Berlin (teleprinter office, call-sign OKH HZPH) and the Courland on the Baltic coast in present-day Latvia. None of the undulator slip or perforated tape has survived for any period of the war.

The decode was produced by a Tunny analogue machine after Colossus, the Robinsons, other machines and/or hand methods had been used to work out both the pin positions (which were raised and which flush, i.e. wheel-breaking) for that day, and the wheel-settings (or starting positions) for the individual transmission. The pin positions and the message settings would be passed to the Decoding Room, where a Tunny machine would produce a decode by deciphering the message or messages in a transmission.

This is the plain-language decode, but, as can be seen, except for short sections containing recognizable German words or abbreviations, it is far from plain. This is because it is printed on what was known as a shiftless printer so the teleprinter punctuation and instruction characters would be printed in the basic teleprinter code. The sequences such as '++M– –.' (representing 'shift to figures', 'shift to figures', 'full stop', 'shift to letters', 'shift to letters', 'SPACE') were of vital importance for building up the statistics needed for wheel-breaking and wheel-setting on Colossus and Robinson. Note the operator always repeats the 'shift' commands. Also note that '+' is used instead of '5' to represent 'figures-shift'; '-' instead of '8' to represent 'letters-shift'; '.' instead of '9' for 'SPACE'.

After the decode had been produced it would be passed to Hut 3 for translation and, if necessary, rewritten (to hide the source and to provide only essential information) and annotated (providing back references to people, units and topics in any message) before being sent to operational commands. (Copies of these teleprints do survive and are easily accessible at the National Archives in London (DEFE series), however, in many cases, it would be difficult to distinguish intelligence from Fish and from Enigma.) The full text of the translated decode would also be forwarded to armed forces headquarters and military intelligence units. Apparently, none of these full texts survives. Additionally, a number of reports were written based on Fish decodes by Hut 3 and the Sixta (traffic-analysis section), which do survive and are mainly open to the public (see Further Reading). A few of these reports do indicate the name of the Fish link and the date of the message, but provide a very short summary of the content and only as related to the subject of the report.

At the time this particular message was sent, Army Group North and other German armed forces units were isolated in the Courland pocket (Kurland in German), while the Russian army was attacking East Prussia and Koenigsberg to the south and west of the pocket. A small number of the German armed forces units were being shipped from the Courland to help with defence of the Reich, and many messages were being sent regarding shipping arrangements. This message was probably one of the messages sent regarding shipping arrangements as the list of addressees in the header includes several naval units.

According to the official British history (British Intelligence in the Second World War, Vol 3, 646–7), 'The decrypts had established by then that the Germans were not carrying out a general evacuation from Courland and that the divisions they were withdrawing could not possibly be assembled for a counter-offensive in East Prussia or

Poland.' Only enough shipping was available for the transportation of one division a week of the twenty-six divisions that Stalin estimated he had surrounded in the Courland as reported to the Yalta conference with Churchill and Roosevelt. The lack of shipping also meant that German citizens could not be evacuated from Koenigsberg and East Prussia. One decrypt from 22 January 1945 'specified the removal of the civilian population by sea was not to be allowed to interfere with the evacuation of service personnel or the shipping needed for the withdrawal of divisions from Courland'.

The text of the decode is given below in three forms. First, it has been directly copied from the original and shows the message in basic teleprinter code; I have taken the pencilled-in corrections as the correct text. Second, the teleprinter punctuation and shift commands have been removed and the characters are shown as either letters or numerals as appropriate; this version is presented in a continuous stream. Third, the message has been formatted and annotated to give an indication of the information available. What appears to be the message towards the end makes little sense. Clearly, the experts at Bletchley Park would have been able to derive substantially more than I have from my guesswork.

Decoded on Tunny Machine XII

Decoded on 5/2/45

Sent on 4/2/45 (note error on original in illustration 21 showing 4/2/44)

Sent from Berlin (HZGH) to Army Group North teleprinter office (HZPH) in the Courland on Whiting link.

Time started 00.14

Time ended 00.20

Frequency 2,386 Kc/s

Serial number KN/WB6573 (KN probably indicates that the transmission was intercepted at Knockholt)

```
FUSE.++Z.AA--KR++AA--.MKSN.NR++M.OWQO.TMW
N.RTSPPPP.K--HZGH++X--FF++Q.QQOPTL.VV--.AN.
KR++M--.MKSN.NR++M.OWQO.TMWN.RT.PPPP.K--H
ZPH++X--FF++Q.QQOPTL.VV.--AN.KR++M--.HEERES
GR++M--.KURLAND.++.VV--.GLTD++C--.KR++M--.O
KM.SKL++M--.QU++M--.SECHS.UEBER.ADM++M--.H
AMBURG++M---.KR.MOK.OST.O++P--.QU++MA—.KR.
ADM++M--.WESTL++M--.HAMBURG++MA--.KRH/-I.O
STSO++++M--.QU++M--.SECTSASEBER.ADM++M--.H
AMBURG++MA--.KR.MOK.OST.O++M--.QU++MA--.K.
UEBER.ADM++M--.HAMBURG++MA--.KR.MOK.OST.
O++M--.QU++MA--.KR.ADM++M--.WESTL++M--.OST
SEE++MA--.KR.SEE1RAFCHEF.OSTSEE++MA--.KR.M
VO++M--.B++M--.CH++M--.GEN++M--.ST++M--.D++
M--.HEERES++M--.KR.MVO.H++M-K.GR++M--.NORD
.PILLAU++MA--.KR.OKW++M--.WESTB.EBNS.A.HEI
M++M--.STAB.SKAND++MA--.NORD.PILLAU++MA--.
KR.OKW+JDV-WEXSTB.AINS.A.IIIM++M--.STAB.SK
AND++MA--.KR.H++M--.GR++M--.KURLAND++MA--.
KR.SEETRASTJ+M--.LIBAU.++.A.AA--ROT++AA.--R
GEHEIM++AA--.STETTIN.EC.J+C.RXW.WQPP—.GUWE
```

```
.++WWPV--.ASKARI++MA.WRPP-G.GUFBINNEN++M
A--.STETTIN.AUS++C.RXWM--.RHEINLAND++MC.W
RPP--.BUKAREST.NACH.GIBAU++VV--.KMD++M--ST
ETTIN.GEH++M.QTQYXRT--.S.++Z.-.BEI.DIR.WA4.ES
```

```
FUSE_+_--KR--_MKSN_NR.9219.5.2._45'000_(HZGH/
FF1_11905)_==_AN_KR._MKSN_NR.9219_5.2.45_000
0_(HZPH/FF1_11905)==_AN_KR._HEERESGR._KURL
AND_==_GLTD:KR._OKM_SKL._QU._SECHS_UEBER
_ADM._HAMBURG._KR_MOK_OST_00_QU.-K
R_ADM._WESTL._HAMBURG.0_KRHI_OSTSO._QU.
SECTSASEBER_ADM._HAMBURG.-_KR_MOK_OST_0.
_QU.=_K_UEBER.ADM._HAMBURG.=_KR.MOK.OST_
0._QU.=_KR_ADM.WESTL._OSTSEE._KR.SEEIRAFCH
EF_OSTSEE.=_KR_MVO._B._CH._GEN._ST._HEERES.
=_KR_MVO_H.K._GR._NORD_PILLAU._KR.OKW._WE
STB_EBNS_A_HEIM._STAB.SKAND._NORD_PILLAU.
=_KR_OKW_JDV_WEXSTB_AINS_A_IIIM._STAB_SKA
ND.-_KRH._GR._KURLAND.-_KR_SEETRASTJ._LIBA
U__-_--_STETTIN_EC_J:4/22100_GUWE220=_ASKARI
.-_2400G_GUFBINNEN._STETTIN_AUS:_4/2._RHEIN
LAND.:2400_BUKAREST_NACH_GIBAU==_KMD.STE
TTIN_GEH.1516/45_S+_BEI_DIR_WA
```

FUSE = —KR—MKSN NR.9219.5.2.45'000 (HZGH/FF1 11905)== ['FUSE' – meaning unknown; KR is possibly a security rating, or perhaps it is a mistake and should read AN KR, in which case it would probably mean 'To HQ'; MKSN is possibly a Marine teleprinter call-sign; there follows serial number, date, time of origin and call-sign – this line is possibly a mistake, with two further errors, one in the 000 and the other in HZGH. If this is the case then the next line repeats the details with corrections, AN KR, 0000 and HZPH. The HZPH/FF1 is the sending teleprinter office call-sign (OKH Zossen at this time).]

AN KR. MKSN NR. 9219 5.2.45 0000 (HZPH/FF1 11905)==
AN KR. HEERESGR. KURLAND== [to Army Group Courland]
GLTD: [means 'also being sent to' on other landline or wireless links]
KR. MOK OST 00. [KR probably means 'Kommandatur', i.e. command headquarters]
KR ADM. WESTL HAMBURG –
KR. MOK. OSTO QU.= [OST = 'East']
K UEBER ADM HAMBURG. = [UEBER = over or above; ADM probably = Admiral]
KR.MOK. OST O QU.=
KR.ADM.WESTL.OSTSEE [OSTSEE = Baltic Sea]
KR. SEEIRAFCHEF OSTSEE.=
KR.MVO. B CH GEN. ST. HEERES [HEERES = Army]
KR MVO H. K. GR NORD PILLAU. [H. K. GR NORD = Army Group North, Pilau is a Baltic Sea port in East Prussia]
KR. OKW.WESTLB EBNS A HEIM. STAB. SKAND. NORD PILLAU=
KR OKW JDV WEXSTB AINS A IIIM. STAB SKAND – [STAB = Staff]
KR H. GR. KURLAND. – [= Army Group Courland]
KR SEETRASTJ. LIBAU – [Libau is a Baltic Sea port in the Courland]
STETTIN EC J:4/22100 GUWE 220 =

ASKARJ – 2400 GUEBINNED. STETTIN AUS: 4/2. RHEINLAND.:
2400 BUKAREST NACH GIBAU==
KMD. STETTIN GEH. 1516/45 S+ BEI DIR WA [breaks off?]

Appendix P: 'Hitler as seen by Source'

The extracts below come from a fascinating document, entitled 'Hitler as seen by Source', written in May 1945, assessing what could be deduced about Adolf Hitler as shown by Enigma and Geheimschreiber decrypts (referred to as Source and as MSS – Most Secret Source). It makes no claim to give a rounded or complete view of Hitler, only what can be deduced from the communication of orders in Hitler's name that were uncovered in the intercepts. It is important to appreciate that, at that time, no one could be sure that there would be no attempts to carry on a guerrilla struggle by Nazi supporters, perhaps using Hitler as a martyred figurehead. The complete document consists of fifteen closely typed pages and has been substantially reduced in length for this appendix. There is no indication of who the author was – but whoever it was, they crafted the opening sentences with mischievous intent.

That Adolf Hitler was a good man few outside Germany have at any time supposed. But that he had elements of greatness, touches of genius, for diplomacy and even for strategy – this view has sometimes been taken, especially at periods of German success, even in circles that were well-informed... The question is not mere academic history. Men can be more powerful dead than they ever were alive – for good or evil. It may matter a lot to posterity whether Hitler goes down to it, especially in Germany, as sublime or ridiculous; as a man in some ways great, but unfortunate; or as a man in all ways small, except as a popular hypnotist.

Source alone, needless to say, cannot give a full answer. But he can help. His portrait of the Fuehrer lacks the gayer colour of diplomats' despatches or prisoners' reports. But it has one advantage: what there is of it, is true.

The first point in the assembled MSS evidence on Hitler that surprises even the regular reader of Source since 1940, is the growth in the quantity of that evidence as the War draws to its close... Other causes contribute, but the main reason is simple. The longer the War lasted, the more the Fuehrer tried to take control. The worse things went, the more he meddled: the more he meddled, the worse things went...

Infallibility grew upon him... no one would criticize the first [Hitler] directive ever reported by Source [Jan 1942] on the need for economy in war-decorations... Again, it was reasonable enough to desire that visitors to the Fuehrer's HQ should first be deloused. It would be hard to find any great harm in his general attention to questions of supply, to Flak protection, or to the structure of American tanks...

But [the effect of Hitler's intervention] was more important than that, instead of maintaining German morale by making frequent speeches... the Fuehrer insisted more and more on being, not orator, but [the] general. There his interventions were lethal. [And this is where Source grows most interesting.] We can watch them multiply. Their tone grows more and more peremptory. They spread over the whole field of strategy. They encroach increasingly in tactics, down to divisions, even to pill-boxes...

His secret was simple. He was fanatically determined, completely aware of what he wanted, entirely unscrupulous, and extremely reckless [which took him to success in war in Poland, Scandinavia and north-western Europe]... Then began the real war – and the change in Hitler. The gifted demagogue must needs become a general. The greatness of Germany that he had built up for six years on the platform, he now proceeded to disintegrate for five more on the battlefield. To this the German Generals... submitted and succumbed. This seems the essential truth in the story Source has to tell.

[In September 1941] he merely 'expresses views'... [but] the process continues with a certain growth in the tone of superiority ... [November 1941] 'early attack on Tobruk as intended by Rommel with agreement of the Duce is desirable. But the Fuehrer considers that it cannot begin until [Luftwaffe] supporting units have supplies enough'... [January 1942] 'the Fuehrer demands higher railway performance in the East'... [June 1942] 40 tanks to be sent over to [Panzer] Army Afrika, 'on express orders of the Fuehrer'... [Crete then became a major area of worry for Hitler]

He was soon to have sounder cause for worry. Alamein and Stalingrad were at hand... The general tone, however, is still far from the angry hectoring of later days – it remains the tone of a man who thinks he has bright suggestions to offer, but still appears to respect his generals on the spot. Further, these directives are still of a fairly general nature. Simultaneously the Fuehrer was presiding over [his siege of] Stalingrad. An excellent example of his banal and fuzzy suggestions, calculated to irritate, but not yet to drive to despair, his commanders in the field, is provided by [a signal] of 22/11. The Fuehrer 'judges' the crisis as follows: 'The situation will be restored if the Rumanians hold west of Kletskaya, and if further Russians do not pour through gap'. Then follow rather futile orders for dropping leaflets on the Rumanians and also (more practically) rations. And the Fuehrer 'attaches decisive importance' to reconnaissance. Similarly [a signal] of 29/1/43 still gives the impression of a fidgety individual anxious to say something, rather than having anything particular to say. Stalingrad and 4 Panzer Army are to be supported by air. 'The weather conditions are also to be taken into account in deciding on operations. Should the weather prevent operations to Stalingrad, but allow of bombing in support of 4 Panzer Army, then the latter will be carried out. Similarly, if the weather excludes operations in support of 4 Panzer Army, but allows of the supplying of Stalingrad, Stalingrad will be supplied'...

1943 was to be a very different year. January opened with more premonitions: 'The Fuehrer is anxious' about a Russian crossing of the Dnieper'... 'The Fuehrer fears an attack in the area Ivnbaba-Feodosia'... June produced a special Hitler order about large-scale mining on the Italian front, and July a great wordy document from him about rear defences there. But now the interest shifts west.

The attitude of Hitler, in MSS documents, shows a violent stiffening from Normandy on. One has the impression of a growing despair (whether or no he owned it to himself), a growing distrust of his generals, as either knaves or fools who would let him down whenever he gave them a chance... But the more numerous and minute his orders, the less possible they become to carry out; the more they were disobeyed, the more ubiquitous become his interferences, his threats, his flying-court-martials.

9/8: Hitler to CinC West: Attack of XLVII Panzer Corps was too early, therefore too weak. To be resumed elsewhere. 'I give the following orders. Surprise attack by Eberbach. Another attack under LXXXI Corps. Time of attack is envisaged to be reported. I reserve the right of sanction. I reserve to myself, for the present, decision on employment of 11 Panzer division.' He has now got down to commanding divisions.

13/8: Hitler to 7 Army [about proposed withdrawal to avoid encirclement in the Falaise pocket]. Flat refusal by Hitler. 'The proposed withdrawal yields too much ground, without compelling reason.' Thus he ensured the disaster of the Falaise pocket.

[During the autumn], though the spate of Fuehrer orders persists, they are of a longer-term nature, and concerned with administration, man-power, defence-lines, morale, punishments of waverers, scatterings of oak-leaves [i.e military decorations], swords and crosses, and designation of more and more 'fortresses' to be held to the last round. The Ardennes offensive of 16/12 shows little trace, in MSS... but the new year proved that he had formed no lasting good resolutions. On 5/1 'the Fuehrer demanded speedier information about the situation at strategic schwerpunkte [focal points]'.

[On 21/1 orders were issued that] 'All commanders down to divisions are personally responsible to me for ensuring that: every decision on an operational movement; every intended attack; every offensive scheme on quiet fronts; every intended withdrawal; every intended abandonment of a position, local strongpoint, or fortress is to be reported to me early enough to enable me to intervene...' No document in all MSS throws more light than this on the Fuehrer's ruling passion, his itch for managing...

On 10/1/45 Hitler was personally ordering the transfer of two Jagdtiger specially suited to cope with pillboxes to XXXIX Corps for 10 SS Panzer Division...

This, then, seems the keynote of the Fuehrer's character, as brought out by MSS, and also the chief secret of his failure – sheer meddlesomeness... The surprising thing is not that the Corporal's strategy should have been of no high order, nor that some of his orders should be simply childish and unpractical... It is not these that can surprise. We know our Hitler. But it does remain a psychological curiosity to find the master of Europe fussing about the transformation into Cadre Abteilungen of three miserable [Luftwaffe] Works Battalions in [Air Group] Kiev; or personally concerning himself with the withdrawal of a solitary Flak [unit] from Monfalcone to Hungary; or making it the subject of a Fuehrer order that the island of Vis should henceforth be called by its other name of Liosa.

It would have been a serious failing even had Hitler's military gifts been of the first order, to constantly to cramp the liberty of subordinates... the growing complexities of the modern world and modern war make it more vital than ever to concentrate on essentials. And when among all his other too numerous activities, he tried also to run battles at the front, like Louis XIV conducting campaigns against Marlborough from Versailles, or George III against the Americans from St James's, the wonder is not that for him, as for them, disaster followed, but that the most experienced general staff in the world could endure these bunglings year after year, with only one feeble attempt at revolt. True Hitler had the facilities of wireless; but that only made his interference worse.

Source: HW13/58, 24/5/1945, 'Hitler as seen by Source' [CX/MSS./S177]

Appendix Q: Newmanry Staffing

A – Daily staffing per shift of the Newmanry, April 1945

7 Cryptographers:
1 Duty Officer in charge of setting
1 Wheel man in charge of wheel-breaking
1 in charge of Cribs and Robinson work
2 to supervise Colossus setting
2 to supervise Colossus wheel-breaking

67 Wrens:
7 Registrars
17 Tunny operators
2 Robinson operators
20 Colossus operators
15 Computers
1 Cribs assistant
5 'Room 11' maintaining contact with Knockholt

5 Engineers

23 Miscellaneous:
2 Research cryptographers
2 Research Wrens
13 Construction engineers
6 Administrative staff

Total: 102

B – The Newmanry cryptographers

Date of Arrival		Jun 43–Jul 44	Aug 44–May 45
Professional mathematicians & research students		8	4
Other University mathematicians		3	11
Others		2	1
Previous Cryptographic experience		12	3
of which:			
Enigma		8	2
Fish		3	1
Age on joining	over 30	5	2
	25–30	3	3
	20–25	3	5
	under 20	1	6
British		11	13
American		2	3
Total		13	16

Source: 'General Report Tunny' (National Archives, London) pp. 276–278

Appendix Q

Fish statistics

Period	Transmission received at Knockholt	Tapes received at Bletchley Park	Tapes set on Chi's	Decodes (messages)	Decodes in thousands of characters	Keys broken
1942						
Nov–Dec	12180	–	–	872	4467	4+
1943						
Jan–Mar	16615	–	–	991	3386	10+
Apr–Jun	23970	73	2	965	3063	15+
Jul–Sep	21550	272	17	745	3047	19+
Oct–Dec	34740	955	199	733	3145	18+
1944						
Jan–Mar	28000	1670	1205	680	3189	13
Apr–Jun	6215	4160	1446	1044	4695	19
Jul–Sep	5210	4450	1638	1139	6860	80*
Oct–Dec	6922	5496	2182	1861	9607	160*
1945						
Jan–8 May	12325	10555	4332§	4478	21972	374*
Totals	**167727**	**27631**	**11021**	**13508**	**63431**	**718**

Source: General report on Tunny, page 394
Table shows the amount of material used and the results obtained.
The table does not show the strong correlation between success and high motor settings

+ = all broken by means of depths
* = over half of these were broken by rectangles
§ = of these, 1040 were set mechanically on all 12 wheels

A Note on Sources

The main sources for this book have been files held at the National Archives (formerly the Public Record Office) at Kew, West London and all of which are open to the public. The most important files are in the HW series. HW5 contains the two volumes of *General Report on Tunny* (HW5/24 and HW5/25) and several other useful files. The HW11 series contains a number of useful histories of GC&CS written after the end of the war in 1945 for internal use. HW3, HW13 and HW43 contain many useful files covering relevant aspects. There are also relevant files in other series, including HW62 and HW50. The amount of material on German signals operations is vast and I have consulted only a fraction of the total.

All these series have seen substantial releases of previously secret material relating to the overall Fish story since mid-2000. The *Technical Description of Colossus I* (HW25/24) was one of several relevant documents released in the summer of 2004. Two relevant files on the Testery and the Sixta (traffic analysis) remain closed (though I was provided by GCHQ with photocopies of a few declassified pages of HW43/63, namely on limitations used on the Lorenz SZ/42 machines, and on the structure of wireless teleprinter networks of German army and other services). The DEFE series holds on microfiche the intelligence teleprints sent to Allied operational intelligence units of Ultra material. The FO and ADM series also contain relevant material.

The HW14 series, however, provided much of the most interesting detail, filling out the official tone of the end of the war histories. This series contains correspondence kept, presumably by a secretary, either to the director or the deputy director. It is a complete miscellany of types of correspondence from tiny slivers of paper to complete multi-page reports and covers the entire gamut of GC&CS operations from 1939 to 1945. The items are often quite frustrating: a note stating that a report on a particularly appropriate subject was attached, but without the report; plenty of items that consist of nothing but abbreviations and reference numbers and so could not be 'decoded' in the time that could be spared. Perhaps one item in one hundred or fewer was applicable to the Fish story, but I have no doubt missed a good many. Each file in the series (of which there are over 140, each of which holds at least a couple of hundred individual items) contains one or more notices stating that an item or items has been withheld. Of course, there is no way of telling if these items relate to Fish or not, but it does mean that in total at least some 700 individual items from this one series of files, which are exclusively about GC&CS from 1939 to 1945, still remain secret today, sixty years since the end of the war.

Since restrictions have been lifted, a number of key figures, such as Tom Flowers, Alan Coombs, William Tutte, Jack Good, Shaun Wylie and Donald Michie have written papers which provide excellent insights into technical issues and important personal, social and organizational details about the Fish story. A number of key people, in particular Max Newman and Tom Flowers, have recorded audio accounts (held in the main either at the Science Museum or at the Imperial War Museum in London).

There are also plenty of reminiscences being collected, especially by the Bletchley Park Museum, from surviving veterans. While providing valuable insight into the atmosphere of GC&CS, it has to be kept in mind that the strong imposition of the 'need to know' principle and consequent compartmentalisation limited the knowledge of veterans to their own tasks. And there is another reason why this category of source is one of the most difficult to assess. The veterans had to suppress all knowledge of what they had done for at least thirty years, and many of the details for another twenty-five – a total of fifty-five years. The danger is that the memories now being recalled are those that can be drawn out after that long a period of suppression, and are inevitably filtered through more recent events. One example will illustrate the problem. It comes from a recent publication, Marion Hill's *Bletchley Park People*, a collection of reminiscences. In it, a Post Office engineer who was based at Bletchley Park is cited as saying that he

> believes that he can pinpoint the actual moment when Alan Turing conceived the idea of the modern computer. 'The engineers, deciding the "the Prof" should see the workshops where the real work was done and grabbed him. "He wore his usual faraway look as he went in. One lad picked up a valve and said, 'Now, Prof, this is what we call a thermionic valve. It's an electronic device.' [Turing] just stood there goggle-eyed, then all of a sudden his face changed. He just sort of went rigid, stared into the middle-distance, and still holding this valve in this hand said, 'You know, I could make a computer with these.' We think, and I certainly think, that's where the computer started.

The scene, I'm afraid, owes more to the style of Hollywood biopics than history. No doubt the story of the encounter, even Turing's strange countenance, is an account of a real event. But the attribution of the conception of the computer to this chance encounter with an electronic valve owes much to hindsight and the much later acquired knowledge of the idea that Turing 'invented the computer'. Not only did the invention of the computer involve more people than Turing himself. But, also, Turing knew of valves before the war and he was most certainly not just a thinker. He loved tinkering and experimenting, getting his hands dirty playing with soldering irons and bits of wire. The conception of the computer developed over stages, from Turing's pre-war theoretical and practical work, and through the feverish years of 1939–45. This example illustrates the care that has to be taken with recent reminiscences of matters that had to be forgotten for over half a century.

Abbreviations:
AHC – Annals of the History of Computing
BISWW – British Intelligence in the Second World War
IWM – Imperial War Museum
POEEJ – Post Office Electrical Engineers Journal

Notes

Introduction

1 HW3/29
2 D Kahn, *Codebreakers: The Comprehensive History of Secret Writing from Ancient Times to the Internet*, 2nd edition, New York 1996, 486
3 P Strathern, *Turing and the Computer*, London 1997

Chapter one – Wireless War One

1 R Bruce Scott, *Gentlemen on Imperial Service: A Story of the Trans-pacific Telecommunications Cable*, Victoria, British Columbia 1994, 35–6
2 CAB 8/3, 5–8–1904, 'Protection of Cable Landing Place at Fanning Island'
3 G Lawford & L Nicholson (eds), *The Telcon Story 1850–1950*, London 1950, 84
4 CAB18/16, 8/8/1901
5 D Headrick, *The Invisible Weapon: Telecommunications and International Politics 1851–1945*, Oxford 1991, 21–2
6 Headrick, *Invisible Weapon*, 36
7 CAB8/1, 18/8/1886; CAB18/16, 19/3/1891
8 CAB16/14, 11/12/1911
9 The USA also followed a somewhat similar route to Britain from treating cables as neutral to seeing them as vital military, diplomatic and commercial assets that needed to be fully owned and which avoided foreign territory. A Hezlet, *The Electron and Sea Power*, London 1975, 20, records that: 'In the Spanish–American War of 1898 both governments depended on the cable systems of the world for communication with their outlying squadrons of warships. The US Navy at first believed it best not to cut any cables but to declare them neutral for use by both belligerents... After the American

naval victory in Manila Bay, Commodore Dewey tried to arrange with his enemy for both sides to use the [Spanish cable] to Hong Kong. When this was refused he cut it [and was forced to use a dispatch vessel]... His adversary, however, was isolated altogether, much to the advantage of the United States; shortly afterwards the Navy Department changed its policy and ordered cables to Cuba to be cut... Subsequently the US Government took care that the new cable to be laid from the Pacific coast to the Philippines touched land only at places where the USA had sovereignty. Wake Island, at the time unclaimed, was annexed by the USA for this purpose.'

10 Scott, *Imperial Service*, 36–9; K Yates, *Graf Spee's Raiders: Challenges to the Royal Navy, 1914–1915*, London 1995, 81–86; P Halpern, *A Naval History of World War I*, London 1994, 76–82

11 W J Baker, *A History of the Marconi Company*, London 1970, 158

12 ADM 137/4065

13 G Basalla, *The Evolution of Technology*, Cambridge 1988, 124–5; D Landes, *The Unbound Prometheus: Technological Change and Industrial Development from 1750 to the Present*, Cambridge 1969, 234–48

14 J Clapham, *The Economic Development of France and Germany, 1815–1914*, Cambridge 1936, 308

15 ADM 137/4065

16 R Asprey, *The German High Command at War: Hindenburg and Ludendorff and the First World War*, London 1993

17 J Ferris (ed), *The British Army and Signals Intelligence during the First World War*, Stroud 1992, 3–4

18 J Terraine, *White Heat: The New Warfare 1914–1918*, London 1982, 103, 148–50, 312

19 P Beesly, *Room 40: British Naval Intelligence 1914–18*, London 1982; P Hopkirk, *On Secret Service East of Constantinople: The Plot to bring down the British Empire*, Oxford 1994

20 Headrick, *Invisible Weapon*, 160. Headrick is citing an Italian historian, Alberto Santoni, who points to the intercepted wireless messages cited above, suggesting that they were decoded before Room 40 was set up. However, the messages are recorded in longhand in a bound volume at the National Archives, ADM137/4065, and contain an entry on the first pages stating that they were decoded in November 1914; this appears to contradict Santoni's suggestion of decoding as early as March 1914. However, it is clear that the messages were all intercepted by official naval wireless stations in Britain and overseas from that date onwards. Furthermore, at least some of the stories about the way that the codes were acquired are clearly false (one that was supposed to have been fished out of the sea shows no sign of water damage at all, for example). And

there is substantial evidence of Admiralty activities in wireless and awareness of the possibilities of interception, and there are still files relating to First World War codebreaking activities that are held secret (see note 23 below). Santoni may have exaggerated his case, but it cannot be entirely dismissed. A Santoni, *Il primo Ultra Secret: L'influenza delle decrittazioni britanniche sulle operazioni navali della Guerra 1914–1918*, Milan 1985. A Santoni, *The First Ultra Secret: The British Cryptanalysis in the Naval Operations of the First World War*, Revue internationale d'histoire militaire, no 63, 1985

21 Beesly, *Room 40*, 2

22 R Pocock, *The Early British Radio Industry*, Manchester 1988

23 B Tuchman, *The Zimmerman Telegram*, London 1958, 186. For the Zimmerman telegram see also: Beesly, *Room 40* and D Kahn, *The Codebreakers: The Comprehensive History of Secret Communication from Ancient Times to the Internet*, New York 1996. At the time of writing, six files on the Zimmerman telegram held at the National Archives in Kew, London, remain closed.

24 D Landes, *Prometheus Unbound*, 430–1

25 Kahn, *Codebreakers*, 360–4; S Budiansky, *Battle of Wits: The Complete Story of Codebreaking in World War II*, London 2000, 29–30

26 Beesly, *Room 40*, 25; H Bonatz, *Die Deutsche Marine-Funkaufklaerung 1914–1945*, Darmstadt 1970

27 In Japan, multi-stage telecommunications switches were used instead of rotor wheels in cipher machines; these effectively performed the same function.

28 Kahn, *Codebreakers*, 420–1

29 HW25/8, Enigma marketing material

30 H Bonatz, *Deutsche Marine Funkaufklaerung*, 87

Chapter two – Codes and Ciphers

1 ADM 51/2462

2 ADM 1/414

3 Grimble, *The Sea Wolf: The Life of Admiral Cochrane*, Edinburgh 2000, 81.

4 J Elting, *Swords around a Throne: Napoleon's Grand Armée*, London 1997, 104–5

5 In most countries the electric telegraph soon led to the demise of the visual telegraph, although it endured longest, and in state service, in France, the country of its invention, being used until the 1850s.

6 S Maffeo, *Most Secret and Confidential: Intelligence in the Age of Nelson*, London 2000, 69

7 F B Wixon, *Codes, Ciphers and Other Cryptic Clandestine Communications*, New York 2000, 410, 431

Notes

8 D Kahn, *Codebreakers: The Comprehensive History of Secret Communication from Ancient Times to the Internet*, 2nd edn, New York 1996, 741–2

9 In this sense, the gap between the visual telegraph and the electric telegraph using Morse detected via a sounder is somewhat less dramatic than it seems in that both depend on human recognition of signals.

10 G Siemens, *History of the House of Siemens*, Vol 1, *The Era of Free Enterprise*, Munich 1957, 252–6; Baudot developed the five-unit code idea from a technique used by two German scientists, Carl Gauss and Wilhelm Weber, who worked on an electric telegraph system in 1833, J Freebody, *Telegraphy*, London 1958, 7–8; K Beauchamp, *History of Telegraphy*, London 2001, 395–9

11 Siemens, *House of Siemens*, Vol 1, 252

12 POEEJ, Vol 49 Part 3, October 1956, 170. Baud rate is not necessarily identical with digital bit rate; above about 50 Baud/bits-per-second, they tend to diverge as transmission/modulation techniques are used that allow more than one code item to be transmitted by a single system signal, so that the unit of modulation need not change for every bit.

13 Two terminological points: first, to distinguish between two different uses of the word space throughout the following chapters, 'space' will signify one possible state of the signal units in the Baudot code, and 'SPACE' will signify a gap between characters, usually, of course, but not always, between two words; second, the Enigma machine dealt only with the letters of the alphabet, but the shift function of the Baudot code allows for 'figures', i.e. numerals, punctuation marks and machine instructions – thus the use of the generic term 'characters' rather than 'letters'.

14 In fact, the German wireless teleprinter system that forms the core of the Colossus story required two separate sets of teleprinters and cipher machines at each end, one set at each end for transmission and one for reception.

15 The top row of the teleprinter keyboard, 'Q', 'W', 'E', etc., was shared with the numerals '1', '2', '3' and so on; the lower rows, 'A', 'S', 'D', etc., and 'Y', 'X', 'C', etc., are shared with punctuation marks, etc., for example, 'M' is shared with '.' (full stop) and 'N' with ',' (comma). Note that there is a reversal of the positioning of 'Y' and 'Z' on German- and English-language keyboards.

16 Freebody, *Telegraphy*, 7–8

17 Like many technological definitions, the descriptions of codes and ciphers as, respectively, fixed and changing means of encoding/enciphering, applies only to the most characteristic codes or ciphers. As one moves towards the edges, the definitions become hazier and need to be surrounded by qualifications.

18 WO 6/69/8, Newcastle to Raglan, 8/6/1854

19 D Swade, *The Cogwheel Brain: Charles Babbage and the Quest to Build the First Computer*, London 2000, 182–3

20 Kahn, *Codebreakers*, 191, 230–6

21 Both the American Civil War and the Franco-Prussian War had featured the tapping of telegraph lines and codebreaking. But it was the Russo-Japanese war of 1904/05 that saw the first real use of telegraph and radio communications as weapons, just as the conflict prefigured the massed artillery, machine-gun and trench system of the First World War. Japanese interception of Russian naval radio transmissions in plain language led directly to the defeat of Russia's fleet at Tsushina, and defeat in the war led to the 1905 revolution, itself a precursor of the revolutions of 1917.

22 Kahn, *Codebreakers*, 401

23 H Cragon, *From Fish to Colossus: How the German Lorenz Cipher was Broken at Bletchley Park*, Dallas Texas 2003

24 D Davies, *The Early Models of the Siemens and Halske T52 Cipher Machine*, Cryptologia, Vol 7, No 3, July 1983, pp 235–6; D Davies, *New Information on the History of the Siemens and Halske T52 Cipher Machines*, Cryptologia, Vol 18, No 2, April 1984

25 D Davies, *The Lorenz Cipher Machine*, Cryptologia, Vol 19, No 1, January 1995, pp 39–41

26 W Mache, *Geheimschreiber*, Cryptolgia, Vol 10, No 4, October 1986. The Germany Navy originally referred to the T52 as the Geheimfernschreib-maschine (secret teleprinter). Later, it was referred to as the Geheimzusatz der Siemens Fernshreibmaschine (secret attachment of the Siemens teleprinter), and by the Luftwaffe as the Schluesselzusatz der Siemens-Fernschreibmaschine (cipher attachment of the Siemens teleprinter). Another naval name was the Schluesselfernschribermaschine (cipher teleprinter), in abbreviations, SFM. Other secret writing machines were reported to be made by Olivetti and by Dr Rudolf Hell (who was also inventor of the 'Hellschreiber', which was not a cipher device but a coding technique for transmitting telegraphy signals – see Chapter eight); these machines were referred to as the Olivetti-Geheimschreiber and the Hell-Geheimschreiber. However, despite the intricacies of these names and the various models, British intercepts show that the German armed forces referred to all these machines as Geheimschreiber.

27 However, there was no reason why an on-line Enigma machine could not be developed, and, indeed, the German armed forces did use such a machine albeit not widely, and the British developed an Enigma-type machine that worked with a teleprinter, the Type X. The distinction between the Geheimschreiber and the Enigma is in the way they were deployed, not in design principle.

Notes

Chapter three – Between the Wars

1 G Siemens, *History of the House of Siemens*, Vol 2, *The Era of the World Wars*, Munich 1957, 24

2 Siemens, *House of Siemens*, Vol 2, 25–7

3 D Aldcroft, *From Versailles to Wall Street 1919–1929* (Vol 3 of W Fischer (ed), *History of the World Economy in the Twentieth Century*), London 1977, 209

4 Siemens, *House of Siemens*, Vol 2; S von Weiher & H Goetzeler, *Weg und Wirken der Siemens-Wirke im Fortschritt der Elektrotecknik 1847–1972*, Munich 1972; F C Delius, *Unsere Siemens-Welt: Eine Festschrift zum 125 jaehrigen Bestehen des Hauses S.*, Berlin 1976

5 Siemens, *House of Siemens*, Vol 2, 165–74

6 K Wildhagen (ed), *Erich Fellgiebel, Meister operativer Nachrichtenverbindungen: Ein Beitrag zur Geschichte der Nachrichtentruppe*, Hannover 1970; K Macksey, *The Searchers: Radio Intercept in Two World Wars*, London 2003, 53–4

7 K-A Muegge, *Die operativen Fernmeldverbindungen des deutsche Heeres 1939*, in Wildhagen, *Fellgiebel*, 42

8 H Guderian, *Panzer Leader*, London 1952

9 K-A Muegge, *Fernmeldverbindungen*, 54

10 M van Creveld, *Command in War*, Cambridge Mass, 1985, 192–3

11 I am grateful to Andrew Emmerson for pointing out to me the English term 'transposition' for the technique used for the German Drehkreuzachse system.

12 Air Ministry, *The Rise and Fall of the German Air Force 1933–1945*, originally written in 1948 and published by the National Archives (PRO), London 2001, 40–1

13 Air Ministry, *Rise and Fall*, 395

14 Wildhagen, *Fellgiebel*, 27

15 Wildhagen, *Fellgiebel*, 22–3

16 Muegge, *Fernmeldverbindungen*, 54

17 HW3/16, 'A brief history of events relating to the growth of the "Y" Service'. This document was written by Kenworthy just before his retirement in 1957. 'Y' Service was the wireless interception service of GC&CS and the armed services.

18 The main requirement, apart from accurate deflection of the needle, was for the paper tape to be passed through the inking point at a constant speed as signals sometimes had to be measured with a ruler.

19 Special Branch is the name used for the sections of the British police that handle political and subversive activities.

20 M Smith, *The Emperor's Codes: Bletchley Park and the Breaking of Japan's Secret Ciphers*, London 2001, 64–8

21 HW3/81, 3/1/32
22 HW3/81, 3/1/32
23 For the relationship between the Metropolitan Police and the Foreign Office, HW3/16; HW3/79; HW3/80 and HW3/81
24 HW3/80, 17/11/37
25 HW3/80, 23/10/37
26 HW3/81, October 1939
27 HW3/163, 'The interception of German teleprinter communications by Foreign Office Station, Knockholt', document written by Kenworthy in 1946

Chapter four – Wireless War Two

1 R Overy & A Wheatcroft, *Road to War*, London 1999, 203
2 J Lukacs, *Five Days in London: May 1940*, London 1999, 2; J Lukacs, *The Duel: Hitler versus Churchill, 10 May – 31 July 1940*, London 1990, 40–5
3 HW11/2
4 HW11/19
5 HW11/19
6 S Bungay, *Most Dangerous Enemy: A History of the Battle of Britain*, London 2000, 391
7 R Overy, *The Air War, 1939–1945*, London 1980, 32
8 M Postan, *British War Production*, London 1975, 360
9 BISWW, I, 176–7
10 BISWW, I, 177
11 R Overy, *Air War*, 22–3
12 Hitler also underestimated British determination to pursue the war. A year later (see Chapter five) he would seriously underestimate the strength of the Soviet Union, with dire consequences. These gross errors are all the more ironic given that 'Much that was successful in Hitler's career was due to his opponents' underestimation of his abilities', J Lukacs, *The Hitler of History: Hitler's Biographers on Trial*, New York 1997, 134
13 R Overy, *War and Economy in the Third Reich*, Oxford 2002, 175–256
14 R Bennett, *Behind the Battle: Intelligence in the War with Germany 1939–1945*, London 1999, 3
15 Bennett, *Behind the Battle*, 38–45
16 HW14/147
17 D Stafford, *Churchill and Secret Service*, London 1997, 2–3
18 HW1/155
19 G Welchman, *The Hut Six Story: Breaking the Enigma Codes*, Shropshire 2000, 127
20 HW14/147
21 HW13/81, 7/1/42 – The appearance of Treasury control was still needed. On 7 January 1942, RN Hind Hopkins of the Treasury wrote to F Ashton-

Gwatkin of the Foreign Office regarding a request to transfer a single police officer, Sergeant Janes of the Metropolitan Police, to the Foreign Office. 'I have laid before the Lords Commissioners of His Majesty's Treasury [your letter] and subsequent semi-official correspondence regarding the employment of certain Metropolitan Police officers on wireless interception work on behalf of the Foreign Office. In reply I am to request you to inform the Secretary of State for Foreign Affairs that My Lords sanction the charge to the Foreign Office of the expenditure involved by the employment of Station Sergeant Janes, the senior operator at Denmark Hill, on special work at West Wickham.' Not one of the more earth-shattering decisions of the war, but no doubt Messrs Ashton-Gwatkin and Hind Hopkins felt that they were making a vital contribution to the war effort.

Chapter five – A Window on a War

1 M van Creveld, *Technology and War: From 2000 B.C. to the Present*, London 1991; M van Creveld, *Command in War*, London 1985, 103–47

2 M Howard, *The Franco-Prussian War: The German Invasion of France, 1870–1871*, London 1961, 212

3 G Wawro, *The Austro-Prussian War: Austria's War with Prussia and Italy in 1866*, London 1996, 283

4 HW11/3 The volumes making up this history form the HW11 series files held at the PRO; some material from the volumes has been published in the multi-volume official history, *British Intelligence in the Second World War: Its Influence on Strategy and Operations (BISWW)*.

5 HW11/3

6 I Kershaw, *Hitler*, Vol 2, *Nemesis 1936–1939*, London 2000, 368

7 I Krumpelt, *Das Material und die Kriegfuehrung*, Frankfurt A/M 1968; R Overy, *Russia's War: A History of the Soviet War Effort, 1941–1945*, London 1998

8 *BISWW*, Vol 3 Part 1, 145–6

9 K Wildhagen (ed), *Erich Fellgiebel, Meister operativer Nachrichtenverbindungen: Ein Beitrag zur Geschichte der Nachrichtentruppe*, Hannover 1970, 44, 81–2

10 W Bodemann, *Mitarbeiter von General Fellgiebel bei der in 7 und bei Chef HNW*, in Wildhagen, *Fellgiebel*, 242–5

11 A Praun, *Erich Fellgiebel, der Meister operativer Nachrichten-Verbindungen*, in Wildhagen, *Fellgiebel*, 18–34

12 K-H Muegge, *Die operativer Fernmeldverbindungen des deutsche Heeres 1939*, in Wildhagen, *Fellbiebel*, 67

13 Muegge, *Fernmeldverbindungen*, 87. Muegge says that the Geheimschreiber was not widely available at the time of the Polish invasion.

14 J Keegan, *Six Armies in Normandy: From D-Day to the Liberation of Paris*, London 1982, 243

15 HW14/46

16 The sort of sounds described will be familiar today to anyone who uses a tone phone to 'dial' the numbers to make a telephone call, or who answers a phone when it rings only to hear a wailing fax device or modem trying to talk to what it thinks is a similar machine.

17 HW14/14, 8/4/41

18 HW14/16, 23/6/41

19 H Cragon, *From Fish to Colossus: How the German Lorenz Cipher was broken at Bletchley Park*, Dallas, Texas, 2003, 22. Cragon cites the name of the paper, which is held in the US National Archives, NARA RG457, Box 185, G Morgan, 'Theory and Analysis of a Letter-Subtractor Machine', unknown date. It dealt with a letter-subtractor system based on a twenty-six-letter code rather than the Baudot code. I have not seen a copy of this paper.

20 HW14/16, 23/6/41

21 HW14/15, 13/5/41

22 HW14/17, 1/7/41

23 HW14/17, 1/7/41

24 HW3/163, 'The interception of German teleprinter communications by Foreign Office Station, Knockholt' by Harold Kenworthy, March 1946

25 HW14/36; HW14/34

26 HW14/26

27 W Churchill, *The Second World War*, Abridged edition, London 1959, 447–9

28 J Lukacs, *The Hitler of History: Hitler's Biographers on Trial*, New York 1997, 150; I Kershaw, *Hitler*, Vol 2, 301–8

29 R Moseley, *Mussolini's Shadow: the Double Life of Count Galeazzo Ciano*, London 1999, 129

30 G Gordetsksy, *Grand Delusion: Stalin and the German Invasion of Russia*, London 1999, 172

31 R Overy, *Russia's War*, 94–5

32 I Kershaw, *Hitler*, Vol 2, 447

33 R-D Mueller and G Ueberschaer, *Hitler's War*, 88–94; M van Creveld, *Supplying War: Logistics from Wallenstein to Patton*, Cambridge 1977, chapter 5; B Wenger (ed), *Zwei Wege nach Moskau: Vom Hitler-Stalin Pakt zum 'Unternehmen Barbarossa'*, Munich 1991; J Erickson, *The Road to Stalingrad: Stalin's War with Germany*, Vol 1, London 1985; E Wagner (ed), *Der Generalquartiermeister: Briefe und Tagebuchaufzeichnungen des Generalquartiermeisters des Heeres General der Artillerie Eduard Wagner*, Munich 1963; I Krumpelt, *Das Material und die Kriegfuehrung*, Frankfurt/M 1968

Notes

34 D Glantz & J House, *When Titans Clashed: How the Red Army Stopped Hitler*, Edinburgh 2000, 61

35 I Megargee, *Inside Hitler's High Command*, Kansas 2000, 133

36 R-D Mueller & G Ueberschaer, *Hitler's War*, 103–4

37 G Wawro, *The Austro-Prussian War: Austria's War with Prussia and Italy in 1866*, Cambridge 1996, 19

38 Kershaw, *Hitler*, Vol 2, 283

39 B Liddel Hart, *History of the Second World War*, London 1970, 157

40 L Grenkevich, *The Soviet Partisan Movement, 1941–1944*, London 1999, 95–7, 153–214

41 Grenkevich, *The Soviet Partisan Movement*, 227–8

42 HW14/35, 21/4/42

Chapter six – NoMo

1 M Urban, *The Man Who Broke Napoleon's Codes*, London 2001

2 HW14/37, 12/5/42

3 It took time and much debate before the role of traffic analysis was properly understood at GC&CS. See G Welchman, *The Hut Six Story: Breaking the Enigma Codes*, Shropshire 2000. The HW 13 and 14 series files contain numerous reports on traffic analysis. However, despite this, its role was only belatedly appreciated for Fish. (See Chapter twenty-one.)

4 HW14/36; HW14/34

5 G Gluender, *Wireless and 'Geheimschreiber' Operator in the War, 1941–1945*, Cryptologia, Vol 26, No 2, April 2002, 81–96. Some British sources suggest that the name was derived from the shape of the aerial, but no German sources are cited to support this interpretation.

6 HW14/36; HW14/37

7 HW14/155, 10/5/42. An extraordinary choice given its closeness to the German codename, as was the later Fish-related codename series assigned to versions of the Geheimschreiber (Tunny, Sturgeon, Thrasher) and wireless links (Codfish, Octopus, etc.). The codenames should not have reflected the original source in any way.

8 HW14/45

9 HW14/42

10 HW14/36; HW14/35

11 GRT, 4–5

12 HW14/34

13 HW14/36

14 HW14/22

15 HW14/36

Chapter seven – 'If the Wind Meets It'

1 *The Mabinogion*, Everyman Edition. The Coroniaid were traditionally fairies or spirits.

2 However, these (binary) digital signals were transmitted by analogue signalling techniques.

3 It is possible to use various techniques to indicate more than one signalling unit in a signalling phase, so Baud rate, the rate of change of signalling, and bit rate, i.e. the number of message units transmitted per second, are not necessarily identical.

4 HW14/42

5 Freebody, *Telegraphy*, 2, 14, 17, 514

6 HW14/42

7 Variable-length codes are more efficient in terms of number of code signals needed for an average message, but machine telegraphy involved ensuring machines worked in step and quite possibly shared transmission capacity in multiplex mode. These factors also have to be taken into account in defining the most practically efficient code form. Similarly, after the war when the computer was in development, mathematicians established that tertiary or base-3 coding was slightly more efficient for use in computers than binary or base-2 (other bases were less efficient, especially decimal or base-10). But, despite its marginally greater efficiency, tertiary has not made any real impact on physical computer design (despite some attempts, for example, in the Soviet Union in the 1960s and 1970s, where three-way electronics were developed for tertiary computers). This is because the enormous advantage of manufacturing and using two-way, solid-state devices outweighs the small mathematical benefit of three-way techniques.

8 I am indebted to Brian Oakley for details of this story. The Post Office was asked if the exchange could be attached to the national telephone network but permission was refused, so it was connected without official approval, and apparently without the Post Office ever being aware of the illegal activities. There is considerable confusion over the spelling of Wynn Williams's name; it often appears as Wynne-Williams in Bletchley Park documents and post-war accounts.

9 In Germany before and during the Second World War, Konrad Zuse, a young engineer, alighted on binary digital techniques for a series of computing machines that he built. He arranged for a friend to recover Liebniz's writings on binary for him when he calculated that a binary system would suit his needs best, K Zuse, *Der Computer – Mein Lebenswerk*, Berlin 1990, 33

10 A Hodges, *Alan Turing: The Enigma*, London 1983, 138–40

11 The key to Reeves's invention was his idea for regenerating the pulses without the signal becoming degenerated by increased noise, as happens

with analogue amplification. The idea of digitalizing speech by periodic sampling had already been proposed but, using analogue amplification, corrupted signals would have become too great a problem. Reeves's system samples speech 8,000 times a second and coded the value in eight binary bits (originally 8,000 times a second and five bits). This equals 64,000 bits per second (8x8,000), or 64Kbps in modern terms, and is the standard unit of modern digital telecommunications lines, such as ISDN (Integrated Services Digital Network), and the building block for core network lines in Europe. The US equivalent was designed around seven bits with the same number of samples, equalling 56,000 (56Kbps), the modern US digital standard. These values are also reflected in the standard maximum modem speed available over dial-up connections. Pulse code modulation is now being challenged by 'packetized' voice transmission coding technology (for example, 'voice over internet protocol', VOIP), which employs a different form of digital transmission (using fewer bits due to improved techniques) and a different form of switching ('packet' as opposed to 'circuit' switching).

12 P Young, *Power of Speech: A History of Standard Telephone and Cables 1883–1983*, London 1983, 75–6
13 Quoted in, J Bray, *The Communications Miracle: The Telecommunications Pioneers from Morse to the Information Highway*, London 1995, 206–7
14 Bray, *Communications Miracle*, 200–1
15 HW13/208, US report on British 'Y' Service, August 1942
16 HW14/42
17 HW14/34; HW14/36
18 HW14/35
19 HW14/35
20 HW14/42

Chapter eight – Knockholt
1 HW14/56
2 HW3/163, Report entitled, 'The interception of German Teleprinter Communications by Foreign Office Station, Knockholt', by Harold Kenworthy, March 1946
3 HW14/56, 23/10/42
4 HW14/56, 3/10/42
5 HW14/34; HW14/35; HW14/56
6 HW3/163
7 HW14/56
8 HW14/56
9 HW14/61; HW14/62
10 HW14/59, 22–11–42

11 HW14/63

12 HW14/66, 1/2/43

13 HW14/67, 14/2/43

14 HW14/63

15 HW14/67, 1/2/43

16 HW14/60; HW14/61; HW14/62; HW14/63; HW14/64

17 HW14/36

18 HW14/21, 16/10/41

Chapter nine – 'HQIBPEXEZMUG'

1 HW14/42; HW14/44

2 Tiltman's Military Section had been charged, along with the Research Section under Gerry Morgan, with trying to break the Geheimschreiber.

3 HW14/26, 7/1/42

4 HW14/67, 18/2/43

5 A Stripp, *Codebreaker in the Far East: How Britain Cracked Japan's Top Secret Military Codes*, Oxford 1995, 139–41

6 M Smith, *Station X: The Codebreakers or Bletchley Park*, London 1998, 77

7 HW25/4 and HW25/5, *The General Report on Tunny*, 'GRT'. This chapter draws in particular on chapter 41 of the report, 'The First Break', pp 297–303. GRT is the source of all quotes in this chapter that are not given specific references. See Further Reading for details of this document.

8 HW14/47, 2/6/42

9 HW14/24, 12/12/41

10 HW14/46, 29/5/42

11 S Wylie, *Breaking Tunny and the birth of Colossus*, in M Smith & R Erskine, *Action This Day*, London 2001, 323

12 Smith, *Station X*, 144

13 W Tutte, *Fish and I*, University of Waterloo, New Zealand, 16 June 1998

14 Tutte, *Fish and I*

15 Tutte, *Fish and I*

16 It does not matter whether the two key streams act consecutively on the plain-language character, or whether they are combined before being applied to the plain character.

17 HW14/50, 25/8/42

18 R Churchhouse, *Codes and Ciphers: Julius Caesar, the Enigma and the Internet*, Cambridge 2002, 158–9

Chapter ten – Fishing the Depths

1 C McKay & B Beckman, *Swedish Signal Intelligence 1900–1945*, London 2003, 133

2 McKay & Beckman, *Swedish Signal Intelligence*, 167

Notes

3 HW14/22, 15/11/41

4 HW14/25, 8/12/41, 21/12/41

5 See: www.nsa.gov/docs/venona/docs/Apr41/apr41.htm (Report from Baron)

6 This section draws heavily on *General Report on Tunny*, chapter 42, 'Early Hand Methods', pp 304–12 and chapter 43, 'Testery Methods 1941–1944', pp 313–19, and chapter 44, 'Statistical Hand Methods', pp 320–4

7 GRT, 304

8 D Michie, *Colossus and the Breaking of the Wartime 'Fish' Codes*, Cryptologia, Vol 26, No 1, January 2002, 18

9 M Smith, *Station X*, 146

10 GRT, 305

11 GRT, 306

12 GRT, 307

13 W Tutte, *Fish and I*, University of Waterloo, New Zealand, 19 June 1998

14 GRT, 258

15 R Jenkins, *Churchill*, London 2001, 632

16 Smith, *Station X*, 153

17 Smith, *Station X*, 153–4

18 HW50/63

19 GRT, 312

20 Michie, Cryptologia, Vol 26, No 1, January 2002, 22

21 GRT, 320

22 I am indebted to Brain Oakley for pointing out this technique to me.

23 GRT, 320

24 HW50/63

25 HW13/53, 16/8/43 (CX/MSS/S.70)

26 GRT, 320

27 GRT, 323

28 Michie, Cryptologia, Vol 26, No 1, January 2002, 37

Chapter eleven – Herring and the Cat's Whiskers

1 N Hamilton, *The Full Monty*, Vol 1, *Montgomery of Alamein 1887–1942*, London 2001, 533

2 Hamilton, *Full Monty*, 584

3 Hamilton, *Full Monty*, 661

4 Hamilton, *Full Monty*, 606–7

5 P Calvocoressi & G Wint: *Total War: Causes and Courses of the Second World War*, London 1972, 355. Calvocoressi was at Bletchley Park during the war. The book was published before the release of information about Ultra. He says (p 362) that Montgomery 'had certain advantages denied to his predecessors... [including] Last but not least, British intelligence was

giving British field commanders unparalleled assistance... It is one of Montgomery's claims to fame that he was extraordinarily quick to weigh up, appreciate and act upon intelligence received, so that the campaigns which he fought provide an excellent illustration of generalship and intelligence in partnership in action.' Enigma intelligence was, in fact, available to Montgomery's predecessors. The comment is interestingly worded, given that we now know just what this 'unparalleled' intelligence was.

6 B Liddell Hart, *History of the Second World War*, London 1970, 299

7 I Hernon, *Britain's Forgotten Wars: Colonial Campaigns of the 19th Century*, London 2003 provides a good selection of examples.

8 H Strachan, *European Armies and the Conduct of War*, London 1983, 55

9 P Ziegler, *Omdurman*, London 1973; J Pollock, *Kitchener*, London 2001

10 HW50/63, 20/8/45

11 HW50/63, 20/8/45

12 *BISWW*, Vol 2, 582–609

13 HW50/63, 20/8/45

14 A Moorehead, *Desert War: The North African Campaign 1940–1943*, London 2002, 626–30

15 Playfair et al, *History of the Second World War: The Mediterranean and Middle East*, Vol 4, *The Destruction of Axis Forces in Africa*, London 1966, 457–9

16 Moorehead, *Desert War*, 630

17 *BISWW*, Vol 1, vii. Access for the authors of the official history to secret files required their agreement that the secret services would have a say over what could be published. The authors state, 'The need to apply this restriction to the published history has at no point impeded our analysis of the state of intelligence and of its impact, and it has in no way affected our conclusions. It has, however, dictated the system we have adopted when giving references to our sources... It would have served no useful purpose to give precise references to the domestic files of the intelligence-gathering bodies, which are unlikely ever to be opened. We have been permitted – indeed, encouraged – to make use of these files in our text and we have done so on a generous scale, but in their case our text must be accepted as being the only evidence of their contents that can be made public.' The provision of such references would, in fact, have served a very useful purpose for historians, especially as some of the then secret documents have now been released.

18 HW14/77, 25/5/43

19 HW14/77, 26/5/43

20 HW14/77, 26/5/43

21 HW14/79, 14/6/43

22 HW14/84, 20/8/43

Notes

23 HW14/84, 18/9/43; the report continues: 'Part two – What is true of 10's is also true of OC's [commando troops]. This will be elaborated in final report... No doubt in my mind that navy cooperates and will cooperate even more provided army can be induced to see need for our kind of document to be handled with special safeguards and priorities. Briefly, they consider that commando three nought was necessary and efficient but that it is now too small, and that there is no need of a fighting body to collect material of use of B[letchley] P[ark]. Thus, their views agree with Wiseman's and others. Basic principles are... complete interservice understanding as regards transport... [of captured] high speed comms [equipment] by W/T and aircraft.'

24 HW3/164

25 HW13/216

26 HW13/214

27 Fish Notes, # 46, 12/6/44. This report and others in the series can be seen at www.codesandciphers.co.uk.

28 *BISWW*, Vol 1, viii

29 HW14/73, 11/4/43

Chapter twelve – 'Hier ist so traurig'

1 HW14/58, 8/11/42

2 HW14/59, 29/11/42

3 HW11/3; HW13/216, 5/10/43

4 These examples of Codfish messages come from HW13/196.

5 G Gluender, *Wireless and 'Geheimschreiber' Operator in the War, 1941–1945*, Cryptolgia, Vol 26, No 2, April 2002, 86

6 H Heiber & D Glantz, *Hitler and his Generals: Military Conferences 1942–1945*, London 2002, 777

7 R-D Mueller & G Ueberschaar, *Hitler's War in the East: A Critical Assessment*, Oxford 2002, 126

8 A Beevor, *Stalingrad: The Fateful Siege 1942–1943*, London 1998, 398–400

9 U Herbert, *Hitler's Foreign Workers: Enforced Foreign Labour in Germany under the Third Reich*, Cambridge 1997, 256–64

10 *BISWW*, Vol 2, 624

11 HW13/193 The entire text of this appreciation has also been reproduced as an appendix in *BISWW*, II, 764–5. The Ultra reference number was CX/MSS/2499/T14; also referred to, regarding the delay, in CX/MSS/S.62, 7/6/43. These different references have different translations, though with similar meanings, of the original German-language message (which, as with other intercepts, has not been released, and has probably been destroyed).

12 R Cross, *The Battle of Kursk: Operation Citadel*, London 2002, 92–5 (originally published as *Citadel: The Battle of Kursk*, 1993)

13 D Glantz, *The Role of Intelligence in Soviet Military Strategy in World War II*, Novato California 1990, 108

14 M Smith, *Station X: The Codebreakers of Bletchley Park*, London 1998, 153–4

15 *BISWW*, Vol 3, part 1, 18–19

16 G Megargee, *Inside Hitler's High Command*, Kansas 2000, 157

17 K-A Muegge, *Die operativen Fernmeldverbindungen des Deutschen Heeres 1939*, in K Wildman, *Erich Fellgiebel: Meister operativer Nachrichtenverbindungen, Ein Beitrag zur Geschichte der Nachrichtentruppe*, Hannover 1970, 43

18 HW13/53 (CX/MSS/S.58)

19 A Hezlet, *The Electron and Sea Power*, London 1975, 7

20 T Royle, *Crimea: The Great Crimean War 1854–1856*, London 1999, 256

21 HW13/193, 15/12/43

22 Heiber & Glantz, *Hitler and his Generals*, 341, 27/12/43

23 Gluender, *'Geheimschreiber' Operator*, Cryptologia, Vol 26, No 2, 81–96

24 For examples of the sort of discussion had by Hitler and his general staff, see Heibner & Glantz, *Hitler and his Generals*, 119–31: May 1943, 'In view of this situation, I consider it necessary to take precautions against a possible attack on the Peloponnesian Peninsula… So we have to move a panzer division there, whether we like it or not. The only question is where do we bring it from… The Italians can't be relied upon. On the other hand, I'm convinced that relatively few forces would be required if some sort of mess were to develop in Italy… I have come to the conclusion that the Balkans are an even greater threat to us than Italy… I would still reconsider whether we can make do in Sicily without any additional troops. I hope to keep the 16th [Panzer Division] in Italy and move others to Sardinia. This requires careful consideration… I'm always afraid of having too much on my plate.'

25 J Fest, *Speer: The Final Verdict*, London 2001, 163–72

26 HW13/193, 10/10/43 (CX/MSS/S76)

27 HW13/53, 25/5/43 (CX/MSS/8.60)

28 HW13/53, 30/8/43 (CX/MSS/S.73)

29 HW13/52, 4/11/42 (CX/MSS/S30)

30 HW41/155, 10/6/43

31 HW13/213, 9/10/43

32 HW13/213, 7/9/43

33 HW13/53,16/8/43 (CX/MSS/S.70)

Chapter thirteen – Making the Difference

1 I Kershaw, *Hitler*, Vol 2, *1936–1945, Nemesis*, London 2000, 527

2 H Heibland & D Glantz, *Hitler and his Generals: Military Conferences 1942–1945*, London 2002, 418

3 HW5/24 & HW5/25 – *General Report on Tunny*. Except where other sources are cited, all the quotations in this chapter come from this report, especially from Chapter 12, 'Cryptographic Aspects', Chapter 13, 'Machines' and Chapter 15, 'Organisation'. See Further Reading for more information about the report and its availability.

4 W Tutte, *Fish & I*, University of Waterloo, New Zealand, 19 June 1998

5 It is important to appreciate the role of the shift function in order to understand the otherwise confusing use of the characters 3, 5, 8, 9, M, N and / in this section. In the plain-language and cipher texts processed by the Geheimschreiber they are used as arbitrary signs in the basic teleprinter code representing machine commands such as shift and do not represent the characters 3, 5, 8, 9, or /. In letters-shift, M and N do represent m and n, but in figures-shift they represent full stop and comma.

6 This transparency also exists at the unit level and this feature was exploited in Tutte's 'double-delta' technique which depended on the statistical likelihood of a dot or a cross in both units 1 and 2 of a 'delta plain' of a message.

7 H Cragon, *From Fish to Colossus: How the German Lorenz Cipher was Broken at Bletchley Park*, Dallas 2003, 65

8 Tutte, *Fish and I*

Chapter fourteen – The Robinson Family

1 HW14/87, 10/9/43, 'Report on "Machine Co-ordination and Development Section"... to deal with all matters arising from the development of new machinery as an aid to Cryptography [under Gordon Welchman]... Mr Welchman should be consulted on all questions of machine aids (other than the BTM machines in Mr Freeborn's Section). He will be responsible to me [Travis] for their construction and supply.' A committee consisting of Welchman, Turing, Newman, Freeborn, Wynn-Williams and Major Morgan was to meet monthly.

2 HW14/66 1/2/43

3 H Strachan, *The First World War*, Vol 1, *To Arms*, Oxford 2001, 108

4 Max Newman Papers, Box 1, Folder 1, 26/2/1918 (Hermann Neumann born 9/9/1864 at Bromberg, died 5/10/1926)

5 Max Newman Papers, Box 1, Folder 1, September 1923

6 Max Newman Papers, Box 3, Folder 1, 13/5/42

7 Max Newman Papers, Box 3, Folder 1, 24/5/42; 1/6/42; 15/7/42; 26/7/42; 15/8/42

8 HW14/139, 2/9/42

9 Randell, *Colossus*, 12

10 GRT 276

11 HW14/139 1/2/43. GRT, 28, gives June 1943 as the date for the setting up of the Machine Section, while GRT 318 gives the date as July 1943.

12 GRT, 28

13 HW14/62, 26/12/42

14 GRT, 33

15 M Bragg, *RDF1: The Location of Aircraft by Radio Methods 1939–1945*, Paisley 2002, 224

16 HW14/25, 28/10/41; 25/12/41. 'Dr Wynne Williams suggests that the TRE at Swanage is the best place for carrying on further investigation and possibly for constructing prototype machines. If you are in agreement with this view, it is necessary to obtain further approval, and who would bear the cost? You will of course appreciate the need for absolute secrecy.'

17 The section on the Robinson technical details draws on three main sources: *The General Report on Tunny*, GRT (see Further Reading); B Randell, *Colossus* (see Further Reading) 1974; and T Sale, *The Rebuilding of Heath Robinson* (see www.codesandciphers.co.uk).

18 HW14/70, 12/3/43

19 J Lee, *Computer Pioneers*, Washington DC, 1995, 490

20 A C Chamberlin, *Reminiscences of Bletchley Park*. My thanks to John Chamberlain for supplying me with a copy of his father's handwritten account of his days as a cryptographer and of wartime colleagues.

21 HW14/77, 29/5/43

22 GRT 33. There were two limitations in the logical design of the Robinsons. First, a pattern could not be extended, so it was necessary to contract the de-Chi. This wasted evidence but was quite feasible if no limitation was in use on the Tunny machine. Second, stepping was uniform, so to set wheels arbitrarily was laborious in the extreme, and a wheel which had been stepped had to remain at a fixed setting, so its tape had to be replaced by one of a different length (GRT 329).

23 HW14/79, 18/6/43

24 HW14/79, 18/6/43

25 Randell, *Colossus*, 17–18

26 J Good, *Enigma and Fish*, in F Hinsley and A Stripp (eds), *Codebreakers: The Inside Story of Bletchley Park*, Oxford 1993, 162

27 HW14/79, 18/6/43

28 D Michie, *Colossus and the Breaking of the Wartime 'Fish' Codes*, Cryptologia, Vol 26, No 1, January 2002, 52–4

29 GRT, 34

30 GRT, 34

31 GRT, 35

32 GRT, 276

33 HW14/85, 19/8/43

34 HW43/2, *The Cryptanalytic Contribution to the War in the West*

35 Max Newman Papers, Box 3, Folder 3

Notes

Chapter fifteen – Inventing the Electronic Computing Machine

1 G Ifrah, *The Universal History of Numbers*, Vol 3, *The Computer and Information Revolution*, London 2000, 217

2 This chapter draws on four main sources: HW25/24 (*Technical Description of Colossus I*); Imperial War Museum, audio archive tape number 18332, interview with Tommy Flowers, 1998; *Annals of the History of Computing*, Vol 5, which contained several articles on Colossus; and B Randell, 'The Colossus', paper presented to International Research Conference on the History of Computing, Los Alamos Scientific Laboratory, University of California, 10–15 June 1976, also available in PRO file HW25/23; it is noteworthy that this file was retained as classified material and only opened to the public in August 2003 – twenty-seven years after it had already been published in the public domain.

3 Dollis Hill was also home to Cabinet War Rooms 2, CWR2, the back-up to the main control centre off Downing Street (today open as a museum). A third centre, CWR3, was based at Virginia Water some distance outside London. They were equipped with communications facilities, ready for immediate use in an emergency, but there was never any need to use either of the alternative control centres.

4 IWM, 18332

5 *Annals of the History of Computing*, 5/241

6 IWM, 18332

7 W Keister et al, *The Design of Switching Circuits*, Bell Laboratory Series, New York 1951, 68

8 M Davis, *The Universal Computer: The Road from Leibniz to Turing*, York 2000, 120

9 R Scarth, *Echoes From the Sky: A Story of Acoustic Defence*, Hythe 1999

10 Randell, *Colossus*, 8

11 HW62/5, 4/6/43; 8/6/43

12 HW62/5, 4/6/43; HW62/5 contains several other documents on this dispute; see also HW62/4, 4/10/42, 31/10/42, and HW14/77, 29/5/43

13 HW62/4, 4/10/42

14 HW62/5, 4/6/43

15 HW62/5, 4/6/43

16 HW62/5, 8/6/43

17 Randell, *Colossus*, 11

18 *Annals of the History of Computing*, 5/244

19 IWM, 18332

20 HW14/70, 12/3/43, 'For the more ambitious machine they now propose to use tape for the message and valves only for the fixed wheels. This does away with the main objection to their first scheme (lack of flexibility in use).

About 1,000 valves are still needed and they recognize that there will be teething troubles.'

21 Randell, *Colossus*, 20

22 Max Newman Papers, Box 3, Folder 3

23 IWM, 18332

24 HW14/77, 29/5/43

25 IWM, 18332

26 *Annals of the History of Computing*, 5/259

27 *Annals of the History of Computing*, 5/253

28 There may be an element of the 'not invented here' syndrome at work in Coombs's comments on the Wynn Williams counter. The Post Office engineers did have a tendency to denigrate the work of others.

29 *Annals of the History of Computing*, 5/254–5

30 HW25/34

31 HW25/24

32 Another very useful contemporaneous development by British valve manufacturers was a valve which was suitable for outputting a current powerful enough to operate an electro-magnetic relay. These were used for passing results of counts to the display or printer via such relays. The same valve was also used for signal transfer within Colossus.

33 *Annals of the History of Computing*, 5/247

34 *Annals of the History of Computing*, 5/259

35 IWM, 18332

36 *Annals of the History of Computing*, 5/245

37 IWM, 18332

38 The claim is made on the official caption which accompanies the set of photos of Colossus released in 1975. At the end of the war, Colossus was set up in such a way as to perform a crude conditional branching by manipulation of the input stream from the paper tape, but it was an artificial technique, not a practical one, and was not part of the basic functional architecture of Colossus. This experiment cannot be interpreted to substantiate the assertion made in the 1975 release. The assertion has, naturally enough, given its official origin, been repeated widely in accounts of Colossus. It is not clear why the claim was made in 1975.

39 *Annals of the History of Computing*, 5/239

40 *Annals of the History of Computing*, 5/245

41 HW25/24

42 IWM, 18332

43 HW62/6, 2/1/44

Chapter sixteen – 'Colossus Arrives Today'

1 It is usually claimed that Colossus was named after its arrival at Bletchley Park,

but in recently released documents it is called Colossus while still at Dollis Hill. For example, a memo from Welchman, in HW62/5 dated 7/12/43, states: 'Flowers valve engine, known as Colossus, is also nearing completion.'

2 HW14/67, 18/2/43
3 Allied merchant shipping loss figures from J Ellis, *The World War II Data Book*, London 2003, 267
4 *BISWW*, Vol 3, part 1, 75
5 HW41/155, 23/6/43
6 HW41/155, 23/6/43
7 HW13/122, 9/6/43 (CX/MSS/HF/92)
8 *BISWW*, Vol 3, part 1, 77
9 R Bosworth, *Mussolini*, London 2002, 374
10 R Bennett, *Ultra and Mediterranean Strategy, 1941–1945*, London 1989; R Bennett, *Behind the Battle: Intelligence in the War with Germany, 1939–1945*, London 1999, 70–135; R Bennett, *Intelligence Investigations: How Ultra Changed History*, London 1996, 34–51, 93–115, 129–45
11 *BISWW*, Vol 3, part 1, 177
12 Bennett, *Behind the Battle*, 211–19
13 HW14/84, 2/8/43
14 HW13/53, 16/8/43 (CX/MSS/S.70)
15 HW14/93, 13/12/43
16 HW14/93, 12/12/43; HW14/94, 20/12/43
17 HW14/84, 2/8/43
18 HW14/94, 20/12/43
19 HW14/86, 21/8/43
20 HW14/92, 24/11/43
21 HW14/84, 19/8/43
22 HW50/63
23 HW50/63
24 HW14/86, 22/8/43
25 HW14/88, 18/9/43
26 HW14/82, 28/11/43
27 HW14/96, 18/1/44
28 GRT, 329
29 GRT, 319
30 *Annals of the History of Computing*, Vol 5, No 3, July 1983
31 HW62/6, 3–4–44
32 HW62/6, 1–5–44

Chapter seventeen – Fish Dialects

1 *General Report on Tunny* (GRT), 279 (see Further Reading)
2 HW14/100, 27/3/44

3 GRT, 322–3

4 HW14/97, 7/2/44

5 J Good, *Enigma and Fish*, in F Hinsley & A Stripp (eds), *Codebreakers: The Inside Story of Bletchley Park*, Oxford 1993, 162–3

6 Wylie, *Breaking of Tunny*, 332

7 HW14/97, 4/5/44

8 There was a trade-off, however, with dottage, i.e. the number of flush pins on the motor wheel with thirty-seven pin positions. A low dottage made Chi-setting harder, but motor-setting easier, while a high dottage made Chi setting easier and motor setting harder. 'Fortunately, machine and hand methods are complementary in this respect. When dottage is high, the Psis are easy to set by hand and then the setting of the motor is a routine job.' GRT, 100

9 GRT, 63

10 GRT, 62

11 HW14/97, 4/5/44

12 HW14/97, 4/5/44

13 GRT, 80

14 The reader who wants to know more is guided to the 500-page *General Report on Tunny*, which covers in some detail this and other mathematical aspects (see Further Reading).

15 GRT, 95

16 Limitations usually required more or different processing, but some limitations allowed short rather than long runs, GRT, 104–5

17 GRT, 92

18 GRT, 17

19 GRT, 17–18

Chapter eighteen – Fish – Landing the Catch

1 That conclusion, drawn from the official history of British Intelligence, *BISWW* Vol 3 parts 1 and 2, is not accepted by everyone. For example, S Ambrose, *Eisenhower: Soldier and President*, London 2003, 111, says that 1943 'had been a year of great gains on the map. The forces under Eisenhower's command had conquered Morocco, Algeria, Tunisia, Sicily and South Italy. The strategic gains, however, had been small at best. Germany had not lost any territory that was critical to its defence. It had not been forced to reduce its divisions in France or Russia. Taken as a whole, Eisenhower's campaigns from November 1942 to December 1943 must be judged a strategic failure.' This seems to omit an important issue – would the German troops in North Africa and Italy have been kept there without Allied intervention, or would they have been used in France and/or Russia?

2 F Ruge, *Rommel in Normandy*, London 1979, 144

Notes

3 C D'Este, *Decision in Normandy: The Unwritten Story of Montgomery and the Allied Campaign*, London 1994, 86

4 HW14/98, 23–2–44; R Bennett, *Ultra in the West: The Normandy Campaign of 1944–45*, London 1979

5 *BISWW*, Vol 3, part 2, 4/5; *BISWW* Vol 5, 104–32

6 HW14/73, 16/4/43

7 H Heiber & D Glantz (eds), *Hitler and his Generals: Military Conferences 1942–1945*, London 2002, 311–14, 920

8 'Army Y' refers to the Allied wireless interception and direction-finding service that was based close to fighting army units and used to intercept low-level messages of fighting units.

9 *BISWW*, Vol 3, part 2, 19

10 HW13/217, 13/3/44

11 Fish Notes Report, 17/4/44 (see www.codesandciphers.co.uk)

12 *BISWW*, Vol 3, part 2, 53–4, 779

13 *BISWW*, Vol 5, 130/131

14 *BISWW*, Vol 3, part 2, 78. But see also R Bennett, *Ultra in the West* and *Behind the Battle: Intelligence in the War with Germany 1939–1945*, London 1999. In the first of these books, Bennett does not mention the Geheimschreiber, Fish or Colossus. However, he frequently refers to Fish decodes stating or implying that they were Enigma intercepts. He sometimes uses a non-committal phrase. For example, he says (pp 48–9) the following: 'During [the spring of 1944] the cryptographers managed to break a number of isolated days' traffic in hitherto impregnable army keys. It was so difficult to do this that they were sometimes held up for a week or more, but the effort was abundantly worthwhile. Most of the decodes quoted in this chapter were obtained in this way; they conveyed information of immense value and their lateness seldom detracted much from it.' It is clear, from the detail of the decodes, that Bennett is here referring to the decodes that we now know were the products, not of Enigma decryption, but of the Geheimschreiber. It is possible that Bennett was using carefully crafted words ('hitherto impregnable army keys') to give the impression that he was referring to Enigma keys, while not actually saying so. On page 100, Bennett says 'a transient difficulty with army keys deprived until towards the end of July of the tank returns and supply pro-formas which had been invaluable during the first few weeks [after D-Day]'. Again, this is clearly a reference to Fish material, but Bennett places it in a context which implies that it is Enigma material, although the phrasing ('army keys') does leave open the possibility that Bennett is discreetly hiding the Fish operation. However, later on in the book, referring to the period of the Germans' Ardennes offensive in late 1944, he says, 'It was therefore unfortunate that Ultra could not

immediately give clear and unequivocal answers to the questions being asked of it and only arrived at them more stutteringly than usual and with greater hesitation and delay. In the present state of public knowledge [1979], no certain reason can be assigned for this. Nevertheless, a plausible hypothesis may be advanced to explain it: small amounts of traffic in army keys were identified and intercepted (most army communications were now going by landline). Granted greater security of army signals procedure, its small quantity would normally have made this traffic unremunerative (in terms of Bombe time) or impossible to break. But the high value of the intelligence it might contain, and recent increases in the number and sophistication of the Bombes, might now render some of it at least decodable if enough Bombe-time could be spared from the regular daily tasks of breaking the Red and Light Blue... Time was found after these tasks had been accomplished, but lower priority on the Bombes and the relative clumsy cryptographic methods imposed by the paucity of material caused inescapable delays and brought a few days' keys out in the wrong time sequence. If all this is true (and, in the total absence of accessible evidence about the internal history of Hut 6, it must be stressed that it is no more than intelligent guesswork), then there is ground for thankfulness that the cryptographers were able to provide us with any information at all about major changes in OB West's dispositions than for regret that much of it was late and at first difficult to interpret.' This is clearly not careful wording, designed to hide the Fish story, but Bennett's interpretation of what he knew. He may well have been prepared to use careful phrasing to hide what was still considered to be sensitive, but it is most improbable that he would have made up an explanation that would later be shown to be incorrect. The conclusion can only be that Bennett, an intelligence officer during the war in Hut 3, never knew of the wireless teleprinter/Geheimschreiber/Fish/Colossus operation. This is an indication of just how strong were the rules about not sharing any information outside one's immediate job at Bletchley Park. At least some – and probably most – of the intelligence officers in Hut 3 who did know about Enigma were not allowed to know about Fish, although they may well have been privy to the intelligence revealed by Fish decodes. Hut 3 did have a Fish traffic analysis section. Also, in his later books, when some knowledge of Fish was publicly available, Bennett consistently downplayed the role of Fish, devoting just two paragraphs to it in an appendix in his last book, *Behind the Battle*, published in 1999. He makes a number of questionable judgements and provides a misleading picture of the contribution of the cracking of the Geheimschreiber. For example, he states 'that it was mainly used on the Russian front'. Of its decodes, he asserts 'the great bulk of them consisted of long lists of

Notes

supplies needed or sent, and the like, but important operational items were also found among them' (p 292). In addition there are lots of places where Bennett omits information about decodes being from Fish links. For example, regarding the intercept of the Fish message detailing Guderian's tour, Bennett states, Allied 'pre-invasion bombing had more urgent tasks than telephone lines, the cutting of which would compel the use of radio, although it seemed that some of the best Ultra was the consequence of raids. Cases in point were the interception of the whole programme of a tour to be made in April and May by General Guderian, Inspector-General of Panzer Troops, to the bases of all the Panzer divisions in France and to the tank training ground at Mailly-le-Camp (eighty miles west of Paris), from which much information about the strength, equipment and readiness for battle of the German armour was derived' (pp 249–52). Bennett does not attribute this message to Fish, and misleadingly suggests that it was the consequence of a bombing raid, rather than that it gave information about the effectiveness of the raid. Bennett would have had access to the official history, *BISWW*, Vol 3, part 1 & part 2 – indeed, he cites it in some places – and this convincingly demonstrates that the Fish intercepts offered considerably more than just long lists of supplies and the odd 'find'.

15 *BISWW*, Vol 3, part 2, 81
16 HW14/97, 4/5/44
17 HW14/101, 13/4/44
18 HW13/217, 13/3/44
19 B Liddell Hart, *History of the Second World War*, London 1970, 536
20 HW14/101, 13/4/44
21 HW14/103, 5/5/44
22 I Kershaw, *Hitler*, Vol 2, *1936–1945, Nemesis*, London 2000, 640
23 Ruge, *Rommel in Normandy*, 15–16
24 S Mitcham Jnr, *Retreat to the Reich: The German Defeat in France, 1944*, London 2000, 19
25 Ruge, *Rommel in Normandy*, 183
26 A Horne, *The Lonely Leader: Monty 1944–1945*, London 1994, 224
27 HW14/110, 25/8/44
28 Rectangle analysis – rectangling – was another wheel-breaking technique, initially using hand-methods.
29 Fish Notes Report, 2/7/44 (see www.codesandciphers.co.uk)
30 HW14/97, 4/5/44
31 *BISWW*, Vol 3, part 2, 777
32 HW14/97, 4/5/44
33 HW14/105, 5/6/44
34 The concentration of Colossi, Robinsons and other machines at Bletchley

Park meant that it became a worrying target. A memo reporting on the planned expansion also noted, 'It is to be borne in mind that a near miss [from a bomb] would probably throw thousands of [electro-magnetic] relays out of adjustment, and might cause subsidence, which would bend finely adjusted connecting rods, necessitating replacements and lengthy re-adjustments. After a direct hit it would take at least three months to re-start, unless one of the Colossi were near completion at Dollis Hill (but note that about one month's work would be needed after arrival here).' That suggested that a separate, back-up centre should be considered (though, as far as is known, no action was taken to set one up) – HW14/99, 12/3/44.

35 HW50/63

36 HW50/63

37 HW14/123, 7/3/45

38 Bennett, *Behind the Battle*, 165

39 P Hoffman, *History of the German Resistance, 1933–1945*, London 1977, 337

40 Suggestions by some writers that Fellgiebel was supposed to blow up the communications exchange are incorrect. The conspirators – most of whom expected to be able to reach a peace agreement with the Western Allies that would allow them to continue the war with Russia, perhaps jointly with those Allies – put considerable emphasis on making sure that communications with the fronts, especially the eastern front, were not severed. If the coup had succeeded, it would have been essential to have immediate control of an active communications network to effect the coup, not face the immediate need to repair a bomb-damaged main switching node and a loss of control. For Fellgiebel's role in the conspiracy, see P Hoffman, *History of the German Resistance, 1933–1945*; K Wildman, *Erich Fellgiebel: Meister operativer Nachrichtenverbindungen, Ein Beitrag zur Geschichte der Nachrichtren-Truppe*, Hannover 1970.

41 P Hoffman, *History of the German Resistance*, 341

42 S Mitcham Jnr, *Retreat to the Reich*, 60

43 HW13/154, July 1944

44 R-D Mueller & G Ueberschaer, *Hitler's War in the East: A Critical Assessment*, New York 2002, 131

45 R Overy, *The Dictators: Hitler's Germany, Stalin's Russia*, London 2004, 531–532

46 HW13/58, 'Hitler as seen by Source'

47 HW 41/155, 13/3/43

48 D Isby (ed), *The German Army at D-Day: Fighting the Invasion*, London 2004, 30

49 HW14/110, 25/8/44

Chapter nineteen – A Day in the Life of Fish I

1 HW 14/13, 23/3/41

2 HW14/34, 11/4/42

3 HW14/42 July 1942

4 C Wilmot, *The Struggle for Europe*, London 1952, 622

5 A Harvey, *Collision of Empires: Britain in Three World Wars, 1792–1945*, London 1992, 559

6 HW14/21, 21/10/41

7 HW3/152, 'The History of the Wrens at GCCS', Superintendent E Blagrove, 6/10/45

8 M Smith, *Station X: The Codebreakers of Bletchley Park*, London 1998, 158

9 GRT, 281

10 HW14/100, 14/3/44. A memo from Lieutenant-Colonel Wallace, who had replaced Harold Kenworthy as officer in charge of Knockholt, to the director of GC&CS, Edward Travis, from August 1944 observed, 'It was realized [earlier this year] that Knockholt, through inability to handle enough traffic, was likely to prevent us from achieving the full exploitation of Fish that our supply of [radio intercept] machinery would make possible here. Applications were made for the necessary staff and living accommodation, but with discouraging lack of success... The billeting situation for Knockholt is still serious in spite of the Hostel we have organized to accommodate ninety girls. We have pressed the Ministry of Health for help in the Sevenoaks area – so far without success largely due to the bomb-inspired evacuation of that town... If [an] appeal does not produce any result it is proposed to ask you to get action taken at a much higher level. As regards the personnel urgently required, would you be willing to make an immediate high level approach to the Ministry of Labour? We require ninety-one keyboard perforator operators to fill the establishment, but forty at once (trained, partly trained or qualified as typists) would overcome the immediate emergency', HW14/110, 22/8/44.

11 HW14/110, 22/8/44

12 HW14/103, 12/5/44: To Mr John de Grey (liaison between Wireless Co-ordination Section and Bletchley Park) from H S Wallace co-ordinator of non-Morse interception), 'Knockholt should be omitted from your programme of visits. The Director has ruled that all matters affecting FORDE and GCWS are to be dealt with by me personally; and I do not think any general visits to Knockholt are desirable at the present stage.' Whether this was connected with Kenworthy's presence, security issues and/or some other reason(s) is not clear; but see following note, which suggests very close security over non-Morse/Fish may well have been an issue.

13 HW14/121, 14/2/45, A handwritten note attached to the report, signed by a Colonel Jacob, says, 'I think this report should NOT have the distribution

inside BP which the [other] section reports and my covering letter Part I have, so I have marked it "Director only".'

14 HW14/103, 12/5/44; HW14/105, 1/6/44; HW14/112, 18/9/44; HW14/140, 18/9/44
15 HW14/121, 14/2/45
16 GRT, 281
17 HW14/92, 28/11/43
18 Jacob's report concentrated on the slip-reading and reperforating sections. On the Set Room, he observed, 'During my stay some attention was given to the organization of the set-room, particularly as regards the immediate identification of depths, but as far more slip, apparently of reasonable quality, was being delivered to the Slip-room than they could cope with, there seemed little point in going deeper into the work carried out in that department.'
19 An image of a Red Form is reproduced on page 269 of the *General Report on Tunny*.
20 GRT, 325
21 Arthur Chamberlain, *Reminiscenses of Bletchley Park*, March 1992
22 GRT, 282
23 GRT, 464
24 GRT, 284
25 GRT, 284
26 GRT, 326
27 HW14/99, 12/3/44
28 GRT, 370
29 GRT, 370
30 HW14/99, 12/3/44

Chapter twenty – A Day in the Life of Fish II
1 GRT, 327
2 HW14/103, 12/5/44
3 S Wylie, 'The Breaking of Tunny and the Birth of Colossus', in M Smith & R Erskine, *Action This Day*, London 2001, 340
4 GRT, 464–5
5 GRT, 465
6 GRT, 278
7 GRT, 279
8 Max Newman Papers, Box 3, Folder 2
9 AHC, 5/261
10 Wylie, 'The Breaking of Tunny', 339
11 GRT, 278–9
12 GRT, 326

Notes

13 F Block has now been demolished, but H Block survives as part of the Bletchley Park Museum and the room that housed Colossus 9 is currently home to a reconstruction of Colossus 2.

14 M Smith, *Station X*, 150

15 Smith, *Station X*, 150–1

16 NARA NR4628 , Special Fish Report, Box 1417

17 GRT, 102

18 Following a successful wheel-setting run, a de-Chi tape was ordered by the Tapes Registrar and returned. The tapes, a print of the de-Chi stream, and details of the Chi-settings were then sent from the Registry to Room 12 of the Testery which passed them, plus the Red Form, to Room 41 for Psi-setting and after that to Room 40 for motor wheel settings.

19 GRT, 29

20 J Good, 'Enigma and Fish', in F Hinsley & A Stripp (eds), *Codebreakers: The Inside Story of Bletchley Park*, Oxford 1993, 164–5

21 Dragon – GRT, 363–4

22 G Hayward, 'Operation Tunny', in F Hinsley & A Stripp (eds), *Codebreakers*, 183

23 HW50/63

24 HW14/116, 21/11/44; HW14/116, 26/11/44

25 Aquarius overcame a slide by going back to the stream of characters before the slide started, aligning the text to exclude the extra characters, and then defining a restart point. It worked on the de-Chi stream which was read from a paper tape. But, significantly, the tape was read only once, and was then stored in an internal memory made up of 2,000 capacitors. These had to be recycled with power every two minutes to maintain their charge – a positive charge representing a mark (1) and a negative charge a space (0). It could remember up to 218 de-Chi characters before the autopause which caused the slide and 97 characters after it. One cheap, but useful, attachment was a buzzer: 'This is provided to call assistance to avoid imminent catastrophe'. Once Aquarius had done its job, a message analysis truncated by a slide could be re-run on Colossus to draw out as much statistical evidence as possible.

26 HW14/115, 21/12/44; HW14/126, 30/4/45

27 T Watson Jr, *Father, Son and Company: My Life at IBM and Beyond*, London 1990, 112

28 E Black, *IBM and the Holocaust: The Strategic Alliance between Nazi Germany and America's Most Powerful Corporation*, London 2001, 351

29 See in particular, HW25/22 'The Use of Hollerith Machines in Bletchley Park', R Whelan. HW14/15, 12/5/41, 13/5/41; HW14/16, 18/6/41; HW14/21, 18/10/41, 23/10/41; HW14/93, 14/12/43. I am also indebted to Brian Oakley for further details of Bletchley Park's punched card

installation given at a talk to the British Computer Society, entitled 'Beyond Colossus: More Wartime Decoding Machines', Science Museum, May 2002. He suggests that one reason for greater use of punched cards in the USA before the Second World War was that Japanese 'book-codes' were more suited to punched-card processes than the European Enigma-type machines.

30 P Gannon, *Trojan Horses and National Champions: A History of the European Computing and Telecommunications Industry*, London 1997, 33–54, 107–225; M Campbell-Kelly, *ICL: A Business and Technical History*, Oxford 1989, 193–350

31 HW14/35, 21/4/42

32 HW14/16, 25/6/41

33 See note 26.

34 HW3/16

35 D Schmandt-Besserat, *Before Writing*, Vol 1, *From Counting to Cuneiform*, Austin Texas 1992; D Schmandt-Besserat, *How Writing Came About* (abridged version), Austin Texas 1996

36 L Paine, *German Military Intelligence in World War II: The Abwehr*, New York 1984, 44–5

Chapter twenty-one – The Technology and Organization of Fish

1 A Millward, *War, Technology and Society, 1939–1945*, London 1977, 20 174–5, 185

2 R Heilbroner, 'Do Machines Make History?', in *Technology & Culture*, 8 July 1967, 335–45

3 R Heilbroner, 'Technological Determinism Revisited', in M Smith & L Marx, *Does Technology Drive History? The Dilemma of Technological Determinism*, Cambridge Massachusetts 1994, 67–78

4 Millward, *War, Technology and Society*, 181

5 AHC, 5/260

6 GRT, 326

7 GRT, 326

8 T Hughes, 'The Evolution of Large Technological Systems', in W Bijker, T Hughes & T Pinch (eds), *Social Construction of Technological Systems: New Directions in the Sociology and History of Technology*, Cambridge Mass 1989, 51–82

9 HW43/2

10 D Michie, *Colossus and the Breaking of Wartime 'Fish' Codes*, Cryptologia, Vol 26, No 1, January 2002

11 HW43/2

12 HW43/2

13 HW43/2
14 *Computing*, 4/12/03

Chapter twenty-two – Transatlantic Fisheries

1 S Ambrose, *Eisenhower: Soldier and President*, London 2003, 141
2 M Pearton, *The Knowledgeable State: Diplomacy, War and Technology Since 1830*, London 1982; H Strachan, *European Armies and the Conduct of War*, London 1983; M van Creveld, *Technology and War: From 2000 B.C. to the Present*, London 1991
3 D Headrick, *The Invisible Weapon: Telecommunications and International Politics, 1851–1945*, Oxford 1991
4 R Overy, *War and Economy in the Third Reich*, Oxford 1992, 238–64; W Abelshamer, 'Germany: Guns, Butter, and Economic Miracles', in M Harrison (ed), *The Economics of World War II: Six Great Powers in Comparison*, Cambridge 1998
5 Overy, *War and Economy in the Third Reich*, 311–13
6 R Overy, *The Dictators: Hitler's Germany, Stalin's Russia*, London 2004, 537
7 P Geyl, *Encounters in History*, London 1963, 332
8 A Millward, *War, Technology and Society, 1939–1945*, London 1977, 40
9 Overy, *The Dictators*, 496–7
10 P Beesly, *Room 40: British Naval Intelligence, 1914–18*, London 1982
11 R Ratcliff, '*Searching for Security: The German Investigations into Enigma's Security*', in D Alvarez (ed), *Allied and Axis Signals Intelligence in World War II*, London 1999, 146–67
12 C McKay & B Beckmann, *Swedish Signal Intelligence 1900–1945*, London 2003, 157
13 H Heiber & D Glantz, *Hitler and his Generals: Military Conferences 1942–1945*, London 2002, 222–3
14 D Kahn, *Hitler's Spies: German Military Intelligence in World War II*, New York 1978
15 A Harvey, *Collision of Empires: Britain in Three World Wars, 1792–1945*, London 1992, 574
16 R Overy, *Why the Allies Won*, London 1995, 304
17 Heiber & Glantz, *Hitler and his Generals*, 447
18 The case of Russia must be taken into account – it had suffered from Stalin's great purges and an even more thoroughgoing shackling of the intelligentsia to ideology, as well as unconscionably harsh punishment of its troops and workers. But two key countervailing factors were the national determination to expel the invaders, and the availability of large quantities of vital supplies (such as food and trucks) from the United States to supplement Russia's advantages of an enormous population and massive

internal production of heavy weapons. It is an important question, for, as Overy, *Why the Allies Won*, page 2, points out, 'the war was about the very survival of democracy in its besieged heartlands… [yet] the great paradox of the Second World War is that democracy was saved by the exertions of communism', or perhaps that should read, 'the exertions of the peoples that were bound to Stalin's fearful empire'.

19 S Bungay, *The Most Dangerous Enemy: A History of the Battle of Britain*, London 2000, 396

20 J Fest, *Speer: The Final Verdict*, London 2001, 239

21 van Creveld, *Technology and War*, 90

22 D Stafford, *Roosevelt & Churchill: Men of Secrets*, London 1999, 44–5

23 B Smith, *The Ultra-Magic Deals and the Most Secret Special Relationship 1940–1946*, Presido 1993

24 HW14/46, 29/5/42

25 HW14/46, 13/5/42

26 HW14/47, 2/6/42

27 Stafford, *Roosevelt & Churchill*, 142, 224

28 HW14/59, 30/11/42

29 'The Fish Special Report', by A Small, American National Archive NR4628, Box 1417

30 C Burke, 'Automating American Cryptanalysis 1930–45: Marvelous Machines, a Bit Too Late', in D Alvarez (ed), *Allied and Axis Signals Intelligence in World War II*, London 1999, 18

31 Burke, *Automating American Cryptanalysis*, 32

32 Burke, *Automating American Cryptanalysis*, 30–1

33 GRT, 472

34 GRT, 480

35 GRT, 480

36 GRT, 480

37 Burke, *Automating American Cryptanalysis*, sheds a little light on this. He says, page 39 note 48, 'the 5202 had the advantage of being relatively small and, importantly, centred on film in order to avoid the problems associated with the use of large numbers of electronic tubes.' Yet the important advantage of Colossus was that it overcame these problems and harnessed the potential of electronics.

38 Burke, *Automating American Cryptanalysis*, 33

39 Headrick, *The Invisible Weapon*, 265–8. Headrick also points to a different approach to networks, with Britain wanting to prolong its view that one, or a few, reliable companies should manage a large, integrated network, providing service to all-comers, but giving British government traffic priority, while the USA preferred to install a model of multiple cable owners, with 'channels' leased by users, say a US government department, for possibly

exclusive use. Network operating structures have evolved considerably and now feature aspects of both approaches.

Chapter twenty-three – Siginstitutionalization

1 *BISWW*, Vol 3, part 2, 438

2 *BISWW*, Vol 3, part 2, 365

3 *BISWW*, Vol 3, part 2, 368

4 H van der Zee, *The Hunger Winter: Occupied Holland 1944–5*, London 1982, 24

5 HW14/119, 4/1/45. 'Dear Travis, Thank you for writing about your fresh difficulty. I am sorry to hear that you are faced with this new and extreme difficulty. We in the War Office are content to know that you and your team will tackle it with your usual enthusiasm. We feel confident that you will shortly make some headway, even though we realize that you can never give us the volume that you did before.' War Office HW14/120, 23/1/45

6 HW50/63

7 HW 14/118, 19/12/44

8 C Wilmot, *The Struggle for Europe*, London 1952, 611

9 HW13/56, 22/12/44 (CX/MSS/S143) provides a summary and analysis of Ultra information between September and December 1944 regarding 'Fortress Area West'.

10 HW13/56, 3/3/45 (CX/MSS/S159) provides a summary and analysis of Ultra information on German defensive measures on the Rhine.

11 HW13/13, 20/12/44 (CX/MSS/EC76)

12 HW13/13, 12/12/44 (CX/MSS/EC76)

13 HW13/22, 5/6/44 (CX/MSS/HF95)

14 HW13/56, 5/2/45 (CX/MSS/S154) 'The success achieved by the Russian winter offensive makes it desirable to know how far the Germans foresaw their adversary's intentions. Fortunately, Source has given us sufficient material to make this possible, so that there is no need to estimate the extent of the Germans' knowledge from their actions. Not only would this be unreliable; it would, as the data prove, conceal the truth.'

15 R Overy, *The Dictators: Hitler's Germany, Stalin's Russia*, London 2004, 527–8

16 I Kershaw, *Hitler, Vol 2, 1936–1939, Nemesis*, London 200, 564–5

17 HW13/56, 22/12/44

18 HW13/56, 22/12/44; HW13/56, 3/3/45

19 *BISWW*, Vol 3 part 2, 668, 672–3, 681, for examples of relevant messages

20 HW13/56, 3/3/45

21 HW50/63

22 HW14/122, 1/45; HW14/123, 13/3/45; HW14/124, 21/3/45; HW14/125, 4/4/45

23 HW14/122, 28/2/45

24 HW14/125, 4/4/45; HW14/126, 29/4/45 – 'Fish output good. Momentary drop in traffic due to changing locations. But section well occupied'; HW14/126, 22/4/45, 'Fish going well with Knockholt slightly improving.'

25 HW13/57, 9/3/45 (CX/MSS/S160)

26 HW43/63 (see A Note on Sources)

27 The 'Chi' branch name is not related to the Chi stream/wheels of the Geheimschreiber, and is purely coincidental.

28 HW13/22, 15/6/44 (CX/MSS/HF93)

29 HW14/135, 5/10/45

30 Kershaw, *Hitler*, Vol 2, 465

31 HW13/213, 5/2/45, 13/3/45, 26/3/45, 31/3/45, 2/4/45

32 Kershaw, *Hitler*, Vol 2, 811–12

33 H Heiber & D Glantz, *Hitler and his Generals: Military Conferences 1942–1945*, London 2002, 729

34 Kershaw, *Hitler*, Vol 2, 814

35 HW14/127, 5/5/45, 5/5/45, 7/5/45

36 HW14/140, 8/6/45

37 R Aldrich, *The Hidden Hand: Britain, America and Cold War Secret Intelligence*, London 2001

38 HW14/83, 7/43

39 HW14/110, 29/8/44

40 HW14/110, 16/8/44

41 For example, HW14/54, 5/10/42

42 HW14/110, 16/8/44

43 HW14/122, 19/2/45

44 HW14/128, 17/5/45; HW14/128, 20/5/45; HW14/128, 28/5/45; HW14/122, 2/45

45 Aldrich, *Hidden Hand*, 28, 38–40

46 HW14/126, 21/4/45; HW14/127, 14/5/45; HW14/127, 26/5/45; HW14/127, 27/3/45

47 HW13/129, 7/6/45

48 HW14/102, 21/4/44; HW14/115, 11/11/44

49 HW14/137, 22/11/45, Hellschreiber traffic was also an important category and was widely used by the press.

50 HW14/110, 29/8/44; HW14/111, 14/9/44

51 HW14/111, 13/9/44

52 HW14/119, 5/1/45

53 HW14/125, 10/4/45

54 HW14/131, 5/7/45

55 HW14/125, 10/4/45

56 HW14/132, 31/7/45; HW14/133, 10/8/45; also HW14/133, 13/8/45, lists

seven categories of 'Non-Tunny work done on Tunny Machines up till 13 August 1945' – which implies the Tunny analogue decoding machines rather than the Colossi.

57 See for example, D Kahn, *Codebreakers: The Comprehensive History of Secret Writing from Ancient Times to the Internet*, 2nd edition, New York 1996

58 HW/14/126, 24/4/45

59 J Bamford, *Body of Secrets: How America's NSA and Britain's GCHQ Eavesdrop on the World*, London 2002; *The Puzzle Palace: A Report on America's Most Secret Agency*, London 1983

60 HW62/6, 3/6/45; 17/7/45; 16/7/45

61 HW62/6, 3/6/45

62 HW14/83, 7/43; HW14/84, 2/8/43

63 HW14/83, July 1943

64 HW14/120, 31/1/45

65 HW14/128, 17/5/45

66 HW14/137, 22/11/45

67 HW14/121, 4/2/45

68 HW14/136, 22/10/45

69 HW14/130, 22/6/45; HW14/130, 10/7/45

70 HW14/131, 9/7/45

Chapter twenty-four – Colossus – The Legacy

1 S Hughes, *The Archeology of an Early Railway System: The Brecon Forest Tramroad*, Aberystwyth 1990, 129–31

2 J Page, *South Wales*, Vol 8 of A Patmore (ed), *Forgotten Railways*, Newton Abbot 1988; D Barrie, *South Wales*, Vol 12 of *A Regional History of the Railways of Great Britain*, Nairn 1994. Neither of these works mentions Parson's Folly, not even as a historical curiosity, let alone as a stepping stone to the modern railway.

3 P Strathern, *Turing and the Computer*, London 1997, 8

4 C Barnett, *The Verdict of Peace: Britain Between her Yesterday and her Future*, London 2001, 350

5 B Randell, 'The Colossus', paper presented to the International Research Conference on the History of Computing, Los Alamos Scientific Laboratory, California, June 1976, defines Colossus as 'at least a special-purpose program-controlled electronic digital computer'.

6 Unfortunately, this tendency to describe Eniac as the first electronic computer is not confined to popular accounts, but is also common in academic works. However, there are some significant exceptions, and a few works exist which, even based on the limited information available at the time of their writing, accord Colossus a role in the development of the

computer, see in particular, P Ceruzzi, *Reckoners: The Prehistory of the Digital Computer, from Relays to the Stored Program Concept, 1935–1945*, London 1983; K Flamm, *Creating the Computer: Government, Industry and High Technology*, Washington DC 1988; J Cortada, *The Computer in the United States: From Laboratory to Market, 1930–1960*, London 1993.

7 W Aspray, *John von Neumann and the Origins of Modern Computing*, London 1990, 27, 258–9

8 HW14/116, 20/11/44 – the memo on 'desirability of scientific Ultra information being made available to top Washington scientists' names Bush and E L Bowles and recommends they should be informed. The memo also requests permission to brief on two problems relating to the Japanese War (hydrogen peroxide stabilization and radar) but does not mention any of the specific Ultra issues. 'If Bush not indoctrinated prior to departure, request authority to do so here.'

9 A Cohen, Introduction to reprint of 'Engineering Research Associates', *High Speed Computing Devices*, 1950, reprint edition, Volume 4 of the Charles Babbage Institute Reprint Series for the History of Computing, Los Angeles/San Francisco 1983, xii

10 Randell, 'The Colossus', Section 9

11 Max Newman Papers, Box 3, Folder 5

12 P Gannon, *Trojan Horses and National Champions: A History of Europe's Computing and Telecommunications Industry*, London 1997. The same error of promoting a national champion in mainframe technology was made in France, Germany, Italy and the Netherlands. The successful challengers to IBM's position came from those who developed alternatives to the mainframe, and were again US companies, enjoying US government support and a market of eager commercial and military users.

13 Max Newman Papers, Box 4, Folder 6

14 R Morris, *Between the Lines: A Personal History of the British Public Telephone and Telecommunications Service, 1870–1990*, London 1994, 21

15 *Computer Weekly*, 28/7/77

Epilogue

1 S Levy, *Crypto: Secrecy and Privacy in the New Code War*, London 2000, 325–8

Appendix K – Sturgeon and Thrasher

1 HW43/2, 'Organizational problems at Bletchley Park'

2 Fish Notes Report, 7/5/44 (see www.codesandciphers.co.uk)

3 HW 43/63 (This document remains classified and is not open to public access as it is considered to contain information that would be of current value for codebreaking activities. I was supplied by GCHQ with photocopies

of a limited number of pages not considered to be sensitive. These pages covered the information in this section on the Sturgeon and Thrasher links used by the Wehrkreis, SS, GAF and navy.)

4 HW43/63
5 HW43/63
6 BISWW, Vol 2, 477
7 GRT, 494
8 HW43/63
9 HW14/93, 13/12/43
10 HW43/63
11 HW43/63

Further Reading

Codebreaking and the Second World War

The author's website – www.colossus-book.co.uk – contains several downloads with further examples, diagrams, maps and appendices which expand on themes pursued in this book. It will also be used to provide updates about the Fish and Colossus story if/when new documents are released, as well as links to other useful websites.

The best overall account of the Allied codebreaking operations during the Second World War is Stephen Budiansky, *Battle of Wits*. A good, short overview of GC&CS and Bletchley Park is provided by Michael Smith, *Station X*. Two collections of papers, M Smith & R Erskine, *Action This Day*, and F Hinsley & A Stripp, *Codebreakers*, offer a broad variety of views of different aspects of the Bletchley Park story. Michael Smith, *The Emperor's Codes*, is an account of codebreaking in the Far East during the war.

On the Fish story, there exist several files held at National Archives, Kew, West London, which provide more detail. The 500-page *General Report on Tunny* covers the cryptographic aspects of considerable detail, but generally requires a fairly advanced knowledge of statistics and probability theory (it can be seen in a facsimile version on the www.AlanTuring.net/tunny_reports website). I have seen several mentions of plans to publish this document in book form, which would be very useful, especially if it also contained the next document. The *Technical Description of Colossus I* (HW25/24) is of a much more manageable length and provides a lot of detail on technical aspects of Colossus. There is also a copy of Professor Brian Randell's 1975 account of *Colossus*, which, though now superseded in cryptographic and technical detail, still contains a wealth of useful material. For a guide to other files in the National Archive, see A Note on Sources. The *Annals of the History of Computing*, Vol 5, contains papers on Colossus by Flowers and Coombs. They were forced to hide the purpose to which Colossus was put, but provide a lot of information that is usefully supplemented by the *Technical Description of Colossus I*.

The www.codesandciphers.co.uk website contains some excellent material on Colossus and the Robinsons, including simulator software that allows a user to perform virtual runs on Colossus; it also holds several useful US documents cited in this book. This site is run by Tony Sale who has reconstructed a version of Colossus and this can be seen at the Bletchley Park Museum Trust at Bletchley. A trip to see the machine in operation is highly recommended. Other exhibits include a Lorenz SZ42 and a reconstruction of a Bombe.

There are plenty of books about Enigma, but there is, surprisingly, no overall account, especially of the machinery and the different versions of the Bombe (or the use of punched-card machines). A good introduction to the non-cryptographic aspects of the story is Hugh Sebag-Montefiore, *Enigma*, which provides a thrilling narrative of the acquisition of naval codebooks and Enigma rotor wheels, needed to crack the naval Enigma keys. Gordon Welchman's *Hut Six Story* covers the basic techniques of the Bombe and provides much intimate background; however, it is disappointing for its reticence over Colossus – especially as Welchman was Assistant Director, Mechanization from 1943 and thus in charge of the Newmanry. Andrew Hodge's superb biography

Turing: The Enigma, though now in need of updating, remains essential, and gripping, reading.

Highly detailed accounts are available in Ralph Bennett's books, *Ultra in the West*, *Ultra and Mediterranean Strategy* and *Behind the Battle*, of the intelligence, derived from Enigma and Fish, that was sent to the operational commands (but he does not consider the intelligence that informed strategy but was not forwarded to commands). He looks for detectable effects of intelligence and how it was used. Even more detailed and voluminous are the three 'volumes' in four 'parts' of the official British history, *British Intelligence in the Second World War*. These volumes provide a comprehensive account of Enigma and Fish and other sources of intelligence (two further volumes in the series cover counter-intelligence and strategic deception, volumes four and five respectively). Patrick Beesly, *Very Special Intelligence*, covers the codebreaking war from the naval point of view, with naturally a special emphasis on Enigma intelligence. For the German intelligence and codebreaking services, see David Kahn, *Hitler's Spies*.

There are several books on codebreaking which mainly cover the same ground in different ways. Simon Singh's *The Code Book* is a good example. David Kahn, *The Codebreakers*, is massive, very expensive and not an easy read. An excellent, readable account of post-war 'public key cryptography' is available in Steven Levy, *Crypto*; it includes the role played by GCHQ.

The role of communications in modern warfare is covered in two books by Martin van Creveld, *Command in War* and *Technology and War*. Maurice Pearton's *The Knowledgeable State* is an excellent short introduction to the industrialization of war from the early nineteenth century. Hew Strachan's *European Armies and the Conduct of War* is also essential for viewing military develop-ments in historical perspective.

Telecommunication is a subject that has been poorly covered by historians. Most books are technically oriented and the general style of works is to concentrate heavily on the early technical inventions of the various technologies (usually written from national perspectives). Daniel Headrick's pioneering work, *The Invisible Weapon*, is a rare exception and provides a solid analysis of the politics of international telecommunications from the first international submarine telegraph cables up to the end of the Second World War. He puts the Allied codebreaking efforts firmly into a longer historical context. Roland Pocock's *The Early British Radio Industry* offers a short, interesting account of the struggle for leadership of the international wireless industry up to 1914.

The lack of detail about Colossus has led to distortion of the accounts of its role in computer history. However, three notable exceptions are Kenneth Flamm, *Creating the Computer*, Paul Ceruzzi, *Reckoners*, and James Cortada, *The Computer in the United States*. Although written before much detail was available, these books offer realistic appraisals of various aspects of the role of Colossus in computer history.

Index

Index

Index

Index

Index

Index

Index

Index

Index